COMPLEX INTEGRATION

COMPLEX INTEGRATION

By

S.C. Sharma

DPH

DISCOVERY PUBLISHING HOUSE
NEW DELHI-110 002

First Published - 2007

Reprinted - 2023

ISBN: 978-81-8356-209-6

Published by:

DISCOVERY PUBLISHING HOUSE

4383/4B, Ansari Road, Darya Ganj

New Delhi-110 002 (India)

Phone: +91-11-23279245, 23253475, 43596065

E-mail: discoverypublishinghouse@gmail.com

orderdphbooks@gmail.com

web: www.discoverypublishinggroup.com

Printed at:

Infinity Imaging Systems

Delhi

Preface

This book Complex Integration is written for the students of mathematics statistics, engineering and physics of all Indian Universities studying at degree and post-graduate level. The whole subject matter has been dealt in a simple and lucid manner to make the subject attractive to the reader questions have been selected from examination papers of various universities I.A.S and P.C.S.

I feel indebted to various authors on the subject whose books have been consulted in preparing the present volume. Suggestions for the improvement of the book will be gratefully acknowledge.

Author

CONTENTS

1

COMPLEX INTEGRATION

INTRODUCTION

In real variable, a distinction is made between definite and indefinite integrals-the former being regarded as the limit of a sum and the latter as a process inverse to differentiation. We make a similar distinction between definite and indefinite integrals of a complex variable. Definite integrals of complex variable are usually known as line integrals. As in the case of real variable, an indefinite integral of a complex variable is a function whose derivative equals a given analytic function in a region. The indefinite integrals of many elementary functions can be obtained by inversion of known derivation formulae. However, the theory of definite integrals of a real variable does not extend straight way to the domain of complex, variable. For example, in the case of real variable, the path of integration of

$$\int_a^b f(x)dx$$

is always along the real axis from x = a to x = b. But in the case of a complex function f(z), the path of the definite integral

$$\int_a^b f(z)dz$$

may be along any curve joining the points z = a and z = b. Thus generally the value of the integral depends upon path of integration. However, we shall see that this variation in the value of definite integral will disappear in some special circumstances. We shall prove that if f(z) is analytic in a simply connected region D, then

$$\int_a^b f(z)dz$$

is independent of the path in D joining a and b where a, b are points in D. We shall express complex definite integrals in terms of real integrals. This will be more convenient to the reader who is familiar with the theory of definite integrals of real continuous functions.

The theory of line integrals, alongwith the theory of power series and residues forms a very useful and important part of the theory of functions of a complex variable. These theories contain some of the most powerful theorems which have application in both pure and applied mathematics. We shall present some of the most essential gradients of the theory of complex integrals in this and the succeeding chapters.

SOME BASIC DEFINITIONS

Partitions

Let [a, b] be a closed interval where a, b are real numbers.

Divide [a, b] into n sub-intervals

$$[a = t_0 , t_1], [t_1, t_2], [t_2, t_3] \dots [t_{n-1}, t_n = b] \qquad \dots (1)$$

by inserting n – 1 intermediate points $t_1, t_2 \dots\dots, t_{n-1}$ satisfying the inequalities

$$a = t_0 < t_1 < t_2 < \dots . < t_{n-1} < t_n = b.$$

Then the set

$$P = \{t_0, t_1, t_2, \dots, t_n\} \qquad \dots (2)$$

is called a partition of the interval [a, b] and the greatest of the numbers

$$t_1 - t_0, t_2 - t_1, \dots, t_n - t_{n-1}$$

is called the norm of the partition P and shall be denoted by $|P|$. Thus the norm of the partition P is the maximum length of the sub-intervals given in (1).

Arcs and Closed Curves

The equation $z = z(t) = x(t) + iy(t)$ ...(3)

where t runs through the interval $a \le t \le b$ and x (t), y (t) are continuous functions of t, represents an arc L in the complex plane. The parametric representation x = x (t), y = y (t) is also used.

Essentially an arc is the set of all image points of a closed finite interval under a continuous mapping.

An arc L is said to be differentiable if $z'(t)$ exists and is continuous. The term continuously differentiable is also sometimes used. If in addition to the existence of $z'(t)$, we also have $z'(t) \neq 0$, then we say that L is regular or smooth. Geometrically speaking, a smooth arc has at every point a tangent whose direction is determined by arg $z'(t)$.

As a matter of fact, as t increases from a to b, z continuously traces out the arc L and at the same time arg $z'(t)$ varies continuously since $z'(t)$ changes continuously without vanishing. Thus the inclination of a tangent to a smooth arc varies continuously as the point of contact moves along the arc.

An arc L is said to be Piecewise differentiable if among it's various representations there exists at least one representation, say (3), such that the interval [a, b] can be divided into a finite number of sub-intervals

$$[a, a_1], [a_1, a_2], ..., [a_{n-1}, b]$$

on each of which z′ (t) exists; and if, in addition, z′ (t) ≠ 0 on any of these sub-intervals, then L is said to be piecewise regular (or piecewise smooth).

We say that an arc L is simple or a Jordan arc if $z(t_1) = z(t_2)$ only when $t_1 = t_2$.

If the points corresponding to the values a and b coincide, the arc is said to be a closed curve.

If L is the arc $z = z(t)$, $a \le t \le b$, then the arc defined by

$$z = z(-t), \; -b \le t \le -a$$

is said to be the opposite arc of L and is denoted by –L or sometimes by L^{-1}.

Rectifiable Arcs

Let an arc L be defined by

$$z = z(t) = x(t) + iy(t), \; a \le t \le b.$$

Consider any partition

$$P = \{t_0, t_1, ..., t_n\} \text{ of } [a, b]$$

Corresponding to this partition L is divided into n sub arcs

$$I_k = \text{Arc } z_{k-1} z_k \; (k = 1, 2, ... n)$$

where $z_k = z(t_k) \; (k = 0, 1, ..., n)$.

We join each of the points $z_0, z_1, ..., z_n$ to the next point by straight lines (as indicated in the following figure 1.1 for n = 6). In this way, we obtain a polygonal curve. The length of this polygonal curve is evidently

$$\sum_{k=1}^{n} |z_k - z_{k-1}|.$$

Fig. 1.1

We say that the arc L is rectifiable if the least upper bound (or supremum) of the sums

$$|z_1 - z_0| + |z_2 - z_1| + ... + |z_{n-1} - z_n| \quad ...(4)$$

taken ever all partitions P is finite *i.e.*, if

$$\sup_P \sum_{k=1}^{n} | z_k - z_{k-1} | = l < \infty$$

The non-negative real number l is called the length of the arc L. Also we say that L is non-rectifiable if the sums (4) become arbitrarily large for suitably chosen partitions. In this case we may say that L has no length (or, if preferred, infinite length). It can be shown that the length of a polynomial arc corresponding to a partition P inscribed in a rectifiable arc L approaches the length of L as the norm of the partition P approaches zero.

Functions of Bounded Variation

It is easy to see that

$$|x(t_k) - x(t_{k-1})| \leq |z(t_k) - z(t_{k-1})|$$

$$|y(t_k) - y(t_{k-1})| \leq |z(t_k) - z(t_{k-1})|$$

$$|z(t_k) - z(t_{k-1})| = |x(t_k) + iy(t_k) - x(t_{k-1}) - iy\,(t_{k-1})|$$

$$= |x(t_k) - x(t_{k-1}) + i\,\{y(t_k) - y\,(t_{k-1})\}|$$

$$\leq |x(t_k) - x(t_{k-1})| + |i|\,|y(t_k) - y\,(t_{k-1})|$$

or $|z(t_k) - z(t_{k-1})| \leq |x(t_k) - x(t_{k-1})| + |y(t_k) - y(t_{k-1})|$ $\quad [\because |i| = 1]$

It follows from these inequalities that the sum

$$|z(t_1) - z\,(t_0)| + |z(t_2) - z(t_1)| + ... + |z(t_n) - z(t_{n-1})|$$

and the sums

$$|x(t_1) - x(t_0)| + |x(t_2) - x(t_1)| + ... + |x(t_n) - x(t_{n-1})|$$

$$|y(t_1) - y(t_0)| + |y(t_2) - y(t_1)| + ... + |y(t_n) - y(t_{n-1})|$$

bounded at the same time.

We say that the functions x (t) and y (t) are of bounded variation if the latter two of above three sums are bounded for all partitions P of [a, b].

In can be shown that a necessary and sufficient condition for an arc defined by

$$z = z(t) = x(t) + iy\,(t),\ a \leq t \leq b$$

to be rectifiable is that the functions x (t) and y (t) should be of bounded variation in [a, b].

It is not hard to show that a smooth arc L is rectifiable and that its length l is given by the familiar formula

$$l = \int_a^b \sqrt{\left[x'(t)^2 + y'(t)^2\right]}dt \qquad \text{... (5)}$$

or equivalently by

$$l = \int_a^b |z'(t)|\, dt. \qquad \text{... (6)}$$

Contours: *A contour is a continuous chain of a finite number of regular arcs.*

If the contour is closed and does not intersect itself, it is a piecewise smooth curve called a closed contour. The boundaries of triangles and rectangles are examples of closed contours. It is evident that a contour is rectifiable : its length is the sum of lengths of smooth arcs comprising the contour.

Simply and Multiply Connected Regions

A region in which every closed curve can be shrunk to a point without passing out of the region is called a simply connected region otherwise it is said to be multiply connected.

COMPLEX INTEGRALS

Let L be a rectifiable arc defined by

$$z = z(t) = x(t) + iy(t),\ a \le t \le b$$

and let f(z) be a function of a complex variable z defined and continuous of L. Consider an arbitrary partition.

$$P = \{a = t_0, t_1, t_2, ..., t_n = b\}$$

of [a, b] and form the sum

$$S_P = (z_1 - z_0)\, f(\zeta_1) + ... + (z_k - z_{k-1})\, f(\zeta_k) + ... + (z_n - z_{n-1})\, f(\zeta_n)$$

$$= \sum_{k-1}^{n} (z_k - z_{k-1}) f(\zeta_k) \qquad \text{...(1)}$$

where $z_k = z(t_k)$, $\zeta_k = z(a_k)$, $t_{k-1} \le a_k \le t_k$.

Thus to form the sum S_p, we choose an arbitrary point ζ_κ on each arc joining the points zk–1 to zk and add the terms of the form (zk – zk–1) $f(\zeta_\kappa)$

where κ varies from 1 to n.

For convenience, we shall write zk – zk – 1 = Δz_k.

Thus (1) can be written as

$$S_P = \Sigma f(\zeta_\kappa)\Delta zk. \qquad \text{... (2)}$$

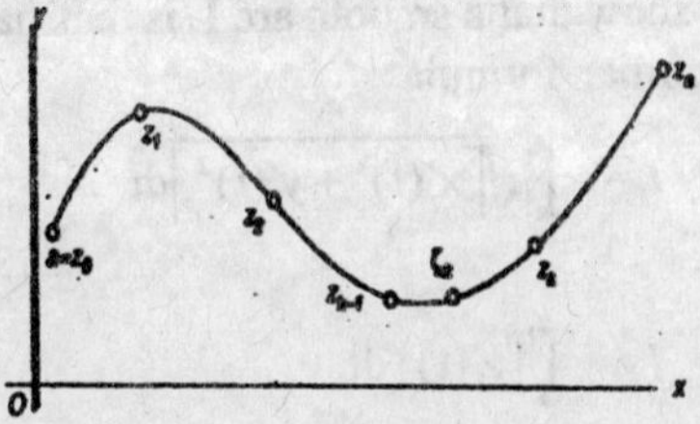

Fig. 1.2

If the sum S_P taken over all possible partitions P tends to a unique limit I as n tends to infinity and simultaneously as the norm |P| tends to zero, then we say that f(z) is integrable from a to b along the arc L, and we write

$$I = \int_L f(z)dz.$$

Also $\int_L f(z)dz$ is called the complex line integral or simply line integral of f(z) along L or the definite integral of f(z) from a to b along L.

Thus $\int_L f(z)dz = \underset{k\to\infty}{\text{Lim}\ |P| \to 0} \sum_{k=1}^{n} f(\zeta_k)(zk - zk - 1)$ ...(3)

Example:

Using the definition of an integral as the limit of a suns evaluate the following integrals

(i) $\int_L dz$ (ii) $\int_L |dz|$ (iii) $\int_L z dz$

where L is any rectifiable arc joining the points

$$z = \alpha \text{ and } z = \beta.$$

Solution:

We first note that the integrals exist since the integrand is continuous on in each case.

(i) By definition, we have

$$\int_L f(z) = \lim_{n\to\infty} \sum_{k=1}^{n} (z_k - z_{k-1})$$

$$= \lim_{n\to\infty} [z_1 - z_0 + z_{.} - z_1 + ...+ z_n - z_{n-1}]$$

$$= \lim_{n\to\infty} [z_n - z_0] = \beta - \alpha \text{ since } z_0 = \alpha,\ z_n - \beta.$$

In particular if L is closed, then $\alpha = \beta$ and $\int_L dz = 0$

(ii) $\int_L |dz| = \sum_{k=1}^{n} (zk - zk - 1)$

$$= \lim_{n\to\infty} [|z_1 - z_0| + |z_2 - z_1| + ...+ |zn - zn-1|]$$

$$= \lim_{n\to\infty} [\text{Chord } z_1z_0 + \text{chord } z_2z_1 + ... + \text{chord } z_nz_{n-1}]$$

$$= [\text{arc } z_1z_0 + \text{arc } z_2z_1 + ... + \text{arc } z_nz_{n-1}]$$

$$= \text{Arc length of L.}$$

(iii) We have

$$I = \int_L z\,dz = \lim_{n\to\infty} \sum_{k=1}^{n} \zeta_k (z_k - z_{k-1}) \quad ...(1)$$

where ζ_k is any point on the sub-arc joining z_{k-1} to z_k. Since ζ_k is arbitrary, we set $\zeta_k = z_k$ and $\zeta_k = z_{k-1}$ successively in (1) and get

$$I = \lim_{n\to\infty} \sum_{k=1}^{n} z_k (z_k - z_{k-1}) \text{ and } \lim_{n\to\infty} \sum_{k=1}^{n} z_k = 1 (z_k - z_{k-1}).$$

Adding these two, we get

$$2I = \lim_{n\to\infty} \sum_{k=1}^{n} (z_k - z_{k-1})(z_k + z_{k-1})$$

$$= \lim_{n\to\infty} \sum_{k=1}^{n} (z_k{}^2 - z^2{}_{k-1})$$

$$= \lim_{n\to\infty} \sum_{k=1}^{n} \left[z_1^2 - z_0^2 + z_2^2 - z_1^2 + ... + z_n^2 - z_{n-1}^2\right]$$

$$= \lim_{n\to\infty} \sum_{k=1}^{n} \left(z_n^2 - z_0^2\right) = \beta^2 - \alpha^2 \text{ since } z_0 = \alpha,\ z_n = \beta.$$

Hence $I = \frac{1}{2}\left(\beta^2 - \alpha^2\right).$

In particular if L is closed, then $\alpha = \beta$ and $\int_L z\,dz = 0.$

REDUCTION OF COMPLEX INTEGRALS OF REAL INTEGRALS

Theorem:

Let the arc L be defined by

$$z = z(t) = x(t) + iy(t),\ a \le t \le b$$

be continuously differentiable and let

$$f(z) = u(x, y) + iv(x, y)$$

be continuous over L. Then (i) L is rectifiable and

(ii) $\int_L f(z)dx = \int_a^b \{u[x(t), y(t)]x'(t) - v[x(t), y(t)]y'(t)\}dt$

$$+i\int_a^b\{v[x(t),y(t)]x'(t)+u[x(t),y(t)]y'(t)\}$$

Proof:

(i) We first prove L is rectifiable. Let

$$P = \{a = t_0, t_1, ..., t_n = b\}$$

be any partition of the interval [a, b]. Writing

$$z_k = z(t_k) = x(t_k) + iy(t_k),$$

we have

$$\sum_{k=1}^{n}|z_k - z_{k-1}| = \Sigma|z(t_k) - z(t_{k-1})$$

$$= \Sigma\ |[x(t_k) - x(t_{k-1})] + i[y(t_k) - y(t_{k-1})]|$$

$$\leq \Sigma\ |x(t_k) - x(t_{k-1})| + \Sigma|y(t_k) - y(t_{k-1})|. \qquad ...(1)$$

By Lagrange's mean value theorem of Differential Calculus, there exist numbers α_k, $\beta_k \in]\ t_{k-1}, t_k\ [$ such that

$$x(t_k) - x(t_{k-1}) = (t_k - t_{k-1})\ x'(\alpha_k) \qquad ...(2)$$

$$y(t_k) - y(t_{k-1}) = (t_k - t_{k-1})\ y'(\beta_k) \qquad ...(3)$$

Again since z(t) is continuous differentiable the derivatives x′(t) and y′(t) are continuous on [a, b] and consequently they are bounded on [a, a]. Therefore there exists a number M such that

$$|x'(t)| \leq M,\ |y'(t)| \leq M \qquad ...(4)$$

for all $t \in (a, b)$.

It follows from (1), (2), (3) and (4) that

$$\Sigma\ |z_k - z_{k-1}| \leq \Sigma M|t_k - t_{k-1}| + \Sigma M|t_k - t_{k-1}|$$

$$= 2M\ \Sigma(t_k - t_{k-1}) \text{ since } t_k > t_{k-1}$$

$$= 2M\ [t_1 - t_0 + t_2 - t_1 + ... + t_0 - t_{n-1}]$$

$$= 2M\ [t_n - t_0] = 2M\ (b - a). \qquad ...(5)$$

The inequality (5) implies that the arc L is rectifiable.

(ii) We consider the sum

$$S = \Sigma(z_k - z_{k-1})f(\zeta_k)$$

where ζ_k is a point on the arc joining z_{k-1} and z_k. If τ_k is the parameter of ζ_k, then evidently τ_k lies between z_{k-1} and z_k. We write

$$f[z(t)] = u[x(t), y(t)] + iv\ [x(t), y(t)] = \phi(t) + i\psi(t)$$

so that $\phi(t) = u\ [x(t), y(t)]$ and $\psi(t) = v[x(t), y(t)]$. ... (6)

We then have

$$S = \Sigma[x(t_k) + iy(t_k) - x(t_{k-1}) - iy\ (t_{k-1})]\ [\phi(\tau_k) + i\psi(\tau_k)]$$
$$= \Sigma[x(t_k) - x(t_{k-1}) + i\{y(t_k) - y(t_{k-1})\}]\ [\phi(\tau_k) + i\psi(\tau_k)]$$

Using (2) and (3), we have

$$S = \Sigma[(t_k - t_{k-1})]x'(a_k) + i(t_k - t_{k-1})y'(\beta_k)\ [\phi(\tau_k)\ i\psi(\tau_k)]$$
$$= \Sigma(t_k - t_{k-1})\ x'(\alpha_k)\ \phi(\tau_k) - \Sigma(t_k - t_{k-1})\ y'(\beta_k)\ \psi(\tau_k)]$$
$$+\Sigma(t_k - t_{k-1})\ x'(\alpha_k)\ \psi(\tau_k) + i\Sigma(t_k - t_{k-1})\ y'(\beta_k)\ \psi(\tau_k)$$
$$= S_1 + S_2 + i\ (S_3 + S_4) \qquad ...(7)$$

where $S_1 = \Sigma(t_k - t_{k-1})\ x'(\Sigma_k)\ \phi(\tau_k),$

$$S_2 = -\Sigma(t_k - t_{k-1})\ y'(\beta_k)\ \psi(\tau_k)$$
$$S_3 = \Sigma(t_k - t_{k-1})\ x'(\alpha_k)\ \psi(\tau_k)$$
$$S_4 = \Sigma(t_k - t_{k-1})\ y'(\beta_k)\ \phi(\tau_k).$$

We now consider the sums S_1, S_2, S_3, S_4 one by one. After a slight manipulation, we get

$$S_1 = \Sigma(t_k - t_{k-1})\ x'(\alpha_k)\ \phi(\tau_k)$$
$$= \sum_{k=1}^{n}(t_k - t_{k-1})x'(\tau_k)\phi(\tau_k)$$
$$+\sum_{k=1}^{n}(t_k - t_{k-1})[x'(\alpha_k) - x'(\tau_k)]\phi((\tau_k). \qquad ...(8)$$

Now x′(t) is uniformly continuous since it is continuous on the closed interval [a, b]. Hence to every $\varepsilon > 0$, there exists $\delta > 0$ such that $|x'(h) - x'(k)| < \varepsilon$ whenever $|h - k| < \delta$.

If follows that for any partition P of [a, b] with norm $\leq \delta$, we have

$$|\Sigma(t_k - t_{k-1})[x'(\alpha_k) - x'(\tau_k)]\ \phi(\tau_k)|$$
$$\leq\Sigma(t_k - t_{k-1})\ M_1 = \varepsilon M_1\ (b - a) \qquad ...(9)$$

where M_1 is a number such that

$$|\phi(t)| \leq M_1\ \forall\ t \in [a, b]$$

[Since f(z) is continuous over L, $\phi(t)$ and $\psi(t)$ are continuous on [a, b] and consequently they are bounded. Hence there exists a M_1 such that $\phi(t) \leq M_1\ \forall\ t \in [a, b]$.

Now letting $n \to \infty$ and the norm |P| tend to zero, we conclude from (9) that the second sum on the right of (8) tends to zero and the first sum tends to the integral

$$\int_a^b \phi(t)x'(t)dt$$

Then $\quad \lim S_1 = \int_a^b \phi(t)x'(t)dt.$

Similarly $\quad \lim S_2 = -\int_a^b \psi(t)y'(t)dt$

$$\lim S_3 = \int_a^b \psi(t)x'(t)dt$$

and $\quad \lim S_4 = \int_a^b \phi(t)y'(t)dt.$

Combining these results, we see that S tends to the limit.

$$\int_a^b [\phi(t)x'(t) - \psi(t)y'(t)]dt + i\int_a^b [\psi(t)x'(t) - \phi(t)y'(t)]dt$$

Thus $\int_L f(z)dz = \int_a^b [\phi(t)x'(t) - \psi(t)y'(t)]dt$

$$+ i\int_a^b [\psi(t)x'(t) - \phi(t)y'(t)]dt \qquad ...(10)$$

Substituting the values of $\phi(t)$ and $\psi(t)$ from (6) in (10), we get the result stated in the theorem.

We may write (10) as a definite integral

$$\int_L f(z)dz = \int_a^b f(z(t))z'(t)dt \qquad ...(11)$$

or in terms of real line integrals as

$$\int_L f(z)dz = \int_L (udx - vdy) + i\int_L (udy + vdx) \qquad ...(12)$$

or $\int_L f(z)dz = \int_L (u + iv)(dx + idy) \qquad ...(13)$

SOME PROPERTIES OF COMPLEX INTEGRALS

Property I:

$$\int_L [f(z) + \psi(z)]dz = \int_L f(z) + \int_L \phi f(z)dz.$$

It can be easily generalized for a finite number of functions.

Property II:

$$\int_L f(z)dz = -\int_{-L} f(z)dz$$

whereby –L we mean the curve L traversed in the opposite direction.

Property III:

$$\int_{L_1+L_2} f(z)dz = \int_{L_1} f(z)dz + \int_{L_2} f(z)dz$$

where the final point of L_1 coincides with the initial point of L_2.

In general, if

$$L = L_1 + L_2 + ... + L_n$$

where the final point of L_k coincides with the initial point of

$$L_{k+1} \ (k = 1, 2, ..., n-1),$$

then
$$\int_L f(z)dz = \int_{L_1} f(z)dz + \int_{L_2} f(z)dz + ... + \int_{L_n} fn(z)dz.$$

Property IV:

$$\int_L cf(z)dz = c\int_L f(z)dz$$

where c is any complex constant.

Property V:

$$\int_L [c_1 f_1(z) c_2 f_2(z) + ... + c_n f_n(z)]dz$$

$$= c_1 \int_L f_1(z)dz + c_2 \int_L f_2(z)dz + ... + c_n \int_L f_n(z)dz.$$

This follows from the properties III and 11

The proofs of the properties follow directly by the definition of a complex integral as the limit of a sum and are left as an exercise for the readers.

Property VI:

An Important Inequality

$$\left|\int_L f(z)dz\right| \le \int_L |f(z)||dz|$$

Proof:

From IV, we have

$$R\left[c\int_L f(z)dz\right] = R\left[\int_L cf(z)dz\right]$$

Since c is arbitrary, we may set $c = e^{-i\theta}$ where θ is real but arbitrary. Then

$$R\left[e^{-i\theta}\int_L f(z)dz\right] = R\left[\int_L e^{-i\theta}(z)dz\right]$$

$$= \int R\left[e^{-i\theta}f(z)dz\right]$$

$$\le \int_L |e^{-i\theta}f(z)dz|$$

[Since real part of complex number cannot exceed its absolute value]

$$= \int_L |f(z)||dz|. \qquad ...(1)$$

Again since θ is arbitrary, we may set

$$\theta = \arg \int_L f(z)dz.$$

Then $\int_L f(z)dz = \left|\int_L f(z)dz\right| e^{i\theta}$

and the left hand side of(1)

$$= R\left[e^{-i\theta}\left|\int_L f(z)dz e^{i\theta}\right|\right] = \left|\int_L f(z)dz\right|$$

Hence $\left|\int_L f(z)dz\right| \le \int_L |f(z)||dz|.$

Example 1:

Evaluate $\int_L \frac{dz}{z-a}$ *where L represents a circle*

$$|z-a| = r.$$

Solution:

The parametric equation of L is

$$z = a + r\cos t + ir\sin t = a + re^{it}$$

where $0 \le 1 \le 2\pi$. We have

$$z(t).\frac{dz}{dt} = rie^{it}.$$

Hence using the formula (ii) of the preceding theorem, we get

$$\int_L \frac{dz}{z-a} dz = \int_0^{2\pi} \frac{1}{z-a}.\frac{dz}{dt} dt$$

$$= \int_0^{2\pi} \frac{1}{re^{it}} \int_0^{2\pi} dt = 2\pi i.$$

Example 2:

Prove that the value of the integral of 1/z along a semi-circular arc $|z| = 1$ *from −1 to + 1 is −πi or πi according as the arc lies above or below the real axis.*

Solution:

The parametric equation of the circle

$$|z| = 1 \text{ is } z = e^{it}$$

so that $\frac{dz}{dt} = ie^{it}$

where $0 \leq t \leq 2\pi$

As z moves from – 1 to 1 along the upper semi-circular arc, t varies from π to 0. Hence in this case, we have

$$I_1 = \int_{CBA} \frac{dz}{z} = \int_{\pi}^{0} \frac{ie^{it}dt}{e^{it}} = i\int_{\pi}^{0} dt = \pi i \quad ...(1)$$

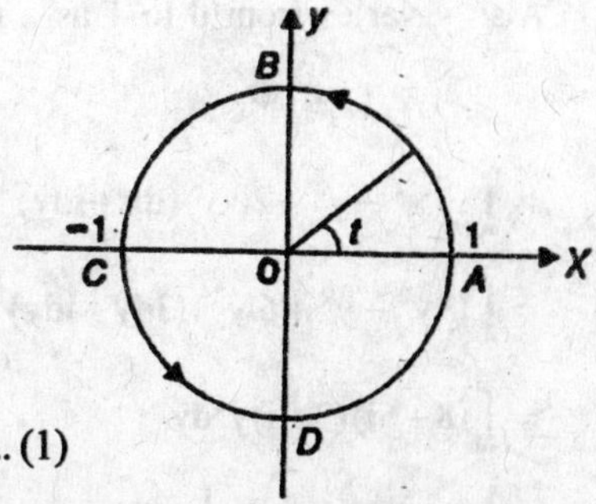

Fig. 1.3

Also if z moves along the lower semi-circle from –1 to 1, t varies from π to 2π and we have

$$I_2 = \int_{CBA} \frac{dz}{z} = \int_{\pi}^{2\pi} \frac{ie^{it}dt}{e^{it}} = i\int_{\pi}^{2\pi} dt = \pi i \quad ...(2)$$

Remark:

Since $\int_{CBA} \frac{1}{z} dz = -\pi i$, we have

$$\int_{ABC} \frac{1}{z} dz = \pi i \quad ...(3)$$

Hence from (2) and (3), we have

$$\int_{ABCDA} \frac{1}{z} dz = \int_{ABC} \frac{1}{z} dz + \int_{CDA} \frac{1}{z} dz$$

$$= \pi i + \pi i = 2\pi i.$$

Thus, the integral of 1/z round the entire circle | z | = 1 is 2πi.

Example 3:

Integrate z^2 along the straight line OM and also along the path OLM consisting of two straight line segments OL and OM where O is the origin, L is the point z = 3 and M the point

$$z = 3 + i.$$

Hence show that the integral of z^2 along the closed path OLMO is zero.

Solution:

We have $z^2 = (x + iy)^2 = x^2 - y^2 + 2ixy$. ...(1)

On the line OM, x = 3y

so that $dx = 3\,dy$.

Also y varies from 0 to 1 as z moves along OM from O to M.

$$\therefore \quad I_1 = \int_{OM} z^2\,dz$$

$$= \int_{OM} (x^2 - y^2 + 2ixy)(dx + idy)$$

$$= \int_0^1 (9y^2 - y^2 + 6iy^2)(3dy + idy)$$

$$= \int_0^1 (8+6i)(3+i)y^2 dy$$

$$= \frac{1}{3}(8+6i)(3+i) = \frac{1}{3}(18+26i) = 6 + \frac{26}{3}i.$$

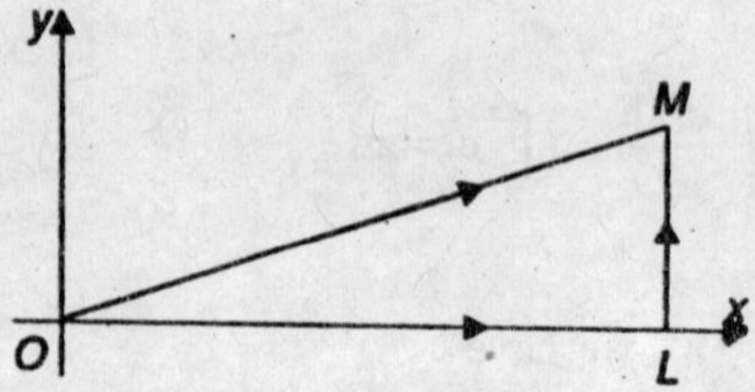

Fig. 1.4

Now we consider the integral of z^2 along the path OLM. We observe that on OL, $y = 0$ so that $dy = 0$ and along LM, $x = 3$ so that $dx = 0$. Also as z moves along OL from 0 to L, x varies from 0 to 3 and as z moves along LM from L to M, y varies from 0 to 1.

Hence,

$$I_2 = \int_{OLM} z^2\,dz = \int_{OL} z^2 dz + \int_{LM} z^2 dz$$

$$= \int_{OL} (x^2 - y^2 + 2ixy)(dx + idy)$$

$$+ \int_{LM} (x^2 - y^2 + 2ixy)(dx + idy)$$

$$= \int_0^3 x^2 dx - \int_0^1 (9 - y^2 + 6iy).idy$$

$$= \left[\frac{x^3}{3}\right]_0^3 + i\left[9y - \frac{y^3}{3} + 6i\frac{y^2}{2}\right]_0^1$$

$$= 9 + i\left[9 - \frac{1}{3} + 3i\right] = 9 + \frac{26}{3}i - 3 = 6 + \frac{26}{3}i. \qquad ...(2)$$

Thus $I_1 = I_2$ in this case.

Also since $\int_{OM} z^2 dz = 6 + \frac{26}{3}i$, we have

$$\int_{MO} z^2 dz = -\left(6+\frac{26}{3}i\right). \quad \text{...(3)}$$

Hence $\int_{OLMO} z^2 dz = \int_{OLM} z^2 dz + \int_{MO} z^2 dz = 0$ by (2) and (3).

Remark:

We have seen in examples 2 and 3 above that the integral of 1/z round the circle | z | = 1 is $2\pi i \neq 0$ whereas the integral of z^2 round the closed contour OLMO is zero. As a matter of fact the function 1/z is not analytic at z = 0 which is an interior point (the centre) of the circle | z | = 1 whereas the function z^2 is analytic throughout the interior and the boundary of the triangle OLM. We shall prove a general result known as *Cauchy's fundamental theorem* which states:

If f(z) is analytic at all points within and on the closed contour C, then

$$\int_C f(z)dz = 0.$$

EXERCISES

1. Show that the integral of $\bar{z}$ along a semi-circular arc | z | = 1 from – 1 to + 1 has the value – πi or πi according as the arc lies above or below the real axis.

2. Evaluate $\int_L \bar{z}\,dz$ from z = 0 to z = 4 + 2i along the curve L defined by (i) $z = t^2 + it$ (ii) the line from z = 0 to z = 2i and then the line from z = 2i to z = 4 + 2i.

   Ans. (i) $10-\frac{8}{3}i$,

   (ii) 10 – 8i.

3. Evaluate $\int_L \frac{dz}{z-a}dz$ where L is the semi-circle

   $z = 2e^{it}$, $0 \le t \le n$.

   Ans. –4 + 2ni.

4. Evaluate $\int_L \frac{dz}{z}$

   where L represents the square described in the positive sense with sides parallel to the axes and of length 2a and having its centre at the origin.

   Ans. 2ni.

AN ESTIMATION OF A COMPLEX INTEGRAL

Theorem. Let f(z) be continuous on a contour L of length l and let $|f(z)| \le M$ on l. Then

$$\left| \int_L f(z)dz \right| \le Ml.$$

Proof:

We have $S_P = \sum_{k=1}^{n} (z_k - z_{k-1})(z_k)$.

Since the modulus of the sum is less than or equal to the sum of the moduli, we have

$$\begin{aligned} |S_P| &= |\Sigma(z_k - z_{k-1})\, f(z_k)| \\ &\le \Sigma\, |(z_k - z_{k-1})\, f(z_k)| \\ &= \Sigma\, |z_k - z_{k-1}|\, |f(z_k)| \\ &\le M\, \Sigma\, |z_k - z_{k-1}| \end{aligned}$$

$$\therefore \lim |\Sigma\, (z_k - z_{k-1})\, f(z_k)|$$

$$\le \lim M\, \Sigma\, |z_k - z_{k-1}|$$

$$\text{or } \left| \int_L f(z)dz \right| \le M \int_L |dz| = Ml.$$

LINE INTEGRALS AS FUNCTIONS OF ARCS

We have seen that a line integral $\int_L f(z)dz$ over an arc L can be put in the form

$$\int_L (u + iv)(dx + idy)$$

General line integrals of the form

$$\int_L p\,dx + q\,dy$$

are often studied as functions (or functionals) of arc L under the assumption that p, q are defined and continuous in a domain D such that L is free to vary in D. There is an important class of integrals characterized by the property that the integral over an arc depends only on its end points. This means that if the two arcs L_1 and L_2 have the same initial point and the same final point, then

$$\int_{L_1} p\,dx + dx + q\,dy = \int_{L_2} p\,dx + q\,dy.$$

Theorem I:

The following statements are equivalent:

(i) A line integral of f(z) over an arc L depends only on the end points of L.

(ii) The integral of f(z) over any closed curve is zero.

Proof:

Let the integral of f(z) over any closed curve be zero and let L_1 and L_2 be any two arcs with the same end points. Then $L_1 - L_2$ is a closed curve so that

$$\int_{L_1 - L_2} f(z)\,dx = 0$$

which is equivalent to

$$\int_{L_1} f(z)\,dx - \int_{L_2} f(z)dz = 0$$

Hence $$\int_{L_1} f(z)\,dx - \int_{L_2} f(z)dz.$$

Conversely, let the integral over any two arcs with the same end points be the same and let Γ be any closed curve. Then Γ and $-\Gamma$ have the same end points and consequently

$$\int_{\Gamma} f(z) = \int_{-\Gamma} f(z)dz = -\int_{\Gamma} f(z)dz.$$

$$\therefore \quad 2\int_{\Gamma} f(z)dz = 0, \text{ that is, } \int_{\Gamma} f(z)dz = 0$$

Theorem II:

The line integral $\int p\,dx + q\,dy$, *defined in a domain D, depends only on the end points of Γ if and only if there exists a function U (x, y) in D such that*

$$\frac{\partial U}{\partial x} = p \text{ and } \frac{\partial U}{\partial y} = q.$$

Proof:

The 'if' Part: Suppose there exists a function U(x, y) in D such that

$$\frac{\partial U}{\partial x} = p, \frac{\partial U}{\partial y} = q.$$

Then if a, b are the end points of L, we have

$$\int_L p\,dx + q\,dy = \int_L \frac{\partial U}{\partial x}dx + \frac{\partial U}{\partial y}dy$$

$$= \int_a^b \left(\frac{\partial U}{\partial x}x'(t) + \frac{\partial U}{\partial y}y'(t)\right)dt$$

$$= \int_a^b \frac{d}{dt} U(x(t), y(t)dt$$

$$= U(x(b), y(b)) - U(x(a), y(a)). \quad ...(1)$$

Since the right hand side of (1) depends only on the end points a and b, the sufficiency is established.

The 'only if' Part: Let the line integral

$$\int_L p\,dx + q\,dy$$

depend only on the end points of L. We choose a fixed point (x_0, y_0) in D and let (x, y) be an arbitrary point in D. We join (x_0, y_0) to (x, y) by a polygonal arc L, contained in D, whose sides are parallel to the coordinate axes (see the figure). We now define a function U by

$$U(x, y) = \int_L p\,dx + q\,dy.$$

By hypothesis, the integral depends only on the end points and so it is well defined.

Further, if we choose the last segment of L horizontal, we can keep y constant (so that dy = 0) and suppose that x varies without changing the other segments. Choosing x as a parameter on the last segment, we obtain

$$U(x, y) = \int^x p(x, y)\,dx + \text{const.} \quad ...(2)$$

[Note that dy = 0 implies that $\int q\,dy$ is constant]

We do not specify the lower limit since it is immaterial for our purpose. From (2), we see that

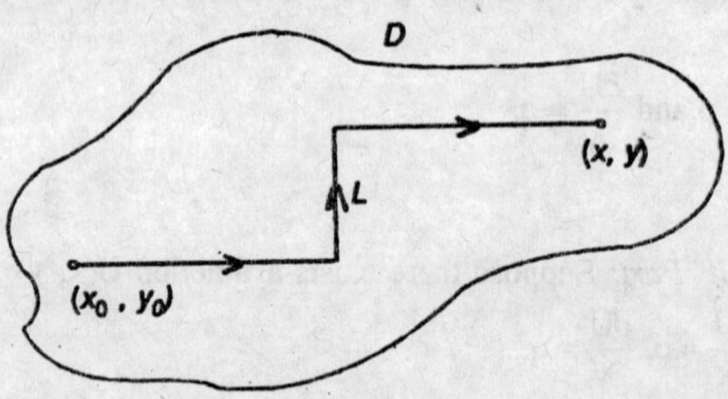

Fig. 1.5

Similarly, if we choose the last segment vertical, then it can be shown that $\frac{\partial U}{\partial y} = q.$

This proves the necessity.

Remark:

(i) It is customary, to write

$$dU = \left(\frac{\partial U}{\partial x}\right)dx + \left(\frac{\partial U}{\partial y}\right)dy \qquad \text{... (1)}$$

and we say that an expression p dx + q dy is an exact differential if it can be written in the form (1). Using this terminology, the above theorem can be stated as:

An integral depends only on the end point if and only if the integrand is an exact differential.

(ii) We now determine the conditions under which

$$f(z)\,dz = f(z)\,dx + if(z)\,dy$$

is an exact differential. By definition of an exact, differential, there must exist a function F(z) in D such that

$$\frac{\partial F(z)}{\partial x} = f(z) \text{ and } \frac{\partial F(z)}{\partial y} = if(z).$$

It follows that

$$\frac{\partial F}{\partial x} = -i\frac{\partial F}{\partial y}$$

which is a Cauchy-Riemann equation.

Also f(z) is by assumption continuous (otherwise $\int_L f(z)dz$ would not be defined). Hence F(z) is analytic.

(iii) From the discussion in (i) and (ii), we conclude:

The integral $\int_L f(z)dz$, with continuous f, depends only on the end points of L if and only if f is the derivative of an analytic function in D.

For example, for n ≥ 0, the function $(z - a)^n$ is the derivative of $(z - a)^{n+1}/(n + 1)$ which is an analytic function in the whole complex plane. If F is any closed curve, then it follows from theorem 1 and remark (iii) above that

$$\int_L (z-a)^n\,dz = 0 \qquad \text{... (1)}$$

If n is negative, but ≠ – 1, then also $\int_L (z-a)^n\,dz = 0$ for all closed curve Γ which do not pass through a, since in the complementary region of the point a the infinite integral is still analytic and single-valued. If n = –1, then (1) does not always hold.

$$\int_{\Gamma} \frac{dz}{z-a} = 2\pi i$$

where Γ is any circle $|z - a| = r$.

CAUCHY'S FUNDAMENTAL THEOREM

We first prove weaker version of Cauchy's fundamental theorem usually known as Cauchy Goursat theorem.

Theorem I:

(Cauchys Theorem): *Let D be a simply connected region and let f(z) be single valued continuously differentiable function on D i.e. f′(z) exists and is continuous at each point of D. Then*

$$\int_C f(z)dz = 0$$

where C is any closed contour contained in D.

Proof:

In the proof of this theorem, we shall make use of Green's theorem for a plane which states

If P (x, y), Q (x, y), $\frac{\partial P}{\partial y}, \frac{\partial Q}{\partial x}$ are all continuous functions within a domain D and if C is any closed contour in D, then

$$\int_C (p\,dx + Q\,dy) = \iint_D \left(\frac{\partial Q}{\partial x} - \frac{\partial P}{\partial y} \right) dx\,dy$$

Now $\int_C f(z)\,dz = \int_C (u\,dx - v\,dy) + i \int_C (v\,dx + u\,dy)$. ...(1)

We have $f'(z) = u_x + iv_x = v_y - iu_y$ ...(2)

[By Cauchy-Riemann Equations]

Since f′(z) is continuously differentiable, it follows from (2) that u_x, u_y, v_x, v_y all exist and are continuous in D. Thus all the conditions of Green's theorem are satisfied. Hence we get from (1)

$$\int_C f(z)\,dz = \iint_D \left(-\frac{\partial v}{\partial x} - \frac{\partial u}{\partial y} \right) dx\,dy + i \iint_D \left(\frac{\partial u}{\partial x} - \frac{\partial v}{\partial y} \right) dx\,dy$$

$$= \iint_D \left(-\frac{\partial v}{\partial x} + \frac{\partial v}{\partial x} \right) dx\,dy + i \iint_D \left(\frac{\partial u}{\partial x} - \frac{\partial u}{\partial y} \right) dx\,dy$$

$= 0.$ [By Cauchy-Riemann equations]

Note: The form of Cauchy's theorem is of much practical utility in applied mathematics in as much as the continuity of the four partial derivatives u_x, u_y, v_x, v_y is generally assumed on physical grounds.

Remark:

In the statement of theorem I above, we assumed the continuity of the derived function f ′(z). It was Goursat who first proved that this condition can be removed from the hypothesis in the theorem. The revised form of the theorem, known as Cauchy -Goursat Theorem, is given -below.

Theorem I:

(Cauchy-Goursat): *We shall give three independent proofs of this important theorem.*

Theorem II:

(Cauchy-Goursat): *Let f(z) be analytic in a simply connected domain D and let C be any closed continuous rectifiable curve in D. Then*

$$\int_C f(z)\,dz = 0.$$

Before proving the theorem, we prove the following Lemma known as Goursat's Lemma.

Lemma:

Let f(z) be analytic within and on a closed contour C. Then for every $\varepsilon > 0$, it is always possible to divide the region within C into a finite number n of squares and partial squares whose boundaries are denoted by S_i (i = 1, 2, ..., n) such that there exists a point z_i within each S_i such that

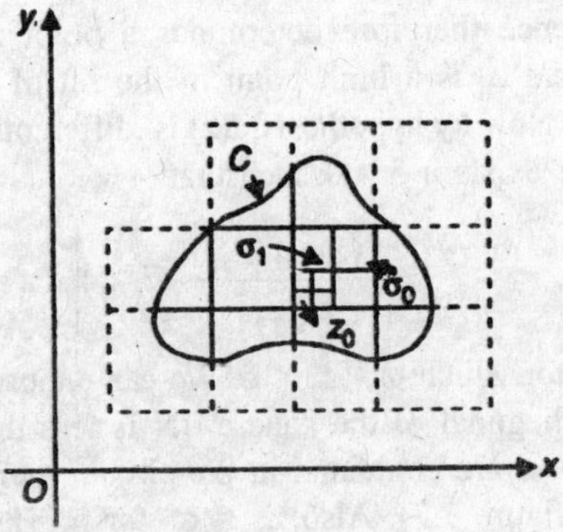

Fig. 1.6

$$\left|\frac{f(z)-f(z_i)}{z-z_i}-f'(z_i)\right|<\varepsilon \qquad \text{... (1)}$$

for each point z ($\neq z_i$) within or on S_i (i = 1, 2, ..., n).

Proof of the Lemma:

Suppose the lemma is false. Then there exists an $\varepsilon > 0$ such that however we subdivide the region within C there will be at least one mesh (either square or partial square) for which (1) does not hold. We shall show that this leads to a contradiction.

We denote by D the closed region consisting of points within and on C. Let the region D be covered by a net work of finite number of meshes (squares or partial squares) by drawing lines, parallel to the coordinate axes (see the figure). They by our assumption, there is at least one mesh for which (1) is false.

Let ao denote the mesh if it is a square and if this mesh is a partial square, let co denote the entire square containing it. We divide co into four equal squares, Then there is at least one of the four smaller squares, say σ_1, containing points of D for which (1) does not hold. We quadrisect a_1 again and proceed as before. If this process ends after a finite number of steps, we have arrived at a contradiction and our lemma is proved.

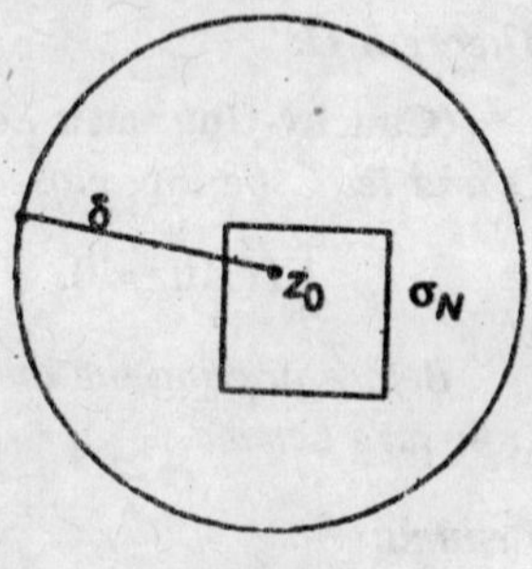

Fig. 1.7

If, however, the process is continued indefinitely, we get a nested sequence of squares $\sigma_0, \sigma_1, \sigma_2, ..., \sigma_n$ ... each contained in the preceding one for which the lemma is false.

This sequence therefore determines a point z_0 common to all these squares such that z_0 is a limit point of the set of points in D. Since D is closed, $z_0 \in D$. Now by hypothesis, f(z) is .differentiable at z_0. Hence for our chosen ε, there exists a $\delta > 0$ such that

$$\left|\frac{f(z)-f(z_0)}{z-z_0} - f'(z_0)\right| < \varepsilon \qquad ...(2)$$

holds for all z for which $|z - z_0| < \delta$. We can choose a positive integer N so large that the diagonal of the square σN is less than δ so that for $n \geq N$, all the squares on are contained in the circular neighbourhood $|z - z_0| < \delta$ of z_0 (see the figure 1.7). Also $z_0 \in \sigma_n$ for n. Thus we have arrived at a contradiction for by taking z_i to be z_0 the inequality (2) is satisfied. This completes the proof of the lemma.

Proof of the Main Theorem:

Let $\varepsilon > 0$ be given. Then by the above lemma, the region within C can be divided into a finite number n of meshes, either squares or partial squares such that a point z_i exists in each mesh for which (1) holds. We denote the boundaries of these meshes by S_i $(i = 1, 2, ...n)$. We can write the inequality (2) in the form

$$f(z) = f(z_i) - z_i f'(z_i) + zf'(z_i) + (z - z_i)\eta_i\,(Z)$$

where $|\eta_i(z)| < \varepsilon$. ... (3)

The value of f(z) at any point z on the boundary S_i is also given by (3). Hence if z is any point on the boundary S_i, then integrating around S_i, we get from (3)

$$\int_{S_i} f(z)\,dz = [f(z_i) - z_i f'(z_i)] \int_{S_i} dz + f'(z_i) \int_{S_i} z\,dz + \int_{S_i} (z - z_i)\eta_i(z)\,dz. \quad ...(4)$$

$$\int_{S_i} dz = 0, \int_{S_i} z\,dz = 0.$$

Hence (3) reduces to $\int_{S_i} f(z)dz$

$$= \int_{S_i} (z - z_i)\eta_i\,dz \quad ... (5)$$

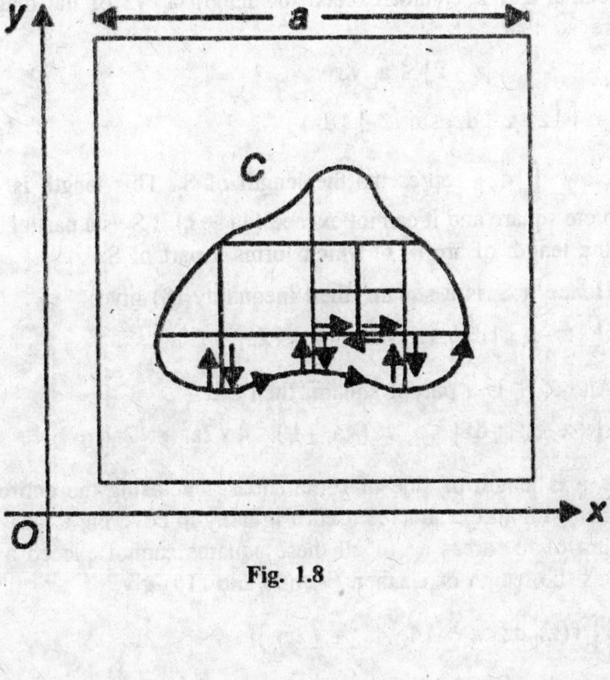

Fig. 1.8

Again, as is evident from the adjoining diagram, the sum of the integrals around all the S_i's is the integral around the closed curve C since the line integrals along the common boundary line of every pair of adjacent meshes cancel each other. Only the integrals along the arcs which form parts of C remain.

Thus $$\int_C f(z)dz = \sum_{i=1}^{n} \int_{S_i} f(z)dz \quad \text{... (6)}$$

Therefore from (5) and (6), we get

$$\int_C f(z)dz = \sum_{i=1}^{n} \int_{S_i} (z - z_i)\eta_i(z)dz$$

so that $$\left|\int_C f(z)dz\right| \le \sum_{i=1}^{n} \left|\int_{S_i} (z - z_i)\eta_i(z)dz\right|$$

$$\le \sum_{i=1}^{n} \int_{S_i} |z - z_i|\,|\eta_i(z)|\,|dz|$$

$$< \varepsilon \sum_{i=1}^{n} \int_{S} |z - z_i|\,|dz| \text{ by (3)} \quad \text{...(7)}$$

The boundary S_i of a mesh either completely or partially coincides with the boundary of a square. We denote by a_i the length of a side of that square. Since z lies on S_i and z_i lies either on or inside S_i the distance between z and z_i cannot exceed the length $a_i\sqrt{2}$ of the diagonal of that square so that

$$|z - z_i| \le a_i\sqrt{2}$$

$$\therefore \int_{S_i} |z - z_i|\,|dz| \le a_i\sqrt{2} \int_{S_i} |dz|. \quad \text{...(8)}$$

Now $\int_{S_i} |dz|$ represents the length of S_i. This length is $4a_i$ if S_i is a complete square and it cannot exceed $(4a_i + l_i)$ if S_i is a partial square where l_i is the length of arc of C which forms a part of S_i.

Hence if S_i is a square, then inequality (8) gives

$$\int_{S_i} |z - z_i|\,|dz| \le a_i\sqrt{2}\,4a_i = 4\sqrt{2}a_i^2. \quad \text{...(9)}$$

And if S_i is a partial square, then

$$\int_{S_i} |z - z_i|\,|dz| \le a_i\sqrt{2}(4a_i + l_i) \le 4\sqrt{2}a_i^2 + \sqrt{2}al_i \quad \text{...(10)}$$

where a is length of side of some square enclosing the entire curve C together with all the squares used originally in covering C. It is evident that the sum of the areas a_i^2 of all these squares cannot exceed a^2. Hence if l denotes the length of C, then (7), (9) and (10) give

$$\left|\int_C f(z)\right| dz < \varepsilon \sum_{i=1}^{n} \left(4\sqrt{4}a_i^2 + \sqrt{2}al_i\right)$$

$$\leq \varepsilon(4\sqrt{4a^2}+\sqrt{2}al) \qquad ...(11)$$

$$= \varepsilon K$$

where K is a constant.

Since ε is arbitrary, it follows from (11) that

$$\int_C f(z)dz = 0.$$

The theorem is thus completely established.

Cor. 1:

Let f(z) be analytic in a simply connected domain D. Then the integral along every rectifiable curve in D joining any two given points of D is the same i.e. it does not depend on the curve joining the two points.

Proof:

Let C_1, C_2, be any two curves in D joining two given points z_1 and z_2. Let C denote the closed curve consisting of C_1 and $-C_2$. Then by Cauchy's theorem we have

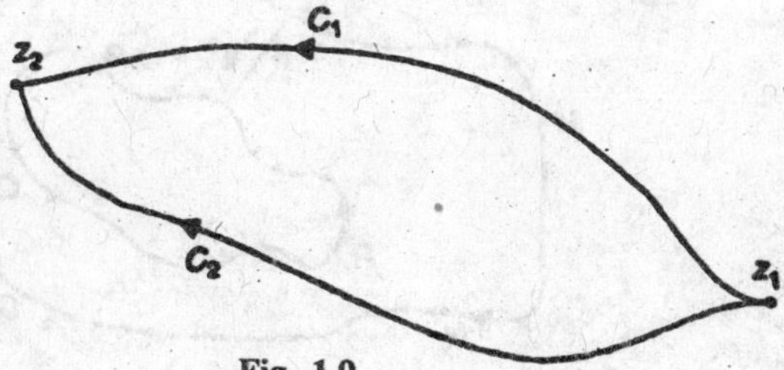

Fig. 1.9

$$\int_C f(z)dz = 0$$

or $\int_{C_1} f(z)dz + \int_{-C_1} f(z)dz = 0$

$$\int_{C_1} f(z)dz - \int_{C_2} f(z)dz = 0$$

or $\int_{C_1} f(z)dz = \int_{C_2} f(z)dz.$

Hence the result.

Note: In view of the above corollary, we may use the symbol $\int_a^b f(z)dz$ for the integral of f(z) along any curve joining a and b.

Cor. 2 : Extension of the Cauchy-Goursat Theorem to Multiply Connected Regions

Let D be a doubly connected region bounded by two simple closed curves C and C_1 such that C_1 is contained in C then

$$\int_C f(z)dz = \int_{C_1} f(z)dz.$$

where C and C_1 are both traversed in the positive sense (*i.e.* anticlockwise direction).

Proof:

We make a cross-cut joining a point L of C to a point P of C_1 as shown in the adjoining future. Then the region formed by LMNOLPQRPL is simply connected. Hence by Cauchy Goursat's theorem, we have

$$\int_{LMNOLPQRPL} f(z)dz = 0$$

i.e.

$$\int_{LMNOL} f(z)dz + \int_{LP} f(z)dz + + \int_{PQRP} f(z)dz + \int_{PL} f(z)dz = 0 \qquad ...(1)$$

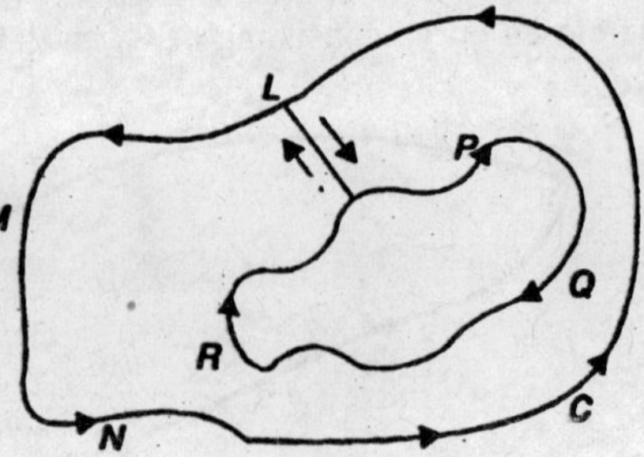

Fig. 1.10

But $\int_{LP} f(z)dz - \int_{PL} f(z)dz$

Hence (1) reduces to

$$\int_{LMNOL} f(z)dz + \int_{PQRP} f(z)dz = 0$$

or

$$\int_C f(z)dz + \int_{-C_1} f(z)dz = 0$$

i.e.

$$\int_C f(z)dz = \int_{C_1} f(z) = 0$$

Thus

$$\int_C f(z)dz = \int_{C_1} f(z)dz.$$

In general if f(z) is analytic in a region bounded by the nonoverlapping simple closed curves C, C_1, C_2, ..., C_m where

$$C_1, C_2, ..., C_m$$

and inside C, then

$$\int_C f(z)dz = \int_{C_1} f(z)dz + \int_{C_2} f(z)dz + ... + \int_{C_m} f(z)dz$$

where C and each C_i is traversed in the anticlock wise direction.

Remark I:

Cauchy's fundamental theorem holds under less restrictive conditions. The following is one of the versions of this thorem.

Let f(z) be continuous on and analytic within a rectifiable Jordan curve C. Then $\int_C f(z)dz = 0$.

Note that in the above statement, it is not necessary for f(z) to be analytic on C. Only the continuity of f(z) is essential on C. However, we shall not try to prove the above assertion.

Remark II:

Conditions stated in theorem II of § 8 are only sufficient but not necessary for $\int_C f(z)dz$ *to vanish. For example consider the integral of* $\frac{1}{z^2}$ *along the circle* γ *defined by* $|z| = d$, $r > 0$. *Setting* $z = re^{i\theta}$, $dz = ri\, e^{i\theta} d\theta$, *we get*

$$\int_\gamma \frac{1}{z^2} dz = \int_0^{2\pi} \frac{ri\, e^{i\theta}\, d\theta}{r^2 e^{2i\theta}} = \frac{i}{r}\int_0^{2\pi} e^{-i\theta}\, d\theta$$

$$= \frac{1}{r}\left[-e^{-i\theta}\right]_0^{2\pi} = \frac{1}{r}\left[e^0 - e^{-2\pi i}\right] = \frac{1}{r}[1-1] = 0$$

Thus the integral of $\frac{1}{z^2}$ along γ vanishes but $\frac{1}{z^2}$ is not analytic at $z = 0$ which is a point (the centre) within γ.

If, however, we assume the continuity of f(z) within and on C, then the vanishing of the integral $\int_C f(z)dz$ will imply analyticity of f(z). We shall prove this assertion later on as a theorem known as Morera's theorem.

SECOND PROOF OF CAUCHY-GOURSAT THEOREM

In this proof we shall use the result of the following lemma.

Lemma:

Let f(z) be continuous on a domain D and let C be any continuous rectifiable curve in D. Their corresponding to even $\varepsilon > 0$, *there exists a polygon* Δ *in D with vertices on C such that*

$$\left|\int_C f(z)dz - \int_\Delta f(z)dz\right| < \varepsilon$$

Theorem:

(Cauchy-Goursat): *Let f(z) be analytic in a simply connected domain D and let C be any closed continuous rectifiable curve contained in D. Then,*

$$\int_C f(z)dz = 0$$

Proof:

Step I: *(Cauchy's Theorem for a Triangle)*—Let Δ be any triangular contour contained in D. Since D is simply connected, the interior of Δ also belong to D. We want to prove

$$\int_\Delta f(z)dz = 0$$

To achieve the desired result, we join the mid-points of the sides of Δ by means of straight lines, thereby obtaining four congruent subtriangles $\Delta^{(1)}$, $\Delta^{(2)}$, $\Delta^{(3)}$ and $\Delta^{(4)}$ as shown in the adjoining figure. We have

$$\int_\Delta f(z)dz = \int_{\Delta^{(1)}} f(z)dz + \int_{\Delta^{(2)}} f(z)dz + \int_{\Delta^{(3)}} f(z)dz + \int_{\Delta^{(4)}} f(z)dz \quad ...(1)$$

The equality (1) follows from the fact that each of the four integrals on the right hand side can be replaced by the sum of three integrals taken along the separate sides of that triangle so that the six of resulting integrals have a sum equal to

$$\int_\Delta f(z)dz$$

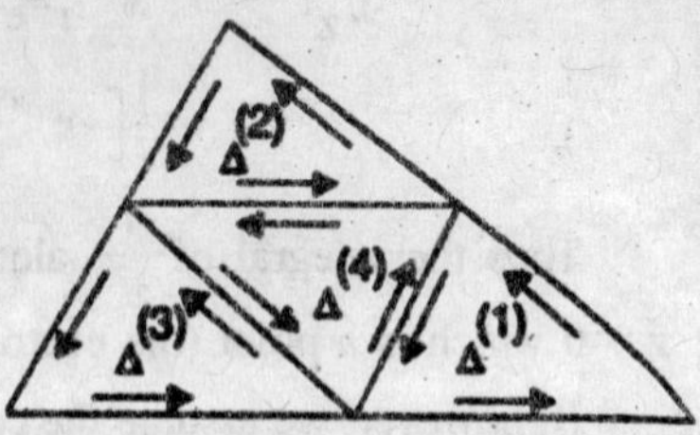

Fig. 1.11

and the remaining six integrals have the sum zero since they can be grouped into three pairs where each pair is taken along the same line segment traversed twice in opposite directions (see the figure).

Since the modulus of a sum is less than or equal to the sum of the moduli, from (1) we have

$$\left|\int_\Delta f(z)dz\right| \le \left|\int_{\Delta^{(1)}} f(z)dz\right| + \left|\int_{\Delta^{(2)}} f(z)dz\right| + \left|\int_{\Delta^{(3)}} f(z)dz\right| + \left|\int_{\Delta^{(4)}} f(z)dz\right| \quad ...(2)$$

We write $\left|\int_{\Delta_1} f(z)dz\right| \geq M$. Then it follows from (2) that at least one of the terms on the right hand side must not be less than $\frac{M}{4}$.

We denote by Δ_1 one of the four triangles $\Delta^{(1)}, \Delta^{(2)}, \Delta^{(3)}, \Delta^{(4)}$ such that At satisfies the inequality

$$\left|\int_{\Delta_1} f(z)dz\right| \geq \frac{M}{4}.$$

Now, we divide the triangle Δ_1 into four congruent triangles by joining the mid-points of Δ_1. As in the case of Δ_1, there exists a triangle Δ_2 amongst these four new triangles such that

$$\left|\int_{\Delta_2} f(z)dz\right| \geq \frac{1}{4}.\frac{M}{4} = \frac{M}{4^2}.$$

Proceeding in this manner, we obtain a sequence of triangles

$$\Delta = \Delta_0, \Delta_1, \Delta_2, \ldots, \Delta_n, \ldots$$

Such that,

(i) Δ_{n+1} is properly contained in Δ_n $(n = 0, 1, 2, \ldots)$.

(ii) the length of $\Delta_n = \frac{1}{2^n} = ln$, say where l is the length of Δ.

(iii) each triangle is contained in D.

(iv) $\left|\int_{\Delta_n} f(z)dz\right| \geq \frac{M}{4^4} (n = 1, 2, 3, \ldots)$

i.e. $\left|\int_{\Delta} f(z)dz\right| \geq 4^n \left|\int_{\Delta_n} f(z)dz\right|$

From (i), (ii), (iii) it follows that there exists a unique point z_0 of D belonging to all the triangles. By hypothesis, f(z) is differentiable at z_0

$$\lim_{z \to z_0} \frac{f(z) - f(z_0)}{z - z_0} = f'(z_0)$$

this means that for a given $\varepsilon > 0$ there exists $\delta > 0$ such that

$$\left|\frac{f(z) - f(z_0)}{z - z_0} - f'(z_0)\right| < \varepsilon.$$

whenever $|z - z_0| < \delta$.

Writing $\frac{f(z) - f(z_0)}{z - z_0} = f'(z_0) = \eta(z)$, ...(3)

we have $|h(z)| < \varepsilon$

whenever $|z-z_0| < \delta$.

Thus for all z satisfying $|z-z_0| < \delta$, we have

$$f(z) = f(z_0) + (z - z_0) f'((z_0) + (z - z_0) \eta(z)$$

where $|h(z)| < \varepsilon$. ...(4)

Since z_0 belongs to all the "nested" triangles and since the triangles become arbitrarily small ($l_n \to 0$ as $n \to \infty$), there exists a positive integer N such that for n > N all the triangles Δ_n arc contained in the circular disc $|z-z_0| < \delta$ so that all their points satisfy the inequality (3).

Now integrating both sides of (4) along the closed curve Δ_n we obtain

$$\int_{\Delta_n} f(z)dz = \int_{\Delta_n} f(z_0)dz + \int_{\Delta_n} (z-z_0)f'(z_0)dz + \int_{\Delta_n} (z-z_0)\eta(z)dz \quad ...(5)$$

As shown in (i) and ((iii) of the example of 3, we have

$$\int_{\Delta_n} f(z_0)dz = f(z_0)\int_{\Delta_n} dz = 0 \quad ...(6)$$

and

$$\int_{\Delta_n} (z-z_0)f'(z)dz$$

$$\int_{\Delta_n} z\,dz - z_0 f(z_0)\int_{\Delta_n} dz = 0 \quad ...(7)$$

To evaluate $\int_{\Delta_n} (z-z_0)\eta(z)dz$, we first observe that the distance between any two points of the triangle Δ_n cannot exceed the perimeter l_n in Δ_n. In other words

$$|z-z_0| \le l_n \forall z \in \Delta_n \quad ...(8)$$

Hence

$$\left|\int_{\Delta_n} (z-z_0)\eta(z)dz\right|$$

$$\le \int_{\Delta_n} |(z-z_0)||\eta(z)||dz|$$

$$< \int_{\Delta_n} l_n.\varepsilon|dz|$$

[By (3) and (8)]

$$= l_n.\varepsilon.l_n \text{ [By ((ii) of example of 3]}$$

$$= \varepsilon l_n^2 = \varepsilon\left(\frac{1}{2^n}\right)^2 \quad ...(9)$$

from (5), (6), (7) and (9), we obtain

$$\left|\int_{\Delta_n} f(z)dz\right| < \varepsilon\left(\frac{l'}{2^n}\right)^2 \quad ...(10)$$

Finally from (4) and (10), we get

$$\left|\int_{\Delta} f(z)dz\right| < 4^n \varepsilon\left(\frac{1}{2^n}\right)^2 = \varepsilon l^2. \quad ...(11)$$

Since ε is an arbitrary small positive number, it follows from (11) that

$$\int_{\Delta} f(z)dz = 0$$

Step II:

(Cauchy's Theorem for a Closed Polygon): *Let C be any closed polygon contained in D.*

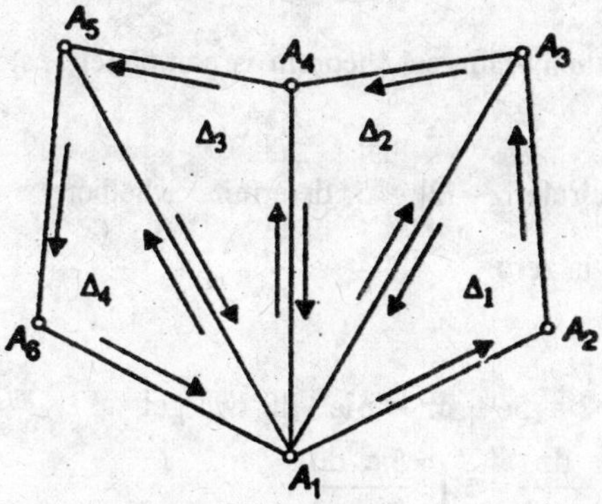

Fig. 1.12

We denote the vertices of C by $A_1, A_2, ..., A_n$ ($n \geq 4$). We divide the polygon in n–2 triangles $\Delta_1, \Delta_2, \Delta_3, ..., \Delta_{n-2}$ by drawing diagonals from on of the vertices, say A_1, to the other vertices. (See the adjoining diagram for n = 6).

Then by Cauchy's theorem for a triangle (step I) and the fact that the integrals along A_1A_3 and A_3A_1, A_1A_4 and A_4A_1, ..., A_1A_{n-1} and $A_{n-1}A_1$ cancel, we see that

$$\int_{\Delta} f(z)dz$$

$$= \int_{\Delta_1} f(z)dz + \int_{\Delta_2} f(z)dz + ... + \int_{\Delta_{n-1}} f(z)dz$$

$$= 0.$$

Step III:

(Cauchy's Theorem for Any Rectifiable Closed Curve): *Let C be any continuous rectifiable closed curve contained in D. Suppose ε > 0 be given. Then by the lemma there exists a polygon A in D with vertices of C such that*

$$\left| \int_C f(z)dz - \int_{\Delta} f(z)dz \right| < \varepsilon.$$

Also by step II, we have

$$\int_{\Delta} f(z)dz = 0.$$

Hence $$\left|\int_C f(z)dz\right| < \varepsilon.$$

Since ε is arbitrary, we have

$$\int_C f(z)dz = 0.$$

Thus the Cauchy-Goursat theorem is completely established.

Example:

If C is the circle |z – 2| = 5, determine whether

$\int_C \frac{dz}{z-3}$ is zero.

Solution:

Putting $z - 2 = 5e^{i\theta}$, $dz = 5ie^{i\theta}\, d\theta$, we get

$$\int_C \frac{dz}{z-3} = \int_0^{2\pi} \frac{5ie^{i\theta} d\theta}{5e^{i\theta} - 1}$$

$$= i\int_0^{2\pi} \left(1 - \tfrac{1}{5}e^{-i\theta}\right) d\theta$$

$$= i\int_0^{2\pi} \left[1 + \frac{1}{5}e^{-i\theta} + \frac{1}{5^2}e^{-2\theta} + \ldots\right] d\theta$$

Now $$\int_0^{2\pi} e^{-mi\theta} d\theta = -\left[e^{-mi\theta}\right]_0^{2\pi} = -\frac{1}{mi}\left[e^{-2\pi mi} - e^0\right]$$

$$= -\frac{1}{mi}[1-1] = 0 \text{ when } m \neq 0.$$

$$\therefore \quad \int_C \frac{dz}{z-3} = i\int_0^{2\pi} d\theta = 2\pi i \neq 0.$$

The reason that the integral is not zero is that $\frac{1}{z-3}$ is not analytic at z = 3 which is an interior point of the circle |z–2| = 5.

A THIRD PROOF OF CAUCHY-GOURSAT THEOREM

Step I:

Cauchy's Theorem for a Rectangle: *By a rectangle R in the complex plane, we shall mean a set of points (x, y) such that*

$a \le x \le b,\ c \le y \le d.$

We think of the perimeter of R as a simple closed curve consisting of four line segments whose direction is chosen in such a manner that the area

R lies to the left of these directed segments. The vertices thus occur in the order (a, c), (b, c), (b, d), (a, d). We shall refer to this closed curve as the boundary curve or contour of R and shall denote it by aR. We now prove Cauchy's theorem for a rectangle, namely :

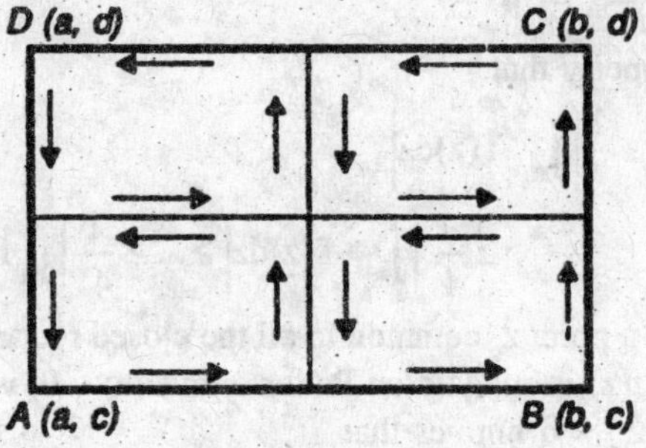

Fig. 1.13

If the function f(z) is analytic on a rectangle R, then

$$\int_{\partial R} f(z)dz = 0.$$

where ∂R denotes the boundary curve of R.

Proof:

We subdivide R into four congruent rectangles $R^{(1)}$, $R^{(2)}$, $R^{(3)}$ and $R^{(4)}$ by joining the mid-points of opposite sides by line segments as shown in the figure. As remarked we shall denote the boundaries of the rectangles by

$$aR^k, K = 1, 2, 3, 4.$$

Observe that $$\partial R = \partial R^{(1)} + \partial R^{(2)} + \partial R^{(3)} + \partial R^{(4)}$$

since the dividing segments cancel in pairs.

$$\int_{\partial R} f(z)dz = \int_{\partial R^{(1)}} f(z)dz + \int_{\partial R^{(2)}} f(z)dz + \int_{\partial R^{(3)}} f(z)dz + \int_{\partial R^{(4)}} f(z)dz \quad ...(1)$$

Clearly for at least one $R^{(k)}$ $(k = 1,...,4)$, we have

$$\left|\int_{\partial R^{(k)}} f(z)dz\right| \geq \left|\frac{1}{4}\int_{\partial R} f(z)dz\right| \quad ...(2)$$

for otherwise

$$\left|\int_{\partial R} f(z)dz\right| = \left|\sum_{k=1}^{4}\int_{\partial R^{(k)}} f(z)dz\right| \leq \sum_{k=1}^{4}\left|\int_{\partial R^{(k)}} f(z)dz\right| < \left|\int_{\partial R} f(z)dz\right|$$

which is impossible.

Let R_1 denote one of the rectangles $R^{(k)}$ for which (2) holds. If several $R^{(k)}$ have this property, the choice must be made according to some definite rule. Repeating the above process indefinitely, we obtain a sequence of rectangles

$$R \supset R_1 \supset R_2 \supset \ldots \supset R_n \supset \ldots$$

with the property that

$$\left|\int_{\partial R_n} f(z)dz\right| \geq \frac{1}{4}\left|\int_{\partial R_{n-1}} f(z)dz\right|$$

$$\geq \frac{1}{4^2}\left|\int_{\partial R_{n-2}} f(z)dz\right| \geq \ldots \geq \frac{1}{4^n}\left|\int_{\partial R} f(z)dz\right| \qquad \ldots(3)$$

There exists a point z_0 common to all the closed rectangles of the above sequence. Since f(z) is analytic on R, for a given $\varepsilon > 0$, we can choose $\delta > 0$ such that $|z - z_0| < \delta$ implies that

$$\left|\frac{f(z)-f(z_0)}{z-z_0} - f(z)\right| < \varepsilon$$

that is, $|f(z) - f(z_0) - (z - z_0) f'(z_0)| < \varepsilon |z - z_0|$. ... (4)

Let $N(z_0, \delta)$ denote the set of all points z for which $|z - z_0| < \delta$. Then for sufficiently large n, we have $R_n \subset N(z_0, \delta)$ and so (4) holds for every $z \in R_n$. Also, we have

$$\int_{\partial R_n} dz = 0 \text{ and } \int_{\partial R_n} z\,dz = 0$$

so that $$\int_{\partial R_n} f(z)dz = 0 \int_{\partial R_n} z\,dz + z_0 f'(z_0)\int_{\partial R_n} dz$$

$$-f'(z_0)\int_{\partial R_n} z\,dz + z_0 f'(z_0)\int_{\partial R_n} dz$$

$$= \int_{\partial R_n} [f(z) - f(z_0) - (z - z_0)f'(z_0)]dz \qquad \ldots(5)$$

If d_n denote the length of the diagonal of Rn, then $z \in R_n$ implies that

$$|z - z_0| \leq d_n. \qquad \ldots(6)$$

Now by (5), we have

$$\left|\int_{\partial R_n} f(z)dz\right| \leq \int_{\partial R} |f(z) - f(z_0) - (z - z_0)f'(z_0)|\,|dz|$$

$$\leq \int_{\partial R_n} \varepsilon |z - z_0|\,|dz| \text{ by (4)}$$

$$\leq \int_{\partial R_n} \varepsilon d_n\,|dz| \text{ by (6)}$$

$$= \varepsilon\, d_n L_n. \qquad \ldots(7)$$

where L_n denotes the arc length of ∂R_n.

If d and L denote the length of the diagonal and the perimeter of R respectively, then it is evident that $d_n = 2^{-n}\, d$ and $L_n = 2^{-n}\, L$.

Then (7) gives, $\left|\int_{\partial R_n} f(z)dz\right| \le \varepsilon\, dL.$ ...(8)

Finally (3) and (8) imply that

$$\left|\int_{\partial R} f(z)dz\right| \le \varepsilon\, dL.$$

Since ε is arbitrary, we have

$$\int_{\partial R} f(z)dz = 0$$

and the theorem is proved.

Step II:

(Cauchy's Theorem in a Circular Disc): *If f(z) is analytic in the open disc A defined by $|z - z_0| < r$, then*

$$\int_C f(z)dz = 0$$

for every closed C in Δ

Proof:

Let O be the centre $z_0 = x_0 + iy_0$ and P any point

$$z = x + iy$$

inside Δ. We define a function F(z) by

$$F(z) = \int_\sigma f(z)dz \quad ...(9)$$

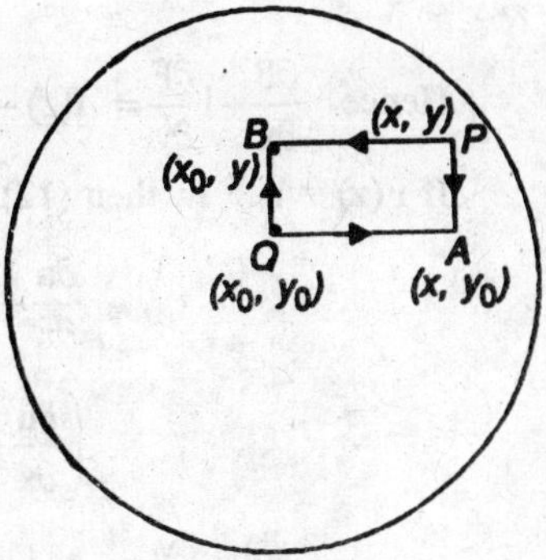

Fig. 1.14

where σ consists of the horizontal segment OA from the centre (x_0, y_0) to (x, y_0) and the vertical segment AP from (x, y_0) to (x, y) see the figure 1.14 above. Thus (9) may be written as

$$F(z) = \int_{OAP} f(z)dz = \int_{OA} + \int_{AP}$$

$$= \int_{x_0}^{x} f(t + iy_0)dt + i\int_{y_0}^{y} f(x + it)dt. \quad ...(10)$$

[Note that on OA, y is constant equal to y_0 and x varies from x_0 to x so that we may set]

$$z = t + iy_0,\ dz = dt$$

on OA. Similarly on AP, x is constant and y varies from y_0 toy so that

$$z = x + it,\ dz = i\ dt \text{ on AP}].$$

By Cauchy's theorem for a rectangle the integral of f(z) along the boundary OAPBO must vanish. This implies that the integrals of f(z) along OAP and OBP are the same. Accordingly the function F(z) may also be defined by

$$F(z) = \int_{OBP} f(z)dz$$

$$= \int_{OB} + \int_{BP} = i\int_{y_0}^{y} f(x_0 + it)dt + \int_{x_0}^{x} f(t + iy)dt \qquad ...(11)$$

By (10), we conclude that

$$\frac{\partial F}{\partial y} = if(x + iy) = if(z).$$

while (11) shows that

$$\frac{\partial F}{\partial x} = f(x + iy) = f(z).$$

Hence $\dfrac{\partial F}{\partial x} + i\dfrac{\partial F}{\partial y} = f(z) - f(z) = 0.$ ...(12)

If F(z) = u + iv, then (12) gives

$$0 = \frac{\partial u}{\partial x} + i\frac{\partial F}{\partial y} + i\left(\frac{\partial u}{\partial y} + i\frac{\partial v}{\partial y}\right)$$

$$= \left(\frac{\partial u}{\partial x} - \frac{\partial v}{\partial y}\right) + \left(\frac{\partial u}{\partial y} + i\frac{\partial v}{\partial x}\right)$$

so that $\dfrac{\partial u}{\partial x} - \dfrac{\partial v}{\partial y} = 0,\ \dfrac{\partial u}{\partial y} + \dfrac{\partial v}{\partial x} = 0,$

and $\dfrac{\partial u}{\partial x} = \dfrac{\partial v}{\partial y}, \dfrac{\partial u}{\partial y} = -\dfrac{\partial v}{\partial x}$

Thus u,v satisfy Cauchy-Riemann equations. Since

$$\frac{\partial F}{\partial x} = f(z)', \frac{\partial F}{\partial y} = if(z)$$

and f(z) continuous, it follows that the four partial derivatives u_x, u_y, v_x and v_y are all continuous. F(z) = u + iv is analytic on Δ. We now find the derivative F′(z).

We know that $F'(z) = \dfrac{\partial F}{\partial x}$

Also as shown above, $\frac{\partial F}{\partial x} = f(z)$. It follows that

$$F' = f(z)$$

and we have proved the following result.

If f(z) is analytic in the disc $|z - z_0| < r$, then there exists another analytic function F(z) in $|z - z_0| < r$ such that

$$F'(z) = f(z).$$

It then follows from our remark after theorem II

$$\int_C f(z)dz = 0$$

for any closed curve C in Δ. This proves Cauchy's theorem for a circular disc.

Step III:

Cauchy's Theorem for Any Closed Curve: *Let f(z) be analytic in a simply connected domain D and let C be any closed contour in D. Then*

$$\int_C f(z)dz = 0.$$

Proof:

Since the closed contour C lies in the interior of D, we can choose $d > 0$ such that the disc $|z - z_0| < 2d$ is entirely contained in D if z_0 is any point of C. Let the domain be covered by a network of squares obtained by drawing two sets of equidistant straight lines parallel to x-axis and y-axis respectively. If we take the distance between adjacent lines to be d, then it is evident that the network of squares of sides obtained in this way has the following property:

Any square whose boundary intersects C at a point z_0 is entirely contained in the disc $|z - z_0| < 2d$.

Let D_0 denote the interior of C. Then we may divide the squares belonging to our net work into two classes:

(i) Those whose interiors consist entirely of points of D_0.

(ii) Those whose interiors also contain points of D which are not in D_0.

Let $C_1, C_2, \ldots, C_n$ denote the perimeters of the squares of the first class and $\Gamma_1, \Gamma_2 \ldots, \Gamma_m$ denote the closed curves which are contained in a square of the second class and consist of sections of C and of parts of the perimeter of the square inside D_0. Then

$$\int_C f(z)dz = \sum_{i=1}^{n} \int_{C_i} f(z)dz + \sum_{j=1}^{m} \int_{\Gamma_j} f(z)dz \qquad \text{...(13)}$$

since the integrals over common boundaries cancel each other.

The integrals over the C_i vanish in view of Cauchy's theorem for rectangles. Also the integrals over the Γ_j vanish by Cauchy's theorem for circular disc since, as pointed out above, each Γ_j is contained in a disc in which f(z) is analytic. Hence, all the integrals on the right-hand side of (13) vanish and consequently.

$$\int_C f(z)dz = 0$$

The Cauchy-Goursat theorem is completely established.

CAUCHY'S INTEGRAL FORMULA

Theorem:

Let f(z) be an analytic function in a simply connected domain D enclosed by a rectifiable Jordan curve C and let f(z) be continuous on C.

Then $$f(z_0) = \frac{1}{2\pi i}\int_C \frac{f(z)}{z-z_0}dz$$

where z_0 is any point of D.

Proof:

We describe a circle γ defined by the equation $z - z_0 = \rho$ where $\rho < d$ (the distance of z_0 from C).

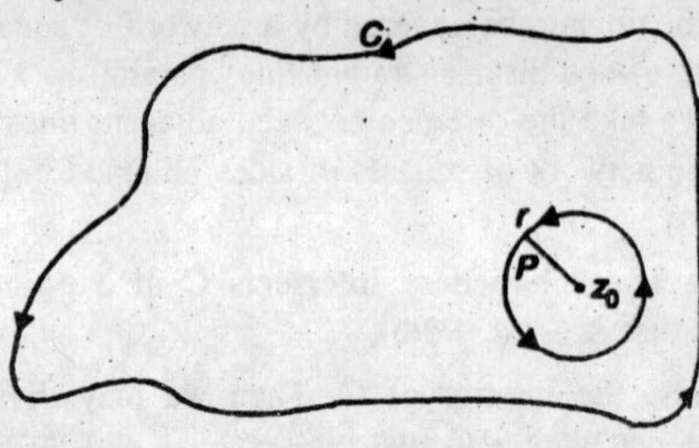

Fig. 1.15

Then the function

$$\phi(z) = \frac{f(z)}{z-z_0} \quad ...(1)$$

is analytic in the doubly connected region bounded by C and V. Hence by Cor. 2 or theorem II, § 7, we have

$$\int_C \phi(z)dz = \int_\gamma \phi(z)dz$$

or $$\frac{1}{2\pi i}\int_C \frac{f(z)}{z-z_0}dz = \frac{1}{2\pi i}\int_\gamma \frac{f(z)}{z-z_0}dz$$

where C and γ are both traversed in the counter-clockwise direction (see the figure 1.15).

It is evident that the integral on the right-hand side of (1) is independent of ρ and so we may choose ρ as small as we please.

Now $$\frac{1}{2\pi i}\int_\gamma \frac{f(z)}{z-z_0}dz$$

$$= \frac{1}{2\pi i}\int_\gamma \frac{f(z)-f(z_0)}{z-z_0}dz + \frac{1}{2\pi i}\int_\gamma \frac{f(z)}{z-z_0}dz \quad \text{... (2)}$$

Writing $z - z_0 = \rho e^{i\theta}$, $dz = \rho i e^{i\theta}\, d\theta$, we have

$$\int_\gamma \frac{f(z_0)}{z-z_0}dz = f(z_0)\int_0^{2\pi} \frac{\rho i e^{i\theta}}{\rho e^{i\theta}} = f(z_0)\int_0^{2\pi} i d\theta = 2\pi i f(z_0).$$

Hence (2) can be written as

$$\frac{1}{2\pi i}\int_\gamma \frac{f(z)}{z-z_0}dz = \int_\gamma \frac{f(z)-f(z_0)}{z-z_0} + f(z_0)dz$$

or $$\frac{1}{2\pi i}\int_\gamma \frac{f(z)}{z-z_0}dz - f(z_0) = \frac{1}{2\pi i}\int_\gamma \frac{f(z)-f(z_0)}{z-z_0}dz. \quad \text{...(3)}$$

Since f(z) is continuous at z_0, for a given $\varepsilon > 0$, there exists a $\delta > 0$ such that

$$|f(z) - f(z_0)| < \varepsilon \quad \text{...(4)}$$

for all z satisfying the inequality $|z - z_0| < \delta$. Since ρ is at our choice, we can take $\rho < \delta$ so that the inequality (4) is satisfied for all points on γ. Hence

$$\left|\frac{1}{2\pi i}\int_\gamma \frac{f(z)-f(z_0)}{z-z_0}dz\right| = \left|\frac{1}{2\pi i}\int_0^{2\pi} \frac{f(z)-f(z_0)}{\rho e^{i\theta}}\rho i e^{i\theta}d\theta\right|$$

$$\leq \int_0^{2\pi} |f(z)-f(z_0)|\, d\theta < \frac{1}{2\pi}\int_0^{2\pi} \varepsilon\, d\theta \text{ by (4)}$$

$$= \frac{1}{2\pi}.2\pi\varepsilon = \varepsilon$$

Thus $$\left|\frac{1}{2\pi i}\int_\gamma \frac{f(z)}{z-z_0}dz - f(z_0)\right| < \varepsilon \quad \text{...(5)}$$

It's then follows from (3) and (5) that

$$\left|\frac{1}{2\pi i}\int_{\gamma}\frac{f(z)}{z-z_0}dz-f(z_0)\right|<\varepsilon. \qquad ...(6)$$

Since ε is arbitrary and the left-hand side of (6) does not depend upon ρ, we conclude that

$$\frac{1}{2\pi i}\int_{\gamma}\frac{f(z)}{z-z_0}dz-f(z_0)=0 \text{ or } \frac{1}{2\pi i}\int_{\gamma}\frac{f(z)}{z-z_0}dz=f(z_0) \qquad ...(7)$$

Finally from (1) and (7), we obtain

$$f(z_0)=\frac{1}{2\pi}\int_{C}\frac{f(z)}{z-z_0}dz. \qquad ... (9)$$

Cor. 1:

Gauss's Mean Value Theorem: *If f(z) is an analytic function on a domain D and if the circular region $|z - z_0| \leq \rho$ is contained in D, then*

$$f(z_0)=\frac{1}{2\pi i}\int_{0}^{2\pi} f(z_0+\rho e^{i\theta})d\theta.$$

In other words, the value of f(z) at the point z_0 equals the average of its values on the boundary of the circle

$$|z - z_0| = \rho.$$

Proof:

Let γ denote the circle $|z - z_0| = \rho$. This equation can be written as

$$z = z_0 + \rho e^{i\theta} \ (0 \leq \theta \leq 2\pi)$$

so that $dz = \rho i e^{i\theta}\, d\theta$.

Hence by Cauchy's integral formula, we get

$$f(z_0) = \frac{1}{2\pi i}\int_{\gamma}\frac{f(z)}{z-z_0}dz=\int_{0}^{2\pi}\frac{f(z_0+\rho e^{i\theta})i\rho e^{i\theta}}{\rho e^{i\theta}}d\theta$$

$$= \frac{1}{2\pi i}\int_{0}^{2\pi} f(z_0+\rho e^{i\theta})d\theta$$

Cor. 2: Extension of Cauchy's Integral Formula to Multiply Connected Regions

We shall consider the case of doubly connected region D bounded by two closed curves C_1 and C_2. If z be any point of D, then we shall prove

$$f(z) = \frac{1}{2\pi i}\int_{C_1}\frac{f(\zeta)d\zeta}{\zeta-z}$$

$$= -\frac{1}{2\pi i}\int_{C_2}\frac{f(\zeta)d\zeta}{\zeta - z}.$$

We make a cross-cut LP connecting the curves C_1 and C_2. Then f(z) is analytic in the region bounded by LMNLPQRPL.

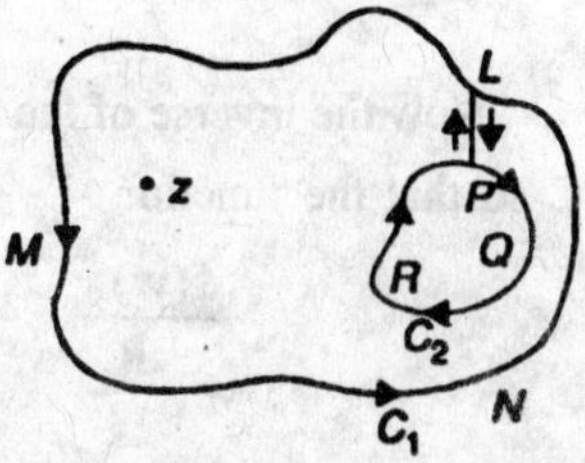

Fig. 1.16

Hence by Cauchy's integral formula

$$f(z) = \frac{1}{2\pi i}\int_{LMNLPQRPL}\frac{f(\zeta)}{\zeta - z}d\zeta$$

$$= \frac{1}{2\pi i}\int_{LMNL}\frac{f(\zeta)}{\zeta - z}d\zeta + \frac{1}{2\pi i}\int_{LP}\frac{f(\zeta)}{\zeta - z}d\zeta$$

$$+\frac{1}{2\pi i}\int_{PQRP}\frac{f(\zeta)}{\zeta - z}d\zeta + \int_{PL}\frac{f(\zeta)}{\zeta - z}d\zeta$$

$$= \frac{1}{2\pi i}\int_{C_1}\frac{f(\zeta)}{\zeta - z}d\zeta - \int_{C_2}\frac{f(\zeta)}{\zeta - z}d\zeta$$

since the integrals along LP and PL cancel.

In particular, if C_1, C_2 are concentric circles with centre z_0 and radii ρ_1, ρ_2 ($\rho_1 > \rho_2$). Then for any point z in the annulus (ring shaped) region, we have

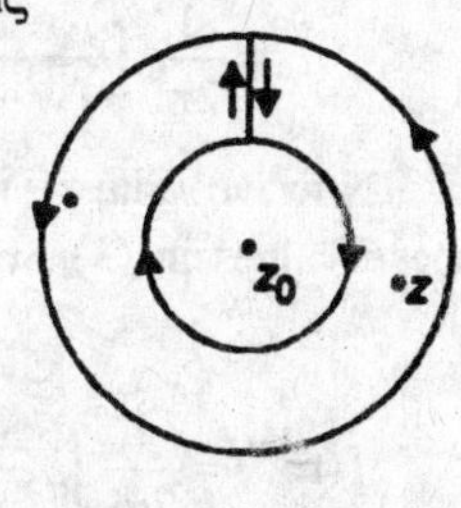

$$f(z) = \frac{1}{2\pi i}\int_{C_1}\frac{f(\zeta)}{\zeta - z}d\zeta - \int_{C_2}\frac{f(\zeta)}{\zeta - z}d\zeta.$$

Fig. 1.17

POISSON'S INTEGRAL FORMULA FOR A CIRCLE

Theorem:

Let f(z) be analytic in the region $|z| < \rho$ and let $z = re^{i\theta}$ be any point of this region. Then

$$f(re^{i\theta}) = \frac{1}{2\pi}\int_0^{2\pi}\frac{(R^2 - r^2)f(Re^{i\phi})}{R^2 - 2Rr\cos(\theta - \phi) + r^2}d\phi$$

where R is any number such that $0 < R < p$.

Proof:

Let C denote the circle $|z| = R$ such that $r < R < \rho$. As given $z = re^{i\theta}$ is any point of the region $|z| < \rho$ where $r < R < p$. Hence, by Cauchy's integral formula, we get

$$f(z) = \frac{1}{2\pi i}\int_C\frac{f(w)}{w - z}dw. \qquad ...(1)$$

Now the inverse of the point z with respect to C is $\dfrac{R^2}{\overline{z}}$ and lies outside C so that the function

$$\frac{f(w)}{w-\dfrac{R^2}{z}}$$

is analytic on and within C. Therefore by Cauchy-Goursat theorem we have

$$0=\int_C \frac{f(w)}{w-\dfrac{R^2}{\overline{z}}} \qquad \text{...(2)}$$

Subtracting (2) from (1), we get

$$f(z)=\frac{1}{2\pi i}\int\left[\frac{1}{w-z}-\frac{1}{w-R^2/\overline{z}}\right]f(w)\,dw$$

$$=\frac{1}{2\pi i}\int_C \frac{z-R^2/\overline{z}}{(w-r)(w-r^2/z)}f(w)\,dw. \qquad \text{...(3)}$$

Now we write $z=re^{i\theta}$, $w=Re^{i\phi}$. Then $\overline{z}=re^{i\theta}$, $dw=Rie^{i\phi}\,d\phi$. Substituting these values in (3), we get

$$f(re^{i\theta})=\frac{1}{2\pi i}\int_0^{2\pi}\frac{\left[re^{i\theta}-\dfrac{R^2}{r}r^{i\theta}\right]f(Re^{i\theta})}{(Re^{i\phi}-re^{i\theta})\left(Re^{i\phi}-\dfrac{R^2}{r}e^{i\theta}\right)}.Rie^{i\phi}d\phi$$

$$=\frac{1}{2\pi i}\int_0^{2\pi}\frac{(r^2-R^2)e^{i\theta}f(Re^{i\theta})i^{i\phi}}{(Re^{i\phi}-re^{i\theta})(Re^{-i\phi}-re^{-i\phi})}d\phi$$

$$=\frac{1}{2\pi}\int_0^{2\pi}\frac{(R^2-r^2)f(Re^{i\phi})}{(Re^{i\phi}-re^{i\theta})(Re^{-i\phi}-re^{-i\theta})}d\phi$$

$$=\frac{1}{2\pi}\int_0^{2\pi}\frac{(R^2-r^2)f(Re^{i\phi})}{R^2-Rr\{e^{i(\theta-\phi)}+e^{-i(\theta-\phi)}\}-r^2}d\phi$$

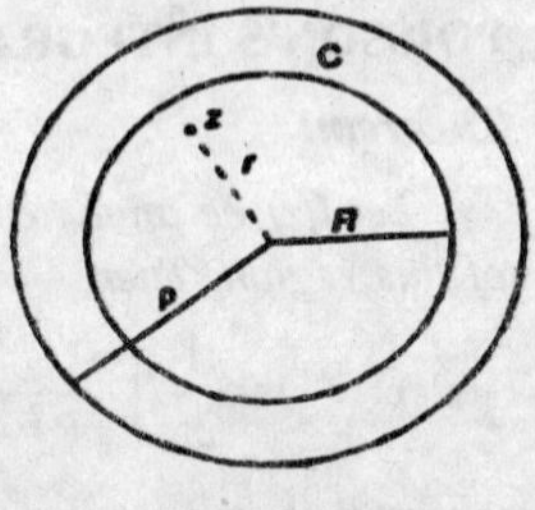

Fig. 1.18

$$=\frac{1}{2\pi}\int_0^{2\pi}\frac{(R^2-r^2)f(Re^{i\phi})}{R^2-2Rr\cos(\theta-\phi)+r^2}d\phi. \qquad \text{...(4)}$$

If we write $f(re^{i\theta}) = u(r,\theta) + iv(r,\theta)$

and $\quad f(Re^{i\theta}) = u(R,\phi) + iv(R,\phi)$

and equate real and imaginary parts in (4), we get

$$u(r,\theta) = \frac{1}{2\pi}\int_0^{2\pi} \frac{(R^2 - r^2)u(R,\phi)}{R^2 - 2Rr\cos(\theta-\phi)+r^2}d\phi \quad \text{... (5)}$$

$$v(r,\theta) = \frac{1}{2\pi}\int_0^{2\pi} \frac{(R^2 - r^2)v(R,\phi)}{R^2 - 2Rr\cos(\theta-\phi)+r^2}d\phi. \quad \text{...(6)}$$

DERIVATIVE OF AN ANALYTIC FUNCTION

Theorem:

Let f(z) be analytic within and on the boundary C of a simply connected region D and let zo be any point within C. Then

$$f'(z) = \frac{1}{2\pi i}\int_C \frac{f(z)}{(z-z_0)^2}dz.$$

Proof:

Let $z_0 + h$ be any point within D near the point z_0 so that h is at our choice. Now by Cauchy's integral formula we have

$$f(z_0 + h) = \frac{1}{2\pi i}\int_C \frac{f(z)}{z - z_0 - h}dz$$

and
$$f(z_0) = \frac{1}{2\pi i}\int_C \frac{f(z)}{z - z_0}dz$$

Therefore

$$f(z_0 + h) - f(z_0) = \frac{1}{2\pi i}\int_C f(z)\left[\frac{1}{z-z_0-h} - \frac{1}{z-z_0}\right]dz$$

$$= \frac{1}{2\pi i}\int_C \frac{hf(z)}{(z-z_0-h)(z-z_0)}dz$$

and so

$$\frac{f(z_0+h)-f(z_0)}{h} = \frac{1}{2\pi i}\int_C \frac{f(z)}{(z-z_0)}dz$$

$$= \frac{1}{2\pi i}\int_C f(z)\left[\frac{1}{(z-z_0-h)} - \frac{1}{(z-z_0)^2}\right]dz$$

$$= \frac{1}{2\pi i}\int_C \frac{hf(z)}{(z-z_0)^2(z-z_0-h)}dz. \quad \text{...(1)}$$

The theorem will be proved if we show the integral on the right hand side of (1) approaches zero as $h \to 0$. For this purpose, we describe a circle y with centre zo and radius p such that y lies entirely within C. (see the figure). Then by the Cor. 2 of Cauchy-Goursat theorem we have

$$\frac{1}{2\pi i}\int_C \frac{hf(z)}{(z-z_0)^2(z-z_0-h)}dz = \frac{1}{2\pi i}\int_\gamma \frac{hf(z)}{(z-z_0)^2(z-z_0-h)}dz \quad ...(2)$$

We now choose h such that the point $z_0 + h$ lies within γ and that $|h| < \frac{1}{2}\rho$. Now the equation of γ is $|z - z_0| = \rho$. Hence for any point z on γ, we have

$$|z-z_0-h| \geq |z-z_0| - |h| \geq \rho - \frac{1}{2}\rho = \frac{1}{2}\rho.$$

Again since f(z) is analytic in D, it is bounded in D so that $|f(z)| \geq M$ for some positive constant M. Using these facts, we get from (1) and (2)

$$\left|\frac{f(z_0+h)-f(z_0)}{h} - \frac{1}{2\pi i}\int_C \frac{f(z)}{(z-z_0)^2}dz\right|$$

$$= \left|\frac{1}{2\pi i}\int_C \frac{hf(z)}{(z-z_0)^2(z-z_0-z)}dz\right|$$

$$\leq \frac{|h|}{2\pi}\int_\gamma \frac{|f(z)|}{|z-z_0|^2|z-z_0-h|}|dz|$$

$$\leq \frac{|h|}{2\pi}\int_\gamma \frac{M}{\rho^2.\left(\frac{1}{2}\rho\right)}|dz| = \frac{|h|M}{\pi\rho^2}2\pi\rho \quad ...(3)$$

[$\because$ the length of γ is $2\pi\rho$)

Hence, when $h \to 0$, the right hand side of (3) also tends to zero and we get

$$\lim_{h\to 0}\frac{f(z_0+h)f(z_0)}{h} = \frac{1}{2\pi i}\int_C \frac{f(z)}{(z-z_0)^2}$$

Thus f(z) is differentiable at z_0 and

$$f'(z_0) = \frac{1}{2\pi i}\int_C \frac{f(z)}{(z-z_0)^2}dz. \quad ...(4)$$

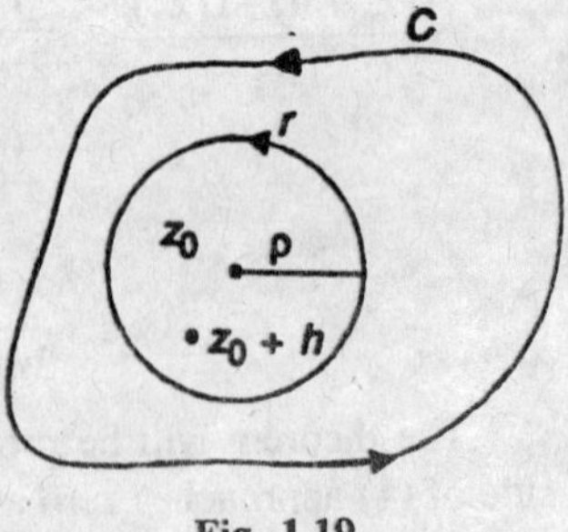

Fig. 1.19

Note: The formula (4) for the derivative $f'(z_0)$ can be written formally by differentiating the integral in Cauchy's integral formula

$$f(z_0) = \frac{1}{2\pi i}\int_C \frac{f(z)}{(z-z_0)^2}dz$$

with respect to z_0 under the integral sign.

Thus $f(z_0) = \int_C \frac{d}{dz_0}\left(\frac{f(z)}{z-z_0}\right)dz = \frac{1}{2\pi i}\int_C \frac{f(z)}{(z-z_0)^2}dz.$

HIGHER ORDER DERIVATIVES

Theorem:

Let f(z) be analytic within and on the boundary C of a simply connected region D and let z_0 be any point within C. Then f(z) possesses derivatives of all orders and these derivatives are themselves all analytic at z_0, their values being given by

$$f^{(n)}(z_0) = \frac{n!}{2\pi i}\int_C \frac{f(z)dz}{(z-z_0)^{n+1}}$$

Proof:

We first show that the first derivative f′(z) is analytic at z_0. We have

$$\frac{f'(z_0+h)-f'(z_0)}{h} = \frac{1}{2\pi i}\int_C \left[\frac{1}{(z-z_0-h)^2} - \frac{1}{(z-z_0)^2}\right]\frac{f(z)}{h}dz$$

$$= \frac{1}{2\pi i}\int_C \frac{2h(z-z_0)-h^2}{(z-z_0-h)^2(z-z_0)^2}.\frac{f(z)}{h}dz$$

$$= \frac{2!}{2\pi i}\int_C \frac{(z-z_0)-h/2}{(z-z_0-h)^2(z-z_0)^2}f(z)dz$$

$$\therefore \quad \frac{f'(z_0+h)-f'(z_0)}{h} = \frac{2!}{2\pi i}\int_C \frac{f(z)}{(z-z_0)^2}dz$$

$$= \frac{2!}{2\pi i}\int_C f(z)\left[\frac{(z-z_0)-h/2}{(z-z_0-h)^2(z-z_0)^2} - \frac{1}{(z-z_0)^2}\right]dz$$

$$= \frac{2!}{2\pi i}\int_C f(z)\left[\frac{\frac{3}{2}h(z-z_0)h^2}{(z-z_0)^3(z-z_0-h)^2}\right]dz$$

$$= \frac{2!}{2\pi i}\int_\gamma \frac{h\left\{\frac{3}{2}(z-z_0)-h\right\}}{(z-z_0)^3(z-z_0-h)^2}f(z)dz$$

where γ is the circle $|z - z_0| = \rho$ lying entirely within C as in 11.

$$\text{Hence}\left|\frac{f'(z_0+h)-f'(z_0)}{h} - \frac{2!}{2\pi i}\int_C \frac{f(z)}{(z-z_0)^3}dz\right|$$

$$\leq \frac{2!}{2\pi}|h|\int_\gamma \frac{\frac{3}{2}|z-z_0|+|-h|}{|z-z_0|^3|z-z_0-h|^2}|f(z)|\,|dz|$$

$$\leq \frac{2!}{2\pi}|h|\frac{\frac{3}{2}\rho+|h|}{\rho^2.\left(\frac{1}{2}\rho\right)^2}.M.2\pi\rho. \qquad ...(1)$$

where M is the upper bound of f(z) in D.

[Note that as in 11, we choose h such that]

$|h| < \frac{1}{2}\rho$ and so $|z - z_0 - h| \geq \frac{1}{2}\rho$ etc.]

Hence when $h \to 0$, the right hand side of (1) also tends to zero and we have

$$\lim_{h\to 0}\frac{f'(z_0+h)-f'(z_0)}{h}=-\frac{1}{2\pi i}\int_C\frac{f(z)}{(z-z_0)}dz.$$

Thus $f'(z)$ is differentiable at z_0 and

$$f''(z_0)=\frac{2!}{2\pi i}\int_C\frac{f(z)}{(z-z_0)^3}dz \qquad ...(2)$$

Therefore the formula holds for n = 2.

Now suppose that the formula is true for n – 1 so that we assume that

$$f^{n-1}(z_0) = \frac{(n-1)!}{2\pi i}\int_C\frac{f(z)}{(z-z_0)^n}dz$$

and $$f^{n-1}(z_0+h) = \frac{(n-1)!}{2\pi i}\int_C\frac{f(z)}{(z-z_0-h)^n}dz$$

$$\therefore\ f^{n-1}(z_0+h)-f^{(n-1)}(z_0) = \frac{(z-1)!}{2\pi i}\int_C f(z)\left[\frac{1}{(z-z_0-h)^n}-\frac{1}{(z-z_0)^n}\right]dz$$

$$= \frac{(z-1)!}{2\pi i}\int_C f(z)\left[\frac{(z-z_0)^n-(z-z_0-h)^n}{(z-z_0)^n(z-z_0-h)^n}\right]dz \qquad ...(3)$$

Now $(z - z_0)^n - (z - z_0 - h)^n$

$= [z - z_0 - (z - z_0 - h)]\,[(z - z_0)]^{n-1}$

$+ (z - z_0)^{n-2}(z - z_0 - h) + ... + (z - z_0 - h)^{n-1}]$

$$= h\sum_{r=1}^{n}(z-z_0)^{n-r}(z-z_0-h)^{r-1}$$

Hence we get from (3)

$$\frac{f^{n-1}(z_0+h)-f^{(n-1)}(z_0)}{h}-\frac{n!}{2\pi i}\int_C \frac{f(z)}{(z-z_0)^{n+1}}dz$$

$$=\frac{n!}{2\pi i}\int_C f(z)\frac{\sum_{r=1}^{n}(z-z_0)^{n-r+1}(z-z_0-h)^{r-1}(z-z_0-h)^{n}}{(z-z_0)^{a+1}(z-z_0-h)^{n}}dz$$

$$=\frac{(n+1)!}{2\pi i}\int_C f(z)\frac{\sum_{r=1}^{n}(z-z_0)^{n-r+1}(z-z_0-h)^{r-1}(z-z_0-h)^{n}}{(z-z_0)^{a+1}(z-z_0-h)^{n}}dz$$

where g is the circle $|z - z_0| = \rho$ lying entirely within C.

$$=\frac{(n-1)!}{2\pi i}\sum_{r=1}^{n}\int_\gamma f(z)\frac{(z-z_0)^{n-r+1}(z-z_0-h)^{r-r+1}}{(z-z_0)^{n+1}(z-z_0-h)^{n-r+1}}$$

$$=\frac{(n-1)!}{2\pi i}\sum_{r=1}^{n}\int_\gamma f(z)\frac{\sum_{s=1}^{n-r}(z-z_0)^{n-r-s}(z-z_0-h)^{s}}{(z-z_0)^{n+1}(z-z_0-h)^{n-r+1}}dz$$

$$=\frac{h(n-1)!}{2\pi i}\sum_{r=1}^{n}\int_\gamma\sum_{r=1}^{n}\frac{f(z)dz}{(z-z_0)^{r+s+1}(z-z_0)^{n-r+1}}$$

As before $|z - z_0 - h| \geq \frac{1}{2}\rho$ and so

$$\frac{f^{(n-1)}(z_0+h)-f^{(n-1)}(z_0)}{h}-\frac{n!}{2\pi i}\int_C \frac{f(z)}{(z-z_0)^{n+1}}dz$$

$$\leq\frac{|h|(n-1)!}{2\pi}\sum_{r=1}^{n}\sum_{s=0}^{n}\frac{M.2\pi\rho}{\rho^{r+s+1}\left(\frac{1}{2}\rho\right)^{n-r-s+1}}$$

$\to 0$ as $a \to 0$

$$\therefore \lim_{h\to 0}\frac{f^{(n-1)}(z_0+h)-f^{(n-1)}(z_0)}{h}$$

$$=\frac{n!}{2\pi i}\int\frac{f(z)}{(z-z_0)^{n+1}}dz$$

or $$f^{(n)}(z_0)=\frac{n!}{2\pi i}\int_C\frac{f(z)}{(z-z_0)^{n+1}}dz.$$

Hence, the formula holds for all values of n. Thus f(z) has derivatives of all orders and these are all analytic at z_0. The theorem is thus completely established.

MORERA'S THEOREM

We now prove an important theorem known as *Morera's theorem*. This theorem may be regarded as a sort of converse of *Cauchy-Goursat theorem*.

Theorem:

(Morera): *Let f(z) be continuous in a simply connected domain D and let*

$$\int_C f(z)dz = 0$$

where C any rectifiable closed Jordan curve in D. Then f(z) is analytic in D.

Proof:

Let z_0 be a fixed point and z any variable point in D and let C_1, C_2 be any two continuous rectifiable curves is D joining z_0 to z. Let C denote the closed rectifiable continuous curve consisting of C_1 and C_2 so that according to the given condition.

$$\int_C f(z)dz = \int_{C_1} f(z)dz + \int_{-C_2} f(z)dz = 0$$

or
$$\int_{C_1} f(z)dz + \int_{C_2} f(z)dz.$$

This shows that the integral along every curve in D joining z_0 to z is the same. Hence taking ~ as the variable of integration, we may write

$$F(z) = \int_{z_0}^{z} f(\zeta)d\zeta. \qquad ...(1)$$

The notation used in (1) for the integral is justified in view of the fact that the integral (1) is path-independent from z_0 to z and depends upon these points z_0, z only.

Let z+h be any point in D near the point z. Then using the notation of (1), we have

$$F(z+h) = \int_{z_0}^{z+h} f(\zeta)d\zeta. \qquad ...(2)$$

Subtracting (1) from (2), we get

$$\begin{aligned} F(z+h) - F(z) &= \int_{z_0}^{z+h} f(\zeta)d\zeta - \int_{z_0}^{z} f(\zeta)d\zeta \\ &= \int_{z_0}^{z+h} f(\zeta)d\zeta + \int_{z}^{z_0} f(\zeta)d\zeta \\ &= \int_{z}^{z+h} f(\zeta)d\zeta. \qquad ...(3) \end{aligned}$$

Now the integral in (3) is path-independent and may he taken along the straight line segment joining z to z + h. Hence,

$$\frac{F(z+h)-F(z)}{h}-f(z)= \frac{1}{h}\int_z^{z+h} f(z)d\zeta-\frac{f(z)}{h}h. \qquad ...(4)$$

$$= \frac{1}{h}\left[\int_z^{z+h} f(\zeta)d\zeta-f(z)\int_z^{z+h} dz\right]$$

$$= \frac{1}{h}\int_z^{z+h}[f(\zeta)-f(z)]d\zeta$$

Since f(ζ) is continuous at z, for a given ε > 0, there exists a δ > 0 such that

$$|f(\zeta)-f(z)|<\varepsilon \qquad ...(5)$$

orfC f(z) dz = fc, f(z) dz.

for every ζ satisfying |ζ – z| < δ.

We now choose h such that |h| < δ. Then, the inequality (5) is satisfied for every point on the line segment joining z to z + h. Hence from (4) and (5) we obtain

$$\left|\frac{F(z+h)-F(z)}{h}-f(z)\right| \le \frac{1}{|h|}\int_z^{z+h}|f(\zeta)-f(z)||d\zeta|$$

$$< \frac{1}{|h|}\int_z^{z+h}\in|f(\zeta)|$$

$$= \frac{1}{|h|}\varepsilon|h|=\varepsilon \qquad ...(6)$$

Since ε is arbitrary, we get from (6)

$$\lim_{h\to 0}\frac{F(z+h)-F(z)}{h}=f(z).$$

Hence F′(z) exists and F′(z) = f(z) ... (7)

The inequality (5) holds for every z ∈ D.

Thus, F(z) possesses the derivative f(z) at every point z ∈ D and consequently F(z) is analytic in D. But the derivative of an analytic function is analytic. If follows that f(z) is analytic it. D as required.

In view of Cauchy-Goursat theorem and Morera's theorem, we may state the following theorem.

Theorem II:

Let f(z) be continuous in a simply connected domain D and let C be any rectifiable closed curve in D. Then necessary and sufficient condition for f(z) to be analytic in D is that

$$\int_C f(z)dz = 0.$$

INDEFINITE INTEGRALS OR PRIMITIVES

Definition:

Let f(z) be a single-valued analytic function on a domain D. Then a function F(z) is said to be indefinite-integral (synonymously, a Primitive or anti-derivative) of f(z) if F(z) is single-valued and analytic in D and

$F'(z) = f(z)\ (z \in D)$.

Theorem I:

A necessary and sufficient condition for a function f(z) to possess an indefinite integral in a simply connected domain D is that the function f(z) is analytic in D. Further, any two indefinite integrals differ by a constant.

Proof:

Necessity: Let f(z) possess an indefinite integral F(z). Then

$$F'(z) = f(z) \qquad \text{... (1)}$$

Thus, F(z) possesses a derivative f(z) at every point $z \in D$ and so F(z) is analytic in D. But the derivative of an analytic function is analytic. It follows from (1) that f(z) is analytic in D.

Sufficiency:

Let f(z) be analytic in D. Let z_0 be any fixed point and z any variable point in D.

Then by the Cor. 1 of Cauchy-Goursat theorem the integral f(z) along every curve in D joining z_0 to z is the same. Hence we may write

$$F(z) = \int_{z_0}^{z} f(z)dz \qquad \text{... (1)}$$

where z is the variable of integration. As in the proof of Morera's theorem, we can show that

$$F'(z) = f(z).$$

Thus, f(z) possesses an indefinite integral F(z) defined by the equation (1). Hence, every analytic function in a simply connected domain possesses an indefinite integral.

We now show that any two indefinite integrals differ by a constant.

Let F(z) and $\psi(z)$ be two indefinite integrals of f(z). Then

$$F'(z) = \psi'(z)(z \in D)$$

or $\psi'(z) - F'(z) = 0$

or $[\psi(z) - F(z)]' = 0$

Hence $\psi(z) - F(z) = c$,

where c is an arbitrary constant. Thus $\psi(z) = F(z) + c$.

Hence, the general indefinite integral of an analytic function f(z) is given by $F(z) + c$

where $F(z) = \int_{z_0}^{z} f(\zeta)d\zeta$.

Example:

If f(z) is analytic in a simply connected region D of the complex plane, show that there exists a function F(z) analytic in D and such that F′(z) = f(z) for z ∈ D.

Solution:

Let f(z) be analytic in D. Let z_0 be any fixed point and z any variable point in D. Then by the Cor. 1 of Cauchy-Goursat theorem the integral f(z) along every curve in D joining z_0 to z is the same. Hence we may write

$$F(z) = \int_{z_0}^{z} f(z)dz \quad \text{... (1)}$$

where z is the variable of integration. As in the proof of Morera's theorem, we can show that

$$F'(z) = f(z).$$

Thus, f(z) possesses an indefinite integral F(z) defined by the equation (1). Hence, every analytic function in a simply connected domain possesses an indefinite integral.

We now show that any two indefinite integrals differ by a constant.

Let F(z) and ψ(z) be two indefinite integrals of f(z). Then

$$F'(z) = \psi'(z)(z \in D)$$

or $\psi'(z) - F'(z) = 0$

or $[\psi(z) - F(z)]' = 0$

Hence $\psi(z) - F(z) = c$,

where c is an arbitrary constant. Thus $\psi(z) = F(z) + c$.

Hence, the general indefinite integral of an analytic function f(z) is given by $F(z) + c$

where $F(z) = \int_{z_0}^{z} f(\zeta)d\zeta$.

Theorem II:

(Fundamental Theorem of Integral Calculus for Complex Functions): *Let f(z) be single-valued analytic function in a simply connected domain D. If a, b ∈ D, then*

$$\int_a^b f(z)dz = F(b) - f(a)$$

where F(z) is any indefinite integral of f(z).

Proof:

Let $\varphi(z) = \int_a^b f(\zeta)d\zeta.$ ... (1)

Then by theorem 1 above, the indefinite integral F(z) of f(z) is given by $F(z) = \varphi(z) + c$

$$\therefore \quad F(b) = \varphi(b) + c \text{ and } F(a) = \varphi(a) + c.$$

Hence $F(b) - F(a) = \varphi(b) - \varphi(a)$. ... (2)

Now from (1), we have

$$\varphi(b) = \int_a^b f(\zeta)d\zeta \text{ and } \varphi(a) = \int_a^a f(\zeta)d\zeta = 0,$$

Then (2) gives

$$F(b) - F(a) = \int_a^b f(\zeta)d\zeta = \int_a^b f(z)dz \qquad ...(3)$$

as required.

Since F(z) is an indefinite integral of f(z), we have by definition $F'(z) = f(z)$. Hence (3) may be written in the form

$$\int_a^b F'(z)dz = F(b) - F(a) \qquad ... (4)$$

Remark:

In view of this theorem, we can evaluate integrals of elementary functions of a complex variable by using formulae similar to those for elementary functions of a real variable. For example,

$$\int_a^b z^n dz = \frac{1}{n+1}\left(b^{n+1} - a^{n+1}\right)(n \neq -1)$$

$$\int_a^b e^z dz = ce^b - e^a$$

CAUCHY'S INEQUALITY THEOREM

Let f(z) be analytic in a domain D and let D contain the interior and the boundary of the circle γ defined by $|z - z_0| = \rho$. if $|f(z)| \le M$ on γ, then

$$|f^{(n)}(z_0)| \le n!\frac{M}{\rho^n}$$

Proof:

By the theorem of 12, we have

$$f^{(n)}(z_0) = \frac{n!}{2\pi i}\int_\gamma \frac{f(z)}{(z-z_0)^{n+1}}dz$$

$$\therefore |f^{(n)}(z_0)| = \left|\frac{n!}{2\pi i}\int_\gamma \frac{f(z)}{(z-z_0)^{n+1}}dz\right|$$

$$\le \frac{n!}{2\pi i}\int_\gamma \frac{|f(z)|}{|z-z_0|^{n+1}}|dz|$$

$$\le \frac{M(n)I}{2\pi}\int_\gamma \frac{|f(z)|}{|z-z_0|^{n+1}} \quad ...(1)$$

Now the equation $|z - z_0| = \rho$ may be written as $z - z_0 = \rho e^{i\theta}\, d\theta$. Thus $|dz| = \rho\, d\theta$.

Hence (1) gives

$$|f^{(n)}(z_0)| \le \frac{M(n)!}{2\pi}\int_0^{2\pi}\frac{\rho\, d\theta}{\rho^{n+1}} = \frac{M(n)!}{2\pi\rho^n}2\pi$$

$$\text{Thus } |f^{(n)}(z_0)| \le n!\frac{M}{\rho^n}.$$

LIOUVILLE'S THEOREM

Definition:

A function which is analytic in every finite region of the z-plane is called an integral function.

Theorem:

(Liouville's Theorem): *Let $f(z)$ be an integral function satisfying the inequality $|f(z)| \le M$ for all values of z where M is a positive constant. Then $f(z)$ is constant.*

Proof:

Let z_1, z_2 be any two points in the z-plate. Let Γ be a circle with centre z_1 and radius R such that the point z_2 is interior to c. Then by Cauchy's integral formula, we have

$$f(z_2) - f(z_1) = \frac{1}{2\pi i}\int_c \frac{f(z)}{z-z_2}dz - \frac{1}{2\pi i}\int_c \frac{f(z)}{z-z_1}dz$$

$$= \frac{z_2 - z_1}{2\pi i} \int_C \frac{f(z)dz}{(z-z_1)(z-z_2)} \quad ...(1)$$

Now we choose R so large that $|z_2 - z_1| < \frac{R}{2}$

The since $|z - z_1| = R$, we have

$$|z - z_2| = |z - z_1 + z_1 - z_2| = |(z - z_1) - (z_2 - z_1)|$$

$$\leq |z - z_1| - |z_2 - z_1| \geq R - \tfrac{1}{2}R = \tfrac{1}{2}R.$$

Also $|f(z)| \leq M$. Hence we get from (1),

$$|f(z_2) - f(z_1)| = \left| \frac{z_2 - z_1}{2\pi i} \int_C \frac{f(z)dz}{(z-z_1)(z-z_2)} \right|$$

$$\leq \frac{|z_2 - z_1|}{2\pi} \int_C \frac{|f(z)|}{|z-z_1|} \frac{|dz|}{|z-z_2|}$$

$$\leq \frac{|z_2 - z_1|}{2\pi} \int_C \frac{M|dz|}{R.\frac{1}{2}R}$$

$$= \frac{M|z_2 - z_1|}{\pi R^2} 2\pi R = \frac{2|z_2 - z_1|M}{R} \quad ...(2)$$

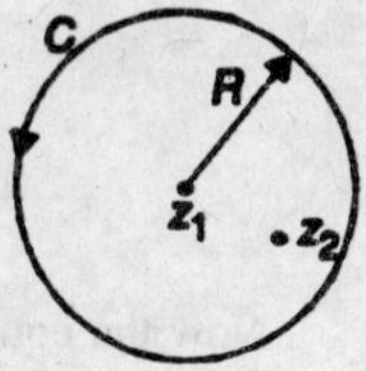

Fig. 1.20

Letting $R \to \infty$, we see that the right hand side of (2) tends to zero and consequently

$$f(z_2) - f(z_1) = 0$$

or $$f(z_2) = f(z_1).$$

This shows that f(z) is constant.

Alternative:

The theorem follows immediately by using Cauchy's inequality.

For n = 1, this inequality becomes $|f'(z_0)| \leq \frac{M}{\rho}$.

Letting $\rho \to \infty$, we see that $f'(z_0) = 0$.

Since z_0 is an arbitrary point, we see that the derivative of f(z) vanishes everywhere and consequently f(z) is a constant.

EXPANSION OF ANALYTIC FUNCTIONS AS POWER SERIES

Taylor and Laurent Theorems

Theorem 1:

(Taylor's Theorem): *Let f(z) be analytic at all points within a circle C_0 with centre z_0 and radius r_0. Then for every point z within C_0, we have*

$$f(z) = f(z_0) + f'(z_0)(z - z_0) + \frac{f''(z_0)}{2!}(z-z_0)+\ldots$$

$$+\frac{f^{(n)}(z_0)}{n!}(z-z_0)^n+\ldots$$

$$= f(z_0)+\sum_{n=1}^{\infty}\frac{(z-z_0)^n}{n!}f^{(n)}(z_0).$$

Proof:

Let z be any point inside the circle C_0 with centre z_0 and radius ρ_0 Let $z - z_0 = r$ and let C be the circle with centre z_0 and radius ρ such that $r < \rho < \rho_0$ so that the point z lies inside C (see the figure 1.21). BY Cauchy's integral formula, we have

$$f(z)=\frac{1}{2\pi i}\int_C\frac{f(\zeta)}{\zeta-z}d\zeta \quad \ldots(1)$$

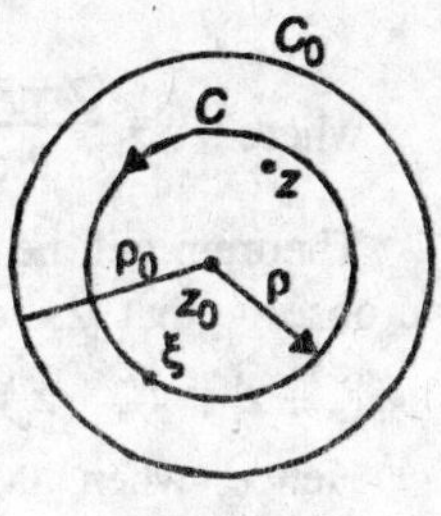

Fig. 1.21

To obtain the desired result, we consider the identity

$$\frac{1}{\zeta-z}=\frac{1}{(\zeta-z_0)-(z-z_0)}$$

$$=\frac{1}{\zeta-z_0}=\left[\frac{1}{1-\frac{z-z_0}{\zeta-z_0}}\right]$$

$$=\left[1+\frac{z-z_0}{\zeta-z_0}+\frac{(z-z_0)^2}{(\zeta-z_0)^2}+\ldots+\frac{(z-z_0)^{n-1}}{(\zeta-z_0)^{n-1}}\right.$$

$$\left.+\frac{(z-z_0)^n}{(\zeta-z_0)^n}\frac{1}{1-\frac{\zeta-z}{\zeta-z_0}}\right]$$

$$=\frac{1}{\zeta-z_0}+\frac{z-z_0}{(\zeta-z_0)^2}+\frac{(z-z_0)^2}{(\zeta-z_0)^2}+\ldots+\frac{(z-z_0)^{n-1}}{(\zeta-z_0)^n}$$

$$+\frac{(z-z_0)^n}{(\zeta-z_0)^n}\frac{1}{\zeta-z} \quad \ldots(2)$$

Multiplying each term in (2) by $\frac{f(\zeta)}{2\pi i}$ and integrating round C, and sing (1), we obtain

$$f(z) = \frac{1}{2\pi i}\int_C\frac{f(z)}{\zeta-z}dz$$

$$= \frac{1}{2\pi i}\int_C \frac{f(z)}{\zeta - z_0} d\zeta + \frac{(z-z_0)}{2\pi i}\int_C \frac{f(\zeta)}{(\zeta - z_0)} d\zeta$$

$$+\frac{(z-z_0)^2}{2\pi i}\int_C \frac{f(\zeta)}{(\zeta-z_0)^3} d\zeta + \frac{(z-z_0)^{n-1}}{2\pi i}\int_C \frac{f(\zeta)}{(\zeta-z_0)^n} d\zeta$$

$$+\frac{(z-z_0)^n}{2\pi i}\int_C \frac{f(\zeta)}{(\zeta-z)(\zeta-z_0)^n} d\zeta$$

Using the result of 12, we obtain

$$f(z) - f(z_0) + (z - z_0).\ f'(z_0) + (z - z_0)^2 \frac{f'(z_0)}{2!}$$

$$+ \ldots + (z-z_0)^{n-1} . \frac{f^{n-1}(z_0)}{(n-1)!} + R_n . \qquad \ldots(3)$$

where $R_n = \frac{(z-z_0)^n}{2\pi i}\int_C \frac{f(\zeta)}{(\zeta-z)(\zeta-z_0)^n} d\zeta.$ ...(4)

Theorem will be proved if we show that $R_n \to 0$ as $n \to \infty$. To prove this, we observe that $|z - z_0| = r$, $|\zeta - z_0| = \rho$ and therefore

$$|\zeta - z| = |(\zeta - z_0) - (z - z_0)| \geq |\zeta - z_0| - |z - z_0| = \rho - r.$$

Hence, when M denotes the maximum value of $f(\zeta)$ on C, we get from (4)

$$|R_n| = \left| \frac{(z-z_0)^n}{2\pi i}\int_C \frac{f(\zeta)d\zeta}{(\zeta-z)(\zeta-z_0)^n} \right|$$

$$\leq \frac{|z-z_0|^n}{|2\pi i|}\int_C \frac{|f(\zeta)|}{|\zeta-z|} \frac{|d\zeta|}{|\zeta-z_0|^2}$$

$$\leq \frac{r^n}{2\pi}\int_C \frac{M|d\zeta|}{(\rho-r)\rho^n}$$

$$= \frac{r^n}{2\pi} \frac{M}{(\rho-r)\rho^n} 2\pi\rho = \frac{M\rho}{\rho-r}\left(\frac{r}{\rho}\right)^n .$$

Since $r < \rho$, the right hand side of (5) tends to zero as $n \to \infty$ and consequently $R_n \to 0$ as $n \to \infty$.

Thus as $n \to \infty$, the limit of the sum of the first n terms on the right-hand side of (3) is f(z). Therefore f(z) is represented by the infinite series

$$f(z) = f(z_0) + \sum_{n=1}^{\infty} \frac{(z-z_0)^n}{n!} f^{(n)}(z_0)$$

known as Taylor's series.

When $z_0 = 0$, this reduces to

$$f(z) = f(0) + \sum_{n=1}^{\infty} \frac{z^n}{n!} f^{(n)}(0)$$

which is known as Maclaurin's series.

Remark:

For the validity of the expansion as a Taylor's series, it is essential that f(y) be analytic at all points inside the circle C_0 for then the convergence of Taylor's series for f(z) is assured.

Hence the greatest radius of C_0 is the distance from the point z_0 to the singularity of f(z) which is nearest to z_0, since we require the function to be analytic at all points within C_0.

Example 1:

Expand log (1 + z) in a Taylor's series about z = 0 and determine the region of convergence for the resulting series.

Solution:

Let $f(z) = \log(1 + z)$.

Then $f'(z) = \dfrac{1}{1+z} f''(z) = \dfrac{1}{(1+z)^2},$

$$f''' = \frac{2!}{(1+z)^3} f^{iv}(z) = -\frac{3!}{(1+z)^4}, \ldots$$

$$\ldots f^{(n)}(z) = (-1)^{n-1} \frac{(n-1)!}{(1+z)^n}$$

Hence $f(0) = \log 1 = 0,\ f'(0) = 1,\ f''(0) = -1,$

$f'''(0) = 2!,\ f^{iv}(0) = -3! \ldots$

$f^{(n)}(0) = (-1)^{n-1}(n-1)!.$

Therefore

$$f(z) = \log(1 + Z) = f(0) + zf'(0) + \frac{z^2}{2!} f'(0) + \frac{z^3}{3!} f''(0) + \frac{z^4}{4!} f^{iv}(0) + \ldots + \frac{z^n}{n!} f^{(n)}(0) + \ldots$$

$$= 0 + z - \frac{z^2}{2!} + \frac{z^3}{3!}.2! - \frac{z^4}{4!}.3! + \ldots + \frac{z^n}{n!}(-1)^{n-1}(n-1)! + \ldots$$

$$= z - \frac{z^2}{2} + \frac{z^3}{3} - \frac{z^4}{4} + \ldots + (-1)^{n-1}\frac{z^n}{n!} + \ldots$$

If u_n denotes the nth term of the series, then

$$u_n = \frac{(-1)^{n-1} z^n}{n}, \; u_{n+1} = \frac{(-1)^n z^{n+1}}{n+1}$$

$$\therefore \qquad \lim_{n\to\infty}\left|\frac{u_n}{u_{n+1}}\right| = \lim_{n\to\infty}\left|\frac{n+1}{nz}\right| = \frac{1}{|z|}.$$

Hence by D′ Alembert's ratio test, the Series converges for

$|z| < 1.$

The series can be shown to converge for $|z| = 1$ except for $z = -1$.

Note that $z = -1$ is the singularity of $\log(1 + z)$ nearest the point $z = 0$. Thus, the series converges for all values of z within the circle $|z| = 1$

Example 2:

Expand the following functions in a Taylor's series about $z = 0$ and determine the region of convergence in each case.

(i) e^z, (ii) sin z, (iii) cos z.

Solution:

(i) Let $f(z) = e^z$. Then $f^{(n)}(z) = e^z$.

Hence $f(0) = e^0 = 1$, $f^{(n)}(0) = e^0 = 1$ for n = 1, 2, 3, ...

Since e^z is analytic for every value of z, we have

$$f(z) = e^z = f(0) + zf'(0) + \frac{z^2}{2!}f''(0) + \ldots$$

$$= 1 + z + \frac{z^2}{2!} + \frac{z^3}{3!} + \ldots$$

$$= \sum_{n=0}^{\infty}\frac{z^n}{n!} \text{ where } |z| < \infty.$$

(ii) Let $\qquad f(z) = \sin z$. Then $f'z = \cos z$, $f''(z) = -\sin z$,

$f'''(z) = -\cos z$, $f^{iv}(z) = \sin z$, $f^{v}(z) = \cos z$ etc.

$\therefore \qquad f(0) = 0$, $f'(0) = 1$, $f''(0) = 0$, $f'''(0) = -1$

$f^{(iv)}(0) = 0$, $f^{(v)}(0) = 1$.

In general, $f^{(2n-1)}(0) = (-1)^{n+1}$.

Since sin z is analytic for all values of z, we have

$$f(z) = \sin(z) = f(0) + zf'(0) + \frac{z^2}{2!}f''(0)+\frac{z^3}{3!}f'''(0)+\frac{z^4}{4!}f^{iv}(0)$$

$$+\frac{z^5}{5!}f^{(v)}(0)+...+\frac{z^{2n-1}}{(2n-1)!}f^{(2n-1)}(0)+...$$

$$= 0+z+0+\frac{z^3}{3!}+0+\frac{z^5}{5!}+...$$

$$+\frac{z^{2n-1}}{(2n-1)!}(-1)^{n-1}+...$$

$$= \sum_{n=0}^{\infty}(-1)^{n+1}\frac{z^{2n-1}}{(2n-1)!} \text{ when} |z|<\infty.$$

(iii) Proceeding as in (ii), we can show that

$$\cos z = 1+\sum_{n=1}^{\infty}(-1)^2\frac{z^{2n}}{(2n)!} \text{ when} |z|<\infty.$$

Example 3:

If the function f(z) is analytic when |z| < R and has the Taylor's expansion $\sum_0^{\infty} a_n z_n$, *then show that for r < R, we have*

$$\frac{1}{2\pi}\int_0^{2a}|f(re^{i\theta})|^2 d\theta \sum_0^{\infty}|a_n|^2 r^2$$

Hence prove that if |f (z)| ≤ M when |z| < R, then

$$\sum_0^{\infty}|a_n|^2 r^{2n} \le M^2.$$

Solution:

Now $|re^{i\theta}| = r < R$ (given).

Since f(z) has the Taylor's expansion $\sum_{n=0}^{\infty} a_n z^n$ when $|z| \le R$, we see that

$$f(re^{i\theta}) = \sum_{n=0}^{\infty} a_m (re^{i\theta})^n = \sum_{n=0}^{\infty} a_n r^n e^{ni\theta} \qquad ...(1)$$

If $\bar{a}_n$, denotes the conjugate of a_n, then

$$\overline{f(re^{i\theta})} = \sum_{m=0}^{\infty} a_m r^m e^{-mi\theta}. \qquad ...(2)$$

Multiplying (1) and (2), we obtain

$$|f(re^{i\theta})|^2 = f(re^{i\theta})\ \overline{f(re^{i\theta})}$$

$$= \sum_{n=0}^{\infty} a_n r^n e^{ni\theta} . \sum_{m=0}^{\infty} \bar{a}_m r^m e^{-mi\theta} . \qquad ...(3)$$

It is easy to see that the two series for $f(re^{i\theta})$ and $\overline{f(re^{i\theta})}$ are absolutely convergent and consequently their product is uniformly convergent for $0 \leq \theta \leq 2\pi$. Therefore the term by term integration is valid.

Now $\int_a^{2\pi} e^{(n-m)i\theta} d\theta = 0$ if $n \neq m$.

$$= 2\pi \text{ if } n = m.$$

Hence integrating both sides of (3), we get

$$\int_0^{2\pi} |f(re^{i\theta})|^2 d\theta = \sum_{n=0}^{\infty} a_n \bar{a}_n r^{2n} \int_0^{2\pi} d\theta = 2\pi \sum_{n=0}^{\infty} |a_n|^2 r^{2n}$$

$$\therefore \frac{1}{2\pi} \int_0^{2\pi} |f(re^{i\theta})|^2 d\theta = \sum_{n=0}^{\infty} |a_n|^2 r^{2n} \qquad ...(4)$$

This prove the first result.

To prove the second result, we are given that

$$|f(z)| \leq M \text{ when } |z| < R.$$

Since $|re^{i\theta}| = r < R$. we have $|f(re^{i\theta})| \leq M$.

Then (4) gives

$$\sum_{n=1}^{\infty} |a_n|^2 r^{2n} \leq \frac{1}{2\pi} \int_0^{2\pi} M^2 d\theta = \frac{1}{2\pi} M^2 . 2\pi$$

Thus $\sum_{n=0}^{\infty} |a_n|^2 r^{2n} \leq M^2$ as desired.

Alternative:

As before, we have

$$\frac{1}{2\pi} \int_0^{2\pi} |f(re^{i\theta})|^2 d\theta = \frac{i}{2\pi} \int_0^{2\pi} \sum_{n=0}^{\infty} a_n r^n e^{ni\theta} \, d\theta$$

$$= \frac{1}{2\pi} \int_0^{2\pi} |\Sigma a_n r^n \cos a\theta + i \Sigma a_n + \sin n\theta^2 \, d\theta$$

$$= \frac{1}{2\pi} \int_0^{2\pi} |(\Sigma a_n r^n \cos a\theta)^2 + (\Sigma a_n r^n + \sin n\theta)^2 \, | d\theta$$

$$= \frac{1}{2\pi} \int_0^{2\pi} \left[\sum_{n=0}^{\infty} a_n r^2 r^{2n} \cos^2 n\theta + \sum_{n=0}^{\infty} a_n r^2 r^{2n} \sin^2 n\theta \right.$$

$$\left. + 2 \sum_{n=0}^{\infty} \sum_{n=0}^{\infty} a_n r_n r^{n+1} \{ \cos s\theta \cos t\theta + \sin s\theta \sin t\theta \right] d\theta$$

$$= \frac{1}{2\pi}\sum_{n=2}^{\infty}\int_0^{2\pi}[a_n r^2 r^{2n} d\theta = \frac{1}{2\theta}\sum_{n=0}^{\infty} a_n a^n r^{2n} 2\pi \quad = \sum_{n=0}^{\infty}[a_2 r^2 r^{2n}]$$

since $\int_0^{2\pi}(\cos s\theta \cos t\theta + \sin s\theta \sin t\theta)d\theta$

$$= \int_0^{2\pi}\cos(s+t)d\theta = \left\{\frac{\sin(s-t)}{s-t}\right\}^{2\pi} = 0 \text{ when } s \neq 1$$

[Note that here we have interchanged summation and integration which is possible in view of the uniform convergence of the series].

The second part can be proved as before.

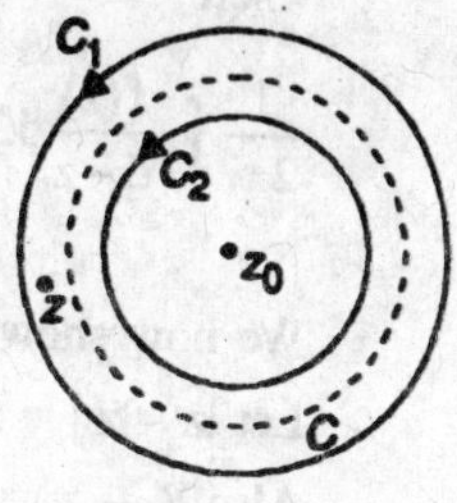

Fig. 1.22

Theorem 2:

(Laurents Theorem): *Let f(z) be analytic in the ring shaped region D bounded by two concentric circles C_1 and C_2 with centre z_0 and radii ρ_1 and ρ_2 ($\rho_1 > \rho_2$) and let z be any point of D. Then*

$$f(z) = \sum_{n=0}^{\infty} a_n (z - z_0)^n + \sum_{n=1}^{\infty} b_n (z - z_0)^{-n}$$

where $a_n = \frac{1}{2\pi i}\int_{C_1}\frac{f(\zeta)}{(\zeta - z_0)^{n+1}}d\zeta, a_n = \frac{1}{2\pi i}\int_{C_2}(\zeta - z_0)^{n-1} f(\zeta)d\zeta$

Proof:

Let z be any point of the ringshaped region D. Then by Cauchy's integral formula for doubly connected region, we have

$$f(z) = \frac{1}{2\pi i}\left[\int_{C_1}\frac{f(z)}{\zeta - z}d\zeta - \int_{C_1}\frac{f(z)}{\zeta - z}d\zeta\right] \qquad ...(1)$$

We consider the first integral in (1). For any point ζ on C_1, we consider the identity

$$\frac{1}{\zeta - z} = \frac{1}{(\zeta - z_0) - (z - z_0)} = \frac{1}{(\zeta - z_0) - \left[1 - \frac{(z - z_0)}{\zeta - z_0}\right]}$$

$$= \frac{1}{(\zeta - z_0)}\left[1 + \frac{z - z_0}{\zeta - z_0} + \left(\frac{z - z_0}{\zeta - z_0}\right)^2 + ... + \left(\frac{z - z_0}{\zeta - z_0}\right)^{n-1}\right.$$

$$\left. + \left(\frac{z - z_0}{\zeta - z_0}\right)^n \frac{1}{1 - \frac{z - z_0}{\zeta - z_0}}\right]$$

$$=\frac{1}{\zeta-z_0}+\frac{z-z_0}{(\zeta-z_0)^2}+\frac{(z-z_0)^2}{(\zeta-z_0)^3}+\ldots+\frac{(z-z_0)^{n-1}}{(\zeta-z_0)^n}+\frac{(z-z_0)^n}{(\zeta-z_0)^n(\zeta-z_0)}$$

$$\therefore \frac{1}{2\pi i}\int_{C_1}\frac{f(\zeta)}{\zeta-z}d\zeta=\frac{1}{2\pi i}\int_{C_1}\frac{f(\zeta)}{\zeta-z_0}d\zeta+\frac{(z-z_0)}{2\pi i}+\frac{1}{2\pi i}\int_{C_1}\frac{f(\zeta)}{(\zeta-z_0)}d\zeta$$

$$+\ldots+\frac{(z-z_0)^{n-1}}{2\pi i}\int_{C_1}\frac{f(\zeta)}{(\zeta-z_0)^n}d\zeta+R_n$$

where $R_n=\dfrac{(z-z_0)^{n-1}}{2\pi i}\displaystyle\int_{C_1}\frac{f(\zeta)d\zeta}{(\zeta-z_0)^n(\zeta-z)}$

$$\frac{1}{2\pi i}\int_{C_1}\frac{f(z)}{\zeta-z}d\zeta=a_0+a_1(z-z_0)+a_2(z-z_0)^2+\ldots$$

$$+a_{n-1}(z-z_0)^{n-1}+R_n \quad \ldots(2$$

We now show that $R_n \to 0$ as $n \to \infty$.

Let $|z - z_0| = r$ so that $\rho_2 < r < \rho_1$.

Also $|\zeta - z| = \rho_1$.

It follows that

$$|\zeta - z| = |(\zeta - z_0) - (z - z_0)|$$

$$\geq |(\zeta - z_0) - (z - z_0)| = \rho_1 - r.$$

Hence $$|R_n| \leq \frac{|z-z_0|^n}{2\pi}\int_{C_1}\frac{|f(\zeta)||d\zeta|}{|\zeta-z_0|^n|\zeta-z|}$$

$$\leq\frac{r^n}{2\pi}\int_{C_1}\frac{M_1|d\zeta|}{\rho_1^n(\rho_1-r)}=\frac{r^n}{2\pi}\frac{M_1.2\pi\rho_1}{\rho_1^n(\rho_1-r)}=\frac{M_1\rho_1}{\rho_1-r}\left(\frac{r}{\rho_1}\right)$$

where M_1 is the maximum value of $f(\zeta)$ on C_1.

Since $r<\rho_1, \left(\dfrac{r}{\rho_1}\right)^n \to 0$ as n -> and consequently R,, --1- 0 as

If then follows from (2) that

$$\frac{1}{2\pi i}\int_{C!}\frac{f(z)}{\zeta-z}d\zeta=\sum_{n=0}^{\infty}a_n(z-z_0)^n \quad \ldots($$

We now consider the second integral in (2). For any point ζ on C_2, consider the identity.

$$-\frac{1}{\zeta-z}=\frac{1}{(z-z_0)-(\zeta-z_0)}=\frac{1}{(z-z_0)}\frac{1}{1-\left(\dfrac{\zeta-z_0}{z-z_0}\right)}$$

$$= \frac{1}{(z-z_0)}\left[1+\left(\frac{\zeta-z_0}{z-z_0}\right)+\left(\frac{\zeta-z_0}{z-z_0}\right)^2+\ldots\right.$$

$$\left.+\left(\frac{\zeta-z_0}{z-z_0}\right)^{n-1}+\left(\frac{\zeta-z_0}{z-z_0}\right)^{n}\frac{1}{1-\frac{\zeta-z_0}{z-z_0}}\right]$$

$$= \frac{1}{z-z_0}+\frac{\zeta-z_0}{(z-z_0)^n}+\frac{(\zeta-z_0)^2}{(\zeta-z_0)^3}+\ldots+\frac{(\zeta-z_0)^{n-1}}{(\zeta-z_0)^n}+\frac{(\zeta-z_0)^n}{(z-z_0)^n(z-\zeta)}$$

$$\therefore -\frac{1}{2\pi i}\int_{C_1}\frac{f(\zeta)}{\zeta-z}d\zeta = \frac{1}{2\pi i(z-z_0)}\int_{C_1}f(\zeta)d\zeta$$

$$+\frac{1}{2\pi i(z-z_0)^2}\int_{C_1}(\zeta-z_0)^2 f(\zeta)d\zeta+\ldots$$

$$+\frac{1}{2\pi i(z-z_0)^n}\int_{C_2}(\zeta-z_0)^{n-1}d\zeta+S_n$$

where $S_n = \dfrac{1}{2\pi i(z-z_0)^n}\displaystyle\int_{C_2}\frac{(\zeta-z_0)^n}{z-\zeta}f(\zeta)d\zeta$

Writing $b_n = \dfrac{1}{2\pi i}\displaystyle\int_{C_2}(\zeta-z_0)^{n-1}f(\zeta)d\zeta$, we have

$$-\frac{1}{2\pi i}\int_{C_2}\frac{f(\zeta)}{\zeta-z}d\zeta = b_1(z-z_0)^{-1}+b_2(z-z_0)^{-2}+\ldots$$

$$+ b_n(z-z_0)^{-n} + S_n \quad \text{...(4)}$$

To show that $S_n \to 0$ as $n \to \infty$, we observe that $z - z_0 = r_1$ $|\zeta - z_0| = \rho_2$ and $\rho_2 < r$ so that

$$|z-\zeta| = |(z-z_0)-(\zeta-z_0)| \geq |z-z_0| - |\zeta-z_0| = r-\rho_2.$$

Hence $|S_n| \leq \dfrac{1}{2\pi|z-z_0|^{n+1}}\displaystyle\int_{C_2}\frac{|\zeta-z_0|^2}{|z-\zeta|}|f(\zeta)d\zeta|$

$$\leq \frac{1}{2\pi r^{n+1}}\int_{C_2}\frac{\rho_2^n}{r-\rho_2}M_2|d\zeta|$$

$$= \frac{1}{2\pi r^{n+1}}\cdot\frac{\rho_2^n M_2}{r-\rho_2}.2\pi\rho_2 = \frac{M_2}{r-\rho_2}\cdot\left(\frac{\rho_2}{r}\right)^{n+1}$$

where M_2 is the maximum value of $f(\zeta)$ on C_2.

Since $\rho_2 < r_1$ $\left(\dfrac{\rho_2}{r}\right)^{n+1} \to 0$ as $n \to \infty$ and consequently $S_n \to 0$ as $n \to \infty$.

Hence we get from (4)

$$-\frac{1}{2\pi r}\int_{C_2}\frac{f(\zeta)}{\zeta-z}d\zeta=\sum_{n=1}^{\infty}b_n(z-z_0)^{-n} \qquad ...(5)$$

From (1), (3) and (5), we finally obtain

$$f(z)=\sum_{n=1}^{\infty}a_n(z-z_0)^n+\sum_{n=1}^{\infty}b_n(z-z_0)^{-n} \qquad ...(6)$$

where $$a_n=\frac{1}{2\pi r}\int_{C_1}\frac{f(\zeta)}{(\zeta-z_0)^{n+1}}d\zeta$$

and $$b_n=\frac{1}{2\pi r}\int_{C_1}(\zeta-z_0)^{n-1}f(\zeta)d\zeta.$$

Remark:

We observe that $b_n = a_{-n}$. Hence if C is any circle of radius ρ with centre z_0 such that $\rho_2 < \rho < \rho_1$ then since the integrand is analytic in the annulus $\rho_2 < z_0\ |\zeta - z_0| < \rho_P$ it is easy to see that

$$a_n=\frac{1}{2\pi r}\int_{C}\frac{f(\zeta)}{(\zeta-z_0)^{n+1}}d\zeta$$

and $$b_n=a_{-n}=\frac{1}{2\pi i}\int_{C}(\zeta-z_0)^{n-1}f(\zeta)d\zeta.$$

Hence the series (6) can he written in the form as follows

$$f(z)=\sum_{n=-\infty}^{\infty}a_n(z-a)^n$$

where $$a_n=\frac{1}{2\pi r}\int_{C}\frac{f(\zeta)d\zeta}{(\zeta-z_0)^{n+1}}$$

Theorem 3:

(Uniqueness Theorem): *Suppose that we have obtained in an to ,;inner or as the definition of f(z) the formula*

$$f(z)=\sum_{n=-\infty}^{\infty}P_n(z-z_0)^n(\rho_2<|z-z_0|<\rho_1)$$

Then the series is necessarily identical with the Laurent's series for f(z).

Proof:

Let C be the circle $|z - z_0| = r$ where $\rho_2 < \rho < \rho_1$. Then the coefficient in the Laurent's expansion is given by

$$a_n=\frac{1}{2\pi i}\int_{C}\frac{1}{(\zeta-z_0)^{n+1}}d\zeta$$

$$= \frac{1}{2\pi i}\int \frac{1}{(\zeta - z_0)^{n+1}} d\zeta \sum_{m=-\infty}^{\infty} P_m (\zeta - z_0)^m d\zeta$$

$$= \frac{1}{2\pi i}\sum_{m=-\infty}^{\infty} P_m \int_C \frac{(\zeta - z_0)^m}{(\zeta - z_0)^{n+1} d\zeta}$$

[Note that the term by term integration is justified since the series converges uniformly on every closed subset of the annulus)

$$= \frac{1}{2\pi i}\sum_{m=-\infty}^{\infty} P_m \int_0^{2\pi} \frac{e^m (e^{mi\theta})}{e^{n+1} e^{(n+1)i\theta}} pie^{i\theta} d\theta$$

where we have put $\zeta - z_0 = \rho e^{i\theta}$

$$= \frac{1}{2\pi i}\sum_{m=-\infty}^{\infty} P_m \int_0^{2\pi} \rho^{m-n} e^{(m-n)i\theta} d\theta$$

Now when $m \neq n$, we have

$$\int_0^{2\pi} e^{(m-n)i\theta} d\theta = \left[\frac{e^{(m-n)i\theta}}{(m-n)^i}\right]_0^{2\pi} = \frac{1}{(m-n)i}[e^{(m-n)2\pi i} - e_0]$$

$$= \frac{1}{(m-n)i}(1-1) = 0.$$

And when $m = n$, we have

$$\int_0^{2\pi} e^{(m-n)i\theta} d\theta = \int_0^{2\pi} d\theta = 2\pi.$$

Hence we get from (1)

$$a_n = \frac{1}{2\pi}.P_n.2\pi = P_n.$$

If follows that the given series is identical with the Laurent's series for f(z).

Example 1:

Show that when $0 < |z| < 4$.

$$\frac{1}{4z - z^2} = \sum_{n=0}^{\infty} \frac{z^{n-1}}{4^{n+1}}$$

Solution:

When $|z| < 4$. We have

$$\frac{1}{4z - z^2} = \frac{1}{4z(1 - z/4)} = \frac{1}{4z}(1 - z/4)^{-1}$$

$$= \frac{1}{4z}\left[1+\frac{z}{4}+\left(\frac{z}{4}\right)^2+\left(\frac{z}{4}\right)^3+...\right]$$

$$= \frac{1}{4z}+\frac{1}{4^2}+\frac{z}{4^3}+\frac{z^2}{4^4}+...$$

$$= \sum_{n=0}^{\infty}\frac{z^{n-1}}{4^{n+1}}$$

Example 2:

Expand $\frac{1}{z(z^2-3z+2)}$ *for the regions*

(1) $0 < |z| < 1$ *(ii)* $1 < |z| < 2$ *(iii)* $|z| > 2$.

Solution

Let $f(z)=\frac{1}{z(z^2-3z+2)}=\frac{1}{z(z-1)(z-2)}$.

Hence resolving into partial functions, we get

$$f(z)= \frac{1}{2z}-\frac{1}{z-1}+\frac{1}{2(z-2)}$$

(i) For $0 < |z| < 1$, we have

$$f(z)=\frac{1}{2z}+(1-z)^{-1}-\frac{1}{4}\left(1-\frac{z}{2}\right)^{-1}$$

$$=\frac{1}{2z}+\left[1+z+z^2+z^3+...\right]-\frac{1}{4}\left[1+\frac{z}{2}+\left(\frac{z}{2}\right)^2+\left(\frac{z}{3}\right)^3+...\right]$$

$$=\frac{1}{2z}+\frac{3}{4}+\frac{7z}{8}+\frac{15}{16}z^2+\frac{31}{32}z^2+...$$

(ii) For $1 < |z| < 2$, we have

$$f(z)=\frac{1}{2z}-\frac{1}{z}\left(1-\frac{1}{z}\right)^{-1}-\frac{1}{4}\left(1-\frac{z}{2}\right)^{-1}$$

$$=\frac{1}{2z}-\frac{1}{z}\left[1+\frac{1}{z}+\frac{1}{z^2}+\frac{1}{z^3}+...\right]-\frac{1}{4}\left[1+\frac{z}{2}+\left(\frac{z}{2}\right)^2+\left(\frac{z}{2}\right)^3+...\right]$$

$$=\left(-\frac{1}{2z}-\frac{1}{z^2}+\frac{1}{z^3}-...\right)-\frac{1}{4}\left[1+\frac{z}{2}+\frac{z^2}{2^2}+\frac{z^3}{2^3}+...\right]$$

(iii) For $|z| > 2$, we have

$$f(z)=\frac{1}{2z}-\frac{1}{z}\left(1-\frac{1}{z}\right)^{-1}+\frac{1}{2}\left(1-\frac{2}{z}\right)^{-1}$$

$$=\frac{1}{2z}-\frac{1}{z}\left(1+\frac{1}{z}+\frac{1}{z^2}+\frac{1}{z^3}+...\right)+\frac{1}{2z}\left(1+\frac{2}{z}+\frac{2^2}{z^2}+\frac{2^3}{z^3}+...\right)$$

$$=(2-1)\frac{1}{z^3}+(2^2-1)\frac{1}{z^4}+(2^3-1)\frac{1}{z^5}+...$$

Example 3:

Expand f(z) $\dfrac{1}{(z+1)(z+3)}$ *in a Laurent's series valid for the regions*

(i) $|z|<1$; *(ii)* $1<|z|<3$; *(iii)* $|z|>3$.

(iv) $1<|z+1|<2$.

Solution:

Resolving into partial fractions, we obtain

$$f(z)=\frac{1}{2(z+1)}-\frac{1}{2(z+3)}$$

(i) For $|z|<1$, we have

$$f(z)=\frac{1}{2}+(1+z)^{-1}-\frac{1}{6}\left(2+\frac{z}{3}\right)^{-1}$$

$$=\frac{1}{2}+\left[1-z+z^2-z^3+...\right]-\frac{1}{6}\left[1+\frac{z}{3}+\left(\frac{z}{3}\right)^2-\left(\frac{z}{3}\right)^3+...\right]$$

$$=\left(\frac{1}{2}-\frac{1}{6}\right)-\left(\frac{1}{2}-\frac{1}{18}\right)z+\left(\frac{1}{2}-\frac{1}{54}\right)z^2-\left(\frac{1}{2}-\frac{1}{162}\right)z^3+...$$

$$=\frac{1}{3}-\frac{4}{9}z+\frac{13}{27}z^2-\frac{40}{81}z^3+...$$

(ii) For $|z|>1$, we have

$$\frac{1}{2(z+1)}=\frac{1}{2z\left(1+\frac{1}{z}\right)}=\frac{1}{2z}\left(1+\frac{1}{z}\right)^{-1}$$

$$=\frac{1}{2z}\left(1-\frac{1}{z}+\frac{1}{z^2}-\frac{1}{z^3}+...\right)$$

$$=\frac{1}{2z}-\frac{1}{2z^2}+\frac{1}{2z^3}-\frac{1}{2z^4}+...$$

For | z | < 3, we have

$$\frac{1}{2(z+3)} = \frac{1}{6(1+z/2)} = \frac{1}{6}(1+z/3)^{-1}$$

$$= \frac{1}{6}\left[1+\frac{z}{3}+\left(\frac{z}{3}\right)^2-\left(\frac{z}{3}\right)^3+\left(\frac{z}{3}\right)^4+...\right]$$

$$= \frac{1}{6}-\frac{z}{18}+\frac{z^2}{54}-\frac{z^3}{162}+\frac{z^4}{1536}-...$$

Hence the Laurent's series for f(z) valid for 1 < | z | < 3 is

$$f(z) = ...-\frac{1}{2z^4}+\frac{1}{2z^3}-\frac{1}{2z^2}+\frac{1}{2z}-\frac{1}{6}-\frac{z}{18}+\frac{z^2}{54}-\frac{z^3}{162}+\frac{z^4}{1536}-...$$

(iii) For | z | > 3.

$$\frac{1}{2(z+3)}-\frac{1}{2(z+3)} = \frac{1}{2z}\left(1+\frac{1}{z}\right)^{-1}-\frac{1}{2z}\left(1+\frac{3}{z}\right)^{-1}$$

$$= \frac{1}{2z}\left[1-\frac{1}{z}+\left(\frac{1}{z}\right)^2-\left(\frac{1}{z}\right)^3+\left(\frac{1}{z}\right)^4-...\right]$$

$$-\frac{1}{2z}\left[1-\frac{3}{z}+\left(\frac{3}{z}\right)^2-\left(\frac{3}{z}\right)^3+\left(\frac{3}{z}\right)^4-...\right]$$

$$= \frac{1}{z^2}-\frac{4}{z^3}+\frac{13}{z^4}-\frac{40}{z^5}+...$$

(iv) Let z + 1 = u. Then 0 < | z + 1 | < 2 implies 0 < | u | < 2 and we have

$$\frac{1}{(z+1)(z+3)} = \frac{1}{u(u+2)} = \frac{1}{2u}\left(1+\frac{u}{2}\right)^{-1}$$

$$= \frac{1}{2u}\left[1-\frac{u}{2}+\left(\frac{u}{2}\right)^2-\left(\frac{u}{2}\right)^3+...\right]$$

$$= \frac{1}{2u}-\frac{1}{4}+\frac{u}{8}-\frac{u^2}{16}+...$$

$$= \frac{1}{2(z+1)}-\frac{1}{4}+\frac{z+1}{8}-\frac{(z+1)^2}{16}+...$$

Example 4:

Expand $f(z) = \dfrac{z+3}{(z^2-z-2)z}$ *in powers of z*

(i) within the unit circle about the origin,

(ii) within the annulus region between the concentric circles about the origin having radii 1 and 2 respectively,

(iii) the exterior to the circle with centre as origin and radius 2 i.e. for | z | > 2.

Solution:

Let $f(z)=\dfrac{z+3}{(z^2-z-2)z}=\dfrac{(z+3)}{z(z+1)(z-2)}$

Hence resolving into partial fractions,

$$f(z)=\frac{3}{2z}+\frac{1}{3(z+1)}+\frac{1}{6(z-2)}$$

(i) For 0 < | z | < 2, we have

$$f(z)=\frac{3}{2z}+\frac{2}{3}(1+z)^{-1}-\frac{5}{12}\left(1-\frac{z}{2}\right)^{-1}$$

$$=-\frac{3}{2z}+\frac{2}{3}\left[1-z+z^2-z^3+\ldots\right]-\frac{5}{12}\left[1+\frac{z}{2}+\frac{z^2}{2^2}+\frac{z^3}{2^3}+\ldots\right]$$

$$=-\frac{3}{2z}\sum_{n=0}^{\infty}\left[\frac{2}{3}(-1)^n-\frac{5}{12}\left(\frac{1}{2}\right)^n\right]z^n$$

(ii) For | z | > 2, we get

$$f(z)=-\frac{3}{2z}+\frac{2}{3z}\left(1+\frac{1}{z}\right)^{-1}+\frac{5}{6z}\left(1-\frac{2}{z}\right)^{-1}$$

$$=-\frac{3}{2z}+\frac{2}{3z}\left[1-\frac{1}{z}+\frac{1}{z^2}-\frac{1}{z^3}+\ldots\right]+\frac{5}{6z}\left[1+\frac{2}{z}+\frac{2^2}{z^2}-\frac{2^3}{z^3}+\ldots\right]$$

$$=-\frac{3}{2z}+\frac{2}{3z}\sum_{n=0}^{\infty}(-1)^n\frac{5}{6z}\sum_{n=0}^{\infty}\left(\frac{2}{z}\right)^n$$

Example 5:

Obtain the Taylor and Laurent's series which represents the function

$$\frac{z^2-1}{(z+2)(z+3)}$$ *in the regions*

(i) | z | < 2, (ii) 2 < | z | < 3, (iii) | z | > 3.

Solution:

We have $f(z)=\dfrac{z^2-1}{(z+2)(z+3)}=\dfrac{5z+7}{(z+2)(z+3)}$

(i) For | z | < 2, we have

$$f(z) = 1+\frac{3}{2}\left(1+\frac{z}{2}\right)^{-1} - \frac{8}{3}\left(1+\frac{z}{3}\right)^{-1}$$

$$= 1+\frac{3}{2}\left[1-\frac{z}{2}+\frac{z^2}{2^2}-\frac{z^3}{2^3}+...\right]-\frac{8}{3}\left[1-\frac{z}{3}+\frac{z^2}{3^2}-\frac{z^3}{3^3}+...\right]$$

$$= 1+\frac{3}{2}\sum_{n=0}^{\infty}(-1)^n\frac{z^n}{2^n}-\frac{8}{3}\sum_{n=0}^{\infty}(-1)^n\frac{z^n}{3^3}$$

$$= 1+\Sigma\left[(-1)^n\left\{\frac{3}{2^{n+1}}-\frac{8}{3^{n+1}}\right\}z^n\right]$$

which is a Taylor's series valid for | z | < 2.

(ii) For 2 < | z | < 3, we have

$$f(z) = 1+\frac{3}{z}\left(1+\frac{2}{z}\right)^{-1} - \frac{8}{3}\left(1+\frac{z}{8}\right)^{-1}$$

$$= 1+\frac{3}{2}\left[1-\frac{2}{z}+\frac{2^2}{z^2}-\frac{2^3}{z^3}+...\right]-\frac{8}{3}\left[1-\frac{z}{3}+\frac{z^2}{3^2}-\frac{z^3}{3^3}+...\right]$$

$$= 1+\frac{3}{2}\sum_{n=0}^{\infty}(-1)^n\frac{2^n}{z^n}-\frac{8}{3}\sum_{n=0}^{\infty}(-1)^n\frac{z^n}{3^n}$$

(iii) For | z | < 3, we write

$$f(z) = 1+\frac{3}{z}\left(1+\frac{2}{z}\right)^{-1} - \frac{8}{z}\left(1+\frac{3}{z}\right)^{-1}$$

$$= 1+\frac{3}{z}\left[1-\frac{2}{z}+\frac{2^2}{z^2}-\frac{2^3}{z^3}+...\right]-\frac{8}{3}\left[1-\frac{3}{z}+\frac{3^2}{z^2}-\frac{3^3}{z^3}+...\right]$$

$$= 1+\frac{3}{2}\sum_{n=0}^{\infty}(-1)^n,\frac{2^n}{z^n}-\frac{8}{3}\sum_{n=0}^{\infty}(-1)^n,\frac{3^n}{z^n}$$

Example 6:

For the function $f(z) = \frac{2z^3+1}{z^2+z}$ *find*

(i) a taylor series valid in the neighbourhood of the point $z = i$,

(ii) a Laurent's series valid within the annulus of which centre is the origin.

Solution:

(i) We have

$$f(z) = 2(z-1) + \frac{1}{z} + \frac{1}{z+1}$$

We write

$$f_1(z) = 2(z-1),\ f_2(z) = \frac{1}{z},\ f_3(z) = \frac{1}{z+1}$$

Taylor's expansion for $f_1(z)$ about z = i is given by

$$f_1(z) = 2(z-1) = f_1(i) + \sum_{n=0}^{\infty} \frac{f_1^{(n)}(i)}{n!}(z-i)^n$$

Now $f_1(i) = 2(i-1)$, $f_1'(i) = 2$ and $f_1^{(n)}(i) = 0$ for $n \geq 2$.

Hence $f_1(z) = 2(i-1) + 2(z-i)$.

Again Taylor's expansion for $f_2(z) = \frac{1}{z}$ about z = i is given by

$$f_2(z) = \frac{1}{z} = f_2(i) + \sum_{n=1}^{\infty} \frac{f_1^{(n)}(i)}{n!}(z-i)^n$$

Now $f_2(i) = \frac{1}{i}$ and $f_2^{(n)}(z) = (-1)^n \frac{n!}{z^{n+1}}$

so that $f_2^{(n)}(i) = \frac{(-1)^n n!}{i^{n+1}}$

Hence $f_2(z) = \frac{1}{i} + \sum_{n=1}^{\infty} \frac{(-1)^n}{i^{n+1}}(z-i)^n \sum_{n=1}^{\infty} \frac{(-1)^n}{i^{n+1}}(z-i)^n$.

Similarly, we can show that

$$f_3(z) = \sum_{n=0}^{\infty} (-1)^n \frac{(z-i)^n}{(1+i)^{n+1}}$$

Thus the Taylor's expansion for f(z) is given by

$$f(z) = 2(i-1) + 2(z-i) + \sum_{n=0}^{\infty}\left[\frac{(-1)^n}{i^{n+1}} + \frac{(-1)^n}{(1+i)^{n+1}}\right](z-i)^n.$$

(ii) For | z | < 1, Laurent's series for f(z) is given by

$$f(z) = 2(z-1) + \frac{2}{z} + (1+z)^{-1}$$

$$= 2(z-1) + \frac{1}{z} + (1 - z + z^2 - z^3 + \ldots).$$

Example 7:

Obtain the Taylor's or Laurent's series which represents the function

$$f(z)=\frac{1}{(1+z^2)(z+2)}$$

when (i) | z | < 1, (ii) 1 < | z | < 2, (iii) | z | > 2.

Solution:

Resolving f(z) into partial fractions, we obtain

$$f(z)=\frac{1}{5}\left[\frac{1}{z+2}-\frac{z-2}{z^2+1}\right]$$

(i) For | z | < 1, f(z) is analytic and so we have

$$f(z)=\frac{1}{5}.\frac{1}{2}\left(1+\frac{z}{2}\right)^{-1}-\frac{1}{5}(z-2)\left(1+z^2\right)^{-1}$$

$$=\frac{1}{10}\left[1-\frac{z}{2}+\frac{z^2}{2^2}+...+(-1)^n\frac{z^n}{2^n}+...\right]$$

$$-\frac{(z-2)}{5}\left[1-z^2+z^4-z^6+...+(-1)^n z^{2n}+...\right]$$

$$=\frac{1}{10}\sum_{n=0}^{\infty}(-1)^n.\frac{z^n}{2^n}-\frac{z-2}{5}\sum_{n=0}^{\infty}(-1)^n.\frac{1}{z^{2n}}$$

This series being in the positive powers of z represents Taylor's expansion for f(z).

(ii) For 1 < | z | < 2, we have

$$f(z)=\frac{1}{5}.\frac{1}{2}\left(1+\frac{1}{2}z^{-1}\right)-\frac{z-2}{5}.\frac{1}{z^2}\left(1+\frac{1}{z^2}\right)^{-1}$$

$$=\frac{1}{10}\left[1-\frac{z}{2}+\frac{z^2}{2^2}-\frac{z^2}{2^2}+...\right]-\frac{z-2}{5z^2}\left[1-\frac{1}{z^2}+\frac{1}{z^4}-...\right]$$

$$=\frac{1}{10}\sum_{n=0}^{\infty}(-1)^n\frac{z^n}{2^n}-\frac{z-2}{5z^2}\sum_{n=0}^{\infty}(-1)^n\frac{1}{z^{2n}}$$

[Note that since | z | > 1,

we have $\frac{1}{|z|}<1$ or $\frac{1}{|z|^2}<1$

so that the binomial expansion of $\left(1+\frac{1}{z^2}\right)^{-1}$ is valid].

The above series being in positive and negative powers of z represents Laurent's expansion for f(z) in the region 1 < | z | < 2.

(iii) For | z | > 2, we have

$$f(z)=\frac{1}{5}.\frac{1}{z}\left(1+\frac{2}{z}\right)^{-1}-\frac{1}{5}(z-2).\frac{1}{z^2}\left(1+\frac{1}{z^2}\right)^{-1}$$

$$=\frac{1}{5z}\left[1-\frac{2}{z}+\frac{2^2}{z^2}-\frac{2^3}{z^3}+...\right]-\frac{z-2}{5z^2}\left[1-\frac{1}{z^2}+\frac{1}{z^4}-\frac{1}{z^6}+...\right]$$

$$=\frac{1}{5z}\sum_{n=0}^{\infty}(-1)^n\left(\frac{2}{z}\right)^n-\frac{1}{5}\left(\frac{1}{z}-\frac{2}{z^2}\right)\sum_{n=1}^{\infty}\frac{(-1)^n}{z^{2n}}$$

Example 8:

Represent the function f(z) = $\frac{z}{(z-1)(z-3)}$ *by a series of negative powers of (z – 1) which converges to f(z), when 0 < | z – 1| < 2.*

Solution:

Let z – 1 = u. Then 0 < | z – 1 | < 2 implies 0 < | u | < 2 and so

$$\frac{z}{(z-1)(z-3)}=\frac{u+1}{u(u-2)}=-\frac{1}{2u}+\frac{3}{2(u-2)}$$

Hence for | u | < 2, we have

$$f(z)=\frac{1}{2u}-\frac{3}{4\left(1-\frac{u}{2}\right)}=-\frac{1}{2u}-\frac{3}{4}\left(1-\frac{u}{2}\right)^{-1}$$

$$=\frac{1}{2u}-\frac{3}{4}\left[1-\frac{u}{2}+\frac{u^2}{2^2}-\frac{u^3}{2^3}+...\right]$$

$$=-\frac{1}{2(z-1)}-\frac{3}{4}\left[1+\frac{z-1}{2}+\frac{(z-1)^2}{2^2}+\frac{(z-1)^3}{2^3}+...\right]$$

$$=-\frac{1}{2(z-1)}-\frac{3}{4}\sum_{n=0}^{\infty}\left(\frac{(z-1)}{2}\right)^n$$

Example 9:

Show that sin {c (z + 1/z) } can be expanded in a series of the type

$$\sum_{n=0}^{\infty}a_n z^n+\sum_{n=0}^{\infty}b_n z^{-n}$$

in which the coefficients of both z^n *and* z^{-n} *are*

$$\frac{1}{2\pi}\int_0^{2\pi} \sin(2c\cos\theta)\cos n\theta\ n\theta.$$

Solution:

The function $f(z) = \sin\left\{c\left(z+\frac{1}{z}\right)\right\}$ is analytic except at z = 0, *i.e.* $\sin\left\{c\left(z+\frac{1}{z}\right)\right\}$ is analytic in the annulus $r \le z \le R$ where r is small and R is large. Therefore f(z) can be expanded in Laurent's series. Thus by Laurent's theorem

$$\sin\left\{c\left(z+\frac{1}{z}\right)\right\} = \sum_{n=0}^{\infty} a_n z^n + \sum_{n=0}^{\infty} b_n z^{-n}$$

$$\text{where } a_n = \frac{1}{2\pi i}\int_C \sin\left\{c\left(z+\frac{1}{z}\right)\right\}\frac{dz}{z^{n+1}}$$

$$\text{and } b_n = \frac{1}{2\pi i}\int_C \sin\left\{c\left(z+\frac{1}{z}\right)\right\} z^{n-1}\, dz$$

where C is any circle with origin as centre. For convenience, we take unity as the radius of C so that

$$z = e^{i\theta},\ dz = ie^{i\theta}\, d\theta.$$

Hence

$$a_n = \frac{1}{2\pi i}\int_C \sin\left\{c\left(z+\frac{1}{z}\right)\right\}\frac{dz}{z^{n+1}}$$

$$= \frac{1}{2\pi i}\int_0^{2\pi} \sin\left\{c\left(c^{i\theta}+e^{-i\theta}\right)\right\}.\frac{ie^{i\theta}d\theta}{e^{(n+1)u\theta}}$$

$$= \frac{1}{2\pi}\int_0^{2\pi} \sin\{2c\cos\theta)e^{-in\theta}d\theta$$

$$= \frac{1}{2\pi}\int_0^{2\pi} \sin(2c\cos\theta)\{\cos n\theta - i\sin\theta)d\theta$$

$$= \frac{1}{2\pi}\int_0^{2\pi} \sin(2c\cos\theta)\cos n\theta d\theta$$

since the integral

$$\int_0^{2\pi} \sin(2c\cos\theta)\sin n\theta d\theta = 0$$

by a property of definite integrals.

Now the function $\sin\left\{c\left(z+\frac{1}{z}\right)\right\}$ remains unaltered if $\frac{1}{z}$ is written for z. It follows that

$$b_n = a_{-n} = \frac{1}{2\pi}\int_0^{2\pi} \sin(2c\cos\theta)\cos(-n\theta)d\theta$$

$$= \int_0^{2\pi} \sin(2c\cos\theta)\cos n\theta d\theta = a_n.$$

Hence $\sin\left\{c\left(z+\frac{1}{z}\right)\right\} = \sum_{n=0}^{\infty} a_n z^n + \sum_{1}^{\infty} b_n z^{-n}$

where $a_n = b_n = \frac{1}{2\pi}\int_0^{2\pi} \sin(2c\cos\theta)\cos n\theta d\theta.$

We may express it also as

$$\sin\left\{c\left(z+\frac{1}{z}\right)\right\} = a_0 + \sum_{n=1}^{\infty} a_n\left(z^n + \frac{1}{z^n}\right)$$

where a_n is as above.

Example 10:

Prove that

$$\cosh\left(z+\frac{1}{z}\right) = a_0 + \sum_{n=0}^{\infty} a_n\left(z^n + \frac{1}{z^n}\right)$$

where $a_n = \frac{1}{2}\int_0^{2\pi} \cosh n\theta \cosh(2\cos\theta)\, d\theta.$

Solution:

The function $\cosh\left(z+\frac{1}{z}\right)$ is analytic everywhere in the whole finite part of the plane except at $z = 0$, *i.e.*, it is analytic in the annulus $r \le |z| \le R$ where r is small and R is large. Hence we can expand f(z) in a laurent's series in the annulus $r < |z| < R$ in the form

$$\cosh\left(z+\frac{1}{z}\right) = \sum a_n z^n + \sum_{n=0}^{\infty} b_n z^{-n}$$

where $a_n = \frac{1}{2\pi i}\int_C \cos\left(z+\frac{1}{z}\right)\cdot\frac{dz}{z^{n+1}}$

and $b_n = \frac{1}{2\pi i}\int_C \cos\left(z+\frac{1}{z}\right) z^{n-1} dz$

where C is any circle with origin as centre.

Taking C to be the circle $|z| = 1$

so that $z = e^{i\theta}$, $dz = ie^{i\theta}d\theta$, we have

$$a_n = \frac{1}{2\pi i}\int_0^{2\pi} \cosh(e^{i\theta}+e^{-i\theta})\frac{ie^{i\theta}\, d\theta}{e^{(n+1)i\theta}}$$

$$= \frac{1}{2\pi i}\int_0^{2\pi} \cosh(2\cos\theta).e^{-ni\theta}d\theta$$

$$= \frac{1}{2\pi i}\int_0^{2\pi} \cosh(2\cos\theta)(\cos n\theta - i\sin n\theta)\, d\theta$$

$$= \frac{1}{2\pi i}\int_0^{2\pi} \cosh(2\cos\theta)\cos n\theta\, d\theta$$

since $\int_0^{2\pi} \cosh(2\cos\theta)\sin n\theta\, d\theta = 0$

by a property of definite integrals.

Now the function $\cosh\left(z+\frac{1}{z}\right)$ remains unchanged by replacing z by $\frac{1}{z}$.

Hence $$b_n = a_{-n} = \frac{1}{2\pi}\int_0^{2\pi} \cosh(2\cos\theta)\cos(-n\theta)\, d\theta$$

$$= \frac{1}{2\pi}\int_0^{2\pi} \cosh(2\cos\theta)\cos n\theta\, d\theta = a_n.$$

Thus $$\cosh\left(z+\frac{1}{z}\right) = \sum_0^{\infty} a_n z^n + \sum_1^{\infty} b_n z^{-n}$$

$$= \sum_0^{\infty} a_n z^n + \sum_1^{\infty} b_n z^{-n} \qquad [\because a_n = b_n$$

$$= a_0 + \sum_1^{\infty} a_n (z^n + z^{-n})$$

$$= a_0 + \sum_1^{\infty} a_n \left(z^n + \frac{1}{z^n}\right)$$

Example 11:

Show that

$$e^{\frac{1}{2}c(z-1/2)} = \sum_{n=-\infty}^{\infty} a_n a^n$$

where $a_n = \frac{1}{2\pi i}\int_0^{2\pi} \cos(n\theta - c\sin\theta)\, d\theta.$

Solution:

The function $e^{\frac{1}{2}c(z-1/2)}$ is analytic at every point except at $z = 0$ an $z = \infty$ *i.e.* it is analytic in the ring shaped region $r \le |z| \le R$ where r is sma and R is large. Hence it can be expanded as Laurent's series in the forn

$$e^{\frac{1}{2}c(z-1/2)} = \sum_{n=0}^{\infty} a_n z^n + \sum_{n=1}^{\infty} b_n z^{-n}$$

$$\text{where } b_n = \frac{1}{2\pi i}\int_C e^{\frac{1}{2}c(z-1/2)} \frac{dz}{z^{n+1}}$$

where C is any circle with origin as centre.

We take c as the circle | z | = 1 so that

$z = e^{i\theta}$, $dz = ie^{i\theta}\, d\theta$.

$$\therefore \quad a_n = \frac{1}{2\pi i}\int_0^{2\pi} e^{\frac{1}{2}c\left(e^{i\theta}-e^{-i\theta}\right)} \cdot \frac{ie^{i\theta}d\theta}{e^{(n+1)i\theta}}$$

$$= \frac{1}{2\pi i}\int_0^{2\pi} e^{ci\sin\theta} . e^{-ni\theta} d\theta$$

$$= \frac{1}{2\pi i}\int_0^{2\pi} e^{-i(n\theta - c\sin\theta)} d\theta$$

$$= \frac{1}{2\pi i}\int_0^{2\pi} [\cos(n\theta - c\sin\theta) - i\sin(n\theta - c\sin\theta)]$$

$$= \frac{1}{2\pi i}\int_0^{2\pi} \cos(n\theta - c\sin\theta)d\theta$$

since the integral $\int_0^{2\pi} \sin(n\theta - c\sin\theta)d\theta$ vanishes by the property of definite integrals.

Now the function remains unaltered if c is replaced by – 1/z so that $b_n = (-1)^n a_n$. If follows that

$$e^{\frac{1}{2}c(z-1/2)} = \sum_{n=0}^{\infty} a_n z^n + \sum_{n=1}^{\infty} b_n z^{-n} = \sum_{n=0}^{\infty} a_n z^n + \Sigma(-1)^n a_n z^{-n} = \sum_{-\infty}^{\infty} a_n z^n.$$

Example 12:

Show that if c > 0, then

$$e^{z+c^3/2z^2} = \sum_{n=-\infty}^{\infty} a_n z^n$$

$$\textit{where } a_n = \frac{e^{-(1/2)c}}{2\pi c^n}\int_0^{2\pi} e^{c(\cos\theta+\cos^2\theta)} \cos\{c\sin\theta(1-\cos\theta) - n\theta)d\theta$$

Solution:

The function $e^{z+c^3/2z^2}$ is analytic except at z = 0 so that we can expand it as a Laurent's series in the annulus r < | z | < R where r is small and R is large.

Hence we have

$$e^{z+c^3/2z^2} = \sum_{-\infty}^{\infty} a_n z^n$$

$$\text{where } a_n = \frac{1}{2\pi i}\int_C e^{z+c^3/2z^2} \cdot \frac{dz}{z^{n+1}}$$

C being any circle with centre as origin. We take C to be the circle defined by | z | = c so that $z = ce^{i\theta}$.

Thus

$$a_n = \frac{1}{2\pi i}\int_0^{2\pi} \exp\left\{ce^{i\theta} + \frac{c}{2}e^{-2i\theta}\right\}\frac{ice^{i\theta}}{c^{n+1}e^{(n+1)i\theta}}d\theta$$

$$= \frac{1}{2\pi c^n}\int_0^{2\pi} \exp\left\{ce^{i\theta} + \frac{c}{2}e^{-2i\theta} - ni\theta\right\}d\theta$$

$$= \frac{1}{2\pi c^n}\int_0^{2\pi} \exp\left\{c\cos\theta + \frac{c}{2}\cos 2\theta\right\}$$

$$\times \exp\left\{i\left(c\sin\theta - \frac{c}{2}\sin 2\theta - n\theta\right)\right\}$$

$$= \frac{1}{2\pi c^n}\int_0^{2\pi} \exp\left(c\cos\theta + \frac{c}{2}\cos 2\theta\right)$$

$$\times \exp\left[\cos\left(c\sin\theta - \frac{c}{2}\sin 2\theta - n\theta\right)\right.$$

$$\left. + i\sin\left(c\sin\theta - \frac{c}{2}\sin 2\theta - n\theta\right)d\theta\right]$$

$$= \frac{1}{2\pi c^n}\int_0^{2\pi} \exp\left(c\cos\theta + \frac{c}{2}\cos 2\theta\right)$$

$$\times \cos\left(c\cos\theta - \frac{c}{2}\sin 2\theta - n\theta\right)d\theta$$

since the second integral is zero by the property of definite integrals

$$\text{Hence } a_n = \frac{1}{2\pi i}\int_0^{2\pi} \exp\left(c\cos\theta + \left(\frac{c}{2}\right)\cos 2\theta\right)$$

$$\times \cos\{c\sin\theta\,(1 - \cos\theta) - n\theta\}\,d\theta$$

Example 13:

Prove that

$$e^{u/v+vz} = \sum_{n=0}^{\infty} a_n z^n + \sum_{n=1}^{\infty} b_n z^{-n}$$

where $a_n = \frac{1}{2\pi}\int_0^{2\pi} \exp\{(u+v)\cos\theta\} \times \cos\{(v-u)\sin\theta - n\theta\}$

and $a_n = \frac{1}{2\pi}\int_0^{2\pi} \exp\{(u+v)\cos\theta\} \times \cos\{(u-v)\sin\theta - n\theta\}\, d\theta.$

Solution:

Now $f(z) = e^{u/z+vz}$ is analytic except at $z = 0$ and so it can be expanded in the region $r < |z| < R$ as a Laurent's series where r is small and R is finite. Thus

$$f(z) = \sum_{n=0}^{\infty} a_n z^n + \sum_{n=1}^{\infty} b_n z^{-n}$$

$$\text{where } a_n = \frac{1}{2\pi i}\int_C \frac{f(z)}{z^{n+1}} dz,\ b_n = \frac{1}{2\pi i}\int_C z^{n-1} f(z) dz,$$

C being any circle with origin as centre. We take C to be the represented by $|z| = 1$ so that

$z = e^{i\theta}$, $dz = ie^{i\theta}\, d\theta$.

Hence

$$\Rightarrow a_n = \frac{1}{2\pi i}\int_C \frac{e^{u/z+vz}}{z^{n+1}} dz$$

$$\Rightarrow a_n = \frac{1}{2\pi}\int_0^{2\pi} \frac{\exp(ue^{-\theta} + ve^{i\theta})}{e^{i(n+1)\theta}} .ie^{i\theta} d\theta$$

$$\Rightarrow a_n = \frac{1}{2\pi}\int_0^{2\pi} \exp\{(u+v)\cos\theta\}\ \exp\{i(v\sin\theta - u\sin\theta - n\theta)\}d\theta$$

$$\Rightarrow a_n = \frac{1}{2\pi}\int_0^{2\pi} e^{(u+v)\cos\theta}[\cos(v\sin\theta - u\sin\theta - n\theta)$$

$$+ i\sin(v\sin\theta - u\sin\theta - n\theta)d\theta$$

$$\Rightarrow a_n = \frac{1}{2\pi}\int_0^{2\pi} e^{(u+v)\cos\theta}\cos(v\sin\theta - u\sin\theta - n\theta)d\theta,$$

since the second integral vanishes by the property of definite integrals.

[Note that $F(2\pi - \theta) = -F(\theta)$]

where$F(\theta) = e^{(u+v)\cos\theta}\sin(v\sin\theta - u\sin\theta - n\theta)$]

$$\text{and } b_n = \frac{1}{2\pi i}\int_C z^{n-1}.e^{u/z+vz} dz$$

$$= \frac{1}{2\pi i}\int_0^{2\pi} e^{(n-q)i\theta}.e^{(ue^{-i\theta}+ve^{i\theta})}.e^{i\theta} i d\theta$$

$$= \frac{1}{2\pi i}\int_0^{2\pi} e^{(u+v)\cos\theta} . \exp\{i(u\sin\theta - v\sin\theta - n\theta)\}d\theta$$

$$= \frac{1}{2\pi}\int_0^{2\pi} e^{(u+v)\cos\theta}[\cos(u\sin\theta - v\sin\theta - n\theta)$$

$$- i \sin (u \sin\theta - v \sin\theta - n\theta)]d\theta$$

$$= \frac{1}{2\pi}\int_0^{2\pi} e^{(u+v)\cos\theta} \cos\{(u-v)\sin\theta - n\theta)d\theta,$$

the second integral vanishing.

Example 14:

Determine a function which shall be regular within the circle | z | = 1 and shall have on the circumference of this circle the value

$$\frac{(a^2-1)\cos\theta + i(a^2+1)\sin\theta}{a^4 - 2a^2\cos 2\theta + 1}$$

where $a^2 > 1$, and 9 is the vectorial angle at point on the circumference.

Solution:

Suppose f(z) is the desired function. Since f(z) is analytic inside the circle |z| = 1, we can expand it as a Taylor's series at any point z within this circle.

Hence $f(z) = \sum_{n=0}^{\infty} a_n z^n$

where $a_n = 2\pi i \int_C \frac{f(z)}{z^{n+1}} dz,$

C being the circle | z | = 1. On this circle, we have

$$\Rightarrow f(z) = \frac{(a^2-1)\cos\theta + i(a^2+1)\sin\theta}{a^4 - 2a^2\cos 2\theta + 1}$$

$$\Rightarrow f(z) = \frac{a^2(\cos\theta + i\sin\theta) - (\cos\theta - i\sin\theta)}{a^4 - 2a^2\cos 2\theta + 1}$$

$$\Rightarrow f(z) = \frac{a^2 e^{i\theta} = -e^{-i\theta}}{a^4 - a^2(e^{2i\theta} + e^{-2i\theta}) + 1}$$

$$\Rightarrow f(z) = \frac{(a^2 e^{i\theta} - e^{-i\theta})}{(a^2 e^{i\theta} - e^{-i\theta})(a^2 e^{-i\theta} - e^{i\theta})} = \frac{1}{a^2 e^{-i\theta} - e^{i\theta}}$$

$$\text{Thus } f(z) = \frac{1}{a^2 e^{-i\theta}\left(1 - \frac{1}{a^2} e^{2i\theta}\right)}$$

Also $z = e^{i\theta}$ on C so that $dz = ie^{i\theta}\, d\theta$.

$$\therefore \quad a_n = \frac{1}{2\pi i}\int_0^{2\pi} \frac{1}{a^2 e^{-i\theta}\left(1-\frac{1}{a^2}e^{2i\theta}\right)}\cdot\frac{ie^{i\theta}d\theta}{e^{(n+1)i\theta}}$$

$$\Rightarrow a_n = \frac{1}{2\pi i}\int_0^{2\pi} e^{-(n-1)i\theta}\left(1-\frac{1}{a^2}e^{2i\theta}\right)^{-1} d\theta$$

$$a_n = \frac{1}{2\pi i a^2}\int_0^{2\pi} e^{-(n-1)i\theta}\left[1-\frac{e^{2i\theta}}{a^2}+\frac{e^{4i\theta}}{a^4}+\ldots\right]d\theta$$

$a_n = 0$ if n is even (why?)

$$a_n = \frac{1}{2\pi i a^2}\int_0^{2\pi} e^{-(n-1)i\theta}\frac{e^{(n-1)i\theta}}{a^{n-1}}d\theta$$

$$= \frac{1}{2\pi a^{n+1}}.2\pi = \frac{1}{a^{n+1}} \qquad \ldots(1)$$

Hence$f(z) = a_1 z + a_3 z^3 + a_3 z^3 + a_5 z^5 + \ldots$

$$[\because a_0 = a_2 = a_4 = \ldots = 0]$$

$$= \frac{z}{a^2}+\frac{z^3}{a^4}+\frac{z^5}{a^6}+\ldots\ldots \text{ by (1)}$$

$$= \frac{\frac{z}{a^2}}{1-\frac{z^2}{a^2}} = \frac{z}{a^2-z^2}$$

Example 15:

Find a function f(z) which is analytic throughout the circle C and its interior, whose centre is at origin and whose radius is unity and has the value

$$\frac{a-\cos\theta}{a^2-2a\cos\theta+1}+\frac{i\sin\theta}{a^2-2a\cos\theta+1}$$

where $a > 1$ and θ is the vertical angle at points on the circumference of C.

Solution:

Since f(z) is analytic within and on the circle

$$|z| = 1,$$

we may expand it as Taylor's series at any point inside and or the circle so that we have

$$f(z)=\sum_{n=0}^{\infty}a_n z^n$$

where $a_n=\dfrac{1}{2\pi i}\displaystyle\int_C \frac{f(z)}{z^{(n+1)}}dz.$

Now on C, $z = e^{i\theta} = ie^{i\theta}\,d\theta$

and $$f(z) = \frac{a-\cos\theta+i\sin\theta}{a^2-2a\cos\theta+1}$$

$$= \frac{a-e^{-i\theta}}{a^2-a(e^{i\theta}+e^{-i\theta})+1}=\frac{a-e^{-i\theta}}{(a-e^{i\theta})(a-e^{i\theta})}$$

$$= \frac{1}{a-e^{i\theta}}$$

Hence $$a_n = \frac{1}{2\pi i}\int_0^{2\pi}\frac{1}{a-e^{i\theta}}.\frac{ie^{i\theta}d\theta}{e^{(n+1)i\theta}}$$

$$= \frac{1}{2\pi i}\int_0^{2\pi}e^{-ni\theta}\left(1-\frac{e^{i\theta}}{a}\right)^{-1}d\theta$$

$$= \frac{1}{2\pi i}\int_0^{2\pi}e^{-ni\theta}\left[1+\frac{e^{i\theta}}{a}+\frac{e^{2i\theta}}{a^2}+\ldots\right]d\theta$$

$$= \frac{1}{2\pi i}\int_0^{2\pi}e^{-ni\theta}\frac{e^{ni\theta}}{a^n}d\theta,$$

as the other integrals vanish

$$= \frac{1}{2\pi a^{n+1}}\int_0^{2\pi}d\theta=\frac{1}{2\pi a^{n+1}}.2\pi=\frac{1}{a^{n+1}}$$

Hence $$f(z) = \sum_{n=0}^{\infty}\frac{z^n}{a^{n+1}}$$

$$= \frac{1}{a}+\frac{z}{a^2}+\frac{z^2}{a^3}+\ldots=\frac{1/a}{1-z/a}=\frac{1}{a-z}.$$

Example 16:

By using the integral representation of $f^n(0)$, prove that

$$\left(\frac{x^n}{n!}\right)^n=\frac{1}{2\pi i}\int_C\frac{x^n e^{xz}}{n!z^{n+1}}dz,$$

where C is any closed contour surrounding the origin. Hence show that

$$\sum_{n=0}^{\infty}\left(\frac{x^n}{n!}\right)^n=\frac{1}{2\pi i}\int_0^{2\pi}e^{2x\cos\theta}d\theta.$$

Solution:

By Cauchy's formula for the nth derivative of f(z) at z = 0, we have

$$f(z) = \frac{n!}{2\pi i}\int_C \frac{f(z)}{z^{n+1}}dz. \qquad ...(1)$$

We take $f(z) = e^{xz}$. Then $f^{(n)}(z) = x^n e^{xz}$

and so $f^{(n)}(0) = x^n e^0 = x^n$. Substituting in (1), we get

$$x^n = \frac{n!}{2\pi i}\int_C \frac{e^{xz}}{z^{n+1}}dz.$$

∴ Multiplying both sides by $\frac{x^n}{(n!)^2}$, we have

$$\left(\frac{x^n}{n!}\right)^2 = \frac{x^n}{2\pi i.n!}\int_C \frac{e^{xz}}{z^{n+1}}dz.$$

$$= \frac{1}{2\pi i}\int_C \frac{x^n e^{xz}}{n!z^{n+1}}dz. \qquad ...(2)$$

Now we take C to be the circle | z | = 1 so that

$$z = e^{i\theta},\ dz = ie^{i\theta}\,d\theta.$$

Hence summing both sides of (2) from n = 0 to ∞, we get

$$\sum_{n=0}^{\infty}\left(\frac{x^n}{n!}\right)^n = \sum_{n=0}^{\infty}\frac{1}{2\pi i}\int_C \frac{x^n.e^{xz}}{n!z^{n+1}}dz$$

$$= \frac{1}{2\pi i}\int_C e^{xz}\sum_{n=0}^{\infty}\frac{1}{n!}\left(\frac{x}{z}\right)^n\frac{dz}{z}.$$

[∵ Note that the summation and integration can be interchanged because of the uniform convergence of the series $\sum_{n=0}^{\infty}\frac{x^n}{n!z^{n+1}}$]

$$\therefore \quad \sum_{n=0}^{\infty}\left(\frac{x^n}{n!}\right)^n = \frac{1}{2\pi i}\int_C e^{xz}.e^{x/z}.\frac{dz}{z}$$

$$= \frac{1}{2\pi i}\int_0^{2\pi} e^{xe^{-i\theta}}e^{xe^{i\theta}}.\frac{ie^{i\theta}d\theta}{e^{i\theta}}$$

$$= \frac{1}{2\pi}\int_0^{2\pi} e^{x(e^{i\theta}+e^{-i\theta})}d\theta = \frac{1}{2\pi}\int_0^{2\pi} e^{2x\cos\theta}\,d\theta$$

Example 17:

If the function f(z) is analytic and one valued in | z – a | < R, prove that when 0 < r < R.

$$f'(a) = \frac{1}{\pi r}\int_0^{2\pi} P(\theta)e^{-i\theta}d\theta$$

where P(θ) is the real part off (a + re^{iθ}).

Solution:

Since f(z) is analytic in | z – a | < R and r < R, it follows that f(z) is also analytic inside the circle C defined by

$$|z - a| = r.$$

Hence by Cauchy's formula for the derivative, we have

$$\frac{1}{2\pi i}\int_C \frac{f(z)}{(z-a)^2}dz = f'(a)$$

Also f(z) can be expanded as a Taylor's series about z = a in the form

$$f(z) = \sum_{m=0}^{\infty} a_m (z-a)^m.$$

Putting $z - a = re^{i\theta}$, we have

$$f(z) = f(a + re^{i\theta})\sum_{m=0}^{\infty} a_m a^m e^{mi\theta}.$$

Then $\overline{f(z)} = \sum_{m=0}^{\infty} \bar{a}_m a^m e^{-mi\theta}$.

$$\therefore \frac{1}{2\pi i}\int \frac{\overline{f(z)}}{(z-a)^2}dz = \frac{1}{2\pi i}\int_0^{2\pi} \frac{\sum_{m=0}^{\infty}\bar{a}_m a^m e^{-mi\theta}}{r^2 e^{2i\theta}}.rie^{i\theta}d\theta$$

$$= \frac{1}{2\pi}\sum_{m=0}^{\infty}\bar{a}_m a^{m-1}\int_0^{2\pi} e^{-(m+q)i\theta}d\theta$$

$$= 0\left[\because \int_0^{2\pi} e^{-(m+q)i\theta}d\theta = 0\right]. \quad ...(2)$$

Adding (1) and (2), we have

$$f'(a) = \frac{1}{2\pi i}\int_C \frac{f(z) + \overline{f(z)}}{(z-a)^2}$$

$$= \frac{1}{2\pi i}\int_C \frac{2\,\text{real part of } f(z)}{(z-a)^2}dz$$

$$= \frac{1}{2\pi i}\int_0^{2\pi} \frac{\text{real part of } (a + re^{i\theta})}{r^2 e^{2i\theta}}.rie^{i\theta}d\theta$$

$$[\because z = a + re^{i\theta}]$$

$$= \frac{1}{\pi r}\int_0^{2\pi} P(\theta)e^{-i\theta}d\theta$$

where $P(\theta)$ is the real part of $f(a + re^{i\theta})$.

Example 18:

Let $f(z) = \sum_{n=1}^{\infty} \frac{z^2}{(4+n^2z^2)}$.

so that f(z) is finite and continuous for all real values of but f(z) cannot be expanded in a Maclaurin's series. Show that f(z) possesses Laurent's expansion valid in a succession of the ring spaces.

Solution:

We have

$$f(z) = \sum_{n=1}^{\infty} \frac{z^2}{4+n^2z^2}$$

If we consider z to be a real variable, then every term of the above series is positive and so

$$|u_n| = \left|\frac{z^2}{4+n^2z^2}\right| = \frac{z^2}{4+n^2z^2} \leq \frac{z^2}{n^2z^2} = \frac{1}{n^2}$$

$$\therefore f(z) = \sum_{n=1}^{\infty} \frac{1}{n^2} = \frac{\pi^2}{6}$$

$$\left[\text{Note that the sum of the series } \sum_{n=1}^{\infty} \frac{1}{n^2} \text{ is } \frac{\pi^2}{6}\right].$$

Thus $0 < f(z)\ \frac{\pi^2}{6}$ so that f(z) is finite for real values of z.

Also by Weierstrass's M-test the series in (1) converges uniformly for all real values of z. Now each term of the series is continuous since its denominator does not vanish for any real value of z. But as shown above the series in (1) is uniformly convergent for all real values of z. It follows that its sum function f(z) is also continuous for all real values of z. (See the chapter on uniform convergence).

When f(z) is regarded as a function of complex variable z, each term of the series in (1) possesses two singularities, viz.

$$z = \pm \frac{2i}{n} \quad (n = 1, 2, 3, \ldots)$$

This shows that the function f(z) possesses singularities in every neighbourhood of zero, however small that neighbourhood may be. Hence it is not possible to expand f(z) as a Maclaurin's series about the origin.

The function f(z) is evidently analytic in the ring-shaped region defined by

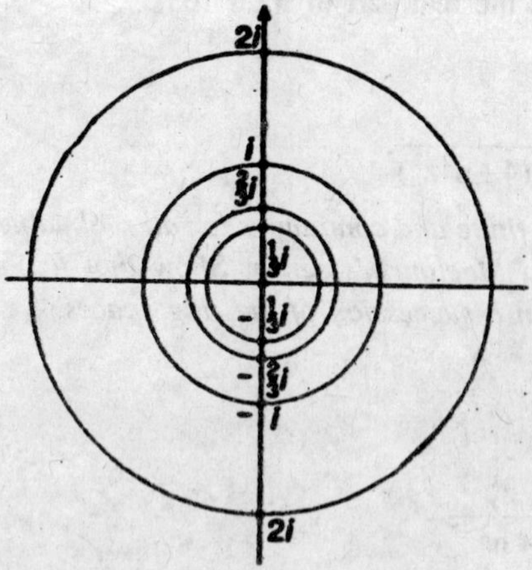

Fig. 1.23

$$\frac{2}{n+1} < |z| < \frac{2}{n}, \quad n = 1, 2, 3, \ldots,$$

since none of the singularities occurs in these regions (see the diagram). Hence f(z) possesses Laurent's expansion valid in a succession of ringspaces defined by

$$\frac{2}{n+1} < |z| < \frac{2}{n}, \quad n = 1, 2, 3, \ldots.$$

EXERCISES

1. Prove that:

$$\frac{1+2z}{z^2+z^3} = \frac{1}{z^2} + \frac{1}{z} - 1 + z - z^2 + z^3, \ldots,$$

where $0 < |z| < 1.$

2. Find two Laurent's series expansions in powers of z of the function f(z) given by

$$f(z) = \frac{1}{z(1+z^2)}$$

Ans. $f(z) = \frac{1}{z} - z + z_2 - z_3 + \ldots$ when $0 < |z| < 1$

$$f(z)=\frac{1}{z^3}-\frac{1}{z^5}+\frac{1}{z^7}-\dots \text{ when } |z|>1.$$

3. Represent a function $f(z)=\dfrac{z}{(z-1)(z-3)}$ by series of positive and negative powers of (z – 1) which converges to f(z) when $0<|z-1|<2$.

Ans. $f(z)=\dfrac{1}{2(z-1)}-\dfrac{3}{4}\sum_{n=0}^{\infty}\left(\dfrac{z-1}{2}\right)^n$

4. Find different developments of $\dfrac{1}{(z-1)(z-3)}$ in powers of z according to the position of the point in the z-plane. Expand the function in Taylor's series about z = 2 and indicate the circle of convergence.

5. Prove that:

$$\tan^{-1} z = z-\frac{z^3}{3}+\frac{z^5}{5}-\dots \text{ when } |z|<1.$$

[Expand by Taylor's theorem about 0]

6. Show that:

$$\log z=(z-1)-\frac{(z-1)^2}{2}+\frac{(z-1)^3}{3}-\dots$$

when $|z-1|<1$.

[Expand log z by Taylor's theorem about z = 1].

7. Expand $f(z)=\dfrac{e^{2z}}{(z-1)^2}$ about z = 1 as a Lurent's series. Also indicate the region of convergence of the series

Ans. $f(z)=\dfrac{e^2}{(z-1)^3}+\dfrac{2e^2}{(z-1)^2}+\dfrac{2e^2}{z-1}+\dfrac{4e^2}{3}+\dfrac{2e^2}{3}(z-1)+\dots$

The series converges for all values of z except 1.

8. Find the expansion of

$$\frac{1}{(z^2+1)(z^2+2)}$$

in powers of z when

(i) $|z|<1$ (ii) $1<|z|<\sqrt{2}$ (iii) $|z|>\sqrt{2}$.

Ans. (i) $\sum_{n=0}^{\infty}(-1)^n\left(1-\dfrac{1}{z^{n+1}}\right)z^{2n}.$

(ii) $\sum_{n=0}^{\infty}(-1)^{n+1}\frac{z^{2n}}{2^{n+1}}+\sum_{n=1}^{\infty}(-1)^{n}\frac{1}{z^{2n+2}}$.

(iii) $\sum_{n=0}^{\infty}\frac{(-1)^{n}(1-2^{n})}{2^{2n+2}}$.

9. Find expansion of $\frac{1}{z^2+3}$ valid for

(i) $|z-1|<2$ (ii) $|z+1|<2$

and hence show that if

$$a_n=(-1)^n\sin\frac{(n+1)\pi}{2}/2^n,\ b_n=2^n\sin\frac{(n+2)\pi}{3}$$

then $\sum_{n=0}^{\infty}a_n(n-1)^n+\sum_{n=1}^{\infty}b_n(z+1)^{-n}=0$

where z lies in the crescent formed by the circles of radius 2 with centres at $z=\pm 1$ to the right of the imaginary axis.

10. Show that in the annulus defined by $a<|z|<b$, the function

$$\left\{\frac{bz}{(z-1)(b-z)}\right\}^{1/2}$$

can be expanded in the form

$$S_0+\Sigma S_n\left(\frac{a_n}{z^n}+\frac{z^n}{b^n}\right)$$

where $S_0=\sum_{i=0}^{\infty}\frac{1.3.5...(2l-1)}{2^{2l+1}l!}\cdot\frac{1.3.5...(2l+2n-1)}{(l+n)!}\left(\frac{a}{b}\right)^{l}$.

11. Obtain the expansions for $\frac{(z-2)(z+2)}{(z+1)(z+4)}$ which are valid when

(i) $|z|<1$ (ii) $1<|z|<4$ (iii) $|z|>1$.

12. Obtain the expansion

$$f(z)=f(z_0)+2\left\{\left(\frac{z-z_0}{2}\right)f'\left(\frac{z-z_0}{2}\right)\right.$$
$$\left.+\frac{(z+z_0)^2}{2^3.3!}f'''\left(\frac{z-z_0}{2}\right)+...\right\}$$

and show the expansion is valid as long as it lies within the neighbourhood of the point $\left(\frac{z+z_0}{2}\right)$.

13. Prove that, if $0 < c < 1$ and $c < |z| < c^{-1}$, then

$$\left\{\frac{(1-cz)(z-c)}{z}\right\}^{1/2}$$

$$= \pm\frac{1}{\pi}\sum_{n=-\infty}^{\infty} z^n \int_0^{\pi} \cos n\theta \sqrt{(1-2c\cos\theta+c^2)}\,d\theta.$$

14. Prove that when $|z| < \frac{1}{2}\pi$.

$$\frac{\sin z}{4z^2-\pi^2} = \sum_{n=0}^{\infty} a_{2n+1} z^{2n+1}$$

where $a_{2n+1} = \frac{(-1)^{n+1}}{\pi^2}\left[\frac{1}{(2n+1)!} - \frac{4}{\pi^2(2n-1)!} + \ldots + \frac{(-4)^n}{x^{2n}}\right]$

and that for $|z| > \frac{1}{2}\pi$,

$$\frac{\sin z}{4z^2-\pi^2} = \sum_{-\infty}^{\infty} b_{2n+1} z^{2n+1},$$

$$\text{where } b_{2n+1} = \begin{cases} a_{2n+1} + \dfrac{2}{n^{2n+3}} & \text{for } n \geq 0 \\ \dfrac{2^{2n+1}}{\pi^{2n+1}} & \text{for } n < 0. \end{cases}$$

15. The function f(z) is analytic in the circle

$$|z| \leq R + \delta,\ \delta > 0$$

and the upper bound of $|f(z)|$ on the circle $|z| = R$ is M. Then Taylor's expansion of f(z) is $\sum_{n=0}^{\infty} a_n z^n$. Prove that

$$\frac{1}{2\pi}\int_0^{2\pi} |f(Re^{i\theta})|^2\, d\theta = \sum_{n=0}^{\infty} |a_n|^2 R^{2n}$$

and deduce that

$$|f^{(n)}(0)| \leq n!MR^{-n}$$

the sign of equality occurring if and only if

$$f(z) = Me^{i\theta} z^n R^{-n}$$

where a is a real constant.

16. The function f(z) is regular when

$$|z| < R'.$$

Show that if

$$|a| < R < R'$$

then $f(a)=\frac{1}{2\pi i}\int_C \frac{(R^2-a\bar{a})f(z)}{(z-a)(R^2-z\bar{a})}dz$

where C is the circle $|z| = R$. Deduce Poisson's formula that, if $0 < r < R$,

$$f(re^{i\theta})=\frac{1}{2\pi}\int_0^{2\pi}\frac{(R^2-r^2)f(Re^{i\phi})}{R^2-2Rr\cos(\theta-\phi)+r^2}d\phi.$$

17. The integral function f(z) satisfies everywhere the inequality

$$|f(z)| \le A|z|^k$$

where A and k are positive constants. Prove that f(z) is a polynomial of degree not exceeding k.

2

THE ZEROS OF AN ANALYTIC FUNCTION

INTRODUCTION

Let f(z) be analytic in a domain D and let zo be a point of D. Then f(z) can be expanded as Taylor's series about $z = z_0$ in the form,

$$f(z) = \sum_{n=0}^{\infty} a_n (z - z_0)^n.$$

If $a_0 = a_1 = a_2 = ... = a_{m-1} = 0$ and am ≠ 0, we say that f(z) has a zero of order m at $z = z_0$. A zero of order one is said to be a simple zero. When f(z) has a zero of order m at $z = z_0$. Taylor's expansion reduces to the form

$$f(z) = \sum_{n=0}^{\infty} a_n (z - z_0)^n = \sum_{n=0}^{\infty} a_{n+m} (z - z_0)^{m+n}$$

$$= (z - z_0)^m \sum_{n=0}^{\infty} a_{n+m} (z - z_0)^n.$$

THE ZEROS AS ISOLATED

Theorem:

Let f(z) be analytic in a domain D. Then unless f(z) is identically zero, there exists a neighbourhood of each point in D throughout which the function has no zero, except possibly at the point itself. In other words, the zeros of an analytic function are isolated.

Proof:

Suppose f(z) has a zero of order m at zo. We can therefore write

$$f(z) = (z - z_0)^m \sum_{n=0}^{\infty} a_{n+m} (z - z_0)^n. \quad ...(1)$$

Let $\phi(z)$ denote the sum of the series in (1) so that

$$\phi(z) = \sum_{n=0}^{\infty} a_{m+n} (z - z_0)^n.$$

We note that $\phi(z0) = am \neq 0$.

Since the series in (1) is uniformly convergent and each term of the series is continuous at z_0, if follows that its sum function $\phi(z)$ is also continuous at z0. Hence for a given $\varepsilon > 0$, we can find as $\delta > 0$ such that

$$|\phi(z) - \phi(z_0)| < \varepsilon \qquad \text{... (2)}$$

whenever $|z - z_0| < \delta$.

Set $\varepsilon = \left|\frac{a_m}{2}\right|$ and let δ_1 be the corresponding value of δ. Then since $\phi(z_0) = a_m$, we get from (2)

$$|\phi(z) - a_m| < \frac{1}{2}|a_m| \qquad \text{... (3)}$$

where$|z - z_0| < \delta_1$.

It follows that $\phi(z) \neq 0$ at any point in the neighbourhood $|z - z_0| < \delta_1$. For if $\phi(z) \doteq 0$, inequality (3) is contradicted. The argument remains valid when rn = 0, in which case $\phi = f$ and $f(z_0) \neq 0$. Hence, the theorem is established.

DIFFERENT TYPES OF SINGULARITIES

In the section, we shall consider functions which are analytic at all points of a bounded domain except at a finite number of points. These exceptional points are called singular points or singularities. We shall classify singularities according to the behaviour of the function in their neigh-bourhoods.

Isolated Singularity

A point zo is said to be an isolated singularity of a function f(z) if f(z) is analytic at each point in some neighbourhood of z_0.

For example the function $f(z) = \frac{z+3}{z^2(z^2+2)}$ possesses three isolated singular points $z = 0$, $z = \sqrt{2}i$ and $z = -\sqrt{2}i$. As another example, the function $\frac{1}{\sin(\theta/z)}$ has an infinite number of isolated singularities all of which lie on the real axis from $z = -1$ to $z = 1$. These isolated singularities are at $z = \pm\frac{1}{n}$, $n = 1, 2, 3,...$ The origin $z = 0$ is also a singularity but it is not isolated since every neighbourhood of 0 contains other singularities of the function.

The function Log z has a singularity at the origin which is not isolated since every neighbourhood of zero contains points on the negative real axis where Log z ceases to be analytic.

Poles, Isolated Essential Singularities and Removable Singularities

Let $z = z_0$ be isolated singularity of a function f(z). Since the singularity is isolated, there exists a deleted neighbourhood

$$0 < |z - z_0| < r$$

in which f(z) is analytic. Then f(z) has a Laurent's expansion

$$f(z) = \sum_{n=0}^{\infty} a_n (z - z_0)^n + \sum_{n=1}^{\infty} b_n (z - z_0)^{-n}$$

The part $\sum_{n=1}^{\infty} b_n (z - z_0)^{-n}$ of the Laurent's series is called the principal part of f(z) at $z = z_0$.

Definition 1:

If the principal part of a function f(z) at $z = z_0$ consists of a finite number of terms, say m, we say that zo is a pole of order m of f(z).

A Pole of Order one is Called a Simple Pole

Thus if z_0 is a pole of order m, then f(z) will have the expansion of the form

$$f(z) = \sum_{n=0}^{\infty} a_n (z - z_0)^n + \frac{b_1}{z - z_0} + \frac{b_2}{(z - z_0)^2} + \ldots + \frac{b_m}{(z - z_0)^m}$$

Definition 2:

If the principal part of f(z) at $z = z_0$ contains an infinite number of terms, then z_0 is called an isolated essential singularity of f(z).

For example 0 is an essential singularity of $e^{1/z}$ since

$$e^{1/z} = 1 + \frac{1}{z} + \frac{1}{2!z^2} + \frac{1}{3!z^3} + \ldots$$

Definition 3:

If the principal of f(z) at $z = z_0$ consists of no terns, then z_0 is said to be a removable singularity of f(z).

In such a case, the singularity can be removed by defining the function f(z) at $z = z_0$ in such a way that it becomes analytic at z_0.

For example the function f(z) defined by $f(z) = \frac{\sin z}{z}$ has removable singularity at 0 since

$$\frac{\sin z}{z} = \frac{1}{z}\left(z - \frac{z^3}{3!} + \frac{z^5}{5!} - \ldots\right) = 1 - \frac{z^2}{3!} + \frac{z^4}{5!} - \ldots$$

Thus $\frac{\sin z}{z}$ contains no negative powers of z. If we set f(z) = 1 at z = 0, then f(z) becomes analytic at 0.

Definition 4:

A function which has poles as its only singularities in the finite part of the plane is called a meromorphic function.

Definition 5:

A function which has no singularity in the finite part of the plane is called an entire function.

For example, ez is an entire function.

A function which has no singularities in the finite part of the plane or at infinity is constant as the following theorem shows:

Theorem:

A function which has no singularity in the finite part of the plane or at infinity is constant.

Proof:

Since the function f(z) has no singularity in the finite part of the plane, we can expand it as a Taylor's series in any circle | z | = R where R is large. Thus

$$f(z) = \sum_{n=0}^{\infty} a_n z^n \qquad ...(1)$$

Again since f(z) has no singularity at z = ∞, $f\left(\frac{1}{z}\right)$ is analytic at z = 0. Further since f(z) has no singularity in the finite part of the plane, $f\left(\frac{1}{z}\right)$ also cannot have any singularity in the finite part of the plane. Hence we may expand $f\left(\frac{1}{z}\right)$ by Taylor's theorem in the form

$$f\left(\frac{1}{z}\right) = \sum_{n=0}^{\infty} b_n z^n \qquad ...(2)$$

Also replacing z by $\frac{1}{z}$ in (1), we have

$$f\left(\frac{1}{z}\right) = \sum_{n=0}^{\infty} \frac{a_n}{z^n} \qquad ...(3)$$

From (2) and (3), we have

$$f\left(\frac{1}{z}\right)=\sum_{n=0}^{\infty}b_n z^n=\sum_{n=0}^{\infty}a_n z^{-n} \quad \text{... (4)}$$

Now (5) can hold only if

$b_n = a_n = 0$ for $n = 1, 2, 3,...$ and $b_0 = a_0$.

It follows that

$f(z) = a_0 = b_0 =$const.

Residue at a Pole

Let z_0 be a pole of order m of f(z) so that

$$f(z)=\sum_{n=0}^{\infty}(z-z_0)^n+\frac{b_1}{(z-z_0)}+\frac{b_2}{(z-z_0)^2}+...+\frac{b_m}{(z-z_0)^m}$$

where $b_m \neq 0$. Then the coefficient b_1 (which may be zero in certain cases) is called the residue of f(z) at z_0. If z_0 is a simple pole, then it is evident that

$$b_1=\lim_{z\to z_0}(z-z_0)f(z)$$

SOME THEOREMS ON POLES AND OTHER SINGULARITIES

Theorem I:

If f(z) has a pole of order m at $z = z_0$, then the function 0 defined by

$\phi(z) = (z - z_0)^m f(z)$

has a removable singularity at z_0 and that $\phi(z_0) \neq 0$.

Also the residue at z_0 is given by

$$\frac{\phi^{(m-1)}(z_0)}{(m-1)!}$$

Proof:

Since f(z) has a pole of order m, we have

$$f(z)=\sum_{n=0}^{\infty}a_n(z-z_0)^n+\frac{b_1}{(z-z_0)}+\frac{b_2}{(z-z_0)^2}+...+\frac{b_m}{(z-z_0)^m} \quad \text{...(1)}$$

when

$0 < | z - z_0 | < r$ $(r > 0)$ and $b_m \neq 0$. Let us write

$$\phi(z) = (z - z_0)^m f(z) \quad \text{... (2)}$$

Thus equation (2) defines the function ϕ in a neighbourhood of z0 except at the point z_0 itself.

Then from (1) and (2), we obtain

$$\phi(z) = \sum_{n=0}^{\infty} a_n (z - z_0)^{n+m} + b_1 (z - z_0)^{m-1} + b_2 (z - z_0)^{m-2} + ... + b_m ...(3)$$

where $b_m \neq 0$. We now define $\phi(z)$ at $z = z_0$ by $\phi(z_0) = b_m$ so that $\phi(z_0) \neq 0$. Then the expansion of $\phi(z)$ in the form (3) is valid throughout a neighbourhood of z_0 including z_0 itself. Now it is easy to see that the series in (3) is a convergent power series. It follows that ϕ is analytic at z_0. Thus we have shown that $\phi(z)$ becomes regular at z_0 by setting $\phi(z_0) = b_m$. Hence $\phi(z)$ has a removable singularity at z_0. We may now write the definition of $\phi(z_0)$ as

$$\phi(z_0) = \lim_{z \to z_0} (z - z_0)^m f(z) = b_m.$$

This limit always exists and is non-zero since $b_m \neq 0$. It follows that $| f(z) | - \infty$ as $z \to z_0$ in any manner.

Further since now $\phi(z)$ becomes analytic at z_0, (3) represents a Taylor's series for $\infty(z)$.Hence coefficient of $(z - z_0)^{m-1} = \dfrac{\phi^{(m-1)}(z_0)}{(m-1)!}$. But the coefficient of $(z - z_0)^{m-1}$ is b1 in (3). Therefore

$$\frac{\phi^{(m-1)}(z_0)}{(m-1)!} = b_1 = \text{residue at } z_0. \qquad ....(4)$$

In particular when zo is a simple pole, then residue at z_0 is

$$\phi(z_0) = \lim_{z \to z_0} (z - z_0) f(z)$$

Theorem II:

Let f(z) be a function such that for some positive integer m, a value $\phi(z_0)$ exists with $\phi(z_0) \neq 0$ such that the function

$$\phi(z) = (z - z_0)m\ f(z)$$

is analytic at z_0. Then f has a pole of order m at z_0.

Proof:

Since $\phi(z)$ is analytic at z_0, it can be expanded in a Taylor's series about z_0 in the form

$$\phi(z) = (z - z_0)^m f(z) = \phi(z_0) + \phi'(z_0)(z - z_0) + ... + \frac{\phi^{(m)}(z_0)}{m!}(z - z_0)^m + ...$$

$$\therefore f(z) = \frac{\phi(z_0)}{(z - z_0)^m} + \frac{\phi'(z_0)}{(z - z_0)^{m-1}} + ... + \frac{\phi^{(m-1)}(z_0)}{(m-1)!} \cdot \frac{1}{z - z_0}$$

$$\sum_{n=m}^{\infty} \frac{\phi^n(z_0)}{n!}(z-z_0)^{n-m} \qquad ...(1)$$

Since $\phi(z_0) \neq 0$, it follows from (1) that f has a pole of order m at z_0.

The residue at z_0 is the coefficient of $\frac{1}{z-z_0}$ in (1)

Thus residue at $\frac{\phi^{(m-1)}(z_0)}{(m-1)!}$.

Remark:

It follows from the above theorem that if a function f(z) can be put in the form $f(z) = \frac{\phi(z)}{(z-z_0)^m}$ where $\phi(z)$ is analytic at z_0 with $\phi(z_0) \neq 0$, then f(z) has a pole of order in at z_0.

Theorem III:

Let a function f(z) be analytic in an open domain D and let $\phi(z)$ be defined by $\phi(z) = \frac{1}{f(z)}$ where $f(z) \neq 0$. Then f has a zero of order in at a point z_0 in D if and only if ϕ has a pole of order in at z_0.

Proof:

The if Part: Let $\phi(z) = \frac{1}{f(z)}$ has a pole of order m at z_0 To show that f(z) has a zero of order m. Since $\phi(z)$ has a pole of order in, we may write

$$\phi(z) = \frac{\psi(z)}{(z-z_0)^m}$$

where $\psi(z)$ is analytic in a neighbourhood of z_0 including z_0 itself and $\psi(z) \neq 0$.

Hence $f(z) = \frac{1}{\phi(z)} = \frac{(z-z_0)^m}{\psi(z)}$ ...(1)

Since $\psi(z)$ is analytic and $\psi(z_0) \neq 0$, it follows that $\frac{1}{\psi(z)}$ is also analytic. It then follows from (1) that f(z) has a zero of order in at z_0.

The only if Part: Suppose that f(z) has a zero of order in at z_0. Then

$$f(z) = (z - z_0)^m \psi(z)$$

where $\psi(z_0) \neq 0$.

Therefore $$\frac{1}{\psi(z)} = \frac{(z-z_0)^m}{f(z)} \qquad ...(1)$$

is analytic in a neighbourhood of z_0 so that it has a Taylor's expansion of the form

$$\frac{1}{\psi(z)} = A_0 + A_1 (z - z_0) + A_2 (z - z_0)2 + ... + A_m(z - z_0)m + \quad ... (2)$$

Since $\phi(z) = \frac{1}{f(z)}$, it follows from (1) and (2) that

$$\phi(z) = \frac{1}{\psi(z)(z-z_0)^m} = \frac{A_0}{(z-z_0)^m} + \frac{A_1}{(z-z_0)^{m-1}}$$

$$+ ... + A_m + \sum_{n=1}^{\infty} A_{m+n}(z-z_0)^n \quad ... (3)$$

The identity (3) shows that $\phi(z)$ has a pole of order m at z_0.

This completes the proof of the theorem.

Theorem IV:

Let z_0 be a pole of f(z), then there exists a neighbourhood of z_0 which contains no other pole of f(z), that is, poles are isolated.

Proof:

Recall that if f(z) has a pole of order m at z0, then there exists a deleted neighbourhood $0 < | z - z_0 | < \rho$ of z_0 in which f(z) is analytic and has a laurent's expansion of the form

$$f(z) = \sum_{n=0}^{\infty} a_n (z - z_n)^n + \sum_{n=1}^{\infty} b_n (z - z_n)^{-n}.$$

Thus in the neighbourhood $0 < | z - z_0 | < \rho$, f(z) contains no other pole. Hence poles are isolated.

Theorem V:

(Riemann): *Let z_0 be an isolated singularity of f(z) and if | f(z) | is bounded on some deleted neighbourhood of z_0, then z_0 is a removable singularity.*

Proof:

Let | f(z) | be bounded on some deleted neighbourhood $N(z_0)$ of z_0. Then $| f(z) | \le M$ where M is the maximum value of f(z) on a circle C defined by $| z - z_0 | = r$ where r is chosen so small that C lies entirely within N (z_0). Then Laurent's theorem gives

$$f(z) = \sum_{n=-\infty}^{\infty} a_n (z - z_0)^n$$

where $a_n = \frac{1}{2\pi i}\int_C \frac{f(z)}{(z-z_0)^{n+1}}dz.$

Now $|a_n| = \left|\frac{1}{2\pi i}\int_C \frac{f(z)}{(z-z_0)^{n+1}}dz\right| \le \frac{1}{2\pi}\int_C \frac{|f(z)||dz|}{|z-z_0|^{n+1}}$

$\le \frac{1}{2\pi}\int_C \frac{M}{r^{n+1}}|dz| = \frac{1}{2\pi}\frac{M}{r^{n+1}}.2\pi r$

$= \frac{M}{r^n} \to 0$ as $n \to \infty$.

Thus, $a_n = 0$ for every negative value of n so that the principal part of f(z) does not contain any negative power of $z - z_0$ in the Laurent's expansion for f(z). It follows that z_0 is a removable singularity of f(z).

The Behaviour of a Function Near an Essential Singularity

Theorem VI:

(Weierstrass's Theorem): *Let z_0 be essential singularity of a function f(z) and let c be an arbitrary constant. Then for every $\varepsilon > 0$ and every neighbourhood $0 < | z - z_0 | < \rho$ of z_0, there exists a point z of this neighbourhood such that*

$$|f(z) - c| < \varepsilon$$

In other words, in every arbitrary neighbourhood of an essential singularity there exists a point (and therefore an infinite number of points) at which the function differs as little as we please from any pre-assigned number.

Proof:

Suppose the theorem is false. Then for a given $\varepsilon > 0$, there exists a constant c and a positive number ρ such that

$$|f(z) - c| > \varepsilon$$

for every z satisfying the inequality $0 < | z - z_0 | < \rho$.

In other words, for $0 < | z - z_0 | < \rho$, we have

$$\left|\frac{1}{f(z)-c}\right| < 1/\varepsilon$$

Then it follows by theorem V that the function $\frac{1}{f(z)-c}$ has a removable singularity at z_0 so that its principal part contains no negative powers of $z - z_0$. Thus in the neighbourhood of z_0, we have

$$\frac{1}{f(z)-c} = a_0 + a_1 (z - z_0) + a_2(z - z_0)^2 + ...$$

If $a_0 \neq 0$, we define

$$\frac{1}{f(z_0)-c} = a_0 \text{ so that } f(z_0) = c + \frac{1}{a_0}.$$

Thus $\frac{1}{f(z)-c}$ becomes analytic and non-zero for $z = z_0$ and consequently f(z) is itself analytic at $z = z_0$. But this contradicts the hypothesis that $z = z_0$ is not an essential singularity of f(z).

Again, let

$a_0 = a_1 = ... = a_{m-1} = 0$ and $a_m \neq 0$.

In this case, we have

$$\frac{1}{f(z)-c} = a_m(z - z_0)^m + a_{m+1} (z - z_0)^{m+1} + ...$$

$$= (z-z_0)^m \sum_{n=0}^{\infty} a_{m+n}(z-z_0)^n.$$

Thus $z = z_0$ is a zero of order m of $\frac{1}{f(z)-c}$ and consequently f(z) – c has a pole of order m at z_0. Since c is merely a constant, it follows that f(z) also has a pole of order m at $z = z_0$ which is again a contradiction.

Hence the theorem must be true.

LIMIT POINTS OF ZEROS

Theorem VII:

Let f(z) be analytic in a domain D and let E be a set of zeros of f(z) having a limit point a in D. Then f(z) vanishes identically in D, that is, f(z) vanishes for all z ∈ D.

Proof:

Since a is a limit point of the set E of zeros of f(z), f(z) vanishes at an infinite number of points in every arbitrarily small neighbourhood of a, that is, f(z) has zeros as near as we please to α. As f(z) is continuous at α, we must have f(α) = 0. But since zeros are isolated, α cannot be a zero of f(z) unless f(z) vanishes identically in D.

Remark:

If f(z) is not analytic and if f(z) is not continuous at z = α, then a must be a singular point of f(z). Thus in this case, a is an isolated singularity but it is not a pole since | f(z) | does not tend to infinity as $z \to \alpha$ in any manner. Thus, we conclude that the limit point of zeros, in this case, is an isolated essential singularity of f(z).

Theorem VIII:

(Identity Theorem) : *If f(z) and g(z) are analytic in a domain D and if f(z) = g (z) on a subset E of a which has a limit point α in D, then f(z) = g(z) in the whole of D.*

Proof:

This theorem is an immediate corollary of the previous theorem. However, we give an independent proof here. Let F(z) = f(z) – g(z). Since f(z) = g(z) on E. It follows that F(z) vanishes on E. Since a is a limit point of E, F(z) must vanish at an infinite number of points in every arbitrary small neighbourhood of a. The continuity of F(z) at α implies that F(α) = 0. But since zeros are isolated, a cannot be a zero of F(z) unless F(z) vanishes identically in D which is equivalent to saying that f(z) = g(z) in the whole of D. This proves the theorem.

The Limit Point of Poles

Theorem IX:

The limit point of a sequence of poles of a function f(z) is a non-isolated essential singularity.

Proof:

Let $z_1, z_2, \ldots, z_n, \ldots$

be a sequence of poles of f(z) having a limit point z_0. Then in every neighbourhood of z_0, there are an infinite number of points at which f(z) becomes unbounded and consequently f(z) cannot be analytic at z_0. Therefore z_0 must be a singularity of f(z). But this singularity is not isolated. We call such a singularity a non-isolated essential singularity or simply an essential singularity of f(z).

Example:

The zeros of the function $\sin \frac{1}{z}$ *are given by*

$$z = \pm\frac{2}{n\pi},\ n = 1, 2, 3, \ldots.$$

The limit point of these zeros is the point z = 0. Thus 0 is an isolated singularity of $\sin \frac{1}{z}$.

Again the function tan $\frac{1}{z}$ has poles at points given by z

$z = \frac{2}{n\pi}$, *n = ± 1, ±3, ±5, ...*

The limit point of this sequence of poles is z = 0 which is therefore a non-isolated essential singularity.

Theorem X:

(Picards Theorem): *An integral function which is constant takes every finite value an infinite number of times with at most one possible exception.*

Proof:

Recall that a function f(z) is called an integral function if f(z) has no singularities except at infinity. We shall not try to prove this theorem but only give an example.

The equation $e^z = A$ has an infinite number of roots if $A \neq 0$ as the reader can easily verify. But if A = 0, this equation has no finite root. Thus, 0 is an exceptional value of e^z.

On the other hand, there exist integral functions with no exceptional values. The function sin z provides a simple example of such a case.

SOLVED EXAMPLES

Example 1:

Find the nature and location of the singularities of the function

$f(z) = \frac{1}{z(e^z - 1)}$. *Prove that f(z) can be expanded in the form*

$\frac{1}{z^2} - \frac{1}{2z} + a_0 + a_2 z^2 + a_4 z^4 + ...$

where $0 < |z| < 2\pi$ *and find the values of* a_0 *and* a_2.

Solution:

Now the singularities of f(z) are given by

$z(e^z - 1) = 0$

or z = 0 and $e^z = 1 = e^{2n\pi i}$ (n = 0, ± 1, ± 2,...)

Hence the singularities of f are at z = 0 and z = $2n\pi i$

(n = + 1, ± 2,...)

Thus z also occurs as a factor of $e^z - 1$. Hence z = 0 is a double pole of f(z).

The other singularities, namely,

$\pm 2\pi, \pm 4\pi, \pm 6\pi, \ldots$

arc simple poles.

It follows that f(z) can be expanded as .a Laurent's series in the region $0 < |z| < 2\pi$ in powers of z. Since z = 0 is a double pole, the principal part of f(z) will consist of two terms only.

Thus the expansion of f(z) will be of the form

$$f(z) = \frac{b_1}{z} + \frac{b_2}{z^2} + a_0 + a_1 z + a_2 z^2 + \ldots$$

$$\text{Now } f(z) = \frac{1}{z(e^z - 1)}$$

$$= \frac{1}{z\left(1 + z + \frac{z^2}{2!} + \frac{z^3}{3!} + \frac{z^4}{4!} + \frac{z^5}{5!} + \ldots - 1\right)}$$

$$= \frac{1}{z^2}\left[1 + \frac{z}{2} + \frac{z^2}{6} + \frac{z^3}{+24} + \frac{z^4}{120} + \ldots\right]$$

$$= \frac{1}{z^2}\left[1 - \left(\frac{z}{2} + \frac{z^2}{6} + \frac{z^3}{24} + \frac{z^4}{120} + \ldots\right)\right.$$

$$+ \left(\frac{z}{2} + \frac{z^2}{6} + \frac{z^3}{24} + \ldots\right) - \left(\frac{z}{2} + \frac{z^2}{6} + \ldots\right)$$

$$\left. + \left(\frac{z}{2} + \ldots\right) + \ldots\right]$$

$$= \frac{1}{z^2}\left[1 - \frac{z}{2} + \left(-\frac{1}{6} + \frac{1}{4}\right)z^2 + \left(-\frac{1}{24} + \frac{1}{6} - \frac{1}{8}\right)z^3\right.$$

$$\left. + \left(-\frac{1}{120} + \frac{1}{3} + \frac{1}{24} - \frac{1}{8} + \frac{1}{16}\right)z^4 + \ldots\right]$$

$$= \frac{1}{z^2}\left[1 - \frac{z}{2} + \frac{z}{12}z^2 + \frac{1}{360}z^4 + \ldots\right]$$

$$= \frac{1}{z^2} - \frac{1}{2z} + \frac{1}{12} + \frac{1}{360}z^2 + \ldots$$

Hence $a_0 = \frac{1}{12}$ and $a_2 = \frac{1}{360}$.

Example 2:

Show that the function e^z has an isolated essential singularity at $z = \infty$.

Solution:

Let $f(z) = e^z$. The nature of the singularity of the function f(z) at $z = \infty$ will be the same as that of the function

$$f\left(\frac{1}{\zeta}\right) \text{ at } \zeta = 0$$

$$\text{Now } f\left(\frac{1}{\zeta}\right) = e^{1/\zeta} = 1 + \frac{1}{\zeta} + \frac{1}{2!\zeta^2} + \frac{1}{3!\zeta^3} + \ldots$$

Here the principal part of $f\left(\frac{1}{\zeta}\right)$ is

$$\frac{1}{\zeta} + \frac{1}{2!\zeta^2} + \frac{1}{3!\zeta^3} + \ldots$$

which consists of an infinite number of terms. Hence $\zeta = 0$ is an isolated essential singularity of $e^{1/\zeta}$ and consequently $z = \infty$ is an isolated essential singularity of e^z.

Example 3:

Show that the function $e^{1/z}$ actually takes every value except zero an infinite number of times in the neighbourhood of $z = 0$.

Solution:

Let $f(z) = e^{1/z}$. In view of theorem VI, it suffices to show that f(z) has an isolated essential singularity at $z = 0$.

$$\text{Now} \qquad e^{1/z} = 1 + \frac{1}{z} + \frac{1}{2!z^2} + \frac{1}{3!z^3} + \ldots$$

$$= 1 + \sum_{n=1}^{\infty} \frac{1}{n!} \cdot \frac{1}{z^n}.$$

Thus the principal part of f(z) is

$$\sum_{n=1}^{\infty} \frac{1}{n!} \cdot \frac{1}{z^n}$$

which contains as infinite' number of terms. Hence $z = 0$ is an isolated essential singularity of f(z) as desired.

Example 4:

(i) The function

$$\frac{e^z}{(z-1)^3}$$

has a pole of order 3 at z = 1.

(ii) The function

$$f(z) = (z-3)\sin\frac{1}{z+2}$$

has a Laurent's expansion

$$f(z) = 1 - \frac{5}{z+2} - \frac{1}{6(z+2)^2} + \frac{5}{6(z+2)^2} + \frac{1}{120(z+2)^4} + \ldots$$

as the reader can easily verify. Since the principal part of f(z) consists of an infinite number of terms, z = –2 is an essential singularity of f(z).

(iii) The function

$$f(z) = \frac{z - \sin z}{z^3}$$

has a Laurent's expansion

$$f(z) = \frac{1}{3!} - \frac{z^2}{5!} + \frac{z^4}{7!} - \ldots$$

about z = 0. Since this expansion contains no negative powers of z, z = 0 is a removal singularity of f(z).

Solution:

Do yourself.

Example 5:

Find the kind of the singularities of the following functions :

(i) $\dfrac{\cot \pi z}{(z-a)^2}$ *at z = 0 and z = ∞.* *(ii) sin z – cos z at z = ∞*

(iii) $\sin\dfrac{1}{1-z}$ at $z = 1$ *(iv)* $\tan\dfrac{1}{z}$ at $z = 0$

(v) $\dfrac{1-e^z}{1+e^z}$ at $z = \infty$. *(vi)* $\operatorname{cosec}\dfrac{1}{z}$ at $z = 0$.

Solution:

(i) Poles of $\dfrac{\cot \pi z}{(z-a)^2} = \dfrac{\cot \pi z}{\sin \pi z (z-a)^2}$

are obtained by equating the denominator to zero *i.e.*

$(z - a)^2 \sin \pi q = 0.$

$\therefore \sin \pi z = 0$ or $(z - a)^2 = 0$

Now $\sin \pi z = 0$ gives $\pi z = n\pi$ or $z = n$

where $n = 0, \pm 1, \pm 2, \pm 3,...$

And $(z - a)^2 = 0$ gives $z = 0$.

Thus $z = a$ is a double pole and

$z = 0, \pm 1, \pm 2, \pm 3,...$

are simple poles. The limit point of these poles is $z = \infty$ and hence $z = \infty$ is a non-isolated essential singularity.

(ii) Let $f(z) = \sin z - \cos z$.

Then zeros of f(z) are given by

$\sin z - \cos z = 0$ or $\tan z = 1$.

Thus $0 = n\pi + \frac{\pi}{4}$ (n=0, ±1, ±2,...)

are zeros of f(z). The limit point of these zeros is evidently at $z = \infty$ which is therefore an isolated essential singularity of (z).

(iii) Let $f(z) = \sin \frac{1}{1-z}$

Now zeros of f(z) are given by

$$\sin \frac{1}{1-z} = 0 \text{ or } \frac{1}{1-z} = n\pi$$

or $$z = 1 - \frac{1}{n\pi} \quad (n = 0, \pm 1, \pm 2,...).$$

Evidently the limit point of these zeros is $z = 1$ which is therefore an isolated essential singularity.

(iv) Let $f(z) = \tan \frac{\sin(1/z)}{\cos(1/z)}$

Hence poles off(z) ai c given by

$\cos\frac{1}{z} = 0$ or $\frac{1}{z} = 2n\pi \pm \frac{\pi}{2}$

or $z = \frac{1}{(2n \pm \frac{1}{2})\pi}$ (n = 0, ±1, ±2,...).

It is evident that, the limit point of these poles is at $z=0$ which is therefore a non-isolated singularity.

(v) Let $f(z) = \dfrac{1-e^z}{1+e^z}$

The poles of f(z) are given by

$1 + e^z = 0$ or $e^z = -1 = e^{(2n+1)\pi i}$

or $z = (2n + 1)\pi i$, $n = 0, \pm 1, \pm 2, ...$

Obviously $z = \infty$ is the limit point of these poles. Hence $z = \infty$ is a non-isolated essential singularity of f(z).

(vi) Poles of cosec $\dfrac{1}{z} = \dfrac{1}{\sin 1/z}$ are given by

$$\sin\frac{1}{z} = 0 \text{ or } \frac{1}{z} = n\pi$$

or $z = \dfrac{1}{n\pi}$ $(n = 0, \pm 1, \pm 2, ...)$.

Evidently $z = 0$ is a limit point of these poles so that $z = 0$ is a non-isolated singularity.

Example 6:

Show that $z = a$ is an isolated essential singularity of the function $\dfrac{e^{c/z(z-a)}}{e^{z/a}-1}$.

Solution:

Let $f(z) = e^{c/z-a} / (e^{z/a} - 1) = \dfrac{e^{c/(z-a)}}{e^{1+(z-a)/a} - 1}$

$$\therefore \qquad f(z) = \frac{1 + \dfrac{c}{z-1} + \dfrac{c^2}{2!(z-a)^2} + \dfrac{c^3}{(z-a)^3} + ...}{e\left[1 + \dfrac{z-a}{a} + \dfrac{(z-a)^2}{a^2} + ...\right] - 1}$$

$$= -\left(1 + \frac{c}{z-1} + \frac{c^2}{2!(z-a)^2} + ...\right)$$

$$\times \left[1 - e\left(1 + \frac{z-a}{a} + \frac{(z-a)^2}{a^2} + ...\right)\right]^{-1}$$

$$= -\left(1+\frac{c}{z-a}+\frac{c^2}{2!(z-a)^2}+\ldots\right)$$

$$\times\left[1\times e\left(1+\frac{z-a}{a}+\frac{(z-a)^2}{2!a^2}+\ldots\right)\right.$$

$$\left.+e^2\left(1+\frac{z-a}{a}+\frac{(z-a)^2}{2!a^2}+\ldots\right)\right].$$

It is evident that the expansion of f(z) contains an in mite number of terms containing negative powers of 1/(z - a). Hence z = a is an isolated essential singularity of f(z).

Example 7:

Show that near z = 1, the function log $(1 + z^2)$ may be expanded in a series of the form

$$\log 2+\sum_{n=1}^{\infty} a_n (z-1)^n$$

and find the value of a_n, the principal value of the logarithm being taken

Solution:

Let f(z) = log $(1 + z^2)$. Now the zeros of I + z^2 *i.e.* z = ± i arc the two branch points of the function f(z). Thus z = ± i and the two singularities o f(z). The distance of the point z = 1 from the nearest singularity is equal to √2. (Note that both z = i and z = – i are at the same distance √2 from z = 1). Therefore in the circular domain | z – 1 | < √2, f(z) can be considered as single-valued and analytic, the particular branch being a value of f(z) fo any z in the domain. The particular branch referred to in the equation is given as the principal value *i.e.* the real value log 2 for z = 1. Since f(z) is analyti inside the circle | z – 1 | = √2, we can expand it as a Taylor's series withi this circle in the form

$$f(z)=\sum_{n=0}^{\infty} a_n (z-1)^n$$

where $a_n = \dfrac{f^n(1)}{n!}$

Now f(z) = log $(1 + z^2)$

so that $f(z) = \dfrac{2z}{1+z^2} = \dfrac{1}{z-i}+\dfrac{1}{z+i}$

$$= (z - i)^{-1} + (z + i)^{-1}$$

Differentiating this n – 1 times, we obtain

$$f^n(z) = (-1)^{n-1}(n-1)!\left[\frac{1}{(z-i)^n} + \frac{1}{(z+i)^n}\right]$$

so that $f^n(1) = (-1)^{n-1}(n-1)!\,[(1-i)^{-n} + (1+i)^{-n}]$.

Put $1 = r\cos\theta$, $1 = r\sin\theta$ so that

$$r = \sqrt{2} \text{ and } \theta = \frac{\pi}{4}$$

$$\therefore\ f^{(n)}(1) = (-1)^{n-1}(n-1)!\,r^{-n}$$

$$[(\cos\theta - i\sin\theta)^{-n} + (\cos\theta + i\sin\theta)^{-n}]$$

$$= (-1)^{n-1}(n-1)!\,r^{-n}$$

$$[(\cos n\theta + i\sin n\theta + \cos n\theta - i\sin n\theta]$$

$$= (-1)^{n-1}(n-1)!\,(\sqrt{2})^{-n}.\,2\cos n\theta$$

$$= 2(-1)^{n-1}(n-1)!(\sqrt{2})^{-n}\cos\frac{n\pi}{4}.$$

$$\therefore\ a_n = \frac{f^n(1)}{n!} = \frac{2}{n}(-1)^{n-1}(\sqrt{2})^{-n}\cos\frac{n\pi}{4}.$$

Example 8:

Consider the singularities of the Junction represented by the series

$$\sum_{n=0}^{\infty}\frac{1}{n!}.\frac{1}{1+(2^n z)^2}$$

and obtain expansion by Laurent's theorem.

Solution:

$$f(z) = \sum_{n=0}^{\infty}\frac{1}{n!}.\frac{1}{1+(2^n z)^2}$$

Now singularities of f(z) are given by

$$(2^n z^2)^2 + 1 = 0 \text{ or } z = \pm\frac{i}{2^n}.$$

where n = 0, 1, 2,3

These singularities are evidently simple poles which lie within the circle $|z| = 1$. Since $z = 0$ is a limit point of these singularities, $z = 0$ is an essential singularity of f(z). Now the function f(z) is analytic on and outside the circle C defined by $|z| = r$ $(r > 1)$ so that f(z) can be expanded as a Laurent's series of negative powers only. It is also evident that f(z) is an even function of z and so its expansion will be of the form

$$f(z)=\frac{b^2}{z^2}+\frac{b_4}{z^4}+\frac{b_6}{z^6}+\ldots=\sum_{m=1}^{\infty}\frac{b_{2m}}{z^{2m}}$$

$$\text{where } b_{2m}=\frac{1}{2\pi i}\int_C z^{2m-1}f(z)dz$$

$$=\frac{1}{2\pi i}\int_C z^{2m-1}\left(\sum_{n=0}^{\infty}\frac{1}{n!}\cdot\frac{1}{1+(2^n z)^2}\right)$$

$$=\frac{1}{2\pi i}\int_C z^{2m-1}\left(\sum_{n=0}^{\infty}\frac{1}{n!}\cdot\frac{2^{-2n}}{2^{-2n}+z^2}\right)$$

We have

$$z^{2m-1}\sum_{n=0}^{\infty}\frac{1}{n!}\cdot\frac{2^{-2n}}{2^{-2n}+z^2}$$

$$=z^{2m-3}\sum_{n=0}^{\infty}\frac{2^{-2n}}{n!}(1+2^{-2n}z^{-2})^{-1}$$

$$=z^{2m-3}\sum_{n=0}^{\infty}\frac{2^{-2n}}{n!}(1-2^{-2n}z^{-2}+2^{-4n}z^{-4}-\ldots)$$

$$=z^{2m-3}\Big[(1-z^{-2}+z^{-4}-\ldots$$

$$+\frac{2^{-2}}{1!}(1-2^{-2}z^{-2}+2^{-4}z^{-4}+\ldots)+\ldots\Big]$$

$$=z^{2m-3}\Bigg[\left(1+\frac{2^{-2}}{1!}+\frac{2^{-4}}{2!}+\frac{2^{-6}}{3!}+\ldots\right)$$

$$-z^{-2}\left(1+\frac{2^{-4}}{1!}+\frac{2^{-8}}{2!}+\ldots\right)+\ldots$$

$$+(-1)^{m-1}(z^{-2})^{m-1}\left(1+\frac{2^{-2m}}{1!}+\ldots\right)+\ldots\Bigg]$$

$$=2^{2m-3}e^{(2^{-2})}-z^{2m-5}e^{(2^{-4})}+\ldots+(-1)^{m-1}z^{-1}e^{(2^{-2m})}+\ldots(1)$$

The reader can easily see that this series converges uniformly for all values of z such that | Z | > 1 and so term by term integration is justified. Now the integral of the terms in (1) along the circle | Z | = 1 is zero except that of the term containing z – 1. We thus have

$$b_{2m} = \frac{1}{2\pi i}\int_C (-1)^{m-1}\frac{1}{z}e^{(2^{-2m})}dz.$$

$$= \frac{(-1)^{m-1}e^{(2^{-2m})}}{2\pi i}\int_0^{2\pi}\frac{1}{e^{i\theta}}d\theta$$

[Putting $z = e^{i\theta}$, $dz = ie^{i\theta}\,d\theta$]

$$= (-1)^{m-1}e^{(-2m)}.$$

Hence for $|z| > 1$, we obtain the expansion

$$f(z) = \sum_{m=1}^{\infty}(-1)^{m-1}e^{(2^{-2m})}.\frac{1}{z^{2m}}$$

$$= \frac{e^{(2^{-2})}}{z^2} - \frac{e^{(2^{-4})}}{z^4} + \frac{e^{(2^{-6})}}{z^6} - \ldots$$

If we put $z = \frac{1}{\zeta}$ in f(z), we observe that $f\left(\frac{1}{\zeta}\right)$ has a zero of second order at $\zeta = 0$. It follows that the given function has a zero of second order at infinity.

Example 9:

Discuss the function represented by the series

$$\sum_{n=0}^{\infty}\frac{1}{n!}.\frac{1}{1+a^{2n}z^2},\ a > 0$$

and obtain expansion by Laurent's theorem.

Solution:

Proceed as in the above example.

Example 10:

The Junction f(z) has a double pole at z = 0 with residue 2, a simple pole at z = 1 with residue 2, is analytic at all other finite points of the plane and is bounded as| z | → ∞. If f(2) = 5 and f(–1) = 2, find f(z).

Solution:

Since f(z) has a simple pole at z = 1 with residue 2, and double pole at z = 0 with residue 2, the principal part of f(z) will be of the form $\frac{2}{z-1} + \frac{2}{z} + \frac{b}{z^2}$ and so f(z) will have a Laurent's expansion of the form

$$f(z)=\sum_{n=0}^{\infty}a_n z^n+\frac{2}{z-1}+\frac{2}{z}+\frac{b}{z^2} \qquad ...(1)$$

As f(z) is bounded when | z | → ∞, there exists a positive constant M such that | f(z) | ≤ M for all values of z. It implies that f(z) has no singularity at z = ∞. Hence, $f\left(\frac{1}{\zeta}\right)$ has no singularity at ζ = 0. Therefore principal part of $f\left(\frac{1}{\zeta}\right)$ will have no term.

Now $f\left(\frac{1}{\zeta}\right)=a_0+\frac{a_1}{\zeta}+\frac{a_2}{\zeta}+...+\frac{2\zeta}{1-\zeta}+2\zeta+b\zeta^2$

Principal part of $f\left(\frac{1}{\zeta}\right)$

$=\frac{a_1}{\zeta}+\frac{a_2}{\zeta}+\frac{a_3}{\zeta}+...$

Hence the principal part of $f\left(\frac{1}{\zeta}\right)$ is will contain no term if

$a_1 = a_2 = a_3 = ... = 0$.

Then (1) takes the form

$$f(z)=a_0+\frac{2}{z-1}+\frac{2}{z}+\frac{b}{z^2} \qquad ...(2)$$

Now by hypothesis,

f(2) = 5 and f(–1) = 2.

Substituting these values in (2), we get

$5 = a_0 + 2 + 1 + \frac{b}{4}$ and $2 = a_0 - 1 - 2 + b$.

These give $a_0 = 1$ and b = 4.

$$f(z)=1+\frac{2}{z-1}+\frac{2}{z}+\frac{4}{z^2}$$

$$\Rightarrow f(z)=\frac{z^3+3z^2+2z-4}{z^2(z-1)}$$

Thus f(z) is determined.

Example 11:

The only singularities of a single valued function f(z) are poles of order 1 and 2 at z = –1 and z = –2 with residues of and 2 respectively at these poles. If f(0) $= \frac{7}{4}$, *f(1)* $= \frac{5}{2}$, *determine the function and expand it in a Laurent's series valid in*

$$1 < | z | < 2.$$

Solution

Proceeding as in the preceding example, we shall have

$$f(z) = a_0 + \frac{1}{z+1} + \frac{2}{z-2} + \frac{b}{(z-2)^2}$$

where $f(0) = \frac{7}{4}$ and $f(1) = \frac{5}{3}$ so that

$$\frac{7}{4} = a_0 + \frac{b}{4} \text{ and } \frac{5}{2} = a_0 - \frac{3}{2} + b,$$

giving $a_0 = 1$ and $b = 3$. Hence

$$f(z) = 1 + \frac{1}{z+1} + \frac{2}{z-2} + \frac{3}{(z-2)^2}$$

Thus f(z) has been found.

Since f(z) is analytic in the region $1 < | z | < 2$, it can be expanded as Laurent's series about any point of this region. Thus

$$f(z) = 1\frac{1}{z}\left(1+\frac{1}{z}\right)^{-1} - \left(1-\frac{z}{2}\right)^{-1} + \frac{3}{4}\left(1+\frac{z}{2}\right)^{-2}$$

[arranged suitably for the validity of bionominal expansion]

$$= 1 + \frac{1}{z}\left(1 - \frac{1}{z} + \frac{1}{z^2} - \frac{1}{z^3} + \ldots\right) - \left(1 + \frac{z}{2} + \frac{z^2}{2^2} + \frac{z^3}{2^3} + \ldots\right)$$

$$+ \frac{3}{4}\left[1 + 2.\frac{z}{2} + 3.\left(\frac{z}{2}\right)^2 + \ldots\right]$$

$$= 1 + \sum_{n=0}^{\infty} (-1)^n . \frac{1}{z^n} - \sum_{n=0}^{\infty} \left(\frac{z}{2}\right)^n + \frac{3}{4}\sum_{n=0}^{\infty} (n+1)\left(\frac{z}{2}\right)^n .$$

$$= 1 + \sum_{n=0}^{\infty} (-1)^n . \frac{1}{z^{n+1}} + \sum_{n=0}^{\infty} \left(\frac{3n-1}{3}\right)\left(\frac{z}{2}\right)^n .$$

Example 12:

The only singularities of a single valued function f(z) are poles of order 2 and 1 at z = 1 and z = 2 with residues 1 and 3 respectively at these poles. If f(0) $= \frac{3}{2}$, *f(–1) = 1, determine the function.*

Solution:

Proceed as in the previous example

$$f(z)=\frac{3z^3-3z^2+3z-3}{(z-2)(z-1)^2}$$

Example 13:

Let $\phi(z)$ and $\psi(z)$ be analytic functions. If $z = a$ is a once repeated root of $\psi(z) = 0$ such that $\phi(a) \neq 0$, the residue of $\phi(z)/\psi(z)$ at $z = a$ is

$6\phi'(a)\ \psi''(a) - 2\phi(a)\ \psi'''(a)$

Solution:

We know that the residue at a pole z = a of order in of the function

$$\frac{F(z)}{(z-a)^m} \text{ is } \frac{F^{(m-1)}(a)}{(m-1)!}$$

Now since z = a is double zero of ψ(z), we have

$\psi(z) = (z - a)^3\ g(z)$

where $\qquad g(a) \neq 0$

$$\therefore \frac{\phi(z)}{\psi(z)}=\frac{\phi(z)}{(z-a)^2 g(z)}$$

Thus $\dfrac{\phi(z)}{\psi(z)}$ has a double pole at z = a and so by the above formula, the residue at z = a is

$$\frac{d}{z}\left[\frac{\phi(z)}{\psi(z)}\right]_{z=a}=\frac{\phi'(a)g(a)-g'(a)\phi(a)}{[g(a)]^2} \qquad ...(1)$$

Now we evaluate g(a) and g'(a).

We have $\psi(z) = (z - a)^2\ g(a)$.

$\therefore \psi'(z) = (z - a)^2\ g'(z) + 2(z - a)\ g(z)$

and$\psi''(z) = (z - a)^2\ g''(z) + 4\ (z - a)\ g'(z) + 2g(z)$

$\psi'''(z) = (z - a)^2\ g'''(z) + 6\ (z - a)\ g''(z) + 6g'(z)$.

Hence$\psi'(a) = 0$, $\psi''(a) = 2g\ (a)$ and $\psi'''(a) = 6g'(a)$.

Thus$g(a) = \dfrac{1}{2}\psi''(a)$ and $g'(a) = \dfrac{1}{6}\ \psi'''(a)$.

Substituting these values in (1), we see that the residue at z = a is

$$\frac{\phi'(a).\frac{1}{2}\psi''(a)-\phi.\frac{1}{6}\psi'''(a)}{\frac{1}{2}[\psi''(a)]^2}$$

$$=\frac{6\phi'(a).\psi''(a)-2\phi(a)\psi'''(a)}{3[\psi''(a)]^2}.$$

THE POINT AT INFINITY

Theorem:

Let f(z) be a function defined in some domain D and let the function g he defined by

$$g(\zeta)=f\left(\frac{1}{\zeta}\right).$$

Then f(i) is analytic or (ii) has a zero of order m or (iii) has a pole of order m or (iv) has a removable singularity or (v) has an essential singularity at $z = \infty$ according as the function g has the same behaviour at $\zeta = 0$ *i.e.* according as g is analytic, has a zero of order m, or has a pole of order m, or has a removable singularity or has essential singularity at $\zeta = 0$.

Proof:

(i) Let $g(\zeta)$ be analytic at the origin. Now

$$\frac{1}{\zeta}\to\infty \text{ as } \zeta\to 0.$$

Since $g(\zeta)=f\left(\frac{1}{\zeta}\right)$,

it follows that f(z) is analytic at $z = \infty$.

(ii) Suppose g has a zero of order m at $\zeta = 0$. Then the Taylor's expansion of $g(\zeta)$ gives

$$g(\zeta)=\sum_{x=m}^{\infty}a_n\zeta^n.$$

But $g(\zeta)=f\left(\frac{1}{\zeta}\right)$. Since $\frac{1}{\zeta}\to\infty$ as $\zeta\to 0$, it follows that the expansion of f(z) at $z = \infty$ is given by

$$g(z)=\sum_{n=m}^{\infty}\frac{a_n}{z^n}$$

This shows that f(z) has a zero of order m at infinity.

(iii) Suppose that g has a pole of order m at $\zeta = 0$ so that laurent's expansion of $g(\zeta)$ at $\zeta = 0$ will be of the form

$$g(\zeta) = \sum_{n=1}^{\infty} a_n \zeta^n + \sum_{n=1}^{n=m} \frac{b_n}{\zeta^n}$$

Then the expansion of f(z) at ∞ will be of the form

$$(z) = \sum_{n=0}^{\infty} \frac{a_n}{z^n} + \sum_{n=2}^{n=m} b_n z^n.$$

This means that f(z) has a pole of order m at infinity.

(iv) Let g have a removable singularity at $\zeta = 0$. Then in the neighbourhood of 0, $g(\zeta)$ will have an expansion of the form

$$g(\zeta) = \sum_{n=0}^{\infty} a_n z^n$$

$$\therefore f(z) = \sum_{n=0}^{\infty} \frac{a_n}{z^n} = a_0 + \frac{a_1}{z} + \frac{a_2}{z^2} + \ldots$$

This shows that f(z) has a removable singularly at infinity.

(v) Finally suppose that g has an essential singularity at the origin. Then the Laurent's expansion of $g(\zeta)$ at $\zeta = 0$ will be of the form

$$g(\zeta) = \sum_{n=0}^{\infty} a_n \zeta^n + \sum_{n=1}^{\infty} b_n \zeta^n$$

$$\therefore f(z) = g\left(\frac{1}{z}\right) = \sum_{n=1}^{\infty} \frac{a_n}{z^n} + \sum_{n=1}^{\infty} b_n z^n.$$

This implies that f(z) has an essential singularity at infinity.

CHARACTERIZATION OF POLYNOMIALS

Theorem I:

Show that a function which has no singularity in the finite part of the plane and has a pole of order n at infinity is a polynomial of degree n.

Proof:

Since f(z) has no singularity in the finite part of the plane, it can he expanded as a Taylor's series about z = 0 in the form

$$f(z) = \sum_{n=0}^{\infty} a_n z^n$$

Thus $f\left(\frac{1}{z}\right)=\sum_{n=0}^{\infty}a_n z^{-n}$. ...(1)

Again since f(z) has a pole of order n at infinity, $f\left(\frac{1}{z}\right)$ has a pole of order n at zero. Hence, Laurent's expansion of $f\left(\frac{1}{z}\right)$ is valid in any region which does not contain 0. Thus, we may write

$$f\left(\frac{1}{z}\right)=F(z)+\sum_{m=0}^{\infty}B_m z^{-m} \qquad ...(2)$$

From (1) and (2), we obtain the identity

$$\sum_{n=0}^{\infty}a_n 2^{-n}=F(z)+\sum_{m=1}^{\infty}B_m z^{-m}$$

It follows that

$F(z) = a_0 =$ coast.

and $a_{n+1} = a_{n+2} = ... = 0$.

Hence $f(z) = a_0 + a_1 z + a_2 z^2 + ... + a_n z^n$

which is a polynomial of degree n.

Theorem II:

A Polynomial of degree n has no singularities in the finite part of the plane but has a pole of order n at infinity.

Proof:

Let $P(z) = a_0 + a_1 z + ... + a_n z^n, a_n \neq 0$ so that P(z) is a polynomial of degree n. Then

$$P\left(\frac{1}{z}\right)=a_0+\frac{a_1}{z}+...+\frac{a_n}{z^n}$$

has a pole of order n at $z = \infty$. Hence by theorem of P(z) has a pole of order n at $z \neq \infty$. Also evidently P(z) has not singularities in the finite part of the plane. Hence the theorem.

Theorem III:

A function f(z) is a polynomial of degree n if and only if f(z) has no singularities in the finite part of the plane and has a pole of order n at infinity.

Proof:

As Theorem I and Theorem II.

Theorem IV:

If a function f(z) is analytic for all finite values of z and as $|z| \neq \infty$,

$$|f(z)| = a(|z|^k)$$

then f(z) is a polynomial of degree $\leq k$.

Proof:

Since f(z) is analytic in the finite part of the plane, we have by Taylor's theorem

$$f(z) = \sum_{n=0}^{\infty} a_n z^n$$

for $|z| < R$.

Let max $|f(z)| = M(r)$ on the circle $|z| = r$ $(r < R)$. Then by Cauchy's inequality, we have

$$|a_n| \leq \frac{M(r)}{r^n} \text{ for all n}$$

$$= \frac{A(|z|^k)}{r^n} \text{ since } M(r) = |f(z)| A |z|^k$$

when $|z| \to \infty$

$$= \frac{Ar^k}{r^n} = Ar^{k-n}.$$

Hence as $r \to \infty$, the right hand side of (1) tend to zero since

$n > k$.

It implies that $a_n = 0$ for $n > k$.

$\therefore \qquad f(z) = a_0 + a_1 z + a_2 z^2 + \ldots + akz^k$

which is a polynomial of degree k.

CHARACTERIZATION OF RATIONAL FUNCTIONS

Theorem I:

If a single-valued Junction f(z) has no singularities other than poles in the finite part of the plant, or at infinity, then f(z) is a rational function.

Proof:

Recall that a function is of the form

$$f(z) = \frac{P(z)}{Q(z)}$$

where F(z) and Q(z) are polynomials.

Let f(z)have poles at $z = z_1, z_2, ..., Z_k$ of orders $m_1, m_2, ..., m_k$ in the finite part of the z-plane. Then

$$f(z) = \frac{P(z)}{(z-z_1)^{m_1}(z-z_2)^{m_2}...(z-z_k)^{m_k}}$$

where P(z) is analytic, for all finite values of z. Therefore

$$P(z) = (z-z_1)^{m_1}(z-z_2)^{m_2}...(z-z_k)^{m_k} f(z).$$

Since P(z) is analytic, we have by Taylor's theorem

$$P(z) = \sum_{n=0}^{\infty} a_n z^n. \qquad ...(1)$$

Putting $z = \frac{1}{\zeta}$ we get

$$P\left(\frac{1}{\zeta}\right) = \sum_{n=0}^{\infty} a_n \zeta^{-n} \qquad ...(2)$$

Now the behaviour of P(z) at infinity is the same as behaviour of $P\left(\frac{1}{\zeta}\right)$ at $\zeta = 0$. Since the singularity of P(z) at $z = \infty$ is a pole, singularity of $P\left(\frac{1}{\zeta}\right)$ at $\zeta = 0$ is also a pole. This implies that the series in (2) will consist of a finite number of terms and consequently the series in (1) will also have only a finite number of terms. Therefore P(z) is a polynomial.

Since the denominator of f(z) is a polynomial, we conclude that f(z) is a rational function.

Theorem II:

A rational number has no singularities other than poles.

Proof:

Let f(z) be a rational function so that we may express it as

$$f(z) = \frac{P(z)}{Q(z)}.$$

where P(z) and Q(z) are two polynomials having no factor in common. Now the singularities of f(z) in the finite part of the plane are given by Q(z) = 0.

But zeros of Q(z) arc the poles of $\frac{1}{Q(z)}$. Hence $\frac{P(z)}{Q(z)}$ can have no other singularities except poles in the finite plane.

To study the behaviour of f(z) near z = ∞, we write (1) in the form

$$f(z) = \frac{a_0 + a_1 z + ... + a_n z^n}{b_0 + b_1 z + ... + b_m z^m} \quad a_n \neq 0, b_m \neq 0$$

$$= z^{n-m} \left[\frac{a_n + \frac{a_{n-1}}{z} + ... + \frac{a_0}{z^n}}{b_n + \frac{b_{m-1}}{z} + ... + \frac{b_0}{z^m}} \right]$$

The expression in (he brackets is regular for large | z | so that we may write

$$f(z) = z^{n-m}\left(c_0 + \frac{c_1}{z} + \frac{c_2}{z^2} + ...\right), \; c_0 \neq 0.$$

where the power series converges for | z | > R if R is sufficiently large. It follows that the behaviour off f(z) near z = ∞ depends on the value of n – m. If n – m ≥ 0, the Laurent expansion of f(z) near z = ∞ contains no positive powers of z and hence f(z) is analytic at z = ∞. If n – m > 0, then there is a pole of order n – m at infinity. We have thus shown that all the singularities of a rational function are poles.

Theorem III:

A single valued function f(z) is a rational function if and only if f(z) has no singularities other than poles either in the finite part of the plane or at infinity.

Proof:

The result follows from the last two theorems.

MAXIMUM MODULUS PRINCIPLE

Theorem I:

Let f(z) be analytic within and on a simple closed contour C. Then | f(z) | reaches its maximum value on C (and not inside C), unless f(z) is a constant. In other words, if M is the maximum value of | f(z) | on and within C, then, unless f is a constant, | f(z) | < M for every point z within C.

(The result stated in the above theorem is known as Maximum Modulus Principle).

Proof:

Since f(z) is analytic and hence continuous within and on C, it follows that | f(z) | must reach its maximum value M at some point on or within C. We suppose that f(z) is not constant. Then we wish to prove that | f(z) | takes the value M at some point on C. Suppose, if possible, this value is not attained on the boundary C but is attained at a point a within C so that | f(a) |, = M. Let P be a circle inside C with centre at a.

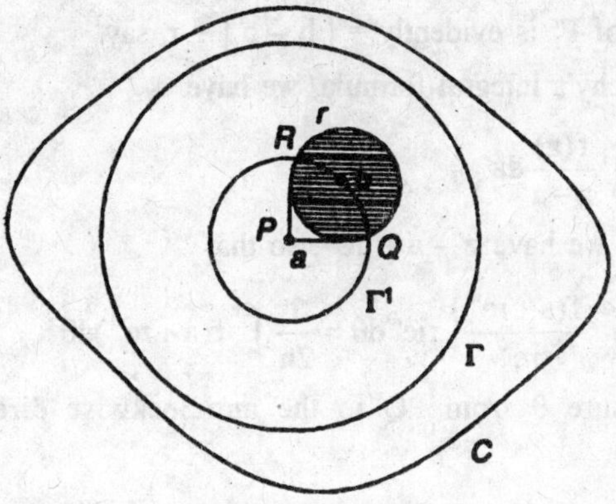

Fig. 2.1

Then, since | f(z) | = M is the maximum value of | f(z) | and f(z) is not a constant, there must exist a point, say b, inside P such that | f(b) | < M.

Let | f(b) | = M - ε where ε > 0.

Since | f(z) | is continuous at b, for our chosen ε > 0, there exists a δ > 0 such that

$$| \, | f(z) | - | f(b) | \, | < \frac{1}{2}\varepsilon \qquad ...(1)$$

whenever | z – b | < 6.

Since | f(z) | – | f(b) | ≤ | | f(z) | – | f(b) | |,

we conclude from (1) that

$$| f(z) | - | f(b) | < \frac{1}{2}\varepsilon$$

$$\text{or} \; | f(z) | < | f(b) | + \frac{1}{2}\varepsilon$$

$$= M - \varepsilon + \frac{1}{2}\varepsilon = M - \frac{1}{2}\varepsilon. \qquad ... (2)$$

$$\text{Thus } | f(z) | < M - \frac{1}{2}\varepsilon$$

for all points z satisfying $| z - b | < \delta$, *i.e.* for all points z inside a circle γ with centre b and radius δ (see the figure).

Now draw a circle Γ' with centre at a such that it passes through b. The arc QR of the circle Γ' lies within γ so that on this arc, we have

$$| f(z) | < M - \frac{1}{2}\varepsilon.$$

On the remaining arc of Γ', we have $| f(z) | \leq M$.

The radius of Γ' is evidently $= | b - a | = r$, say.

By the Cauchy's integral formula, we have

$$f(a) = \frac{1}{2\pi i}\int_{\Gamma'} \frac{f(z)}{z-a}dz$$

Now on Γ', we have $z - a = re^{i\theta}$, so that

$$f(a) = \frac{1}{2\pi i}\int_0^{2\pi} \frac{f(a+re^{i\theta})}{re^{i\theta}}.rie^{i\theta}d\theta = \frac{1}{2\pi}\int_0^{2\pi} f(a+re^{i\theta})d\theta$$

If we measure θ from PQ in the anticlockwise direction and if $\angle QPR = a$, then

$$f(a) = \frac{1}{2\pi}\int_0^a f(a+re^{i\theta})d\theta + \frac{1}{2\pi}\int_a^{2\pi} f(a+re^{i\theta})d\theta$$

$$\therefore | f(a) | \leq \frac{1}{2\pi}\int_0^a | f(a+re^{i\theta}) | d\theta + \frac{1}{2\pi}\int_a^{2\pi} | f(a+re^{i\theta}) | d\theta$$

$$\leq \frac{1}{2\pi}\int_0^a \left(M - \frac{1}{2}\varepsilon\right)d\theta + \frac{1}{2\pi}\int_a^{2\pi} Md\theta$$

$$= \frac{a}{2\pi}\left(M - \frac{1}{2}\varepsilon\right) + \frac{M}{2\pi}(2\pi - a) = M - \frac{a\varepsilon}{2\pi}$$

Thus $M = | f(a) | < M - \frac{a\varepsilon}{4\pi}$ which is absurd since M cannot be less than $M - \frac{a\varepsilon}{4\pi}$. Hence by reduction absurdum, the theorem follows, that is, $| f(z) |$ cannot reach its maximum value at any point within C and so must attain its maximum on C.

Minimum Modulus Principle

Theorem II:

Let f(z) be analytic inside and on a closed contour C and let $f(z) \neq 0$ inside C. Then $| f(z) |$ must reach its minimum value on C (and not *inside C). In other words, if m is the minimum of | f(z) | inside and on C, then unless f is constant*

| f(z) | > m for every point z inside C.

Proof:

Given that f(z) is analytic inside and on C and $f(z) \neq 0$ inside C. Therefore $\frac{1}{f(z)}$ is analytic inside C. By the maximum modulus theorem $\frac{1}{|f(z)|}$ can not reach its maximum value inside C and consequently | f (z) | cannot attain its minimum value inside C. Then since f(z) is continuous on and within C, | f(z) | must attain its minimum value at some point on C.

THE EXCESS OF THE NUMBER OF ZEROS OVER THE NUMBER OF POLES OF A HOMOMORPHIC FUNCTION: THE ARGUMENT PRINCIPLE

Theorem:

If f(z) is homomorphic inside a closed contour C and has no zero on C, then

$$\frac{1}{2\pi i}\int_C \frac{f'(z)}{f(z)}dz = N - P$$

where N is the number of zeros and P the number of poles inside C (a pole or zero of order m must be counted m times).

Proof:

Let a_i (i = 1, 2, ...m) be the zeros of f(z) which lie inside C and r_i be the order of a_i. Further let b_i (i = 1, 2,...n) be the poles of f(z) inside C with s_i as the order of b_i. Then we wish to show that

$$\frac{1}{2\pi i}\int_C \frac{f'(z)}{f(z)}dz = \sum_{i=1}^{n} r_i - \sum_{i=1}^{n} S_i$$

We enclose each zero and pole by non-overlapping circles $A_1, A_2, \ldots A_m$ and $B_1, B_2, \ldots B_n$ respectively each of radii ρ. Since poles and zeros are isolated, it is always possible to find such ρ. Then by the Cor. 2 of theorem I, we have

$$\frac{1}{2\pi i}\int_C \frac{f'(z)}{f(z)}dz = \sum_{i=1}^{n}\int_{A_i} \frac{1}{2\pi i}\frac{f'(z)}{f(z)}dz - \sum_{i=1}^{n}\int_B \frac{f'(z)}{f(z)}dz. \quad \text{...(1)}$$

Now since a_i is a zero of order r_i of f(z), we may write

$$f(z) = (z - a_i)^{r_i}\phi_i(z)$$

where ϕ_i is analytic and non-zero at a_i. Taking logarithm of both sides, we get

$$\log f(z) = r_i \log (z - a_i) + \log\phi_i (z).$$

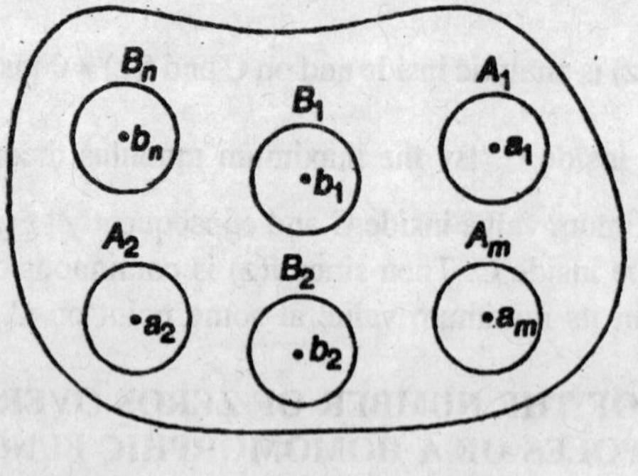

Fig. 2.2

Differentiating, we get

$$\frac{f'(z)}{f(z)} = \frac{r_i}{z-a_i} + \frac{\phi_i'(z)}{\phi_i(z)}$$

Since $\dfrac{\phi_i'(z)}{\phi_i(z)}$ is analytic at $z = a_i$, we have

$$\int_{A_i} \frac{\phi_i'(z)}{\phi_i(z)} = 0.$$

Also $\displaystyle\int_{A_i} \frac{r_i}{z-a_i} dz = r_i \int_0^{2\pi} \frac{\rho i e^{i\theta} d\theta}{\rho e^{i\theta}} = 2\pi i r_i$ [Putting $z - a_i = \rho e^{i\theta}$]

Hence $\displaystyle\sum_{i=1}^{m} \frac{1}{2\pi i} \int_{A_i} \frac{f'(z)}{z-a_i} dz = \sum_{i=1}^{m} \frac{1}{2\pi i} .2\pi i r_i = \sum_{i=1}^{m} r_i$ ...(2)

Again since b_i is a pole of order s_i of f(z), we may write

$$f(z) = \frac{\psi_i(z)}{(z-b_i)^{s_i}}$$

where ψ_i is analytic and non-zero at b_i. Taking logarithm and differentiating, we get

$$\frac{f'(z)}{f(z)} = \frac{\psi_i'(z)}{\psi_i(z)} - \frac{S_i}{z-b_i}$$

Hence as before, we have

$$\int_{B_i} \frac{f'(z)}{f(z)} dz = 0 - 2\pi i s_i$$

$$\therefore \sum_{i=1}^{n} \frac{1}{2\pi i} \int_{B_i} \frac{f'(z)}{f(z)} dz = \sum_{i=1}^{m} \frac{1}{2\pi i}(-2\pi i s_i) = -\sum_{i=1}^{n} s_i. \qquad \text{... (3)}$$

Thus from (1), (2) and (3), we get

$$\frac{1}{2\pi i} \int_C \frac{f'(z)}{f(z)} dz = \sum_{i=1}^{m} r_i - \sum_{i=1}^{n} s_i = N - P. \qquad \text{...(4)}$$

Cor. 1:

$$N - P = \frac{1}{2\pi i} \Delta_C \arg f(z)$$

where Δ_C denotes the variation in arg f(z) as z moves once round C.

Proof:

By the above theorem

$$N - P = \frac{1}{2\pi i} \int_C \frac{f'(z)}{f(z)} dz$$

Letf(z) = $Re^{i\phi}$ so that R = | f(z) |

and ϕ = arg f(z). Then

$$f(z)\, dz = df(z) = d\,(Re^{i\phi}) = e^{i\phi}\,(dR + iR\, d\phi)$$

$$\therefore N - P = \frac{1}{2\pi i} \int_C \left(\frac{dR}{R} + i\, d\phi \right) = \frac{1}{2\pi i} \int \frac{dR}{R} + \frac{1}{2\pi} \int d\phi$$

Now $\int_C \frac{dR}{R} = [\log R]_C = 0$

since log R returns to its original value if z moves once round C.

And $\frac{1}{2\pi} \int_C d\theta = \frac{1}{2\pi} [\phi]_C = \frac{1}{2\pi} \Delta_C \arg f(z).$

Note that arg f(z) does not return to its initial value as z moves round C and so Δ_C arg f(z) is not necessarily zero.

Hence we conclude that

$$N - P = \frac{1}{2\pi} \Delta_C \arg f(z) \qquad \text{... (5)}$$

that is, the excess of the number of zeros over the number of poles of a homomorphic function equals $\left(\frac{1}{2\pi}\right)$ times the increase in arg f(z) as z goes once round C.

This is known as the argument principle.

Cor. 2:

If f(z) is analytic, then P = 0 and we have

$$N = \frac{1}{2\pi i}\int_C \frac{f'(z)}{f(z)}dz = \frac{1}{2\pi}\Delta_C \arg f(z)$$

that is, the number of zeros of an analytic function f(z) within C is $\left(\frac{1}{2\pi}\right)$ *times the increase in arg f(z) as z goes once round C.*

This is the argument principle for an analytic function.

Remark 1:

The reader might be wondering why the variation in arg f(z) as z moves round C is always equal to an integer (*i.e.*, N – P). The reason is not far to seek. If z_0 is any point on C, then we have

$$\Delta_C \arg f(z) = [\arg f(z_0)]^* - \arg f(z_0) \qquad \text{... (6)}$$

where $[\arg f(z_0)]^*$ is the value of the argument after the contour C has been traversed. We know that any two values of an argument can differ by an integral multiple of 2π. It then follows from (6) that

$$\frac{1}{2\pi}\Delta_C \arg f(z) = \frac{1}{2\pi}2\pi m = m$$

where m is an integer.

Remark 2:

The formulae (4) and (5) can be used to count the number of time, Na, a function f(z) takes the values a. In point of fact, f(z) – a = 0 iff f(z) = a and so (4) gives

$$N_a - P = \frac{1}{2\pi i}\int_C \frac{f'(z)}{f(z)-a}dz$$

Similarly (5) shows that

$$N_a - P = \frac{1}{2\pi}\Delta_C \arg [f(z)-a].$$

ROUCHE'S THEOREM

Let f(z) and g(z) be analytic inside and oil a simple closed curve C and let | g(z) | < | f(z) | on C. Then f(z) and f(z) + g(z) have the same number of zeros inside C.

First Proof:

We first observe that neither f(z) nor f(z) + g(z) can vanish on the boundary C. For suppose, if possible, for some point a on C, we have f(a) = 0. Then since | g(a) | < | f(a) |, we conclude that g(a) = 0 so that f(a) = g(a), thus contradicting the hypothesis that | g(z) | < | f(z) | on C. Similarly if f(a) + g(a) = 0, then | f(a) | = | g(a) | which is again a contradiction.

Now suppose $F(z) = \dfrac{g(z)}{f(z)}$ so that g(z) = F(z) f(z). Then

$g'(z) = F(z)\, f(z) + F(z)\, f'(z).$

Let N and M be the number of zeros of f(z) + g(z) and f(z) respectively inside C.

Then since f(z) and f(z) + g(z) are analytic inside and on C, by Cor. 2 of the preceding theorem we have

$$N = \frac{1}{2\pi i}\int_C \frac{f'+g'}{f+g}dz \text{ and M and} = \frac{1}{2\pi i}\int_C \frac{f'}{f}dz$$

$$\Rightarrow \qquad N - M = \frac{1}{2\pi i}\int_C \frac{f'+f'F+fF'}{f+fF}dz - \frac{1}{2\pi i}\int_C \frac{f'}{f}dz$$

$$= \frac{1}{2\pi i}\int_C \frac{f'(1+F)+fF'}{f(1+F)}dz - \frac{1}{2\pi i}\int_C \frac{f'}{f}dz$$

$$= \frac{1}{2\pi i}\int_C \frac{f'}{f}dz - \frac{1}{2\pi i}\int_C \frac{F'}{1+F}dz - \frac{1}{2\pi i}\int_C \frac{f'}{f}dz$$

$$= \frac{1}{2\pi i}\int_C F'(1+F)^{-1}dz$$

$$= \frac{1}{2\pi i}\int_C F'(1+F+F^2-F^3+...)dz$$

[The binomial expansion is justified since

$$\left[\,|g(z)| < |f(z)| \Rightarrow |F(z)| = \left|\frac{g(z)}{f(z)}\right| < 1\right]$$

$$\frac{1}{2\pi i}\int_C (F'-F'F+F'F^2-F'F^3+...)dz$$

$$= \frac{1}{2\pi i}\int_C F'dz - \frac{1}{2\pi i}\int_C F'F dz + \frac{1}{2\pi i}\int_C F'F^2 dz - \quad ...(1)$$

[$\because$ | F | < 1 on C, the series is uniformly convergent on C and term by term integration is justified.]

Now since f(z) and g(z) are analytic and $g(z) \neq 0$ at any point on C, the function $F = \frac{f}{g}$ and is derivative F′ are also analytic within and on C so that each integral in (1) has the value zero. Thus, we conclude that $N - M = 0$ or $N = M$ as required.

Second Proof:

As in the first proof, neither f(z) nor f(z) + g(z) has a zero on C. Let N and M be the number of zeros of f(z) + g(z) and f(z) respectively. Since f(z) and f(z) + g(z) arc analytic inside and on C, by Cor. 2 of the preceding theorem, we have

$$N = \frac{1}{2\pi}\Delta_C \arg(f+g)$$

and $$M = \frac{1}{2\pi}\Delta_C \arg f$$

$$\therefore \quad N - M = \frac{1}{2\pi}[\Delta_C \arg(f+g) - \Delta_C \arg f]$$

$$= \frac{1}{2\pi}\left[\Delta_C \arg f\left(1+\frac{g}{f}\right) - \Delta_C \arg f\right]$$

$$= \frac{1}{2\pi}\left[\Delta_C \left\{\arg f\left(1+\frac{g}{f}\right)\right\} - \Delta_C \arg f\right]$$

$$= \frac{1}{2\pi}\left[\Delta_C \arg f + \Delta_C \arg f\left(1+\frac{g}{f}\right) - \Delta_C \arg f\right]$$

$$= \frac{1}{2\pi}\Delta_C \arg\left(1+\frac{g}{f}\right) \qquad ...(1)$$

Now the theorem will be proved if we show that

$$\Delta_C \arg\left(1+\frac{g}{f}\right) = 0$$

Since $|g| < |f|$, the point $w = 1 + \frac{g}{f}$ always lies inside the circle with centre $w = 1$ and radius unity so that w always lies to the right of the imaginary axis. Hence arg w – arg $\left(1+\frac{g}{f}\right)$ always lies between $-\frac{\pi}{2}$ and $\frac{\pi}{2}$. It follows that arg $\left(1+\frac{g}{f}\right)$ returns to its original value when z describes C. Sine arg $\left(1+\frac{g}{f}\right)$ cannot increase or decrease by a multiple of 2π, we conclude that

$$\Delta_C \arg\left(1+\frac{g}{f}\right)=0$$

Then (1) gives N = M as desired.

SCHWARZ LEMMA

Theorem:

(Schwarz Lemma): *If f(z) is analytic for $|z| < 1$ and satisfies the conditions*

$|f(z)| \leq 1$, $f(0) = 0$ then $|f(z)| \leq |z|$ and $|f'(0)| \leq 1$.

Equality holds only if f(z) is a linear transformation $w = e^{ia}z$ where a is a real constant.

Proof:

Since f(z) is analytic in the disc $|z| < 1$, Taylor's expansion about the origin gives

$$f(z) = c_0 + c_1 z + c_2 z^2 + \ldots$$

By hypothesis f(0) = 0 so that $c_n = 0$.

$$f(z) = c_1 z + c_2 z^2 + \ldots$$

Consider the function

$$g(z) = \frac{f(z)}{z} = c_1 + c_2 z + \ldots$$

In the unit disc $|z| < 1$, g(z) is analytic (if we set $g(0) = c_1 = f(0)$). Let z = a be an arbitrary point of the unit disc. Choose r such that $|a| < r < 1$. Since $|f(z)| \leq 1$, we have on the circle $|z| = r$ the inequality

$$|g(z)| = \frac{|f(z)|}{|z|} \leq \frac{1}{r} \qquad \ldots (2)$$

By the maximum principle, the inequality (2) also holds in the disc $|z| \leq r$ and therefore

$$|g(a)| = \left|\frac{f(a)}{a}\right| \leq \frac{1}{r}.$$

If we let r tend to 1, we see that

$$|g(a)| \leq \left|\frac{f(a)}{a}\right| \leq 1.$$

that is,

$$|f(a)| \leq |a|.$$

In particular, $| g(0) | = | f'(0) | \leq 1$.

Since a is arbitrary, we have

$$| f(z) | \leq | z | \quad \text{... (3)}$$

for every z for which $| z | \leq 1$. If the equality in (3) holds at a single point, it means that $| g(z) |$ attains its maximum and hence that g(z) must reduce to a constant (by maximum modulus principle). Thus $| g(a) | = 1$ can hold only when

$$g(z) = \frac{f(z)}{z} = e^{ia}$$

that is, $f(z) = ze^{ia}$ where a is a real constant. This proves the assertion of the theorem.

Note: The name "Schwarz's lemma" and the above proof are due to C. Caratheodory (1904). The above theorem may therefore be called Caratheodory's inequality.

INVERSE FUNCTION THEOREM

Theorem I:

(Inverse Function Theorem): *Let a function f be analytic at a point $z = z_0$ where $f'(z_0) \neq 0$. Also let $w_0 = f(z_0)$. Then there exists a neighbourhood of the point w_0 in the w-plane in which the function $w = f(z)$ has a unique inverse $z = f(w)$ in the sense that the function F is single-valued and analytic in that neighbourhood and $F(w_0) = z_0$ and*

$$F'(w) = \frac{1}{f'(z)}$$

Proof:

Consider the function $f(z) - w_0$. By hypothesis,

$$f(z_0) - w_0 = 0.$$

Since $f'(z_0) \neq 0$, f is not a constant function and therefore neither $f(z) - w_0$ nor $f'(z)$ is identically zero. Also $f(z) - w_0$ is analytic at $z = z_0$ and so it is analytic in some neighbourhood of z_0. Again since zeros are isolated neither $f(z) - w_0$ not $f'(z)$ has any zeros in some deleted neighbourhood of z_0. Hence there exists $\varepsilon > 0$ such that $f(z) - w_0$ is analytic for $| z - z_0 | \leq \varepsilon$ and $f(z) - w_0 \neq 0$, $f'(z) \neq 0$ for $0 < | z - z_0| \leq \varepsilon$. Let D denote the open disc

$$\{z: | z - z_0 | < \varepsilon\}.$$

and C denote its boundary

$$\{z: | z - z_0 | = \varepsilon\}.$$

Since $f(z) - w_0 \neq 0$ for $| z - z_0 | < \varepsilon$, we conclude that $| f(z) - w_0 |$ has a positive minimum on the circle C. Let

$$\min_{z \in C} | f(z) - w_0 | = m$$

and choose δ such that $0 < \delta < m$. We now show that the function f(z) assumes exactly once in D every value w_1 in the open disc $\Gamma = \{w : | w - w_0 | < \delta\}$. To show this we apply Rouche's theorem to the function $w_0 - w_1$ and $f(z) - w_0$. The condition of the theorem are satisfied. For we have

$$| w_0 - w_1 | < \delta < m = \min_{z \in C} | f(z) - w_0 | \leq | f(z) - w_0 | \text{ on C.}$$

We thus conclude that the functions

$$f(z) - w_0 \text{ and } (f(z) - w_0) + (w_0 - w_1) = f(z) - w_1$$

have the same number of zeros in D. But the function $f(z) - w_0$ has only one zero in D, viz., a simple zero at z_0.

[Note that z_0 is a simple zero since $(f(z) - w_0)' = f'(z) \neq 0$ at z_0].

Hence $f(z) - w_1$ must also have only one zero, say z_1, in D. This means that the function f(z) assumes the value w_1 exactly once in D. It follows that the function $w = f(z)$ has a′ unique inverse, say $z = F(w)$, in D such that F is single-valued and $w = f(F(w))$.

It will now be shown that the function F is analytic in D. For fix w_1 in D, we have $f(z) = w_1$ for a unique z_1 in D. If w is in Γ and $F(w) = z$, then

$$\frac{F(w) - F(w_1)}{w - w_1} = \frac{z - z_1}{f(z) - f(z_1)} = \frac{1}{[f(z) - f(z_1)]/(z - z_1)} \quad ...(1)$$

It is easy to see that Γ is continuous. Hence $z \to z_1$ whenever $w \to w_1$. Since $z_1 \in D$, as shown above $f'(z_1)$ exists and is zero. If we let $w \to w_1$ then (1) shows that

$$F'(w_1) = 1/f'(z_1).$$

Thus $F'(w)$ exists in the neighbourhood Γ of w_0 so that the function F is analytic there and the proof is complete.

Theorem II:

Suppose that the function f(z) is analytic at z_0, f is not a constant, $f(z_0) = w_0$ and that $f(z) - w_0$ has a zero of order n at z_0. If $\varepsilon > 0$ sufficiently small, then there exists a $\delta > 0$ such that for all a for which $| a - w_0 | < \delta$, the equation $f(z) = a$ has exactly n roots in the disc $| z - z_0 | < \varepsilon$

Proof:

The proof of this theorem is on the same lines as that of the previous theorem. Thus we shall see that $f(z) - w_0$ is analytic for $| z - z_0 | \leq \varepsilon$ and that $f(z) - w_0 \neq 0$ for $0 < | z - z_0 | \leq \varepsilon$. Let D denote the open disc $\{z : | z - z_0 | \leq \varepsilon\}$ and C its boundary $\{z : | z - z_0 \leq \varepsilon\}$. Suppose $\min_{z \in C} | f(z) - w_0 | = m$ and choose $\delta > 0$ such that $0 < \delta < m$. We shall show that the function $f(z) - a$ has exactly n zeros in D for every a satisfying

$$| a - w_0 | < \delta.$$

To show this, we apply Rouche's theorem to the functions $w_0 - a$ and $f(z) - w_0$. The conditions of the theorem are satisfied. For we have

$$| w_0 - a | < \delta < m = \min_{z \in C} | f(z) - w_0 | \leq | f(z) - w_0 | \text{ on } C.$$

It follows that the functions

$$f(z) - w_0 \text{ and } (f(z) - w_0) + (w_0 - a) = f(z) - a$$

have the same number of zeros in D. But, as given, $f(z) - w_0$ has a zero of order n at z_0. Since a zero of multiplicity n is counted n times, we may say that the function $f(z) - w_0$ has n zeros in D. Hence the function $f(z) - a$ must also have n zeros in D. In other words, the equation $f(z) = a$ has exactly n roots in D This proves the theorem.

FUNDAMENTAL THEOREM OF ALGEBRA

Theorem I:

(Fundamental Theorem of Algebra): *Let $P(z) = a_0 + a_1 z + ... + a_n z^n$, where $n \geq 1$ and $a_n \neq 0$ so that P(z) is a polynomial of degree one or greater. Then the equation $P(z) = 0$ has at least one root.*

Proof:

The proof of this important theorem follows easily from Liouville's theorem although its proof by purely algebraic methods is extremely difficult.

We shall prove the theorem by contradiction. Suppose the theorem is false so that P(z) is not zero for any value of z. Then the function

$$f(z) = \frac{1}{P(z)}$$

is analytic everywhere. Now we have

$$f(z) = \frac{1}{\frac{a_0}{z^n} + \frac{a_1}{z^{n-1}} + ... + \frac{a_{n-1}}{z} + a_n}$$

$\to 0$ as $z \to \infty$.

Hence for every $\varepsilon > 0$, there exists a $\delta > 0$ such that

$| f(z) | < \varepsilon$ for $| z | > \delta$.

Also since f(z) is continuous in the bounded closed domain $|z| \leq \delta$, it follows that f(z) is bounded in the closed domain $|z| \leq \delta$. Therefore there exists a number K such that

$|f(z)| < K$ for $|z| \leq \delta$.

Let $M = \max(\varepsilon, K)$. Then we see that

$$|f(z)| = \left|\frac{1}{P(z)}\right| < M \text{ for every z.}$$

Hence by Liouville's theorem f(z) is constant. But this is a contradiction since P(z) is not a constant when n = 1, 2, 3, and $a_n \neq 0$. Therefore P (z) must be zero for at least one value of z, that is, the equation P(z) = 0 must have at least one root as desired.

Cor:

Every polynomial equation

$$P(z) = a_0 + a_1 z + a_2 z^2 + ... + a_n z^n = 0$$

where $n \geq 1$, $a_n \neq 0$ *has exactly n roots.*

Proof:

By the fundamental theorem of algebra P(z) = 0 has at least one root, say ai so that $P(a_1) = 0$. Then

$$P(z) = P(z) - P(a_1) = (a_0 + a_1 z + a_2 z^2 + ... + a_n z^n)$$
$$- (a_0 + a_1 \alpha_1 + a_2 \alpha^2 + ... + a_n \alpha^n)$$
$$= a_1(z - a) + a_2(z^2 - a_1^2) + ... + a_n(z^n - a_1^n)$$
$$= (z - a) P_1(z)$$

where $P_1(z)$ is a polynomial of degree n – 1. Then by the fundamental theorem, $P_1(z) = 0$ has again at least one root, say a_2 (which may be equal to a_1). Proceeding as above, we can show that

$$P(z) = (z - a)(z - a_2) P_2(z)$$

where $P_2(z)$ is polynominal of degree n – 2. Continuing in this way we see that P(z) = 0 has exactly n roots.

Alternative: By using Rouches' theorem, we shall show that every polynomial equation

$$P(z) = a_0 + a_1 z + ... + a_n z^n = 0 \quad (n \geq 1, a_n \neq 0)$$

has exactly n roots. We write

$$f(z) = a_n z^n \text{ and } g(z) = a_0 + a_1 z + ... + a_{n-1} z^{n-1}$$

Then $\frac{g(z)}{f(z)} = \frac{1}{a_n}\left(\frac{a_0}{z^n} + \frac{a_1}{z^{n-1}} + \ldots + \frac{a_{n-1}}{z}\right)$

$\to 0$ as $z \to \infty$.

Hence there exists a $\delta > 0$ such that

$$\left|\frac{g(z)}{f(z)}\right| < 1 \text{ for } |z| > b. \qquad \ldots(1)$$

We now take the closed curve C as the circle $|z| = \delta + 1$. Then it follows from (1) that

$|g(z)| < |f(z)|$ on C.

Also evidently f(z) and g(z) are analytic inside and on C. Then by Rouche's theorem f(z) and f(z) + g(z) have the same number of zeros inside C. But $f(z) = a_n z^n$ has n zeros all at the origin. Hence $f(z) + g(z) = a_0 + a_1 z + \ldots + a_{n-1} z^{n-1} + a_n z^n = P(z)$ must also have n zeros. In other words the polynomial equation $P(z) = 0$ has exactly n roots.

Theorem II:

Let P (z) be a polynomial of degree n and let z move round any part of the circle I z I = R where R is large. If 0 is the change in arg z, then the change in arg P (z) will differ from nO by a quantity which tends to zero as R tends to infinity.

Solution:

Let $P(z) = a_0 + a_1 z + \ldots + a_n z^n$, $a_n \neq 0$

we write $P(z) = z^n\left[a_n + \frac{a_{n-1}}{z} + \ldots + \frac{a_0}{z^n}\right]$

so that $\arg P(z) = n \arg z + \arg\left(a_n + \frac{a_{n-1}}{z} + \ldots + \frac{a_0}{z^n}\right)$.

Let C denote the circle $|z| = R$. Now on C, we have

$$\left|\frac{a_{n-1}}{z} + \ldots + \frac{a_0}{z^n}\right| \le \left|\frac{a_{n-1}}{z}\right| + \ldots + \left|\frac{a_0}{z^n}\right|$$

$$= \frac{|a_{n-1}|}{R} + \ldots + \frac{|a_0|}{R}$$

$= r$, say.

Then the point

$$a_n + \frac{a_{n-1}}{z} + \ldots + \frac{a_0}{z^n}$$

evidently lies within or on the circle $|z - a_n| = r$. Let M denote the centre of this circle and OP be a tangent to it where 0 is the origin. If we set

$$\left|\arg\left(a_n + \frac{a_{n-1}}{z} + \ldots + \frac{a_0}{z^n}\right) - \arg a_n\right| = \eta.$$

we see that η cannot exceed the angle MOP and as such can be made as small as we please by taking R sufficiently large *i.e.*, by decreasing r.

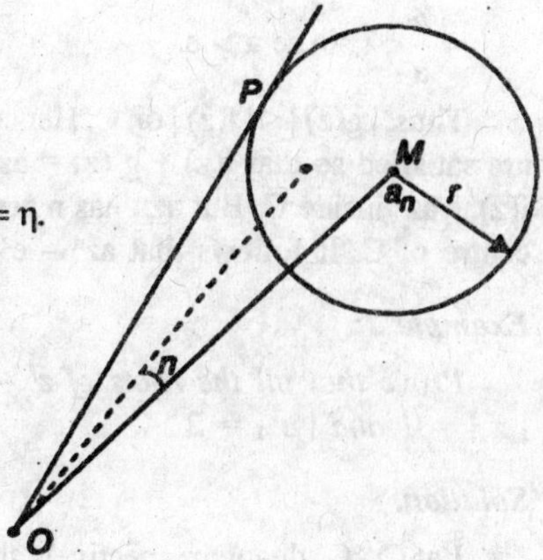

Fig. 2.3

We thus have

arg P(z) = n arg z + arg a_n ± η.

Now as R → ∞, η → 0

so that $\lim_{R\to\infty} \arg P(z) = n \arg z + \arg a_n$. ... (1)

As z varies there is no change in arg an and so we conclude from (1) that the change in arg P(z) tends ton times the change in arg z as R → ∞.

Example 1:

If a > e, use Rouche's theorem to prove that the equation

$$e^z = az^n$$

has n roots inside the circle $|z| = 1$.

Solution:

Let C denote the circle $|z| = 1$. The given equation may he written as

$$az^n - e^z = 0.$$

We write, $f(z) = az^n$ and $g(z) = -e^z$. Then evidently both f(z) and g(z) are analytic within and on C. Also, we have

$$\left|\frac{g(z)}{f(z)}\right| = \frac{|-e^z|}{|az^n|} = \frac{|e^z|}{|a||z|^n} = \frac{|e^z|}{a|z|^n} \quad (\because \text{ a is real + ve})$$

$$= \frac{|1 + z + 1/2!.z^2 + 1/3!z^3 + \ldots|}{a|z|^n}$$

$$= \frac{1 + |z| + 1/2!.|z|^2 + 1/3!|z|^3 + \ldots}{a|z|^n}$$

$$= \frac{1 + 1 + 1 + 1/2! + 1/3 + \ldots}{a}, \text{ as } |z| = 1 \text{ on C},$$

$= \frac{e}{a} < 1$ sin ce a > e.

Thus, $| g(z) | < | f(z) |$ on C. Hence all the conditions of Rouche's theorem are satisfied so that $f(z) + g(z) = az^n - e^z$ has the same number of zeros as $f(z) = az^n$ inside C. But azn has n zeros all located at the origin which is the centre of C. It follows that $az^n - e^z$ has n zeros inside C as required.

Example 2:

Prove that all the roots of $z^7 - 5z^3 + 12 = 0$ lie between the circles $| z | = 1$ and $| z | = 2$.

Solution:

Let C_1, C_2 denote respectively the circles $| z | = 1$ and $| z | = 2$. We write $f(z) = 12$ and $g(z) = z^7 - 4z^3$. Then on C_1, f(z) and g(z) are analytic and

$$\left|\frac{g(z)}{f(z)}\right| = \left|\frac{z^7 - 5z^3}{12}\right|$$

$$\leq \frac{|z|^7 + |-5z^3|}{12} = \frac{|z|^7 + 5|z|^3}{12} = \frac{1+5}{12} = \frac{1}{2} \qquad [\because |z| = 1 \text{ on C}]$$

Thus $\left|\frac{g(z)}{f(z)}\right| < 1$, or $| g(z) | < | f(z) |$ on C_1.

Hence by Rouche's theorem, $f(z) + g(z) = z^7 - 5z^3 + 12$ has the same number of zeros inside C, as $f(z) = 12$. But $f(z) = 12$ has no zeros inside C_2. It follows that $z^7 - 5z^3 + 12$ has no zeros inside C_1.

We next consider the circle C_2. We write $F(z) = z^7$ and $\phi(z) = 12 - 5z^2$. Evidently F(z) and $\phi(z)$ are analytic within and on C_2. Further we have on C_2,

$$\left|\frac{\phi(z)}{f(z)}\right| = \frac{|12 - 5z^3|}{|z|^7}$$

$$\leq \frac{|12| + 5|z|^3}{|z^7|} = \frac{12 + 5.2^3}{2^7} = \frac{52}{128} < 1 \qquad [\because |z| = 2 \text{ on } C_2]$$

Thus $| \phi(z) | < | F(z) |$ on C_2. Hence by Rouche's theorem $F(z) + \phi(z) = z^7 - 5z^3 + 12$ has the same number of zeros as $F(z) = z^7$ inside C_2. But all the seven zeros of z^7 lie inside $| z | = 2$ since they are all located at the origin. It follows that all the seven zeros of $z^7 - 5z^3 + 12$ lie inside $| z | = 2$.

Thus we have shown that the equation $z^7 - 5z^3 - 12 = 0$ has no roots inside $| z | = 1$ but has all the seven roots inside $| z | = 2$. It follows that all the roots of this equation lie between the circles $| z | =$ land $| z | = 2$ as required.

Example 3:

Use Rouche's theorem to show that the equation $z^5 + 15z + 1 = 0$ has one root in the disc $|z| < \frac{3}{2}$ and four roots in the annulus $\frac{3}{2} < |z| < 2$.

Solution:

Let $f(z) = z^5$ and $g(z) = 15z + 1$. On the circle $|z| = 2$, we have

$|f(z)| = |z|^5 = 2^5 = 32$

and $|g(z)| = |15z + 1| \leq 15|z| + 1 = 15 \times 2 + 1 = 31$

Thus $|g(z)| < |f(z)|$ on the circle $|z| = 2$.

It follows by Rouche's theorem that the function

$f(z) + g(z) = z^5 + 15z + 1$

has as many zeros in $|z| < 2$ as the function $f(z) = z^5$. Since the latter function has a zero of order 5 at $z = 0$, it follows that all the five roots of $z^5 + 15z + 1 = 0$ must lie in the disc $|z| < 2$.

On the other hand, since, for

$$|z| = \frac{3}{2}, |z^5 + 1| \leq |z|^5 + 1 \frac{243}{32} + 1 < \frac{45}{2} = |15z|,$$

the function $z^5 + 15z + 1$ has as many zeros in $|z| < \frac{3}{2}$ as the function $15z$, that is, it has exactly one zero there. Consequently four of the zeros of $z^5 + 15z + 1$ must lie in the ring $\frac{3}{2} < |z| < 2$ as required.

Example 4:

Prove that one root of the equation $z^4 + z^3 + 1 = 0$ lies in the first quadrant.

Solution:

Since all the coefficients of the equation $f(z) = z^4 + z^3 + 1 = 0$ are real and positive, it is evident that it cannot be satisfied for any real positive value of z. In other words this equation has no positive roots. It also has no negative root. For if we set $z = -x$ and write

$F(x) = x^4 - x^3 + 1 = 0$, we see that

$F(x) = x^3 (x - 1) + 1 > 0$ when $x > 1$

and $F(x) = x^4 + (1 - x)(x^2 + x + 1) > 0$ when $0 < x < 1$.

Thus, we have shown that the equation f(z) = 0 cannot have any real root. Again this equation cannot have any purely imaginary root. For if we write z = iy, we get $y^4 - iy^3 + 1 = 0$ and it is evident that the real and imaginary parts cannot vanish together.

We shall now show that the equation f(z) = 0 has one complex root in the first quadrant by using argument principle. For this purpose, we shall find change in arg f(z) as z moves round part of the first quadrant bounded by | z | = R where R is large. We write f(z) = w = u + iv.

(i) On the x-axis, when z varies 0 to ∞, w passes along u-axis from 1 to ∞ so that arg f(z) remains constant and equal to zero on positive real axis.

(ii) On the quadrant of the circle | z | = R, we write $z = Re^{i\theta}$ so that

$$f(z) = z^4\left(1+\frac{1}{z}+\frac{1}{z^4}\right)$$
$$= R^4 e^{4i\theta}[1 + f(z)]$$

where F(z) → 0 uniformly when z → ∞. Thus when z moves on the first quadrant of the circle, the change in arg f(z) is $4.\frac{\pi}{2} = 2\pi$.

(iii) Taking z = iy, we have on y-axis

$$f(iy) = y^4 - iy^3 + 1$$

so that $\arg f(iy) = \tan^{-1}\left(\frac{-y^3}{y^4+1}\right)$.

Now the numerator of $\frac{-y^3}{y^4+1}$ vanishes only for y = 0 and the denominator cannot vanish for any real y. Hence as y varies from ∞ to 0 along the imaginary axis, the initial and final values of arg f(z) are zero.

From (i), (ii) and (iii), we conclude that the total change in arg f(z) is

$0 + 2\pi + 0 = 2\pi$.

Hence by argument principle, the number of zeros of f(z) in the first quadrant $= \frac{1}{2\pi} \times 2\pi = 1$.

In other words the equation $z^4 + z^3 + 1 = 0$ has one root in the first quadrant.

Example 5:

Show that the equation

$z^3 + iz + 1 = 0$

has a root in each of the first, second and fourth quadrants.

Solution:

Let $f(z) = z^3 + iz + 1 = 0$. As in the last two examples, we can show that the given equation can have no roots either on real or imaginary axis. We now search for complex roots in the first quadrant. We write

$$f(z) = u + iv \text{ so that}$$

$$u = z^3 + 1 \text{ and } v = z$$

(a) On the x-axis, we write z = x so that u, $= x^3 + 1$ and v = x

$$\therefore \arg f(z) = \tan^{-1} \frac{x}{x^3+1}$$

Now $\lim_{x\to\infty} \frac{x}{x^3+1} = 0.$

When $0 < x < \infty$, both u and v are positive. Also when x = 0, u = 1 and v = 0. Hence as z moves along x-axis from 0 to ∞, the point (u, v) starting from (1, 0) and remaining in the first quadrant moves to ∞ where the curve is parallel to u-axis so that there is no change in arg f(z) as z moves on the real positive axis.

(b) Since the equation is of third degree, as in the last two examples, the change in arg f(z) is $3.\frac{\pi}{2} = \frac{3\pi}{2}$ where z moves along

$z = R^{i\theta}, 0 \le q \le \frac{\pi}{2}$ where $R \to \infty$.

(c) On y-axis, we write z = iy. Then

$f(iy) = -iy^3 - y + 1 = (1 - y) - iy^3$

$$\therefore \quad \arg f(iy) = \tan^{-1} \frac{v}{u}$$

$$= \tan^{-1}\left(\frac{-y^3}{1-y}\right)$$

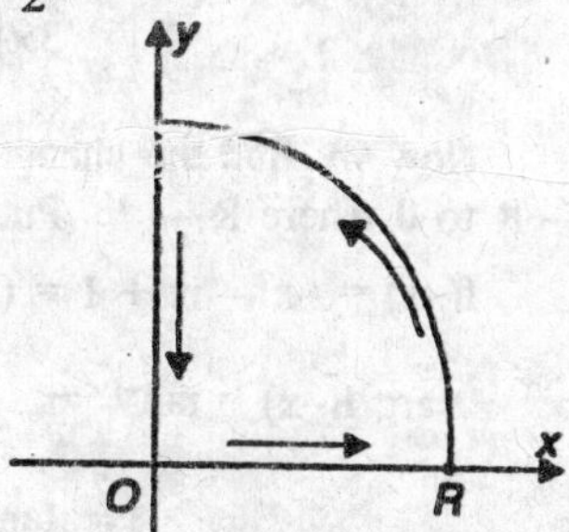

Fig. 2.4

Now numerator of $\frac{-y^3}{1-y}$ is 0 when y = 0 and its denominator vanishes at y = 1. Thus when $1 < y < \infty$, u and v are both negative. At y = 1, u = 0, v = – 1, and when $0 < y < 1$, u is positive and v is negative. At y = 0, u = 1 and v = 0. Thus we see that as y varies from ∞ to 0, the point (u, v) starting from ∞ in the third quadrant where the curve is parallel to v-axis moves to the point (0, –1) and then after remaining in the fourth quadrant comes to the point (1, 0). Hence, the change in arg f(z) as z moves along the imaginary axis is $\frac{\pi}{2}$. Therefore the total change in arg f(z) is .

$$0+\frac{3\pi}{2}+\frac{\pi}{2}=2\pi.$$

Hence by argument principle the number of zeros of f(z) in the first quadrant is

$$\frac{1}{2\pi}\times 2\pi = 1.$$

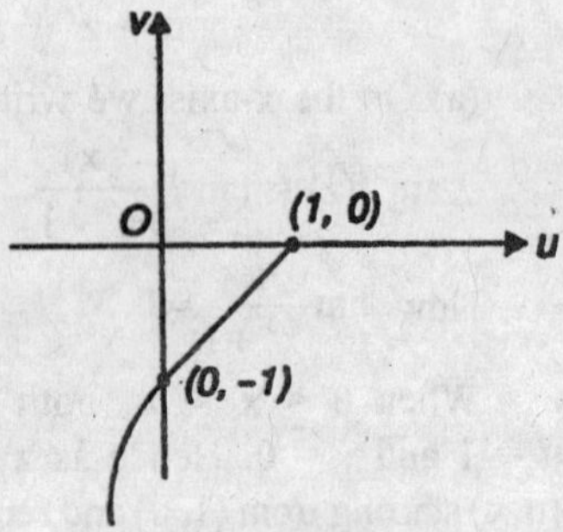

Fig. 2.5

In other words the given equation has one root in the first quadrant.

We now look for the roots of f(z) = 0 in the second quadrant. As seen above, the change in arg f(z) as z moves along the imaginary axis from ∞ to 0 is π/2. Hence, the change in arg f(z) as z moves along the imaginary axis from 0 to ∞ is –π/2. Also the change in arg f(z) along the circle

$$z = Re^{i\theta},\ \frac{\pi}{2}\le\theta\le\pi$$

or $$3\times\left(\pi-\frac{\pi}{2}\right)=\frac{3\pi}{2}.$$

Now we find the change in arg f(z) as z moves on the real axis from – R to 0 where R → ∞. Putting z = – x, we get

$$f(-x) = -x^3 - ix + 1 = (1 - x^3) - tx$$

$$\therefore \arg f(-x) = \tan^{-1}\frac{v}{u}$$

$$= \tan^{-1}\frac{-x}{1-x^3}$$

Now $\lim\limits_{x\to\infty}\frac{u}{v} = \lim\limits_{x\to\infty}\frac{-x}{1-x^3} = 0.$

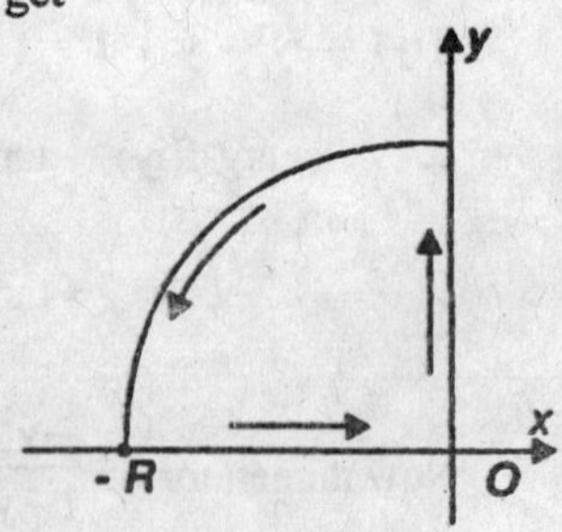

Fig. 2.6

Hence $u = 1 - x^3$ and v = – x.

u = 0 when x = 1 and v = 0 when x = 0.

Also when 1 < x < ∞, u and v are both negative and when 0 < x < 1, u is positive and v is negative. Hence as x varies from ∞ to 1, the point starting from 0 in the third quadrant where the curve is parallel to u-axis, and remaining in the third quadrant comes to the point (0, −1) and when x varies from 1 to 0, the point (u, v) starting from (0, −1) and remaining in the fourth quadrant reaches the point (1, 0). It follows that the change in arg f(z) is n as z moves along the negative real axis from 0 to 0. Hence the total change in arg f(z) as z moves round the second quadrant is

$$-\frac{\pi}{2}+\frac{3\pi}{2}+\pi=2\pi.$$

Therefore by argument principle, the number of zeros of f(z) in the second quadrant is

$$\frac{1}{2\pi}\times 2\pi=1.$$

Thus, the given equation has one root in the second quadrant.

We leave it to the reader to verify that the given equation has one root in the fourth quadrant.

Example 6:

In which quadrant do the roots of the equation

$z^4 + z^3 + 4z^2 + 2z + 3 = 0$

lie?

Solution

Let $f(z) = z^4 + z^3 + 4z^2 + 2z + 3 = 0$

Since all the coefficients of f(z) are real and of the same positive sign, the equation f(z) = 0 has no positive roots. Also if we put z = −x, we have

$f(-x) = x^4 - x^3 + 4x^2 - 2x + 3 = 0$

Now $f(-x) = x^2 (x^2 - x + 4) + 2(1 - x) + 1$

$= x^2[(x - \frac{1}{2})^2 \frac{15}{4}] + 2(1 - x) + 1$

> 0 when $0 < x \le 1$.

And $f(-x) = x^3 (x - 1) + 2x (2x - 1) + 3$

> 0 when $x \ge 1$.

Thus $f(-x) > 0$ for all $x > 0$.

This means that the equation f(z) = 0 has no negative real root. Again putting z = iy, we get

$$f(iy) = y^4 - iy^3 - 4y^2 + 2iy + 3$$
$$= (y^3 - 4y^2 + 3) - iy(2 - y^2).$$

It is evident that the real and imaginary parts of f(iy) cannot vanish together so that equation f(z) = 0 has no purely imaginary root either.

We now search for complex roots of f(z) = 0 in the first quadrant by using argument principle. For this purpose, we find

$$\Delta \arg f(z)$$

i.e. change in arg f(z) as z moves round the part of the first quadrant bounded by | z | = R where R is large. We write

$$f(z) = w = u + iv.$$

(a) On the x-axis, Δ arg f(z) = 0 since as z moves from 0 to ∞ along x-axis, w moves along the real u-axis from 3 to ∞ so that arg f(z) =0 at each point of positive x-axis.

(b) On the quadrant of the circle | z | = R, we write $z = Re^{i\theta}$ so

$$f(z) = z^4\left(1+\frac{1}{z}+\frac{4}{z^2}+\frac{2}{z^3}+\frac{2}{z^4}\right)$$

where F(z) → 0 uniformly as z → ∞. Thus when z moves on the first quadrant, the change in arg f(z) is

$$4.\frac{\pi}{4} = 2\pi.$$

(c) On the y-axis, taking z = iy, we have

$$f(iy) = y^4 - iy^3 - 4y^2 + 2iy + 3$$

so thatarg $f(iy) = \tan^{-1}\left(\frac{-y^3+2y}{y^4-4y^2+3}\right)$

Now the numerator of

$$\frac{-y^3+2y}{y^4-4y^2+3} = \frac{y(2-y^2)}{(y^2-1)(y^2-3)}$$

vanishes at y = 0 and y = √2 and its denominator y = 1 and y = √3. Hence if we write

$$u = y^4 - 4y^2 + 3 \text{ and } v = 2y - y^3$$

$\frac{u}{v}$ varies as follows as y varies from ∞ to 0

y	∞	–,	√3		√2		1		0
v/u	0	–,	∞,	+,	0,	–,	∞,	+,	0

Considering these variations in some detail we observe that (i) when

$$\sqrt{3} < y < \infty,$$

u is positive and v is negative so that the point (u, v) lies in the fourth quadrant, (ii) when $\sqrt{2} < y < \sqrt{3}$, (u, v) lies in the third quadrant (iii) when $1 < y < \sqrt{2}$, (u, v) lies in the second quadrant and (iv) when $0 < y < 1$, (u, v) lies in the first quadrant.

Thus, the arg f(z) decreases by 2π as z moves along the imaginary axis from ∞ to 0.

From (a), (b), (c), we conclude that the total change in arg f(z) is

$$0 + 2\pi - 2\pi = 0$$

Hence, f(z) has no zeros in the first quadrant. Since the coefficients of f(z) are all real, the zeros of f(z) will occur in conjugate pairs and consequently the equation f(z) = 0 will have no roots in the third quadrant. Since the equation is of fourth degree the only possibility left out is that there must be two roots in the second and two in the fourth quadrant.

Example 7:

Show that the equation

$$z^4 + 2z^3 + z^2 + 4z + 5 = 0$$

has no real or purely imaginary roots and that it has one complex root in each quadrant.

Solution:

Let $f(z) = z^4 + 2z^3 + 3z^2 + 4z + 5 = 0$.

Since all the coefficients of f(z) are real and of same sign positive, the given equation has no positive real root. Also if we putso $z = -x$, we have

$$\begin{aligned} f(-x) &= x^4 - 2x^3 + 3x^2 - 4x + 5 \\ &= x^2(z^2 - 2x + 1) + 2(x^2 - 2x + 1) + 3 \\ &= x^2(x-1)^2 + 2(x-1)^2 + 3 \\ &> 0 \text{ for all x.} \end{aligned}$$

This shows that the given equation cannot have any negative real root. Again putting z = iy, we get

$$\begin{aligned} f(iy) &= y^4 - 2iy^3 - 3iy^2 + 4iy + 5 \\ &= (y^4 + 3y^2 + 5y) + 2i(2y - y) \end{aligned}$$

Now f(iy) = 0 if and only if the equations

$$y^4 - 3y^2 + 5 = 0$$

and $$2y - y^3 = 0$$

are satisfied for the same values of y. But these equations are evidently inconsistent for the second equation is satisfied when $y = \sqrt{2}$ but the first is not satisfied for this value. It follows that the equation cannot and have any purely imaginary root either.

Thus, we have shown that the given equation has no roots on the real or imaginary axis. We now search for the complex roots in the first quadrant by using argument principle. For this purpose we find Δ arg f(z) *i.e.* change in arg f(z) as z moves round the part of the first quadrant bounded by $|z| = R$ where R is large. We write,

$$f(z) = (w = u + iv).$$

(a) On the x-axis, Δ arg f(z) = 0 since as z moves from 0 to ∞ along x-axis, w moves along the real u-axis from 5 to ∞ *i.e.* w remains real and positive so that arg f(z) = 0 at each point of the positive x-axis.

(b) On the quadrant of circle the $|z| = R$, we write $z = Re^{i\theta}$ so that

$$f(z) = z^4\left(1+\frac{1}{z}+\frac{4}{z^2}+\frac{2}{z^3}+\frac{2}{z^4}\right)$$

$$= R^4e^{4i\theta}\,[1 + F(z)]$$

where $F(z) \to 0$ uniformly as $z \to \infty$. Thus, when z goes round the first quadrant the change in arg f(z).

$$4.\frac{\pi}{2} = 2\pi.$$

(c) On the y-axis, taking z = iy, we get

$$f(iy) = (y^4 - 3y^2 + 5) + 2i\,(2y - y^3)$$

so that

$$\arg f(iy) = \tan^{-1}\frac{u}{v} = \tan^{-1}\left(\frac{2y(2-y^2)}{y^4-3y^2+5}\right).$$

Now the numerator of the expression in the brackets vanishes for y = 0 and $y = \sqrt{2}$ and its denominator vanishes for no values of y since we have

$$y^4 - 3y^2 + 5 = \left(y^2-\frac{3}{2}\right)+\frac{11}{4} > 0$$

for all y. We now discuss how the point (u, v) moves in the u-v plane as y varies from ∞ to 0. We have

$$u = y^4 - 3y^2 + 5,\ v = 4y - 2y^3.$$

(i) When $\sqrt{2} < y < \infty$. u is positive and v is negative. At $y = \sqrt{2}$, u = 3 and v=0. Also when $y \to \infty$, $u \to \infty$, $v \to \infty$.

This shows that as y varies from ∞ to √2, the point (u, v) starting from ∞ where the curve is parallel to u-axis

$$\left(\text{since } \frac{u}{v} \to 0 \text{ as } y \to \infty\right)$$

and remaining in the first quadrant comes to the point (3, 0) on u-axis. This shows that there is no change in arg f(z) as y varies from ∞ to √2.

(ii) When $0 < y < \sqrt{2}$, a and v are both positive. At $y = 0$, $r = 5$, $v = 0$.

Hence when y varies from √2 to 0, the point (u, v) starting from (3, 0) and remaining in the first quadrant moves to the point (5, 0) on the u-axis so that again there is no change in argument.

Thus the total change in the argument of f(z) is

$0 + 2\pi = 0 = 2\pi.$

Hence by argument principle, the number of zeros of f(z) in the first quadrant is

$$\frac{1}{2\pi} \times 2\pi = 1.$$

In the same way, we can find the number of complex roots in the second quadrant by letting z describe the closed curve consisting of the segment from 0 to R of the imaginary axis, the circle quadrant

$$z = Re^{i\theta} \frac{\pi}{2} \le \theta \le \pi$$

and the segment from –R to 0 of the real axis and then letting $R \to \infty$. We leave it to the reader to verify that there is no change in arg f(z) as z moves along either of the two line segments on the axis and that the change is 2π when z moves along the circle quadrant. Hence, again there is one root in the second quadrant.

Since the coefficients of the given equation are all real, the roots must occur in conjugate parts. Hence there must be one root in each of the third and fourth quadrants.

ANALYTIC CONTINUATION

Definition 1:

Let $f_1(z)$ be analytic in a domain D_1 and suppose that we can find a function $f_2(z)$ which is analytic in a domain D_2 such that D_2 has the part D_{12} in common with D_1. (See the figure 1.30).

If $f_1(z) = f_2(z)$ in the common part D_{12}, then we say that $f_2(z)$ is the direct analytic continuation of $f_1(z)$ from D_1 into D_2 via D_{12}. In fact, we may equivalently say that f_2 is a direct analytic continuation of f_1.

Note that for the purpose of analytic continuation, it is sufficient that the domains D_1 and D_2 have only a small arc in common such as ABC in Fig.

We may regard the aggregate of values of $f_1(z)$ in D_1 and $f_2(z)$ in D_2 as values of a single function f(z) analytic in $D_1 \cup D_2$ such that

$$f(z)\begin{cases} f_1(z) \text{ when } z \in D_1, \\ f_2(z) \text{ when } z \in D_2. \end{cases}$$

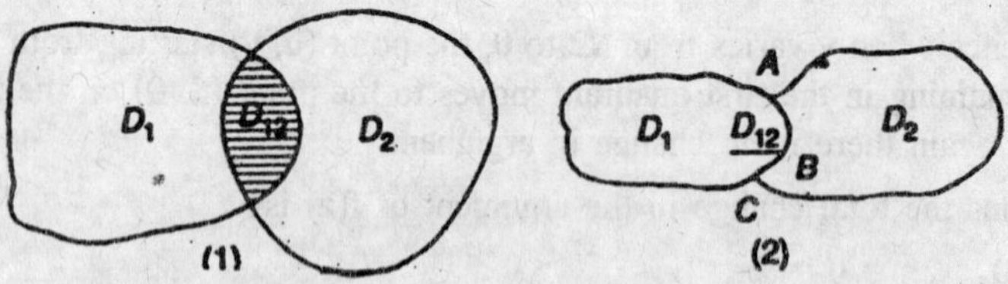

Fig. 2.7

Definition 2:

An analytic function f with its domain of definition D will be called a function element and will be denoted by (f D).

If z is an element of D, then (f, D) is called a function element of z.

Using this notation, we may say that (f_1, D_1) and (f_2, D_2) are direct analytic continuations of each other iff $D_1 \cap D_2 \neq$ and $f_1(z) = f_2(z)$ for all $z \in D_1 \cap D_2$. In this case, we write

$(f_1, D_1) - (f_2, D_2)$.

We will now show that there cannot be two different analytic continuations of a function. For this purpose we shall need a result which we prove in the following theorem.

Theorem I:

Let f(z) be analytic in a domain D and let f(z) vanish over a domain Do which is a part of D. Then f(z) vanishes at each point of the whole domain D.

Proof:

We shall prove the theorem by contradiction. Suppose, if possible, there is a point a in D such that $f(a) \neq 0$. We take a point bin D_0 and join b with a by means of an arc L lying entirely in D. (This is possible since D is connected, being a domain).

On a portion of L near the point b, f(z) will be zero whereas on another portion near the point a, $f(z) \neq 0$. (Why ?) It follows that there exists a point c on L such that f(z) = 0 along the whole arc b c but, there are points on the arc a c as near as possible to c at which f(z) does not vanish. Now since f(z) is analytic and therefore continuous at c, it follows that f(z) must vanish at the point c itself. But this zero at c, is not isolated since the whole arc b c consists of zeros of f(z). Hence f(z) must be identically zero in some neighbourhood N of c and consequently f(z) must vanish at all points of a portion of L adjacement to the point c which lies inside N and which is a part of the arc a c. But this is a contradiction since we have proved that on the arc a c there were points as near as we please to c where f(z) did not vanish. From this contradiction, the theorem follows.

Cor.:

Let $f_1(z)$ and $f_2(z)$ be two functions both analytic in a domain D such that $f_1(z) = f_2(z)$ on a domain D_0 which is contained in D so that

$$f_1(z) - f_2(z) = 0 \text{ in } D_0.$$

Then by the above theorem $f_1(z) - f_2(z) = 0$ in the whole domain D, Thus, we conclude.

If two functions, which are analytic in a domain, coincide in a part of that domain, then they coincide in the whole domain.

Remark:

(i) The result of the theorem holds true if we only assume that f(z) vanishes on an arc L lying entirely in the domain D. As in the proof of the theorem in the case the function f(z) would have vanished in a circle with centre at one of the points of L and consequently it would vanish in the whole domain D.

(ii) The conditions would have been still restricted to the fact that the zeros of f(z) have a limit point z_0 in D so that f(z) has an infinite number of zeros in every arbitrary small neighbourhood of z_0. Since f(z) is continuous at z_0 f(z) must be zero at the point z_0 itself. But this zero is not isolated and consequently f(z) must vanish everywhere in D.

Example:

If the identity $\sin^2 z + \cos^2 z = 1$ holds for all real values of z, show that it holds for all complex values of z.

Solution:

Let $f(z) = \sin^2 z + \cos^2 z - 1$ and let D be the region of z-plane containing a portion of x-axis. Since f(z) is analytic in D such that f(z) = 0 on the portion of x-axis inside D. It follows from the above remark (i) that f(z) = 0 inside D.

i.e. $\sin^2 z + \cos^2 z = 1.$

Since D is arbitrary, the result follows.

Uniqueness of Direct Analytic Continuation

Theorem II:

There cannot be two different direct analytic continuations of a function. In other words, if $f_2(z)$ and $g_2(z)$ are two direct analytic continuations of a function $f_1(z)$, then $f_2(z) = g_2(z)$.

Proof:

Let $f_2(z)$ and $g_2(z)$ be two direct analytic continuations of a function $f_1(z)$ from the domain D_1 into the domain D_2 via D_{12} which is a domain common to both D_1 and D_2. Then by definition of analytic continuation $f_2(z)$ and $g_2(z)$ arc two functions analytic in D_2 such that

$$f_1(z) = f_2(z) \text{ and } f_1(z) = g_2(z)$$

at all points z in D_{12}. In other words $f_2(z) - g_2(z)$ in D_{12}. Thus, $f_2(z)$ and $g_2(z)$ are two functions analytic in the domain D_2 such that they coincide in a part D_{12} of D_2. It then follows from the corollary of theorem I above that $f_2(z) = g_2(z)$ in the whole domain D_2.

Analytic Continuation Along a Chain of Domain

Suppose that we have a chain of function elements.

$$(f_1, D_1), (f_2, D_2), \ldots, (f_k, D_k), \ldots$$

such that D_1 and D_2 have the part D_{12} in common, D_2 and D_3 have the part D_{23} in common and so on. If $f_1(z) = f_2(z)$ in D_{12}, $f_2(z) = f_3(z)$ in

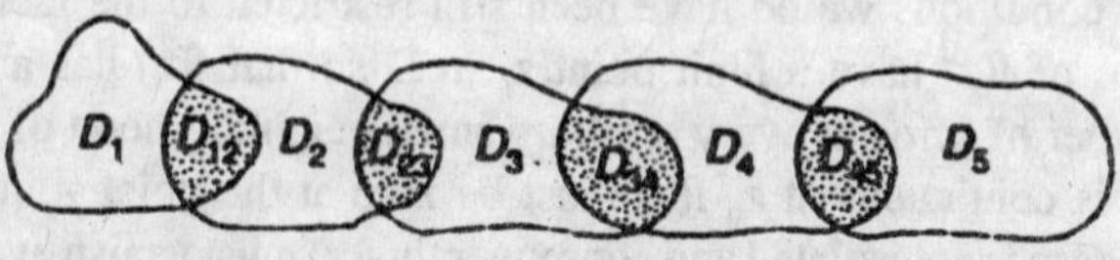

Fig. 2.8

$D_{23}, \ldots, f_{k-1}(z) = f_k(z)$ in $D_{(k-1)k}$ and so on, then we say that (f_k, D_k) is direct analytic continuation of (f_{k-1}, D_{k-1}). In this way, we obtain a chain of function elements,

$$(f_1, D_1), (f_2, D_2), \ldots (f_k, D_k), \ldots$$

such that (f_{k+1}, D_{k+1}) is a direct analytic continuation of (f_k, D_k) for $k = 1, 2, \ldots, (n-1)$. We then say that (f_n, D_n) is the analytic continuation of (f_1, D_1) along the chain of domains $D_1, D_2, \ldots, D_n$. Without loss of generality, we may take these domains as open circular discs.

Analytic Continuation Along a Curve

Definition 3:

Let Γ be a curve in the complex plane with the equation $z = z(t)$, $a \leq t \leq b$: If there is a partition

$a = t_0 < t_1 <...< t_n = b$

and chain (f_1, D_1),... (f_n, D_n) of function elements such that (f_{k+1}, D_{k+1}) is a direct analytic continuation of (f_k, D_k) for

$k = 1, 2, n... n - 1,$

and $z(t) \in D_k$ for $t_{k-1} \leq t \leq t_k$, $k = 1, 2, ...n$,

then (f_n, D_n) is said to be an analytic continuation of (f_1, D_1) along the curve Γ.

Uniqueness of Analytic Continuation Along a Curve

Theorem:

Analytic continuation of a given function element along a given cane is unique. In other words, if (f_n, D_n) and (g_m, E_m) are two continuations of (f_1, D_1) along the same curve Γ defined by

$$z = z(t) : a \leq t \leq b$$

then $$f_n = g_m \text{ on } D_n \cap E_m.$$

Proof:

Suppose there are two continuations of (f_1, D_1) namely,

(f_1, D_1), ... (f_n, D_n)

and (g_1, E_1) , ... (g_m, E_m)

where $g_1 = f_1$ and $E_1 = D_1$.

Then there exist partitions

$a = t_0 < t_1 < ... < t_n = b$

anda $= s_0 < s_1 < ... < s_m = b$

such that

$z(t) \in D_1$ for $1_{i-1} \leq 1 \leq t_i$, $i = 1, 2, ... n$

andz(t) $\in E_1$ for $s_{j-1} \leq t\ s_j$, $j = 1, 2, ... m$.

Our chain is that if $1 \leq i \leq n$, $1 \leq j \leq m$ and

$[t_{i-1}, t_i] \cap [S_{j-1}, S_j] \neq \phi$.

then (f_i, D_i) and (g_j, E_j) are direct analytic continuations of each other. This is certainly true when $i = j = 1$ since $g_1 = f_1$ and $E_1 = D_1$. If it is not true for all i and j, then we may pick from all (i, j) for which the statement is false a pair such that i + j is minimal. Suppose $t_{i-1} \geq S_{j-1}$. [Then $i \geq 2$. For if $i = 1$, then $j = 1$ and we know that the result holds for $i = j = 1$]. Since

$$[t_{i-1}, t_i] \cap [S_{j-1}, S_j] \neq \phi$$

and $\quad S_{j-1} \leq t_{i-1},$

we must have $\quad t_{i-1} \leq S_j.$

Thus $\quad S_{j-1} \leq t_{i-1} \leq S_j.$

It follows that $\quad z(t_{i-1}) \in D_{i-1} \cap E_i \cap E_j.$

In particular, this intersection is non-empty. Now (f_i, D_i) is a direct continuation of (f_{i-1}, D_{i-1}). Moreover, (f_{i-1}, D_{i-1}) is a direct continuation of (g_i, E_j) since i + j is minimal. (Note that

$$t_{i-1} \in [t_{i-2}, t_{i-1}] \cap [S_{j-1}, S_j]$$

so that the hypothesis of the claim is satisfied). Since

$$D_{i-1} \cap D_i \cap E_j \neq \phi,$$

(f_i, D_i) must be direct continuation of (g_j, E_j) which is a contradiction. Hence our claim holds for all i and j. In particular, it holds for $i = n$, $j = m$. This proves the theorem.

Natural Boundary

It may happen that a function cannot be extended analytically beyond the boundary of a certain region. Such a boundary is called a natural boundary.

Complete Analytic Function

Suppose that f(z) is analytic function in a domain D. From all possible analytic continuations of f and all possible continuations of these continuations. In this way we shall arrive at a function F such that for any point ζ, F(ζ) denotes the slow or values obtained for ζ by all possible analytic continuations of F(z) to ζ. The function F obtained in this way is called the complete analytic function. If no analytic continuation of F(z) to ζ is possible, then S is called a singularity of the complete analytic function F(z). Evidently the singularities of f(z) are also singularities of the corresponding complete analytic function F(z).

POWER SERIES METHOD OF ANALYTIC CONTINUATION

We shall now give an element method of analytic continuation by means of power series.

We shall use only circular domain and Taylor's expansion in such domains. This method is explained below.

Suppose that the initial function $f_1(z)$ is represented by the Taylor's series about a point c_1 in the form

$$f_1(z) = \sum_{n=0}^{\infty} a_n^{(1)} (z - c_1)^n \qquad ...(1)$$

convergent within the circle Γ_1 whose equation is $| z - c_1 | = \rho_1$. We now draw a contour L from the point c_1 and perform the analytic continuation of the function along L as follows:

On L we take a point c_2 such that the arc c_1c_2 lies in Γ which is the circle of convergence of the series (1). We then use the series (1) to evaluate the derivatives $f_1^{(n)}(c_2)$ by term by term differentiation and write the expansion valid within a circle Γ_2 defined by $| z - c_2 | = \rho_2$ in form

$$f_2(z) = \sum_{n=0}^{\infty} a_n^{(2)} (z - c_2)^n = \sum_{n=0}^{\infty} \frac{f_n^{(2)}(c_2)}{n!} (z - c_2)^n \qquad ...(2)$$

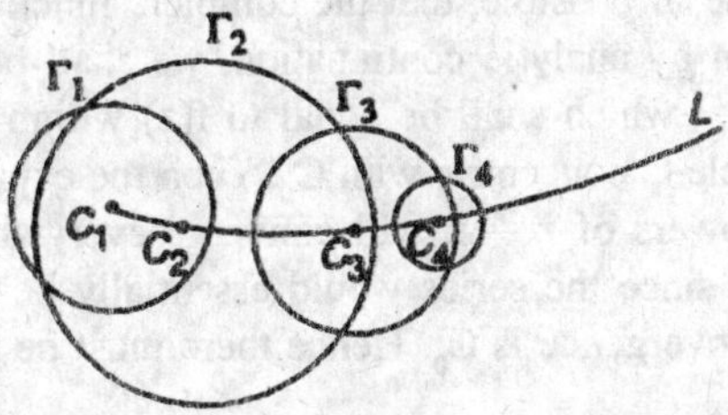

Fig. 2.9

If the circle Γ_2 extends beyond Γ_1, then (2) gives an analytic continuation of $f_1(z)$. At the point c_2, the functions $f_1(z)$ and $f_2(z)$ and all their derivatives have values and these functions will coincide in the region common to the circles Γ_1 and Γ_2.

It is useful to note that the series (2) can be obtained from (1) in the following way.

We rewrite the series (1) in the form

$$\sum_{n=0}^{\infty} a_n^{(1)} [(z - c_2) + (c_2 - c_1)]^n$$

If we now expand $[(z - c_2) + (c_2 - c_1)]^n$ by the binomial theorem and collect terms in like powers of $(z - c_2)$ in (3), we obtain the series (2).

When the first analytic continuation of (1) is performed, we proceed to the next. We take a new point c_2 on L such that $c_2\ c_3$ lies in the circle Γ_2. We then rearrange the series (2) in powers of $(z - c_3)$ by the method explained above and get a new function element

$$f_3(z) = \sum_{n=0}^{\infty} a_n^{(3)}(z-c_3)^n,$$

which is defined in a circle Γ_3 whose equation is $| z - c_3 | = \rho_3$ and so on.

Theorem I:

If the power series c_0

$$f(z) = \sum_{n=0}^{\infty} a_n(z-z_0)^n$$

has a non-zero finite radius of convergence, then the complete analytic function corresponding to f(z) has at least one singularity on the circle of convergence c_σ

Proof:

Suppose, if possible, that the complete function F(z) has no singularity on C_0. Then by analytic continuation, we shall be able to find an analytic function $f_1(z)$ which shall be equal to f(z) within C_0 but will be regular in a larger circle C concentric with C_0. Then the expansion of $f_1(z)$ as a Taylor series in powers of $z - z_0$ will converge everywhere within C. But this is impossible; since the series would essentially be the original series whose circle of convergence is C_0. Hence there must be at least one singularity of F(z) on C_0.

Remark:

In the method of analytic continuation by power series explained before the above theorem, continuations of f(z) was possible only when the circle Γ_2 extended beyond Γ_1. This would happen only when there was no singularity of the complete function on the circle Γ_1 where the arc L intersects it.

If there were a singularity on Γ_1 (which is possible by virtue of the above theorem) where L intersects it, then no analytic continuation is possible along the path L.

We then search for a new path in order to carry out the analytic continuation. If no such path is possible, *i.e.* if the original circle Γ_1 is the natural boundary of f(z), then no analytic continuation of f(z) beyond Γ_1 is possible.

Theorem II:

Let ABC and AB'C be two different paths joining the points A and C. If there is no singularity of the function f(z) inside the closed ABCB'A, then the analytic continuations of f(z) along these different paths will give the same, find power series.

Proof:

We first represent f(z) as a power series which we denote by P, whose circle of convergence is Γ with A as centre.

Let A_1 be any point on the arc ABC inside the circle Γ. We now obtain the analytic continuation of f(z) in the form of a power series which we denote by P_1 whose circle of convergence is Γ_1 with A_1 as centre. Then Γ_1 must extend beyond Γ. Let A_2 be any point inside both the circles Γ and Γ_1 and also inside the curve ABCB'A sufficiently near Al. (See the figure 2.10).

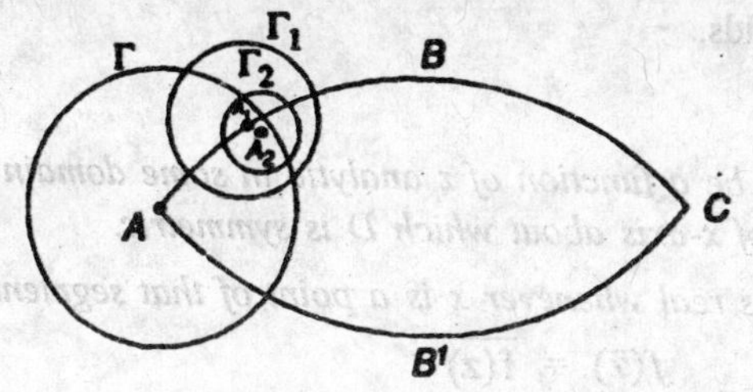

Fig. 2.10

Let P_2 be the power series representation of f'(z) valid inside the circle Γ_2 with A_2 as centres. Since A_2 is very close to A_1, Γ_2 must contain A_1. Then $P_1 = P_2$ over the region shown shaded in the figure since both P_1 and P_2 are equal to P in this region. We r then claim that P_1 is the continuation of P_2. For if Q_1 were the continuation of P_2, then $Q_1 \equiv P_1$ over a domain containing A_1 (Why ?). It follows that the corresponding coefficients of P_1 and Q_1, are the same.

If we repeat this process a sufficient number of times, we can deform the path ABC into the path AB′C provided there is no singularity inside ABCB′A. This means that the analytic continuations of f(z) along the paths ABC and AB′C are the same.

SCHWARZ'S REFLECTION PRINCIPLE

If w = f(z) is a function of z, then it may happen that $\bar{w} = f(\bar{z})$ *i.e.* the reflection of z in the real axis corresponds to one reflection of w in the real axis. For example, if

$$w = f(z) = z^2 + 1$$

then $\quad \bar{w} = \overline{(f(z))} = \overline{(z^2+1)} = \overline{(z^2)} + 1 = \bar{z}^2 + 1$

and $\quad f(\bar{z}) = \bar{z}^2 + 1.$

Hence $\quad \bar{w} = f(\bar{z})$

On the other hand, for the function

$$w = r(z) = z^2 + i, \text{ we have}$$

$$\overline{w} = \overline{(z^2 + i)} = \overline{(z^2)} + \overline{i} = \overline{z}^2 + i$$

and $$f(\overline{z}) = \overline{z}^2 + i,$$

Thus is this case

$$\overline{w} \neq f(\overline{z}).$$

Now following theorem shows under what conditions, the reflection principle holds.

Theorem:

Let f(z) be a function of z analytic in some domain D which contains a segment of x-axis about which D is symmetric.

If f(x) is real whenever x is a point of that segment, then

$$f(\overline{z}) = \overline{f(z)}$$

i.e. f(z) takes conjugate values for conjugate values of z.

Conversely if $f(\overline{z}) = \overline{f(z)}$, *f(x) is real.*

First Proof:

We first observe that since $f(\overline{z}) = f(z)$, the condition $f(\overline{z}) = \overline{f(z)}$ is the same as

$$\overline{f(\overline{z})} = f(z). \qquad \ldots(1)$$

Let the domain D have the segment ABC of the real axis in its interior and let D be symmetrical about ABC. We assume that f(x) is real when x is a point on ABC. We then wish to show that the condition (1) holds. For this purpose we first show that $\overline{f(\overline{z})}$ is analytic throughout D.

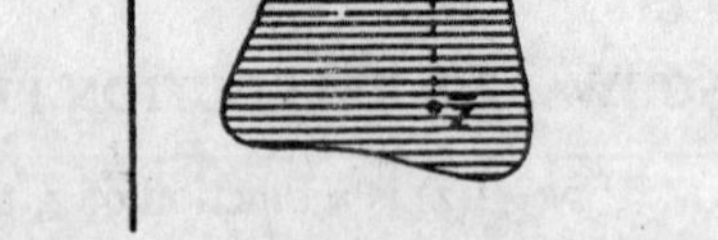

Fig. 2.11

We write

$$F(z) = \overline{f(z)} = U(x, y) + iV(x, y) \qquad \ldots (2)$$

If $$f(z) = u(x, y) + iv(x, y) \qquad \ldots (3)$$

then $$f(z) = u(x, -y) + iv(x, -y) \qquad \ldots (4)$$

and $$\overline{f(z)} = u(x, -y) - iv(x, -y) \qquad \ldots (5)$$

From (2) and (5), we have

$$F(x) = U(x, y) + iv\,(x, y)$$
$$= u\,(x, -y) - iv\,(x, -y) \quad \text{... (6)}$$

Equating real and imaginary parts, we get

$$U\,(x, Y) = u\,(x, \eta),\ V(x, y) = -v\,(x, \eta) \quad \text{... (7)}$$

where $\eta = -y.$

Now $f(x + i\eta)$ is an analytic function of $x + i\eta$ in D so that $u(x, \eta)$, $v(x, \eta)$ and their partial derivatives satisfy the Cauchy-Riemann equations

$$\frac{\partial u}{\partial x} = \frac{\partial v}{\partial \eta}, \frac{\partial u}{\partial \eta} = -\frac{\partial v}{\partial x} \quad \text{...(8)}$$

throughout D. Also from (7) we obtain

$$\left.\begin{aligned} \frac{\partial u}{\partial x} = \frac{\partial u}{\partial x}, \frac{\partial U}{\partial y} = \frac{\partial u}{\partial \eta}.\frac{\partial \eta}{\partial y} = -\frac{\partial u}{\partial \eta} \\ \frac{\partial V}{\partial x} = -\frac{\partial v}{\partial x}, \frac{\partial V}{\partial y} = -\frac{\partial v}{\partial \eta}.\frac{\partial \eta}{\partial y} = \frac{\partial v}{\partial \eta} \end{aligned}\right] \quad \text{...(9)}$$

Then (8) and (9) give

$$\frac{\partial U}{\partial x} = \frac{\partial V}{\partial y} \text{ and } \frac{\partial U}{\partial y} = -\frac{\partial V}{\partial x}$$

and consequently F(z) is analytic in D.

Now by hypothesis, f(x) is real. But by (3),

$$f(x) = u(r, 0) + iv(x, 0).$$

It follows that v (x, 0) = 0 and we get from (6)

$$F(x) = U(x, 0) + iV(x, 0) = u(x, 0) = f(x).$$

In other words, F(z) = f(z) when z is a point on the segment ABC. It then follows from the corollary and the remark (1) of theorem I.

$$F(z) = f(z) \textit{ i.e. } \overline{f(\overline{z})} = f(z)$$

at every point z of D since both the functions are analytic in D. The condition (1) is therefore satisfied.

To prove the converse, let the condition

$$\overline{f(\overline{z})} = f(z)$$

hold. Then from (3) and (6), we have

$$u(x, -y) - iv(x, -y) = u(x, y) + iv(x, y).$$

When this condition is satisfied on the segment ABC, we have $y = 0$ and so

$$u(x, 0) - iv(x, 0) = u(x, 0) + iv(x, 0).$$

Equating imaginary parts, we get

$$-v(x,0) = v(x, 0) \text{ or } v(x, 0) = 0.$$

It follows that $f(x) = u(z, 0)$ and consequently $f(x)$ is real as required.

The proof is now complete.

Second Proof:

Let C be an interior point of D on real segment ABC. Then for sufficiently small values of $| z - c |$, we have

$$f(z) = \sum_{n=0}^{\infty} a_n (z-c)^n$$

All the coefficients a_n are real as shown below.

Since c is real, by hypothesis f(c) is real. But $a_0 = f(c)$ so that ao is real. Now $a_1 = f'(c)$ which can be obtained as the limit of

$$\frac{f(z)-f(c)}{z-c}$$

as $z \to c$ through real values. Since f(z) and f(c) are real, it follows a_1 is also real and so on.

Hence $\bar{a}_n = a_n$ for all n.

Then (1) gives

$$\overline{f(z)} = \overline{\sum_{n=0}^{\infty} a_n (z-c)^n}$$

$$= \sum \bar{a}_n \overline{(z-c)^n}$$

$$= \sum a_n (\bar{z}-c)^n \quad [\because \bar{a}_n = a_n] \quad \text{...(2)}$$

And $$f(\bar{z}) = \sum_{n=0}^{\infty} a_n (\bar{z}-c)^n \quad \text{...(3)}$$

From (1) and (2), we have

$$\overline{f(z)} = f(\bar{z}) \quad \text{... (4)}$$

which holds for all points z inside the circle of convergence of the series (1).

By analytic continuation, the condition (3) must hold for all z in D since the power series about conjugate points will always have conjugate co-efficients.

Example 1:

Show that the function

$f_1(z) = 1 + z + z^2 + z^3 + ...$

can be obtained outside the circle of convergence of the power series.

Solution:

We have $f_1(z) = 1 + z + z^2 + z^3 + ...$ ...(1)

The given series is convergent and defines a function f(z) which is regular only in the open disc $|z| < 1$. But the sum of the series $\frac{1}{1-z}$ is a regular function throughout the whole complex plane except at the point $z = 1$ and consequently, the analytic continuation of $f_1(z)$ is possible.

For this purpose, we take a point c_2 inside the circle Γ_1 defined by $|z| = 1$ such that c_2 does not lie on the line segment joining the points $z = 0$ and $z = 1$.

Then we construct a circle Γ_2 with c_2 as centre and radius ρ_2 equal to the distance of c_2 from the point $z = 1$. This new circle Γ_2 will clearly extend beyond Γ_1.

We now reconstruct the series (1) in powers of $z - c_2$ in the form

$$\sum_{n=0}^{\infty} \frac{(z-c_2)^n}{(1-c_2)^{n+1}} \quad ...(2)$$

This new series has the circle of convergence Γ_2 defined by

$|z - c_2| = |1 - c_2|$.

The sum of the series

$$= \frac{1}{1-c_2}\left[1-\frac{z-c_2}{1-c_2}\right]^{-1} = \frac{1}{1-z}$$

Thus the power series (1) and (2) represent the same function in $\frac{1}{1-z}$ the regions common to the interiors of the circles $|z| = 1$ and $|z - c_2| = |1 - c_2|$. It follows that they are analytic continuations of each other. We now obtain analytic continuation of the function represented by the series (2), and so on.

For example, if we take $c_2 \frac{i}{2}$, then the distance of the point c_2 from $z = 1$ is $\sqrt{\left(\frac{1}{4}+1\right)} = \frac{\sqrt{5}}{2}$. Therefore if we draw a circle with $\frac{i}{2}$ as centre and radius $\frac{\sqrt{5}}{2}$, this circle will extend beyond $|z| = 1$ and will not contain the singularity $z = 1$ in its interior.

In this case the new series is

$$\sum_{n=0}^{\infty}\frac{\left(z-\frac{i}{2}\right)^n}{\left(1-\frac{i}{2}\right)^n}$$

which converges within the

$$\left|z-\frac{i}{2}\right|=\frac{\sqrt{5}}{2}.$$

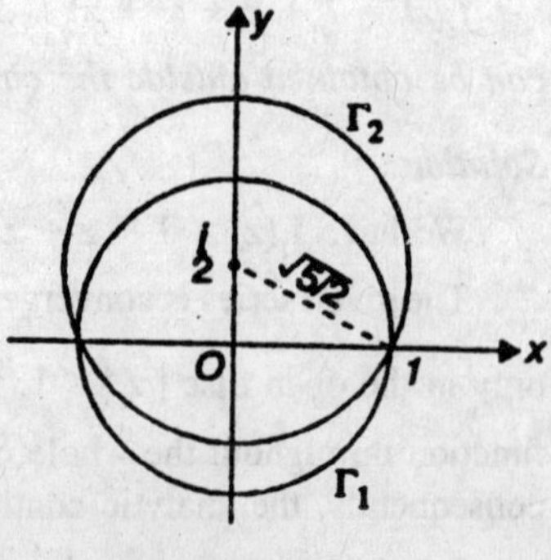

Fig. 2.12

Thus $\sum_{n=0}^{\infty}\frac{\left(z-\frac{i}{2}\right)^n}{\left(1-\frac{i}{2}\right)^{n+1}}$ represents an analytic continuation of $\sum_{n=0}^{\infty} z^n$.

Example 2:

Show that the series

(i) $\sum_{n=0}^{\infty}\frac{z^n}{2^{n+1}}$ *and (ii)* $\sum_{n=1}^{\infty}\frac{(z-1)^n}{2-i^{n+1}}$

are analytic continuations of each other.

Solution:

The series $\sum_{n=0}^{\infty}\frac{z^n}{2^{n+1}}$ converges for all values of z within the circle Γ_2 defined by $|z| = 2$ and has the sum

$$\frac{1/2}{1-z/2}=\frac{1}{2-z}$$

The series $\sum_{n=0}^{\infty}\frac{(z-1)^n}{(2-i)^{n+1}}$ converges for all values of z within the circle Γ_2 defined by

$$|z-i| = |2-i| = \sqrt{5}$$

and has the sum

$$\frac{1/(2-i)}{1-(z-i)/(2-i)}=\frac{1}{2-z}$$

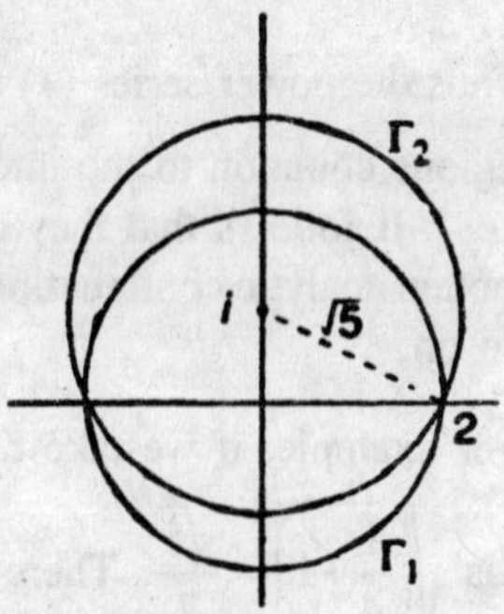

Fig. 2.13

Thus the two power series represent the same function in the regions common to the interiors of the circles

$|z| = 2$ and $|z - i| = \sqrt{5}$.

Hence they represent analytic continuations of each other.

Example 3:

Show that the function

$$f(z) = \frac{1}{a} + \frac{z}{a^2} + \frac{z^2}{a^2} + \frac{z^3}{a^4} + \ldots$$

can be continued analytically.

Solution:

We have

$$f(z) = \frac{1}{a} + \frac{z}{a^2} + \frac{z^2}{a^2} + \frac{z^3}{a^4} + \ldots$$

The series (1) converges within the circle Γ defined by $|z| = |a|$ and has the sum

$$f(z) = \frac{1/a}{1 - z/a} = \frac{1}{a - z} \qquad \ldots(1)$$

The only singularity of f(z) on F is at z = a. Hence the analytic continuation of f(z) beyond Γ is possible. For this purpose we take a point b not lying on the line segment joining z = 0 and z = a. Then we construct a circle Γ_1 with b as centre and radius equal to $|a - b|$. This new circle Γ_1 clearly extends beyond Γ_1 (see the figure 2.14). We now reconstruct the series (1) in powers of z – b in the form

$$\sum_{n=0}^{\infty} \frac{(z-b)^n}{(a-b)^{n+1}} \qquad \ldots(2)$$

This new series has the circle of convergence Γ_1 defined by $|z - b| = |a - b|$.

The sum of the series is

$$\frac{1/(a-b)}{1-(z-b)/(a-b)} = \frac{1}{a-z}$$

Thus the power series (1) and (2) represent the same function in the region common to interior of the circles

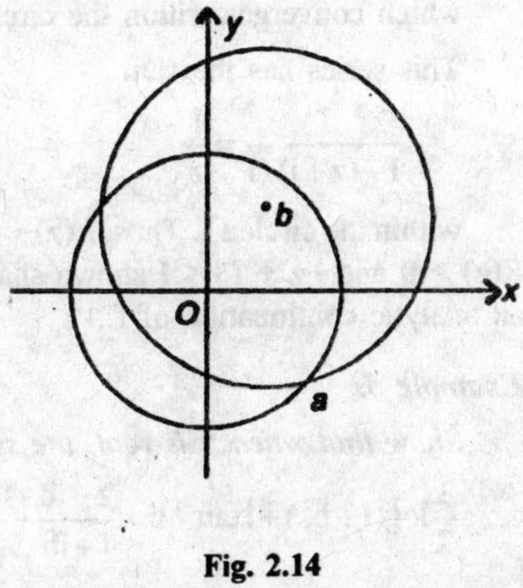

Fig. 2.14

$| z | = | a |$ and

$| z - b | = | a - b |$.

Hence the series (1) represent an analytic continuation of (1).

Example 4:

Show that the function

$$f_1(z) = \int_0^\infty e^{-zt} dt$$

can be continued analytically.

Solution:

We have

$$f_1(z) = \int_0^\infty e^{-z^t} dt = \left[-\frac{1}{z} e^{-z^t} \right] = \frac{1}{z}$$

provided R (z) = 0.

Thus, f_1 is defined only in the domain R(z) > 0. We denote this domain by Γ_1. The only singularity of $f_1(z)$ in the whole complex plane is at z =. 0.

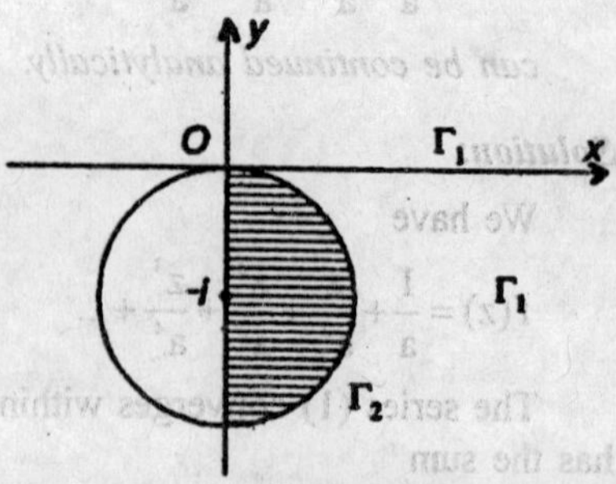

Fig. 2.15

Thus, in order to perform analytic continuation, we shall avoid this singularity. We use the method of power series again.

For example, we represent $f_2(z)$ by the power series

$$f_2(z) = \sum_{n=0}^{\infty} \frac{(z+i)^n}{i^{n-1}}$$

which converges within the circle Γ_2 represented by $| z + i | = 1$.

This series has the sum

$$\frac{1}{1-(z+i)/i} = \frac{1}{z}$$

within the circle Γ_2. Thus, $f_1(z) + f_2(z)$ in the part common to the domains R(z) > 0 and $| z + i | < I$ shown shaded in the figure. Hence f_2 represents an analytic continuation of f_1.

Example 5:

Show that when b is real, the series

$$\frac{1}{2}\log(1+b^2) + i\tan^{-1} b + \frac{z-ib}{1+ib} - \frac{1}{2}\frac{(z-ib)^2}{(1+ib)^2} + \ldots$$

is analytic continuation of the function defined by the sense

$$z-\frac{1}{2}z^2+\frac{1}{3}z^3-...$$

Solution:

The series $z-\frac{1}{2}z^2+\frac{1}{3}z^3-...$

converges within the circle | z | = 1 and has the sum log (1 + z). Its only singularity is at the point z = –1. Again the series

$$\frac{1}{2}\log(1+b^2)+i\tan^{-1}b+\frac{z-ib}{1+ib}+\frac{1}{2}\left(\frac{z-ib}{1-ib}\right)^2+...$$

converges within the circle

$| z - ib | = | 1 + ib | = \sqrt{(1 + b^2)}$

and has the sum

$$\frac{1}{2}\log(1+b^2)+i\tan^{-1}b+\left(1-\frac{z-ib}{1+ib}\right)$$

$$=\frac{1}{2}\log(1+b^2)+i\tan^{-1}b\log\frac{1+z}{1+ib}$$

$$=\frac{1}{2}\log(1+b^2)+i\tan^{-1}b\log(1+z)-\log(1+ib)$$

$$=\frac{1}{2}\log(1+b^2)+i\tan^{-1}b+\log(1+z)-\frac{1}{2}\log(1+b^2)-i\tan^{-1}b$$

= log (1 + z).

Fig. 2.16

Thus, the two series represent the same function in the region common to the interiors of the circles

$$| z | = 1$$

and $\quad | z - ib | = | 1 + ib |$

Hence they represent analytic continuation of each other.

Example 6:

Show that the power series

$$z-\frac{1}{2}z^2+\frac{1}{3}z^3-...$$

may analytically he continued to a wider region by means of the series

$$\log 2-\frac{1-z}{z}-\frac{(1-z)^2}{2.2^2}-\frac{(1-z)^3}{2.2^3}-...$$

Solution:

As in the previous example, the first series converges within the circle $|z| = 1$ and has the sum $\log(1 + z)$. And the second series converges within the circle $\log|z - 1| = 2$ and has the sum

$$\log 2 + \log\left(1 - \frac{1-z}{2}\right)$$

$$= \log 2 + \log\frac{1+z}{2} = \log 2 + \log(1 + z) - \log 2$$

$$= \log(1 + z).$$

Thus, the two series represent the same function in the region common to the circles

$$|z| = 1$$

and $\quad |z - 1| = 2.$

Hence the second series is an analytic continuation of the first series to the circle $|z - 1| = 2$ which evidently extends beyond the circle $|z| = 1$ (see the Figure 2.17).

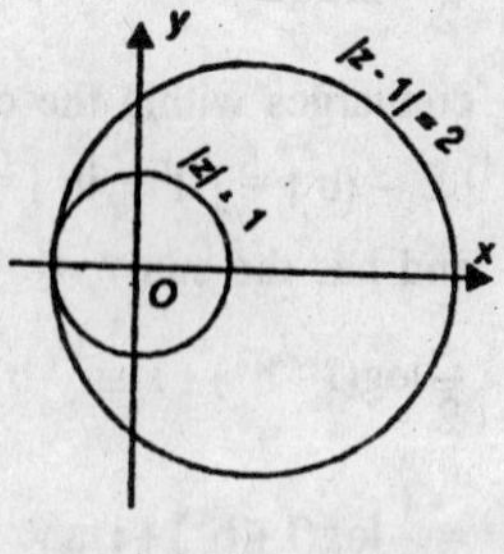

Fig. 2.17

Example 7:

Show that the circle of convergence of the power series

$$f(z) = 1 + z + z^2 + z^4 + z^8$$

is a Natural boundary.

Solution:

The circle of convergence Γ of the power series is

$$|z| = 1.$$

We shall show that every arc Γ, however small contains a singularity of f(z). Now any point on Γ is of the form $e^{i\alpha}$ where

$$0 \le \alpha \le 2\pi.$$

It will now be shown that the point of the form $e^{2\pi pi/2q}$ where p and q are integers is a singularity of f(z). For this purpose, we consider the behaviour of f(z) as z moves upto Γ along the radius through the point $e^{2\pi pi/2q}$. We write the given series in the form

$$f(z) = 1 + z + z^2 + ... + z^{2q} + \sum_{n=q+1}^{\infty} z^{2n}$$

$$f(z) = f_1(z) + f_2(z), \text{ say}$$

Since $f_1(re^{2\pi pi/2q})$ is a polynomial in r of degree 2^q, it tends to a unique limit as $v \to 1$. On the other hand,

$$f_2(re^{2\pi pi/2q}) = \sum_{n=q+1}^{\infty} r^{2^n} \exp\left(\frac{2\pi pi}{2^q}.2^n\right)$$

$$= \sum_{n=q+1}^{\infty} r^{2^n} \exp(2^{1+n-q}.p\pi i)$$

$$= \sum_{n=q+1}^{\infty} r^{2^n}$$

[$\because$ $n > q$, 2^{1+n-q}. p is an even integer so that $\exp(2^{1+n-q}.p\pi i) = 1$]

But the series $\sum_{n=q+1}^{\infty} r^{2^n}$ diverges to ∞ as $r \to 1$. Thus the point $e^{2\pi pi/2^q}$ is a singularity of f(z).

But any arc of Γ, however small, contains a point of the form $e^{2\pi pi/2^q}$ where p and q are integers. Thus the singularities of f(z) are everywhere dense on Γ and consequently Γ constitutes the natural boundary of the given power series.

Example 8:

Show that the unit circle $|z| = 1$ is the natural boundary of the power series

$$f(z) = \sum_{n=0}^{\infty} z^{n!}$$

Solution:

Evidently the function f(z) is analytic within the unit circle $|z| = 1$. Let $z = re^{2\pi pi/q}$ where p and q arc integers and consider the behaviour of f(z) as $r \to 1$ through the real values. We have

$$f(z) = \sum_{n=0}^{\infty} z^{n!} + \sum_{n=q+1}^{\infty} z^{n!}$$

$$= f_1(z) + f_2(z), \text{ say.}$$

Since $f_1(z)$ is a polynomial and therefore tends to a finite limit as $r \to 1$. When $n > q$, q is a divisor of n ! so that

$$z^{n!} = r^{n!}.\exp\left(\frac{2\pi pi}{q}.n!\right) = r^{n!}.$$

Hence, $f_2(z) = \sum_{n=q+1}^{\infty} z^{n!}$ which tends to unity as $r \to 1$. Now proceed as in the preceding example.

Example 9:

The power series

$$z+\frac{1}{2}z^2+\frac{1}{3}z^3+\ldots \text{ and } i\pi-(z-2)+\frac{1}{2}(z-2)^2-\ldots$$

have no comment region of convergence. Prove that they are nevertheless analytic continuations of the same function.

Solution:

The first series defines the function $-\log(1-z)$ with $|z|=1$ as its circle of convergence. The only singularity is at $z = 1$.

The second series defines the function $i\pi - \log[1+(z-2)]$ and has $|z-2| = 1$ for its circle of convergence which touches the circle $|z| = 1$ at $z = 1$ externally as the reader can easily see. This function too has only singularity at $z = 1$. Now

$$i\pi - \log[1+(z-2)] = i\pi - \log(z-1) = i\pi - \log(-1) - \log(1-z)$$
$$= i\pi - i\pi - \log(1-z) = -\log(1-z).$$

Hence the two power series represent the same function $-\log(1-z)$ analytic respectively in the domain $|z| < 1$ and $|z-2| < 1$ which have no region in common. Thus, these series are analytic continuations of the same function although they have no common region of convergence.

Example 10:

The functions defined in the series

$$1+az+a^2z^2+\ldots \text{ and } \frac{1}{1-z}+\frac{(1-a)z}{(1-z)^2}+\frac{(1-a)^2z^2}{(1-z)^3}-\ldots$$

are anahotic continuations of each other.

Solution:

The power series

$1 + az + a^2z^2 + \ldots$

represents the function $\frac{1}{1-az}$ with $|z| = \frac{1}{|a|}$ as its circle of convergence.

The only singularity is at $z = \frac{1}{a}$, $(a > 0)$. Again the series

$$\frac{1}{1-z}+\frac{(1-a)z}{(1-z)^2}+\frac{(1-a)^2z^2}{(1-z)^3}-\ldots \quad \ldots(2)$$

represents the function

$$\frac{1}{(1-z)}\frac{1}{z+(1-a)z/(1-z)}=\frac{1}{1-az}$$

provided $\left|\dfrac{(1-a)z}{(1-z)}\right| < 1$. Now if a is real, then $\left|\dfrac{(1-a)z}{(1-z)}\right| = 1$ gives

$(1-z)(1-\bar{z}) = (1-a)^2 z\bar{z}$, that is

$$1-(z+\bar{z})+z\bar{z} = (1-a)^2 z\bar{z}$$

$$\text{or } a(2-a)z\bar{z}-(z+\bar{z})+1=0$$

Since $z\bar{z} = x^2+y^2$ and $z+\bar{z} = 2x$, this reduces to

$$x^2+y^2-\frac{2x}{a(2-a)}+\frac{1}{a(2-a)}=0$$

$$\text{or}\left(x-\frac{1}{a(2-a)}\right)^2+y^2=\left(\frac{1-a}{a(2-a)}\right)^2 \quad ...(3)$$

which is a circle with centre $\left(\dfrac{1}{a(2-a)}, 0\right)$ and radius $\dfrac{1-a}{a(2-a)}$.

Hence the second series has (3) as its circle of convergence.

We shall assume that $a > 0$. Now there arise the following cases.

Case I:

Let $0 < a < 1$. In this case, the circle (3) touches the circle $|z| = \dfrac{1}{a}$ internally since the distance between their centres is equal to the difference of their radii as the reader can easily verily (see Fig. 2.18). Here the function has not been continued outside the circle $|z| = \dfrac{1}{a}$ although, this circle is not a natural boundary.

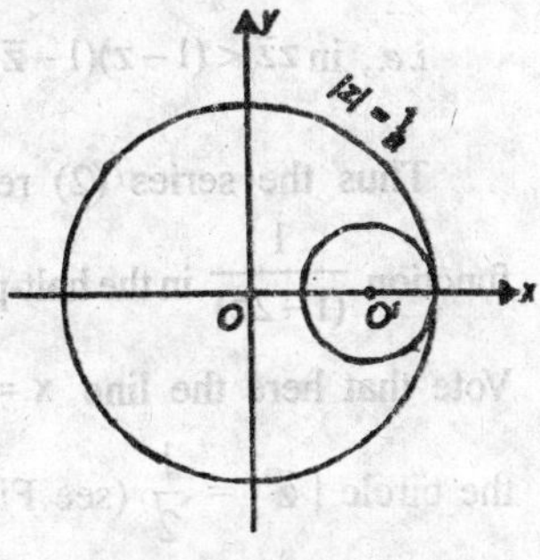

Fig. 2.18

Case II:

Let $1 < a < 2$. In this case the two circles touch externally at $z = \dfrac{1}{a}$ as shown in Fig. 2.19, so that the two series have no common region of convergence. Nevertheless they are analytic continuations of the same function

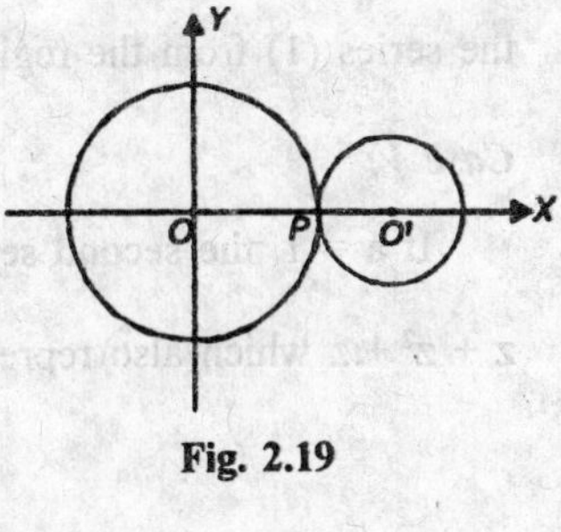

Fig. 2.19

$$\frac{1}{(1-az)}$$

Case III:

Let $a > 2$. In this case, the circle $|z| = \frac{1}{a}$ touches the circle (3) internally as shown in the figure. Hence the second series represents an analytic continuation of the first series to the region which is interior to the circle (3) and has the region $|z| < \frac{1}{a}$ as a common part and also extends beyond it as shown in Fig. 2.20.

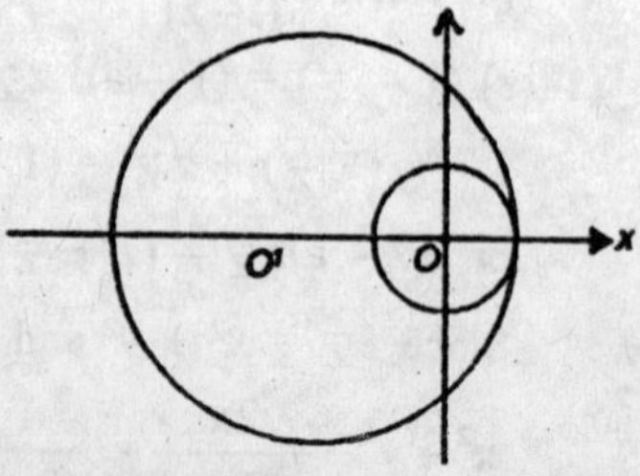

Fig. 2.20

Case IV:

Let $a = 2$. Here the series (1) represents the function $\frac{1}{(1-2z)}$ within the circle $|z| = \frac{1}{2}$. The series (2) defines the same function $\frac{1}{(1-2z)}$ in the region $\left|\frac{1}{1-z}\right| < 1$

i.e., in $z\bar{z} < (1-z)(1-\bar{z})$ or $x < \frac{1}{2}$

Thus the series (2) represents the function $\frac{1}{(1-2z)}$ in the halt-plane $x < \frac{1}{2}$. Vote that here the line $x = \frac{1}{2}$ touches the circle $|z| = \frac{1}{2}$ (see Fig. 2.21).

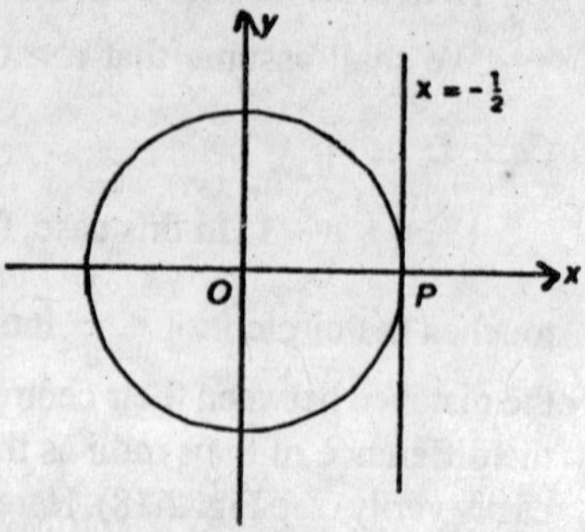

Fig. 2.21

Hence in this case the series (2) represents an analytic continuation of the series (1) from the region $|z| < \frac{1}{2}$ to the half-plant $x < \frac{1}{2}$.

Case V:

If $a = 1$, the second series reduces to $\frac{1}{1-z}$ and the first series is $1 + z + z^2 + \ldots$ which also represents the function $\frac{1}{(1-z)}$.

EXERCISES

1. Discuss the nature of singularities of the following functions and also calculate the residues at the singularities.

(i) $\tan z$ (ii) $\dfrac{1}{z(1-z^2)}$ (iii) $\dfrac{z}{1+z^4}$ (iv) $\dfrac{\sin z}{(z-\pi)^2}$

Ans. (i) Each point $(2n+1)\dfrac{\pi}{2}$ is a pole of order 1 with residue -1 where n is any integer.

(ii) The points 0, 1, −1, are three simple poles with residues 1, $-\dfrac{1}{2}, -\dfrac{1}{3}$ respectively.

(iii) $e^{\pi i/4}, e^{-\pi i/4}, e^{(3\pi i)/4}, e^{(-3\pi i)/4}$ are simple poles with residues $-\dfrac{i}{4}, \dfrac{i}{4}, \dfrac{i}{4}$ and $-\dfrac{i}{4}$ respectively.

(iv) π is a simple pole with residue −1.

2. Find the zeros and discuss the nature of the singularities of

$$f(z) = \frac{z-2}{z^2} \sin \frac{1}{z-1}$$

Also calculate the residue at the poles.

Ans. 2, $1 + \dfrac{1}{n\pi}$ are zeros; 0 is a pole of order 2 and 1 is an essential singularity. The residue at z = 0 is 2 cos 1 −sin 1.

3. If f(z) is an analytic function regular for $|z| \le R$ and $|f(z)| = M$ for $|z| = R$ and f(z) have a zero of order p at z = 0, then prove that

$$|f(re^{i\theta})| \le \frac{Mr^p}{R^p}. 0 \le r \le R.$$

4. Show that the polynomial

$z^5 + z^3 + 2z + 3$

has just one zero in the first quadrant of the complex plane.

5. Show that the equation

$z^4 + 4(1+i)z + 1 = 0$

has one root in each quadrant

6. If $f(z) = \sum\limits_{n=0}^{\infty} z^{2n}$, show that

$f(z) = z + f(z^2)$

and deduce from this that

z = 1 is a natural boundary of this function.

7. Show that $\sum_{n=0}^{\infty} z^{2n}$ can be continued analytically beyond the unit circle.

8. If t a real number the series $\sum_{n=1}^{\infty} \frac{1}{2^n[z-\exp(2int\pi)]}$ represents two different analytic functions, one inside the unit circle and one outside it, the unit circle being a natural boundary of each. If t is rational, the series represents a single rational function.

9. By considering the Laurent expansions of $\frac{1}{1-z^2}$ about the points $z = \pm 1$, show how the function

$$f(z) = \frac{1}{4}\left[\sum_{n=0}^{\infty} \frac{(1-z)^2}{2^n} + \frac{2}{1-z}\right],\ 0 < |1-z| < 2$$

may be continued into the region $0 < |1 + z| < 2$.

[**Hint.**: By partial fractions, we obtain

$$\frac{1}{1-z^2} = \frac{1}{2}\left(\frac{1}{1-z} + \frac{1}{1+z}\right)$$

$$= \frac{1}{4}\left(\sum_{n=0}^{\infty} \frac{(1-z)^2}{2^n} + \frac{2}{1-z}\right),\ 0 < |1-z| < 2$$

$$= \frac{1}{2}\left(\sum_{n=0}^{\infty} \frac{(1+z)^n}{2^n} + \frac{2}{1-z}\right),\ 0 < |1+z| < 2$$

where the restrictions arise from the requirements that the geometric series converges. Evidently the regions $0 < |1 - z| < 2$ and $0 < |1 + z| < 2$ overlap (draw the figure). In this common region the function

$$g(z) = \frac{1}{4}\left(\sum_{n=0}^{\infty} \frac{(1+z)^n}{2^n} + \frac{2}{1-z}\right)$$

is equal to the given function f(z) since both are equal to $\frac{1}{1-z^2}$.

Hence g (z) can be regarded as the continuation of f(z) into the region $0 < |+z| < 2$. Evidently the function $1/(1-z^2)$ can be used to continue either f(z) or g(z) into the whole complex plane apart from the points $z = \pm 1$].

10. State and prove Liouville's theorem and deduce fundamental theorem of Algebra.

3

UNIFORM CONVERGENCE OF SERIES

UNIFORM CONVERGENCE OF A SEQUENCE

Let $S_1(z)$, $S_2(z)$, $S_3(z)$,... be a sequence of one valued functions, each defined in a bounded closed domain D. The sequence of functions $< S_n(z) >$ is said to be convergent at a point z_0 of D_1 if the sequence of complex numbers $S_1(z_0)$, $S_2(z_0)$... tends to a definite finite limit. If the sequence converges at each point of D, it is said to be *point-wise* convergent in D, and the *limit function* S(z) of the sequence is defined at each point of D by the equation

$$S(z) = \lim_{n \to \infty} S_n(z).$$

In other words, if z_0 is any given point of D, for a given e, however small, we can find an integer m such that

$$| S(z_0) - S_n(z_0) | < \varepsilon,$$

for every value of $n \geq m$.

The integer m in general depends on e as well as z_0 so that we may write $m = m(\varepsilon, z_0)$. Thus to each point z of the domain D, and fixed ε, there corresponds a value of $m(\varepsilon, z)$. The aggregate of the values of $m(\varepsilon, z)$ may or may not have an upper bound. If this aggregate has an upper bound, say M, then for every value of z in D, we have for $n \geq M$

$$| S(z) - S_n(z) | < \varepsilon,$$

In such a case we say that sequence $< S_n(z) >$ converges uniformly to S (z) in D.

Definition:

A sequence $< S_n(z) >$ is said to converge uniformly to a function S(z) in D, if for a given e, however small, but positive, there can be found a positive integer m independent of z, such that for $n \geq m$ and for every z in D, we have

$$| S_w(z) - S_n(z) | < \varepsilon$$

It should be noted carefully that the convergence of a sequence < S_n (z) > at every point of D does not necessarily ensure its uniform convergence in D. A sequence may be convergent at every point to an open domain and yet may not be uniformly convergent in that domain.

In other words, a sequence of function $S_n(z)$ is said to converge uniformly in two domain D to the limiting function S(z) if given a positive small number $\in$ we can find a positive integer M($\in$) depending an $\in$ alone, such that for $n \geq m$ the in equality

$|S_n(z) - S(z)| < \in$ holds at each point Z of the domain D.

GENERAL PRINCIPLE OF UNIFORM CONVERGENCE

The definition of uniform convergence of a sequence given in presupposes the knowledge of the limit function of the sequence. It is, however, desirable to express the condition for uniform convergence in a form which is independent of the limit function. This is proved by the following principle of uniform convergence.

Theorem:

The necessary and sufficient condition for the uniform convergence of the sequence $S_1(z)$, $S_2(z)$, $S_3(z)$,... in the bounded closed domain D is that, corresponding to any positive number ε, however small there should exist an integer n_0 independent of z and depending on ε-alone, such that

$$| S_m(z) - S_n(z) | < \varepsilon$$

for all m, $n \geq n_0$ and, all z in D.

UNIFORM CONVERGENCE OF SERIES

The series Σu_n (z) is said to converge uniformly in the bounded closed domain D, if the sequence < $S_n(z)$ > where

$$S_n(z) = u_1(z) + u_2(z) + ... + u_n(z),$$

converges uniformly.

Principle of Uniform Convergence of a Series

Theorem:

The necessary and sufficient condition for uniform convergence of the series $\Sigma u_n(z)$ in the bounded closed domain D is that to every positive number ε, however small, there corresponds a positive integer m, independent of z, such that for every n S m, and every z in D, we have

$$| u_{n+1} (z) + u_{n+2}(z) +...+u_{n+p}(z) | < \varepsilon$$

where p may have any positive integral value.

Proof:

The proof is the same as that of the theorem of we replace the series $\Sigma u_n(z)$ by the sequence $< S_n(z) >$ where

$$S_n(z) = u_1(z) + u_2(z) +...+ u_n(z).$$

Below we give some important tests for uniform convergence of a series.

HARDY'S TESTS FOR UNIFORM CONVERGENCE

We first prove the following lemma.

Lemma:

If in a bounded closed domain D, the function $u_n(z)\ v_n(z)$ tends uniformly to a finite limit as $n \to \infty$ then if one of the series,

$$u_0(z)\ v_0(z) + \sum_1^{\infty} \{u_n (z)-u_{n-1}(z)\} v_n (z)$$

and

$$\sum_0^{\infty} u_n (z)\{v_n (z)-v_{n+1}(z)\}$$

converges uniformly in D, so also does the other.

Proof:

We have the identity

$$u_0(z)\ v_0(z) + \sum_1^{n} \{u_r (z)-v_{r-1}(z)\} v_r (z)$$

$$-\sum_0^{n-1} u_r(z) - v_r(z)\ \{v_{r+1}(z)\} = u_n v_n .$$

Proceeding to the limit as $n \to \infty$, we see that

$$u_0(z)v_0(z) + \lim_{n\to\infty} \sum_1^{n} \{u_r (z) - u_{r-1}(z)\} v_r(z)$$

$$- \lim_{n\to\infty} \sum_0^{n-1} u_r(z)\{v_r(z) - v_{r+1}(z)\}$$

$$= \lim_{n\to\infty} u_n v_n = \text{a finite quantity}$$

Hence if one of the series tends to a finite limit, so does the other. In other words, if one of the series is convergent, so is the other.

Theorem I:

If in a bounded closed domain D :

(i) the series $\Sigma u_n(z)$ has uniformly bounded partial sums,

(ii) the series $\Sigma\{v_n(z) - v_{n+1}(z)\}$ is uniformly and absolutely convergent, and

(iii) $v_n(z)$ tends to zero uniformly as $n \to \infty$, then the series $\Sigma\{u_n(z) - v_n(z)\}$ converges uniformly in D.

Proof:

Let $S_n(z) = u_0(z) + u_1(z) + ... + u_n(z)$. Then from condition (i), it follows that $| S_n(z) | < K$, a finite constant, for all n and all z in D. We then have

$$| S_n(z) v_n(z) | < K | v_n (z) |. \quad ...(1)$$

Using condition (iii), we see from (A) that $S_n(z) v_n(z)$ tends uniformly to zero as $n \to \infty$.

Hence, by the lemma, $\Sigma\{S_n(z) - S_{n-1}(z)\}v_n(z)$, *i.e.*

$\Sigma u_n(z) v_n(z)$ converges in D if $\Sigma S_n(z) \{v_n(z) - v_{n+1}(z)\}$ does.

Now from (ii) it follows that, for a given ε, we can find an integer m, independent of z, such that

$$\sum_{n+1}^{n+p} |v_r(z) - v_{r+1}(z)| v \frac{\varepsilon}{K}$$

for every positive integer p and for all z in D. Hence

$$\left| \sum_{n+1}^{n+p} |S_r(z)\{v_r(z) - v_{r+1}(z)\}| \right|$$

$$\leq \sum_{n+1}^{n+p} |S_r(z)||v_r(z) - v_{r+1}(z)| < K \sum_{r+1}^{n+p} |v_r(z) - v_{r+1}(z)| < \varepsilon.$$

It follows that $\Sigma S_n(z)\{v_n(z) - v_{n+1}(z)\}$ converges uniformly in D.

Hence the result.

Theorem II:

If in a bounded closed domain D

(i) the series $\Sigma u_n(z)$ converges uniformly,

(ii) the serves $\Sigma\{v_n(z) - v_{n+1}(z)\}$ is absolutely convergent and has a bounded sum and

(iii) $v_0(z)$ is bounded, then the series $\Sigma u_n(z)\, v_n(z)$ converges uniformly in D.

Proof:

Let $R_n(z) = U_{n+1}(z) + U_{n+2}(z) + u_{n+3}(z) + ...$

Then from condition (i), $R_n(z)$ tends to zero uniformly as $n \to \infty$. Again from (ii) and (iii), if follows that

$$\sum_0^{\infty} |v_n(z) - v_{n+1}(z)| < K_1 \text{ and } |v_0(z)| < K_2.$$

where K_1 and K_2 are finite positive constants.

$$\text{Hence } |v_n(z)| = \left| v_n(z) - \sum_0^{n-1} \{v_r(z) - v_{r+1}(z)\} \right|$$

$$\leq |v_0(z)| + \sum_0^{\infty} |v_r(z) - v_{r+1}(z)\}$$

$$< K_1 + K_2 < K, \qquad \text{...(1)}$$

where K is finite constant.

We then have $| R_n(z)\, v_n(z) | < K\, | R_n(z) |$

Since $R_n(z)$ tends to zero uniformly as $n \to \infty$, it follows from (2) that $R_n(z)\, V_n(z)$ tends to 0 uniformly in D. Hence

$$u_0(z)\, v_0(z) + \sum_1^{\infty} u_n(z)\, v_n(z) \equiv u_0(z)\, v_0(z) - \sum_1^{\infty} \{R_n(z) - R_{n-1}(z)\} v_n(z)$$

converges uniformly in D, provided

$$\Sigma\, R_n(z)\, [v_n(z) - v_{n+1}(z)] \text{ does so.}$$

Since $R_n(z)$ tends to zero uniformly, for a given ε, we can find an integer m, independent of z such that

$$| R_n(z) | < \varepsilon/K, \qquad \text{...(3)}$$

for all n > m and for all z in D.

$$\therefore \left| \sum_{n+1}^{n+p} R_r(z) [v_r(z) - v_{r+1}(z)] \right| \leq \frac{\varepsilon}{K} \sum_{n+1}^{n+p} |v_r(z) - v_{r+1}(z)| \text{ from (3)}$$

$$< \frac{\varepsilon}{K} \sum_1^{\infty} |v_r(z) - v_{r+1}(z)| < \varepsilon \text{ from (1)}$$

for all z in D and for every positive integer p. It follows that

$$\Sigma\, R_n(z)\, [v_n(z) + v_{n+1}(z)]$$

converges uniformly in D and the result follows.

CONTINUITY OF THE SUM FUNCTION OF A SERIES

Theorem:

If each term of the infinite series $\sum_1^{\infty} u_n(z)$ *be continuous in a bounded closed domain D, and if the series converges uniformly in D, then the sum function S(z) of the series is also continuous in D.*

Proof:

Given that series $\Sigma\, u_n(z)$ is uniformly convergent in D.

We have to show that the sum function $S(z) = \sum_0^{\infty} u_n(z)$ is continuous in D. Let $S_n(z) = u_1(z) + u_2(z) + ... + u_n(z)$.

Then since the series is uniformly convergent in D, we can, for a given ε, find an integer m independent of z, such that

$$| S_n(z) - S(z) | < 1/3\varepsilon,$$

for every $n \geq m$ and every z in D.

In particular, this gives

$$| S_m(z) - S(z) | < 1/3\varepsilon \text{ for every z in D}$$

and

$$| S_m(z_0) - S(z_0) | \leq 1/3\ \varepsilon$$

where z_0 is any point of D.

Now $S_m(z)$ is the sum of finite number m of continuous functions and so it is itself continuous. Hence there exists a positive number δ such that

$$| S_m(z) - S_m(z_0) < 1/3\ \varepsilon \qquad ...(3)$$

for all values of z for which $| z - z_0 | < \delta$ where z is a point of D. From (1), (2) and (3), we see that

$$| S(z) - S\ (z_0) | = | S(z) - S_m(z) + S_m(z) - S_m(z_0) - S_m(z_0) - S(z_0)|$$

$$\leq | S(z) - S_m(z) | + |S_m(z) - S_m(z_0) | + | S_m\ (z_0) - S(z_0) |$$

Hence S (z) is continuous at any point z_0 and is therefore continuous in D.

Continuity of the limit function of a sequence : The above theorem can be stated in the following form also.

If {Sn (z)} is a uniformly .convergent sequence of functions continuous and bounded in a domain D, then the limit function S(z) of the sequence is also continuous in D.

TERM BY TERM INTEGRATION

Theorem:

If (i) the series $\Sigma u_n(z)$ converges uniformly in a closed bounded domain D,

(ii) each $u_n(z)$ is continuous in the closed domain D, then the sum function S(z) of the series is integrable along Γ, a contour of length l lying in D,

$$\text{and } \int_\Gamma \left[\sum_0^\infty u_n(z)\right] dz = \sum_0^\infty \int_\Gamma u_n(z)\, dz$$

i.e., the integral of the sum is equal to the sum of the integrals.

Proof:

Using the notation of we have to show that

$$\int_\Gamma S(z)\, dz = \lim_{n\to\infty} \int_\Gamma S_n(z)\, dz$$

The function S (z) has been shown to be continuous in D in and so is certainly integrated along Γ. Since the series is uniformly convergent in D. We can, for a given ε, find a positive integer m, independent of z, such that for n ≥. m and for every z in D we have

$$| S(z) - S_n(z) | < \varepsilon/l.$$

For such values of a, we have

$$\left|\int_\Gamma \{S(z) - S_n(z)\} dz\right| \le \int_\Gamma |S(z) - S_n(z)| dz < \int_\Gamma \frac{\varepsilon}{l} dz = l \,.\frac{\varepsilon}{l} = \varepsilon.$$

Hence $\int_\Gamma \{S(z) - S_n(z)\} dz \to 0$ as $n \to \infty$

i.e. $\int_\Gamma S(z)\, dz = \lim_{n\to\infty} \int_\Gamma S_n(z)\, dz$

i.e. $\int_\Gamma \sum_0^\infty u_n(z)\, dz = \sum_0^\infty u_n(z)\, dz.$

The theorem is therefore established.

ANALYTICITY OF THE SUM FUNCTION OF A SERIES, TERM BY TERM DIFFERENTIATION

Weierstrass's Theorem :

If (i) the series $\Sigma u_n(z)$ is uniformly convergent on every closed and bounded (i.e. compact) subset of a domain D.

(i) Each u_n (z) is an analytic junction in D, then

(ii) The sum junction S(z) of the series is analytic in D,

(iii) The term by term differentiation is justified.

i.e. $S'(z) = \Sigma u_n'(z)$ *for ail z in D*

and (iii) the series $\Sigma u_n'(z)$ of derivatives converges uniformly to S' (z) in D.

Proof:

Let z_0 be any point of D. Consider a circular neighbourhood

$$|z - z_0| < \rho$$

of z_0 contained in D and let L be any closed contour in this circular domain.

Since Γ is a closed contour, the series $\Sigma u_n(z)$ is uniformly convergent on L. Also the sum function S(z) is continuous in D. Hence term by term integration is justified on L and we have

$$\int_L S(z)\,dz = \int_L u_1(z)\,dz + \int_L u_2(z)\,dz + \int_L u_3(z)\,dz + \dots \qquad \dots(1)$$

Since each $u_n(z)$ is analytic in the circular domain, we have by Cauchy's theorem,

$$\int_L u_n(z)\,dz = 0$$

for all values of n. Then we have from (1),

$$\int_L S(z)\,dz = 0$$

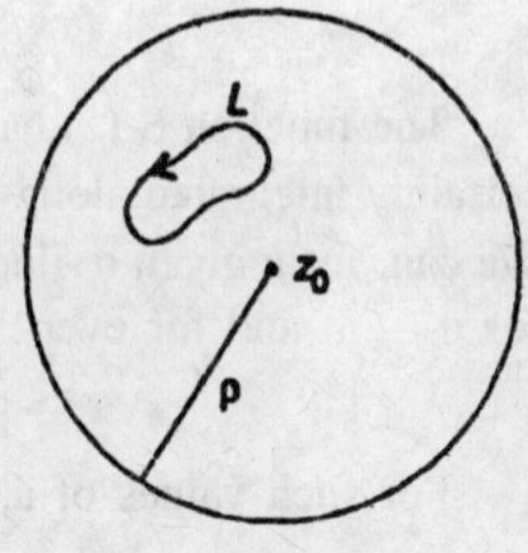

Fig. 3.1

Hence by *Morera's Theorem,* S(z) is analytic in a circular neighbourhood of z_0. As z_0 is any point of D, we see that S(z) is analytic in D. This proves the first result.

To prove the second result, we take a simple closed curve Γ lying in the neighbourhood $|z - z_0| < \rho$ of z_0 and having z_0 in its interiors.

Obviously the series

$$\frac{1}{2\pi i}\frac{S(z)}{(z-z_0)^2} = \frac{1}{2\pi i}\frac{u_1(z)}{(z-z_0)^2} + \frac{1}{2\pi i}.\frac{u_2(z)}{(z-z_0)^2}dz + \dots$$

is uniformly convergent on Γ. Hence integrating term by term, we get

$$\frac{1}{2\pi i}\int_\Gamma \frac{S(z)}{(z-z_0)^2}dz = \frac{1}{2\pi i}\int_\Gamma \frac{u_1(z)}{(z-z_0)^2}dz + \frac{1}{2\pi i}\int_\Gamma .\frac{u_2(z)}{(z-z_0)^2}dz + \dots$$

i.e. $S'(z) = u_1'(z) + u_2'(z) + \dots$

by Cauchy's integral formula for the derivatives.

As z_0 is any point of D, we see that

$$S'(z) = u_1'(z) + u_2'(z) + \dots$$

for every z in D. This proves the second result.

Now it remains to show that $S_n'(z)$ converges uniformly to $S'(z)$ in D within C. For this we construct a closed contour Γ' which lies within C and yet is definitely outside D. Let d denote the shortest distance between Γ' and D. Let z_0 be any point of D, then by Cauchy's integral formula for the derivatives of an analytic function, we have

$$S'(z) - S_n(z) = \frac{1}{2\pi i}\int_\Gamma \frac{S(z)}{(z-z_0)^2}dz - \frac{1}{2\pi i}\int_\Gamma \frac{S_n(z)}{(z-z_0)^2}dz$$

$$= \frac{1}{2\pi i}\int_\Gamma \frac{S(z)-S(z)}{(z-z_0)^2}dz$$

Since $S_n(z)$ converges uniformly to $S(z)$ within and on Γ', we can for a given ε, find an integer m in dependent of z, such that

$$| S(z) - S_n(z) | < \varepsilon.$$

for every $n \geq m$ and every z on Γ'.

Also $| z - z_0 | \geq d$ so

have $\left|\frac{1}{(z-z_0)^2}\right| \leq \frac{1}{d^2}$

Thus we have $\left|\frac{S(z)-S_n(z)}{(z-z_0)^2}\right| \leq \frac{\varepsilon}{d^2}$

$$|S'(z_0) - S_n'(z_0)| = \left|\frac{1}{2\pi i}\int_{\Gamma'} \frac{S(z)-S_n(z)}{(z-z_0)^2}dz\right|$$

$$\leq \frac{1}{2\pi i}\frac{|S(z)-S_n(z)|}{|z-z_0|^2}|dz|$$

$$\leq \frac{1}{2\pi}\int_{\Gamma'}\frac{e}{d^2}|dz| = \frac{1}{2\pi}.\frac{\varepsilon}{d^2}.l = \frac{\varepsilon l}{d\pi d^2}$$

where l is the length of Γ'.

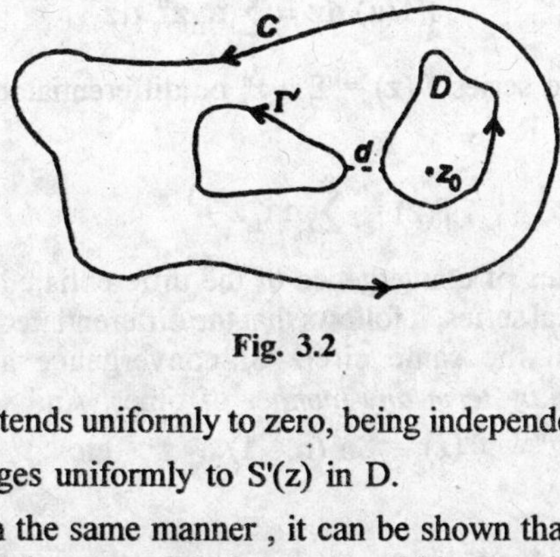

Fig. 3.2

Since $\frac{\varepsilon l}{d\pi d^2}$ tends uniformly to zero, being independent of z_0, it follows that $S_n'(z)$ converges uniformly to $S'(z)$ in D.

Proceeding in the same manner , it can be shown that $S_n''(z)$ converges Uniformly to $S''(z)$ in every closed domain, within C and so on indefinitely. Thus the theorem is completely established.

UNIFORM CONVERGENCE OF POWER SERIES

The power series converges within its circle of convergence and diverges outside it and that on the circle of convergence its behaviour is uncertain. We now prove some theorems on uniform convergence of power series.

Theorem I:

A power series is uniformly convergent within its circle of convergence.

Proof:

The series $\Sigma a_n z^n$ may or may not be uniformly convergent on the circle of convergence, e.g. the series Σz^n is not convergent when $|z| = 1$, *i.e.* on the circle of convergence whereas the series $\sum_{n=2}^{\infty} \frac{z^n}{n(\log n)^2}$ converges for all points on $|z| = 1$ which is the circle of convergence, and hence it is uniformly convergent on and within the circle of convergence by the theorem.

Cor.:

(i) Since each term of the power series $\Sigma a_n z^n$ is continuous and the series is uniformly convergent for $|z| \le r < R$ (R finite), It follows that the sum function of the power series is a continuous function throughout the closed region formed by the interior and boundary of any circle concentric with the circle of convergence and of smaller radius .

(ii) Again it follows from that the series $f(z) = \Sigma a_n z^n$ can be integrated term by term along any contour Γ lying within the circle of convergence, *i.e.* we have

$$\int_\Gamma f(z)\, dz = \sum_0^\infty a_n z^n\, dz$$

(iii) Finally the series $f(z) = \Sigma a_n z^n$ be differentiated term by term for $|z| \le r < R$

i.e.
$$f'(z) = \sum_0^\infty n a_n z^{n-1}$$

Since the radius of convergence of the differentiated series is the same as that of the original series, it follows that the differentiated series is uniformly convergent within the same circle of convergence and series can be *differentiated term by term any number* of times. And so we can write

$f'(z) = S\, na_n\, z^{n-1}$ $.f''(z) = \Sigma n\,(n - I)\, a_n\, z^{n-2}$ etc.

Theorem II:

If a power series $\Sigma a_n z^n$ vanishes identically/or values of z within its circle of convergence, then all the coefficients in the power series vanish separately, i.e. $a_n = 0$ for all n.

Proof:

Let the circle of convergence of power series be

$|z| = R$. Hence the series is convergent for $|z| \leq r < R$, $r > 0$.

Now suppose, if possible, that all the coefficients do not vanish and let a_m be the first coefficient which is not zero.

Then $a_m + a_{m+1} z + a_{m+2} z^2 + \ldots$ vanish for all values of z except zero and converges absolutely when $|z| \leq r < R$. We then have

$$|a_{m+1} + a_{m+2} z + \ldots \left| \leq \sum_{n=1}^{\infty} \right| a_{m+n} | r^{n-1}$$

Hence if $\phi(z) = a_{m+1} z + a_{m+2} z^2 + \ldots$, we can find a positive number

$$\delta \leq r \text{ such that } |\phi(z)| \leq 1/2\, a_m | \qquad \ldots(1)$$

for all values of z for which $|z| \leq \delta$

[It is sufficient to take δ to be the smaller of the number r and

$$\frac{1}{2} |a_m| \Big/ \sum_{n=1}^{\infty} |a_{m+n}| r^{n-1}]$$

Then$| a_m + \phi(z) | \geq | a_m | - \phi(z) |$

$$\geq | a_m | - \phi(z) | \geq \frac{1}{2} | \alpha_\mu | \text{ from (1)}$$

Hence $| a_m + \phi(z) | \neq 0$, when $|z| < \delta$. We have therefore arrived at a contradiction by supposing that some coefficient does not vanish. Hence all the coefficients must have

Cor.:

If one and the same function f(z) can be expanded in a power series in two distinct ways, so that

$$f(z) = \sum_{n=0}^{\infty} a_n z^n = \sum_{n=0}^{\infty} b_n z^n$$

both series being convergent, when $| z [< R$. Then $a_n = b_n$ for all values of n.

If we write $a_n - b_n = c_n$, then, when $|z| < R$,

$$0 = \sum_{n=0}^{\infty} c_n z^n$$

Also $c_n = 0$ for all values of n by the above theorem.

Hence $a_n = b_n$ for all n.

Power Series

A series of the form $\sum_{n=0}^{\infty} a_n z^n$ or $\sum_{n=0}^{\infty} a_n (z-a)^n$, whose terms are variable is called a power series where z is a complex variable and a_n, are complex constants.

The second form car be reduced to the first from merely by changing origin. So the consideration of the series of the second form is always reduced to that of the first form

The form $\sum_{n=0}^{\infty} a_n z^n$ being simpler, we have discussion of power series by considering the form $\sum_{n=0}^{\infty} a_n z^n$

Absolute Convergence of Power Series $\Sigma\ a_n\ z^n$

The power series $\Sigma\ a_n\ z^n$ is said to be absolutely convergent if series $\Sigma\ |a_n\ z^n|$ is convergent

If the series $\sum_{n=0}^{\infty} a_n z^n$ convergent but the series $\sum_{n=0}^{\infty} |a_n\ z|^n$ not converge, then the series $\sum_{n=0}^{\infty} a_n z^n$ is called conditionally convergent.

RADIUS OF CONVERGENT OF POWER SERIES

Applying Cauchy's not test to the series $\Sigma\ |a_n|\ |z|^n$ we find that $\Sigma\ a_n\ z^n$ is convergent or divergent according as limit of nth root of the nth term is less or greater than unity Thus.

$\Sigma\ |a_n|\ |z|^n$ convergent if $\lim_{n\to\infty} |a_n|^{1/n}\ |z| < |$ *i.e.* if $1/R\ .\ \ |z| < |$ where $\lim|a_n|^{1/n} = 1/R$ or if $|z| < R$ and divergent if $|z| > R$

Thus, for every power series $\Sigma\ a_x\ z^n$. There exist a non-negative real number R such that for every $|z| < R$ The series is absolutely convergent, and for every $|z| > R$ the series is not convergent.

Such a number R is called the Radius of convergence of the power series $\Sigma\ a_x\ z^n$. For if we draw a circle whose centre is origin and radius equal to R, then for all values of z with in this circle power series $\Sigma\ a_x\ z^n$ is absolutely convergent and for all values of z outside this circle the power series $\Sigma\ a_x\ z^n$ is divergent.

SOME USEFUL TESTS FOR CONVERGENCE

The following tests whose proofs are trivial should be recollected

Comparison Test : If $\sum|\sqrt{n}|$ converges and $|u_n|\ \Sigma\ |v_n|$ Then $\Sigma|u_n|$ converges absolutely.

Ratio Test : The series Σu_n converges (absolutely) or diverges according as $\lim_{n\to\infty}\left|\frac{u_{n-1}}{u_n}\right| < 1$ or > 1. If this limit equal to 1 the test fails.

Root Test : (n^{th} root test) the series Σu_n converges (absolutely) or diverge according as $\lim_{n\to\infty}\sqrt[n]{(|u_n|)} < 1$ or > 1

If this limit is equal to 1, the test fails.

Series absolutely convergent : The series Σu_n is convergent (absolutely) the series $|\Sigma u_n|$ is convergent.

Theorem 1:

If the power series $\Sigma a_n x^n$ is such that $a_n \neq 0$ for all n and $\lim_{n\to\infty}\left|\frac{a_{n+1}}{a_n}\right| = \frac{1}{R}$, *then $\Sigma a_n x^n$ is convergent (absolutely convergent) for $|x| < R$ and divergent for $|x| > R$..*

Proof:

Let $u_n = a_n x^n$ so that $u_{n+1} = a_{n+1} x^{n+1}$.

$$\therefore \lim_{n\to\infty}\left|\frac{u_{n+1}}{u_n}\right| = \lim_{n\to\infty}\left|\frac{a_{n+1}\,x}{a_n}\right| = \frac{|x|}{R}.$$

By D' Alembert's ratio test, $\Sigma a_n x^n$ converges absolutely, if

$\frac{|x|}{R} < 1$ i.e., $|x| < R$.

Further $\Sigma a_n x^n$ diverges if $|x| > R$. Hence the theorem.

Remark 1:

By Cauchy's second theorem on limits, if $\{a_n\}$ is sequence of positive constants, then

$$\lim_{n\to\infty}(a_n)^{1/n} = \lim_{n\to\infty}\left(\frac{a_{n+1}}{a_n}\right),$$

provided the limit on the R.H.S. exists. It follows that :

If $\lim_{n\to\infty}|a_n|^{1/n} = \frac{1}{R}$, *Then the series $\Sigma a_n x^n$ is convergent (absolutely convergent) for $|x| < R$ and divergent for $|x| > R$..*

In view of the above discussion, the *radius of convergence R of a power series $\Sigma a_n x^n$ may be determined by the following :*

$$R = \lim_{n\to\infty} \left|\frac{a_n}{a_{n+1}}\right| = 1 \div \lim_{n\to\infty} |a_n|^{1/n}$$

$R = \infty$, when $\lim |a_n|^{1/n} = \infty$.

$R = 0$, when $\lim |a_n|^{1/n} = \infty$.

Remark 2:

Every power series converges absolutely within its interval of convergence.

Theorem 2:

If a power series $\Sigma a_n x^n$ converges for $|x| < R$, then it converges uniformly on $[-R + \varepsilon, R - \varepsilon]$, for each $\varepsilon > 0$.

Proof:

Let $x_0 = R - \varepsilon < R$ so that $\Sigma a_n x_0^n$ converges absolutely.

For $|x| \le x_0$, $|a_n x^n| \le |a_n|\ x_0^n$.

Since $\Sigma a_n x_0^n$ converges absolutely, therefore, by Weierstrass's M-test, the series $\Sigma a_n x^n$ converges uniformly on

$[-x_0, x_0] = [-R + \varepsilon, R - \varepsilon]$. Hence the theorem.

Ex.:

Show that a power series converges uniformly on any closed and bounded subinterval of its interval of convergence.

Theorem 3:

If a power series $\Sigma a_n x^n$ converges for $x = x_0$, then

(i) *it is absolutely convergent in the interval* $|x| < |x_0|$

(ii) *it is uniformly convergent in the interval* $|x| \le |x_1|$ *where* $|x_1| \le |x_0|$.

Proof:

(i) Since $\Sigma a_n x_0^n$ converges, so $\lim_{n\to\infty} a_n x_0^n = 0$.

Consequently there exists a positive integer *m* such that

$$\left|a_n x_0^n = 0\right| < 1\ \forall\ n \ge m \text{ or } |a_n| < \frac{1}{|x_0|^n}\ \forall\ n \ge m \qquad ...(1)$$

$$\Rightarrow |a_n x^n| = |a_n|\,|x|^n < \frac{|x|^n}{|x_0|^n}\ \forall\ n \ge m, \text{ by (1)}$$

$$\Rightarrow |a_n x^n| < \left\{\frac{|x|}{|x_0|}\right\}^n \quad \forall\, n \geq m.$$

The series on the R.H.S. converges for $|x| < |x_0|$ (being a geometric series with common ratio < (1), it follows by the comparison test that $\Sigma\, |a_n x^n|$ is convergent for $|x| < |x_0|$.

Hence $\Sigma a_n x^n$ is absolutely convergent for $|x| < |x_0|$.

(ii) Let $M_n = \dfrac{|x_1|^n}{|x_0|^n}$. Then ΣM_n converges, since $|x_1| < |x_0|$ (being a geometric series with common ratio <1).

Using (1), we obtain

$$|a_n x^n| = |a_n|\,|x|^n < \frac{|x|^n}{|x_0|^n} \leq \frac{|x_1|^n}{|x_0|^n},$$

for $|x| \leq |x_1|$ and $n \geq m$

$\therefore |a_n x^n| < M_n \;\forall\, n \geq m$, where ΣM_n converges.

By the Weierstrass M-Test, $\Sigma a_n x^n$ is uniformly convergent in $|x| \leq |x_1|$.

Note : *If a power series whose radius of convergence is 1, then it converges absolutely in]– 1, 1[and uniformly in [–k, k], |k| < 1.*

Theorem 4:

(Cauchy's Product of Two Power Series)

Two power series $\sum_{n=0}^{\infty} a_n x^n$ *and* $\sum_{n=0}^{\infty} b_n x^n$ *can be multiplied to obtain the power series* $\sum_{n=0}^{\infty} c_n x^n$, *where*

$$c_n = a_0 b_n + a_1 b_{n-1} + a_2 b_{n-2} + \ldots + a_n b_0,$$

the result being valid for each x within the common interval of convergence.

The proof of these theorems are omitted.

Some Important Power Series

Consider the following power series :

$$1 + \frac{x}{1!} + \frac{x^2}{2!} + \frac{x^3}{3!} + \ldots + \frac{x^n}{n!} + \ldots\ldots$$

$$1 - \frac{x^2}{2!} + \frac{x^4}{4!} - \ldots + (-1)^n \frac{x^{2n}}{(2n)!} + \ldots\ldots$$

$$x - \frac{x^3}{3!} + \frac{x^5}{5!} - \ldots + (-1)^n \frac{x^{2n+1}}{(2n+1)!} + \ldots\ldots$$

For the first series, $\lim_{n\to\infty}\left|\frac{a_n}{a_{n+1}}\right| = \lim_{n\to\infty}\frac{(n+1)!}{n!} = \lim_{n\to\infty}(n+1) = \infty$.

Thus, the radius of convergence is $R = \infty$ so that the series is everywhere convergent (absolutely and uniformly). Similarly we can verify that the other two power series are also everywhere convergent (absolutely and uniformly). In this section we shall study their exclusive properties and show that the sums of these power series are actually the functions e^x, cos x and sin x respectively.

Theorem 5:

(Abel's Theorem): *If a power series converges at an end point of its interval of convergence, then the power series is uniformly convergent in the interval which includes this end point.*

Remarks:

1. *If a power series with interval of convergence]–R, R[converges at both the end-points – R and R, then the power series is uniformly convergent in [–R, R].*
2. *If a power series converges at the end-point x = R of the interval of convergence]–R, R[, then it is uniformly convergent in]–R, R] or [–R + ε, R], where ε > 0. In particular, the series is uniformly convergent in [0, R].*

Theorem 6:

(Abel's Limit Theorem): *But $\Delta a_n x^n$ be a power series with finite radius of convergence R that $r(x) = \Sigma a_n x^n$, $-R\Delta x<R$. If the series $\Sigma a_n R^n$ converges, be*

$$\lim_{x\to R-} f(x) = \Sigma a_n R^n.$$

Remark 3:

The case R = 1 is of much practical use :

Let $\Sigma a_n x^n$ *be a power series with unit radius of convergence such that* $f(x) = \Sigma a_n x^n$, $-1 \Delta x < 1$. *If the series* $\Sigma a_n x^n$ *converges for x = 1 i.e., if* Σa_n converges, then

$$\lim_{x\to 1-} f(x) = \Sigma a_n.$$

Theorem 7:

Suppose a power series $\Sigma a_n x^n$ converges for $|x| < R$ and that $f(x) = \Sigma a_n x^n$. Then

(i) *f(x) is continuous in]–R, R[.*

(ii) *$\Sigma a_n x^n$ can be integrated term by term on]–R, R[and the integrated series has the same radius of convergence as $\Sigma a_n x^n$.*

(iii) *$\Sigma a_n x^n$ can be differentiated term and term on]–R, [R and $f'(x) = \Sigma n\, a_n x^{n-1}$, $|x| < R$. Further the differentiated series has the same radius of convergence as $\Sigma a_n x^n$.*

Proof:

(i) Since each term of the power series $\Sigma a_n x^n$ is continuous in]–R, R[and the series is uniformly convergent on]–R, R[, so the sum f(x) of the given series is continuous in]–R, R[. (See Theorem 6, p. 165).

(ii) Since each term of $\Sigma a_n x^n$ is continuous in]–R, R[and $\Sigma a_n x^n$ converges uniformly to f(x) in]–R, R[, so $\Sigma a_n x^n$ can be integrated term by termin] –R, R[and the integrated series is $\Sigma \frac{a_n}{n+1} x^{n+1}$. Further

$$\lim_{n\to\infty}\left|\frac{u_n}{u_{n+1}}\right| = \lim_{n\to\infty}\left(\frac{n+2}{n+1}\cdot\frac{a_n}{a_{n+1}}\right) = \lim_{n\to\infty}\frac{a_n}{a_{n+1}} = R,$$

which shows that $\Sigma a_n x^n$ and $\Sigma \frac{a_n x^{n+1}}{n+1}$ have the same radius of convergence.

(iii) We know each term of $\Sigma a_n x^n$ is continuous, has continuous derivative in] – R, R[and $\Sigma a_n x^n$ is uniformly convergent in] – R, R[. Thus the series obtained by differentiating the power series $\Sigma a_n x^n$ is $\Sigma n a_n x^{n-1}$. Further

$$\lim_{n\to\infty}\left|\frac{u_n}{u_{n+1}}\right| = \lim_{n\to\infty}\left|\frac{n\, a_n}{(n+1)\, a_{n+1}}\right| = \lim_{n\to\infty}\left|\frac{a_n}{a_{n+1}}\right| = R.$$

Hence the differentiated series $\Sigma n\, a_n x^{n-1}$ is also a power series which has the same radius of convergence as $\Sigma a_n x^n$.

Note : If *$f(x) = \Sigma a_n x^n$, then $f(x)$ is called the* **sum function** *of the series.*

Theorem 8:

Define cosine and sine functions as sums of power series. Prove that

(i) S(x + y) = S(x)C(y) + C(x)S(y),

(ii) C(x + y) = C(x)C(y) – S(x)S(y),

where C, S denote cosine and since respectively.

Proof:

The *cosine function* is defined as

$$C(x) = 1 - \frac{x^2}{2!} + \frac{x^4}{4!} - ... + (-1)^n \frac{x^{2n}}{(2n)!} + ... \ \forall \ x \in \Re \quad ...(1)$$

The *sine function* is defined as

$$S(x) = x - \frac{x3}{3!} + \frac{x^5}{5!} - ... + (-1)^n \frac{x^{2n+1}}{(2n+1)!} + ... \quad ...(2)$$

$\forall \ x \in \Re$

These two power series are uniformly convergent $\forall \ x \in \Re$ and consequently, the functions C(x) and S(x) are continuous $\forall \ x \in \Re$.

Differentiating term by term the convergent series (2).

$$S'(x) = 1 - \frac{x^2}{2!} + \frac{x^4}{4!} + ...$$

which gives us the uniformaly convergent series (1),

Thus S(x) is variable, $\forall x \in \Re$ and S'(x) = C(x) ...(3)

SimilarlyC'(x) = –S(x). ...(4)

From (1) and (2); S(0) = 0 and C(0) = 1. ...(5)

Let y be any arbitrary but fixed real number. We write

f(x) = S(x + y) – S(x)C(y) – C(x)S(y), ...(6)

g(x) = C(x + y) – C(x)C(y) + S (x) S (y). ...(7)

Differentiating w.r.t. x, we obtain

f'(x) = C(x + y) – C(x)C(y) + S(x)S(y) = g(x), ...(6)

g'(x) = –S(x + y) – S(x)C(y) + C (x) S (y) = –f(x). ...(7)

[Using (3), (4)]

$$\text{Now } \frac{d}{dx}[f^2(x) + g^2(x)] = 2f(x)f'(x) + 2g(x)g'(x)$$

$$= 2f(x)g(x) - 2g(x)f(x) = 0 \quad \forall \ x$$

If follows that $f^2(x) + g^2(z)$ is a constant $\forall$ x

$\Rightarrow f^2(x) + g^2(x) = f^2(0) + g^2(0)$ $\forall$ x

$$= [S(y) - S(0)\,C(y) - C(0)\,S(y)]^2$$

$$+ [C(y) - C(0)\,C(y) + S(0)\,S(y)]^2$$

$$= 0$$ [Using (5)],

$\therefore f^2(x) + g^2(x) = 0 \ \forall \ x \in \Re$ implies the f (x) = 0 and g(x) = 0.

Hence (6) and (7) yield

S (x + y) = S (x) C (y) + C (x) S (y),

$C(x + y) = C(x)\, C(y) - C(x)\, S(y).$

Cor. 1:

$S(-x) = -S(x);\ C(-x) = C(x)$ $\qquad \forall x \in \Re.$

We have $S(-x) = -x - \dfrac{(-x)^8}{3!} + \dfrac{(-x)^5}{5!} - \ldots\ldots$

$$= -\left[x - \frac{x^3}{3!} + \frac{x^5}{5!} - \ldots\ldots\right] = -S(x).$$

Similarly we can prove the second part.

Cor. 2:

$S(x - y) = S(x)\, C(y) - C(x)\, S(y),$

$C(x - y) = C(x)\, C(y) + S(x)\, S(y).$

Replacing y by –y in (i) and (ii)

$S(x-y) = S(x)\, C(-y) + C(x)\, S(-y),$

$C(x-y) = C(x)\, C(-y) - S(x)\, S(-y).$

The desired results follow by Cor. 1.

Cor. 3:

$C^2(x) + S^2(x) = 1$ *or* $\cos^2 x + \sin^2 x = 1$ $\qquad \forall x \in \Re.$

We have $1 = C(0) = C(x - x)$

$$= C(x)\, C(-x) - S(x)\, S(-x)$$

$$= C^2(x) + S^2(x), \text{ by Cor. 1.}$$

Hence $\cos^2 x + \sin^2 x = 1\ \forall x \in \Re.$

Cor. 4:

$C(x) \le 1,\ |S(x)| \le 1,$ $\qquad \forall x \in \Re.$

OR

$|\cos x| \le 1,\ |\sin x| \le 1 : \forall x \in \Re.$

This follows by Cor. 3.

Cor. 5:

$\sin 2x = 2 \sin x \cos x,\ \cos 2x = \cos^2 x - \sin^2 x.$

Replacing y by x in (i) and (ii) of Theorem 8, we obtain

$S(2x) = 2S(x)\, C(x),\ C(2x) = C^2(x) - S^2(x)$

Hence the results follow.

Remark:

It may be noted that the above properties of C(x) and S(x) are simila to those of the trigonometric functions cos x and sin x respectively whic the students do at the elementary, stage. Thus we have

$C(x) \equiv \cos x$ and $S(x) \equiv \sin x$.

Theorem 9:

Let f be a non-zero function continuous on R^+ such that f(xy)

$$= f(x) + f(y) \ \forall \ x, y > 0. \qquad ...(1$$

Show that f(x) $\log_a x$, $x \in \Re^+$ ($a > 0$, $a \neq 1$).

Proof:

For $x > 0$, let us take $t = \log_e x \Leftrightarrow x = e^t$, $t \in \Re$. ...(2

Let $g(t) = f(e^t) \ \forall \ t \in \Re$. Then g is continuous on $\Re$ and

$g(t + s) = f(e^{t+s}) = f(e^t e^3) = f(e^t) + f(e^s)$ by (1)

or $g(t + s) = g(t) + g(s)$.

Here $t, s \in \Re$. $g(t) = ct$, $\forall \ t \in \Re$, c being a constant.

Thus $f(x) = c \log_e x \ \forall x \in \Re^+$, where $c \neq 0$ as f is non-zero.

Let $a = e^{1/e}$. Then $f(x) = \log_a x \ \forall \ x \in \Re^+$ ($a > 0$, $a \neq 1$).

Ex.:

See the exponential function as the sum of a power series and determi its range. Hence define the logarithmic function and deduce that it continuous.

[**Hint.** It can be verified that the exponential function $E : R \to R^+$ strictly increasing on R *i.e.*, E is one-one and onto. Thus E has inver function, say $L : R^+ \to R$. L is called the *logarithmic function,* defined

$E\{L(y)\} = y \ (y > 0)$ or $L\{E(x)\} = x \ (x \in R)$.

In other words, $E(x) = y \Rightarrow I.(y) = x$ or $e^x = y \Rightarrow \log_e y = x$.

Since the function E is differentiable, so its inverse function L is fa differentiable and hence continuous.

Theorem 10:

Define exponential function E(x) as the sum of power series. Show th the domain is the set of all real number Prove that

$E(x + y) = E(x) E(y)$ for all $x, y \in \Re$.

If e denotes E(1), prove that $E(x) = e^2$ for all real x.

Proof:

The exponential function E(x) is defined as the sum of the power series

$$E(x) = 1+\frac{x}{1!}+\frac{x^2}{2!}+...+\frac{x^n}{n!}+..... \qquad ...(1)$$

We have $R = \lim_{n\to\infty}\left|\frac{a_n}{a_{n+1}}\right| = \lim_{n\to\infty}\frac{(n+1)!}{n!} = \lim_{n\to\infty}(n+1) = \infty$.

Thus, the radius of convergence of the above power series is $R = \infty$ that the power series is everywhere convergent *i.e.*, E(x) is defined $\forall\, x \in \mathfrak{R}$. This shows that the domain of the exponential function is $\mathfrak{R}$.

It is clear that the function E(x), defined by (1), is continuous and has derivatives of all orders, for each $x \in \mathfrak{R}$.

Differentiating (1), we get

$E'(x) = E(x)$ and so $E'(x) = E(x)$, $E'(x) = E(x)$ etc.

In fact $E^{(n)}(x) = E(x)$ $\qquad \forall\, n \in N$.

By Taylor's Theorem, for all real values t and x

$$E(t) = E(x) + \frac{E'(x)}{1!}(t-x)+\frac{E''(x)}{2!}(t-x)^2+.......$$

$$\text{or } E(t) = E(x) + \frac{E(x)}{1!}(t-x)+\frac{E(x)}{2!}(t-x)^2+.......$$

Replacing t by x + y, we get

$$E(x+y) = E(x)\left\{1+\frac{y}{1!}+\frac{y^2}{2!}+........\right\} = E(x)E(y)$$

Thus, $E(x + y) = E(x)\, E(y)\ \forall\, x, y \in \mathfrak{R}$. $\qquad$ ...(2)

From (1), $E(1) = 1+\frac{1}{1!}+\frac{1}{2!}+...+\frac{1}{3!}+......$

The above series on the right converges to a number which lies between 2 and 3.

We denote this number by e so that E(1) = e.

The property (2) can be extended as

$E(x_1 + x_2 + ... + x_n) = E(x_1)\, E(x_2)...E(x_n)$ $\qquad$ ...(3)

for any positive integer n and $\forall\, x \in \mathfrak{R}$.

Taking $x_1 = x_2 = ... = x_n = x$ in (3), we obtain

$E(nx) = \{E(x)\}^n\ \forall\, x \in \mathfrak{R},\ \forall\, n \in N$. $\qquad$ ...(4)

For $x = 1$, we obtain

$$E(n) = e^n \ \forall\ n \in N \qquad (\because E(1) = e) \qquad \ldots (5)$$

Taking $x = m/n$ (m and n being positive integers) in (4),

$E(m) = \{E(m/n)\}^n$ or $e^m = \{E(m/n)\}^n$, by (5)

$\therefore\ E(m/n) = (e^m)^{1/n} = e^{m/n}$.

Thus, $E(q) = e^n$ for all positive rationals q. . . .(6)

Let x be any *positive irrational* number. Then there always exists a sequence $\{x_n\}$ of positive rational numbers such that $x_n \to x$.

Using (6), $E(x_n) = e^{xn}$ $\qquad \forall\ n \in N$.

Since $x_n \to x$ as $n \to \infty$ and E is a continuous function $\forall\ x \in \Re$, therefore

$E(x) = e^n$ for all positive irrationals. . . . (7)

From (6) and (7), we conclude that

$E(x) = e^x$ for all positive reals. . . . (8)

Taking $y = -x$ in (2), we get

$E(0) = E(x)E(-x)$ or $1 = E(x)\ E(-x)\ (x \geq 0)$ $\quad [\because E(0) = 1$, by (1)].

or $E(-x) = \dfrac{1}{E(x)} = \dfrac{1}{e^x} = e^{-x}$, using (8)

Hence, $E(x) = e^x \quad \forall\ x \in \Re$.

Theorem 11:

Let f be a continuous function on $\Re$ such that

$f(x + y) = f(x) + f(y)\ \forall\ x, y \in \Re$. . . . (1)

Show that $f(x) = e^x$ for some constant c and $\forall\ x \in \Re$.

Proof:

Putting $y = x$ in (1), $f(2x) = 2\ f(x)$.

In fact $f(nx) = nf(x)\ \forall\ x \in \Re,\ \forall\ n \in N$.

Replacing x by x/n, we get

$f(x) = nf(x/n)$ or $f(x/n) = (1/n) = (1/n)\ f(x)\ \forall\ x \in \Re$.

For any integers p and p $(q > 0)$, it follows that

$$f\left(\frac{p}{q}x\right) = \frac{p}{q} f(x).\ \forall\ x \in \Re.$$

Thus, $f(rx) = r\ f(x)$, for any rational number r. . . . (2

Let us write $f(1) = c$. Taking $x = 1$ in (2), we get

$f(r) = cr$, for every rational number r. . . . (3)

Let α be any irrational number. Then there exists a sequence $\{r_n\}$ of rational numbers such that $r_n \to a$

$\Rightarrow f(r_n) \to f(a)$, continuity of f

$\Rightarrow f(a) = \lim f(r_n) = \lim cr_n = c \lim r_n = ca$, using (3).

Hence $f(x) = cx \ \forall \ x \in \mathfrak{R}$.

Theorem 12:

Define cos x as a power series and determine its domain. Prove that there exists a least positive number π such that $\cos\left(\frac{1}{2}\pi\right) = 0$.

Proof:

cos x is defined as the sum of the power series

$$1-\frac{x^2}{2!}+\frac{x^4}{4!}-...+(-1)^n\frac{x^{2n}}{(2n)!}+.....$$

Its radius of convergence is

$$R = \lim_{n\to\infty}\left|\frac{a_n}{a_{n+1}}\right| = \lim_{n\to\infty}\left|\frac{(2n+2)!}{(2n+1)!}\right| = \lim_{n\to\infty}(2n+2) = \infty.$$

Thus, this power series is convergent for $\forall \ x \in \mathfrak{R}$ and so the domain of cos x is $\mathfrak{R}$.

$$\cos x = 1-\frac{x^2}{2!}+\frac{x^4}{4!}-\frac{x^6}{6!}+\frac{x^8}{8!}+.......... \quad \forall \ x \in \mathfrak{R} \qquad ...(1)$$

$\therefore \cos 0 = 1 > 0$ and

$$\cos 2 = 1-\frac{2^2}{2!}+\frac{2^4}{4!}-\frac{2^6}{6!}+\frac{2^8}{8!}+..........$$

$$=1-\frac{2^2}{2!}\left(1-\frac{2^2}{3.4}\right)-\frac{2^6}{6!}\left(1-\frac{2^2}{7.8}\right)-........$$

Since the brackets are all positive, therefore

$$\cos 2 < 1-\frac{2^2}{2!}\left(1-\frac{2^2}{3.4}\right) = -\frac{1}{3} \text{ and so } \cos 2 < 0.$$

Thus, we see that cos x is a continuous function in the closed interval [0, 2], where cos 0 and cos 2 are of opposite signs. By Intermediate value theorem, there exists at least one number $\alpha \in]0, 2[$ such that $\cos\alpha = 0$. We now proceed to show that α is unique.

Let, if possible, $\beta \in]0, 2[$ satisfy $\cos \beta = 0$ so that

$\cos \alpha = \cos \beta = 0,\ 0 < \alpha, \beta < 2.$

By Rolle's theorem, there exists some number λ, $\alpha < \lambda < b$, such that $-\sin \lambda = 0$.

$\therefore \sin \lambda = 0,\ 0 < \lambda < 2.$ . . . (2)

By definition,

$$\sin x = x - \frac{x^3}{3!} + \frac{x^5}{5!} - \frac{x^7}{7!} + \ldots\ldots \quad \forall\, x \in \Re$$

$$\therefore \quad \sin \lambda = \frac{\lambda}{1!}\left(1 - \frac{\lambda^2}{2.3}\right) + \frac{\lambda^5}{5!}\left(1 - \frac{\lambda^2}{6.7}\right) + \ldots\ldots > 0, \text{ for } 0 < \lambda < 2.$$

This contradicts (2).

Thus, there exists one and only one that of the equation $\cos x = 0$ lying between 0 and 2. *i.e.*, $\cos \alpha = 0,\ 0 < \alpha < 2$.

We denote α as $\frac{1}{2}\pi$. Hence $\frac{1}{2}\pi$ is the *least positive root* of the equation $\cos x = 0$ *i.e.*, $\cos \frac{1}{2}\pi = 0$.

Also, therefore, we have $\cos x > 0$ when $0 \le x < \frac{1}{2}\pi$.

Theorem 13:

Let f be a non-zero continuous function on $\Re$ such that

$f(x + y) = f(x) f(y)\ \forall\, x, y \in \Re.$ . . . (1)

Show that $f(x) = e^{cx}$, for some constant $c \neq 0$.

Proof:

It is given that $f(x) \neq 0\ \forall\, x \in \Re$. From (1)

$$f(x) = f\left(\frac{1}{2}x\right) f\left(\frac{1}{2}x\right) \text{ or } f(x) = \left\{f\left(\frac{1}{2}x\right)\right\}^2 > 0\ \forall\, x \in \Re.$$

Let $g(x) = \log_e f(x)\ \forall\, x \in \Re$. Then by (1),

$g(x + y) = g(x) + g(y)\ \forall\, x, y \in \Re.$ . . . (2)

Now g, being the composition of two continuous functions f(x) and $\log_e x$, is itself continuous on R and g satisfies (2).

It follows that

$g(x) = cx\ \forall\, x \in \Re$, c being a constant

$\Rightarrow \quad \log_e f(x) = cx$

$\Rightarrow \quad f(x) = e^{cx} \ \forall \ x \in \Re.$

SOLVED EXAMPLES

Example 1:

Show that

$$\frac{1}{2}[\log(1+x)]^2 = \frac{x^2}{2} - \frac{x^3}{3}\left(1+\frac{1}{2}\right) + \frac{x^4}{4}\left(1+\frac{1}{2}+\frac{1}{3}\right) + \ldots, -1 < x < 1.$$

Solution:

By the above example,

$$\log(1+x) = x - \frac{x^2}{2} + \frac{x^3}{3} + \frac{x^4}{4} + \ldots, -1 < x < 1.$$

and $(1+x)^{-1} = 1 - x + x^2 - x^3 + x^4 - \ldots\ldots, -1 < x < 1.$

Both the series are absolutely convergent in $]-1, 1[$, ($\because$ R = 1), so their Cauchy's product will converge to $(1+x)^{-1} \log(1+x)$. Thus

$$(1+x)^{-1}\log(1+x) = x - x^2(1+½) + x^3(1+½+½) - \ldots\ldots, \quad -1 < x < 1$$

Integrating, we get

$$\frac{1}{2}[\log(1+x)]^2 = \frac{x^2}{2} - \frac{x^3}{3}\left(1+\frac{1}{2}\right) + \frac{x^4}{4}\left(1+\frac{1}{2}+\frac{1}{3}\right) - \ldots\ldots, -1 < x < 1$$

where the constant of integration vanishes.

Since the series on the right converges at x = 1, so by Abel's theorem the above expansion is valid for $-1 < x \leq 1$.

Example 2:

Find the radius of convergence of $\sum_{n=1}^{\infty} nx^{n-1}$

Solution:

Here $\lim_{n\to\infty}\left|\frac{a_n}{a_{n+1}}\right| = \lim_{n\to\infty}\frac{n}{n+1} = 1$.

Hence the radius of convergence = 1.

Example 3:

Find the radius of convergence of the series

$$x + \frac{x^2}{2^2} + \frac{2!}{3^3}x^2 + \frac{3!}{4^6}x^6 + \ldots\ldots$$

Solution :

$$a_n = \frac{(n-1)!}{n^n},\ a_{n+1} = \frac{n!}{(n+1)^{n+1}}$$

$$\therefore\ R = \lim_{n\to\infty}\left|\frac{a_n}{a_{n+1}}\right| = \lim_{n\to\infty}\frac{(n-1)!}{n!}\frac{(n+1)^{n+1}}{n^n}$$

$$= \lim_{n\to\infty}\left(\frac{n+1}{n}\right)^{n+1} = \lim_{n\to\infty}\left(1+\frac{1}{n}\right)^n\left(1+\frac{1}{n}\right) = e.$$

Hence the radius of convergence = e.

Example 4:

Show that the series

$$1+\frac{x}{2}+\frac{x^2}{3}+\frac{x^3}{4}+......$$

is uniformly convergent in [–1, k], 0 < k < 1.

Solution:

We have

$$\lim_{n\to\infty}\left|\frac{a_n}{a_{n+1}}\right| = \lim_{n\to\infty}\left(\frac{n+1}{n}\right) = \lim_{n\to\infty}\left(1+\frac{1}{n}\right) = 1.$$

The radius of convergence is R = 1 and so the given series is uniformly convergent in]–1, 1[.

For x = 1, given series $\sum\frac{1}{n}$, which is divergent.

However for x = 1, given series becomes $1-\frac{1}{2}+\frac{1}{3}+\frac{1}{4}+.......$, which is convergent by Leibnitz's Test. Hence by Abel's Theorem, given power series is uniformly convergent in [–1, 1[or [–1, k], where 0 < k < 1.

Example 5:

Prove that

$$\int_0^x \frac{dt}{1+t^n} = x - \frac{x^{n+1}}{n+1} + \frac{x^{(2n+1)}}{2n+1} - ....,\ - < x < 1,\ n > 0.$$

Solution:

For n > 0, we have

$(1 + t^n)^{-1} = 1 - t^n + t^{2n} - t^{2n} + ...$

It is clear that the series on the right has its radius of convergence R = 1.

This series can be integrated term by term on]–1, 1[and the integrated series will also have the radius of convergence as unity. Thus

$$\int_0^x \frac{dt}{1+t^n} = x - \frac{x^{n+1}}{n+1} + \frac{x^{(2n+1)}}{2n+1} - \text{.........}, \; - < x < 1. \qquad \text{....(1)}$$

At x = 1, the series on the right is convergent, by Leibnitz's test.

Hence, (1) is true for $-1 < x \leq 1$.

Example 6:

Show that

$$\log(1+x) = x - \frac{x^2}{2} + \frac{x^3}{3} - \frac{x^4}{4} + \text{......}, \; -1 < x \leq 1$$

and deduce that

$$\log 2 = 1 - \frac{1}{2} + \frac{1}{3} - \frac{1}{4} + \text{......}$$

Solution:

We know

$$(1+x)^{-1} = 1 - x + x^2 - x^3 + \text{........}, \quad -1 < x < 1. \qquad \text{...(1)}$$

Its radius of convergence is R = 1.

Thus the power series is absolutely convergent for $|x| < 1$ and uniformly convergent for [–k, k], $|k| < 1$.

The integrated series is also convergent absolutely in]–1, 1[and uniformly in [–k, k], $|k| < 1$.

Integrating (1), we get

$$\log(1+x) = c + x - \frac{x^2}{2} + \frac{x^3}{3} - \frac{x^4}{4} + \text{......}, \; 1 < x < 1.$$

Putting x = 0 gives c = 0. This

$$\log(1+x) = x - \frac{x^2}{2} + \frac{x^3}{3} - \frac{x^4}{4} + \text{......}, \; 1 < x < 1.$$

The series on the R.H.S. is convergent for x = 1 (by Leibnitz's test). Hence by Abel's theorem,

$$\log(1+x) = x - \frac{x^2}{2} + \frac{x^3}{3} - \frac{x^4}{4} + \text{......}, \; 1 < x < 1.$$

At x = 1, by Abel's limit theorem, we get

$$\log 2 = \lim_{x \to 1-} \log(1+x) = 1 - \frac{1}{2} + \frac{1}{3} - \frac{1}{4} + \text{......}$$

Example 7:

Show that

(i) $\tan^{-1} x = x - \frac{x^3}{3} + \frac{x^5}{5} \frac{x^7}{7} + \text{.......}, -1 < x \le 1$

(ii) $\frac{\pi}{4} = 1 - \frac{1}{3} + \frac{1}{5} - \frac{1}{7} + \text{......}$

(iii) $\frac{1}{2} (\tan^{-1} x)^2 = \frac{x^2}{2} - \frac{x^4}{4}\left(1 + \frac{1}{3}\right)$

$$+ \frac{x^6}{6}\left(1 + \frac{1}{3} + \frac{1}{5}\right) + \text{........}, -1 < x \le 1.$$

Solution:

We know

$(1 + x^2)^{-1} = 1 - x^2 + x^4 - x^6 + \text{......}, \quad |x| \le 1.$ ...(1)

Radius of convergence is

$$R = \lim_{n\to\infty} \left|\frac{a_n}{a_{n+1}}\right| = 1.$$

Thus, the series is convergent absolutely for all x such that $|x| < 1$, and is uniformly convergent in $[-k, k]$, $|k| < 1$.

The integrated series is also convergent absolutely in $]-1, 1[$ and uniformly in $[-k, k]$, $|k| < 1$.

Integrating (1), we get

$$\tan^{-1} x = \left(x - \frac{x^3}{3} + \frac{x^5}{5} - \frac{x^7}{7} + \text{.......}\right) + C, \quad |x| < 1.$$

where C is constant of integration.

Putting x = 0, we get C = 0 and so

$$\tan^{-1} x = x - \frac{x^3}{3} + \frac{x^5}{5} - \frac{x^7}{7} + \text{.......}, \quad |x| < 1.$$

Now the series

$x - \frac{x^3}{3} + \frac{x^5}{5} - \frac{x^7}{7} + \text{.......}$ is convergent at $x = \pm 1$.

[$\because$ for $x = 1$, $1 - \frac{1}{3} + \frac{1}{5} - \frac{1}{7} \text{......}$ is an alternating series which converges, by Leibnitz's test, Similarly it is convergent for $x = -1$].

By Abel's Theorem, it is uniformly convergent in [–1, 1].

Hence, $\tan^{-1} x = x - \frac{x^3}{3} + \frac{x^5}{5} - \frac{x^7}{7} + \ldots, -1 < x \le 1.$

(ii) Putting x = 1,

by Abel's Limit Theorem,

$$\frac{\pi}{4} = \tan^{-1} 1 = \lim_{x \to 1-0} \tan^{-1} x = 1 - \frac{1}{3} + \frac{1}{5} - \frac{1}{7} + \ldots\ldots$$

(iii) We have

$$\tan^{-1} x = x - \frac{x^3}{3} + \frac{x^5}{5} - \frac{x^7}{7} + \ldots, -1 < x \le 1.$$

and $(1 + x^2)^{-1} \tan^{-1} x = x - x^2 + x^4 - x^6 + \ldots\ldots, 1 < x < 1.$

By part (i), both the series are absolutely convergent in]–1, 1[, so they can be multiplied and their Cauchy's product will be equal, to

$$(1 + x^2)^{-1} \tan^{-1} x = x - \left(1 + \frac{1}{3}\right)x^2 + \left(1 + \frac{1}{3} + \frac{1}{5}\right)x^2 \quad -1 < x < 1.$$

Integrating, we get

$$\frac{1}{2}(\tan^{-1} x)^2 = \frac{x^2}{2} - \frac{x^4}{4}\left(1 + \frac{1}{3}\right) + \frac{x^6}{6}\left(1 + \frac{1}{3} + \frac{1}{5}\right) - \ldots\ldots, \quad -1 < x < 1$$

Here the constant of integration vanishes on taking x = 0.

By Leibnitz's Test, the series on the R.H.S. converges for x = 1. Hence the above expansion is valid for $-1 < x < 1$.

Example 8:

Find the radius of convergence of the series

$$\frac{1}{2}x + \frac{1.3}{2.5}x^2 + \frac{1.3.5}{2.5.8}x^2 + \ldots\ldots$$

Solution:

$$R = \lim_{n \to \infty} \left|\frac{a_n}{a_{n+1}}\right|$$

$$= \lim_{n \to \infty} \frac{1.3.5\ldots\ldots(2n-1)}{2.5.8\ldots\ldots(3n-1)}, \frac{2.5.8\ldots\ldots(3n-1)(3n+2)}{1.3.5\ldots\ldots(2n-1)(2n+1)}$$

$$= \lim_{n \to \infty} \frac{3n+2}{2n+1} = \frac{3}{2}.$$

Example 9:

Show that

$$\sin^{-1} x = x + \frac{1}{2}\frac{x^3}{3} + \frac{1.3}{2.4}\frac{x^5}{5} + \frac{1.3.5}{2.4.6}\frac{x^7}{7} + \ldots\ldots, 1<x<1.$$

Deduce that

$$\frac{\pi}{2} = 1 + \frac{1}{2}.\frac{1}{3} + \frac{1.3}{2.4}.\frac{1}{5} + \frac{1.3.5}{2.4.6}.\frac{1}{7} + \ldots\ldots$$

Solution:

We know that

$$\frac{1}{\sqrt{1-x^2}} = (1-x^2)^{-1/2}$$

$$= 1 + \frac{1}{2}x^2 + \frac{1.3}{2.4}x^4 + \frac{1.3.5}{2.4.6}x^6 + \ldots\ldots\ldots, |x| < 1.$$

The series on the R.H.S. is a power series with radius of convergence 1 and so it is absolutely convergent in]–1, 1[and uniformly convergent for [–k, k], | k | < 1. The integrated series is also convergent in]–1, 1[and uniformly convergent for [–k, k], | k | < 1. Integrating, we get

$$\sin^{-1} x = c + x + \frac{1}{2}.\frac{x^3}{3} + \frac{1.3}{2.4}.\frac{x^5}{5} + \frac{1.3.5}{2.4.6}.\frac{x^7}{7} + \ldots\ldots, |x| < 1$$

Putting x = 0, we get c = 0.

$$\therefore \sin^{-1} x + \frac{1}{2}.\frac{x^3}{3} + \frac{1.3}{2.4}.\frac{x^5}{5} + \frac{1.3.5}{2.4.6}.\frac{x^7}{7} + \ldots\ldots, -1 < x < 1 \quad \ldots(1)$$

For x = 1, the nth term of the series of the R.H.S. of (1) is

$$u_n = \frac{1.3.5\ldots\ldots\ldots\ldots(2n-1)}{2.4.6\ldots\ldots\ldots 2n(2n+1)}.$$

$$u_{n+1} = \frac{1.3.5\ldots\ldots\ldots\ldots(2n+1)}{2.4.6\ldots\ldots\ldots(2n+2)(2n+3)}.$$

$$\therefore \frac{u_n}{u_{n+1}} = \frac{(2n+2)(2n+3)}{(2n+1)^2}.\ n\left(\frac{u_n}{u_{n+1}} - 1\right) = \frac{6n^2+5}{(2n+1)^2}$$

$$\lim_{n\to\infty} n\left(\frac{u_n}{u_{n+1}} - 1\right) = \frac{3}{2} > 1.$$

So by Raabe's Test, the series is convergent for x = 1. Hence

$$\sin^{-1} x = x + \frac{1}{2}.\frac{x^3}{3} + \frac{1.3}{2.4}\frac{x^5}{5} + \frac{1.3.5}{2.4.6}\frac{x^7}{7} + \ldots\ldots, - < x < 1.$$

(ii) At x = 1, by Abel's Limit Theorem

$$\frac{\pi}{2} = \lim_{x\to 1-} \sin^{-1} x = 1 + \frac{1}{2}.\frac{1}{3} + \frac{1.3}{2.4}.\frac{1}{5} + \frac{1.3.5}{2.4.6}\frac{1}{7} + \ldots\ldots$$

Example 10:

Prove that the power series

$$1 + \frac{a.b}{1.c}x + \frac{a(a+1)\, b(b+1)}{1.2c\,(c+1)}x^2 + \ldots\ldots$$

has unit radius of convergence.

Solution:

$$a_n = \frac{a(a+1)\ldots\ldots(a+n-1)\, b(b+1)\ldots\ldots(b+n-1)}{1.2\ldots\ldots(n+1)\, c(c+1)\ldots\ldots(c+n-1)}$$

(omitting the first term)

$$a_{n+1} = \frac{a(a+1)\ldots\ldots(a+n)\, b(b+1)\ldots\ldots(b+n)}{1.2\ldots\ldots(n+1)\, c(c+1)\ldots\ldots(c+n)}$$

$$R = \lim_{n\to\infty}\left|\frac{a_n}{a_{n+1}}\right| = \lim_{n\to\infty}\frac{(n+1)\,(c+n)}{(a+n)\,(b+n)}$$

$$= \lim_{n\to\infty}\frac{(1+1/n)\,(1+c/n)}{(1+a/n)(1+b/n)} = 1.$$

Example 11:

Find the domain of convergence of the series

$$\text{(i)}\ \sum\frac{x^n}{n^2}, \quad \text{(ii)}\ \sum\frac{(-1)^n (x-1)^n}{2^n(3n-1)}.$$

Solution:

(i) $a_n = \frac{1}{n^3}$, $a_{n+1} = \frac{1}{(n+1)}$ so that

$$\lim_{n\to\infty}\frac{a_n}{a_{n+1}} = \lim_{n\to\infty}\left(\frac{n+1}{n}\right)^3 = 1. \text{ Thus } R = 1.$$

For x = 2, the given series is $\sum\frac{(-1)^{n+1}}{n}$, which is convergent by Leibnitz's Test. Hence the exact interval of convergence is]0, 2].

(iii) The given power series is about the point x = –2.

$$\lim_{n\to\infty}\left|\frac{a_n}{a_{n+1}}\right| = \lim_{n\to\infty}\frac{n!}{n^n}\frac{(n+1)^{n+1}}{(n+1)!} = \lim_{n\to\infty}\left(\frac{n+1}{n}\right)^n$$

$$= \lim_{n\to\infty}\left(1+\frac{1}{n}\right)^n = e.$$

$\therefore R = e$ and the interval of convergence is $]-2-e, -2+e[$.

Example 12:

Show that

(i) $\log(1-x) = -x - \frac{x^2}{2} - \frac{x^3}{3} - \ldots, \; -1 \le x < 1.$

(ii) $\log 2 = 1 - \frac{1}{2} + \frac{1}{3} - \frac{1}{4} + \ldots\ldots\ldots$

(iii) $\frac{1}{2}[\log(1-x)]^2 = \frac{x^2}{2} + \left(1+\frac{1}{2}\right)\frac{x^3}{3} + \left(1+\frac{1}{2}+\frac{1}{3}\right)\frac{x^4}{4} + \ldots, \; -1 < x < 1.$

Solution:

(i) We know that

$(1-x)^{-1} = 1 + x + x^2 + x^3 + \ldots, \; |x| < 1.$ ...(1)

Its radius of convergence is 1. So the above power series converges absolutely for $|x| < 1$ and uniformly for $[-k, k\backslash, |k| < 1$.

The integrated series is also convergent absolutely for $|x| < 1$ and uniformly for $[-k, k], \; |k| < 1$,

Integrating, we get

$-\log(1-x) = x + \frac{x^2}{2} - \frac{x^3}{3} + \ldots + c$

Putting $x = 0$, we get $c = 0$.

$\therefore \log(1-x) = -x - \frac{x^2}{2} - \frac{x^3}{3} - \ldots\ldots, \; -1 < x < 1.$

By Leibnitz Test, the power series on the R.H. S. converges at $x = -1$. So by Abel's Theorem.

$\log(1-x) = -x - \frac{x^2}{2} - \frac{x^3}{3} - \ldots\ldots, \; -1 < x < 1.$ ...(2)

(ii) At $x = -1$, by Abel's Limit Theorem

$\log 2 = \lim_{x\to -1-} \log(1-x) = 1 - \frac{1}{2} + \frac{1}{3} - \frac{1}{4} + \ldots$

(iii) both the series given on the R.H.S. of (1) and (2) are absolutely convergent in]–1, 1[, so their Cauchy's product will converge to $(1 - x)^{-1}$ log (1 – x). Thus

$$(1 - x)^{-1} \log (1 - x) = - [x + (1 + \frac{1}{2}) x^2 + (1 + \frac{1}{2} + \frac{1}{2}) x^2 + ...],$$
$$- 1 < x < 1$$

Integrating, we get

$$\frac{1}{2} [\log (1 - x)]^2 = \frac{x^2}{2} + \left(1 + \frac{1}{2}\right) x^3 + \left(1 + \frac{1}{2} + \frac{1}{3}\right) \frac{x^4}{4} + ...$$
$$- 1 < x < 1,$$

where the constant of integration vanishes.

Since the series on the right converge at x = –1, so by Abel's theorem, the above expansion is valid for $- 1 < x < 1$.

Example 13:

Find the radius of convergence and the exact interval of convergence of the following power series :

(i) $\sum \frac{(n+1)}{(n+2)(n+3)} x^{n,}$

(ii) $\sum \frac{(n!)^2 x^{2n}}{(2n)!}$.

Solution:

(i) $a_n = \frac{(n+1)}{(n+2)(n+3)}, \; a_{n+1} = \frac{(n+2)}{(n+3)(n+4)}$

$$\therefore \; R = \lim_{n \to \infty} \left| \frac{a_n}{a_{n+1}} \right| = \frac{(n+1)(n+4)}{!\,(n+2)^2} = 1.$$

Thus, the given series converges for $|x| < 1$ and diverges for $|x| > 1$. We now check at the end points x = 1, – 1.

For x = 1, the nth term of the series is

$$u_n = \frac{(n+1)}{(n+2)(n+3)} \sim \frac{n}{n^2} = \frac{1}{n}, \text{ which diverges.}$$

However, for x = – 1, the given series is an alternating series for which $u_{n+1} < u_n \; \forall \; n$ and $\lim_{n \to \infty} u_n = 0$. Thus, by Leibnitz's test, the series converges for x = –1.

Hence the interval of convergence is [–1, 1[.

(ii) We have $a_n = \frac{(n!)^2}{(2n)!}, a_{n+1} = \frac{[(n+1)!]^2}{(2n+2)!}$.

Then $\frac{a_n}{a_{n+1}} = \frac{(n!)^2}{\{(n+1)!\}^2} \frac{(2n+2)!}{(2n)!} = \frac{(2n+2)(2n+1)}{(n+1)^2}$

$$R = \lim_{n\to\infty} \left|\frac{a_n}{a_{n+1}}\right| = \lim_{n\to\infty} \frac{\left(2+\frac{2}{n}\right)\left(2+\frac{1}{n}\right)}{(1+1/n)^2} = 4.$$

It follows that the given series converges for $|x| < 4$ diverges for $|x| > 4$. Hence the interval of convergence is $]-4, 4[$.

Example 14:

Show that the series $\Sigma x^n/n^2$ is uniformly convergent in [–1, 1].

Solution:

We have $a_n = \frac{1}{n^2}, a_{n+1} = \frac{1}{(n+1)^2}$ so that

$$\lim_{n\to\infty} \left|\frac{a_n}{a_{n+1}}\right| = \lim_{n\to\infty} \frac{(n+1)^2}{n^2} = \lim_{n\to\infty} \left(1+\frac{1}{n}\right) = 1$$

The radius of convergence is R = 1 and so the given series is uniformly convergent in]–1, 1[.

For x = 1, given series is $\sum \frac{1}{n^2}$, which is convergent.

For x = –1, given series becomes

$$-1+\frac{1}{2^2}-\frac{1}{3^2}+\frac{1}{4^2}-.......$$

This is an alternating series for which $u_{n+1} \le u_n \ \forall\ n$ and

$$\lim_{n\to\infty} u_n = \lim_{n\to\infty} \frac{1}{n^2} = 0.$$

So by Leibnitz's Test, the series to convergent or x = –1. Hence by Abel's Theorem, given power series is uniformly convergent in [–1, 1].

Example 15:

Show that the following series

$$x+\frac{1}{2}\frac{x^2}{3}+\frac{1.3}{2.4}\frac{x^5}{5}+\frac{1.3.5}{2.4.6}\frac{x^7}{7}+......$$

is uniformly convergent in [–1, 1].

Solution:

Ignoring the first term, we have

$$a_n = \frac{1.3.5......(2n-1)}{2.4.6.....2n\ (2n+1)},\ a_{n+1} = \frac{1.3.5.....(2n-1)\ (2n+1)}{2.4.6......2n(2n+2)\ (2n+3)}$$

$$\therefore\ \lim_{n\to\infty} \frac{a_n}{a_{n+1}} = \lim_{n\to\infty} \frac{(2n+2)\ (2n+3)}{(2n+1)^2} = 1.$$

Since the radius of convergence is R = 1, given power series is uniformly convergent in]–1, 1[. For x = 1, we see that the D'Alembert's Ratio Test fails. Now

$$\lim_{n\to\infty}\left(\frac{a_n}{a_{n+1}}-1\right) = \lim_{n\to\infty} \frac{n(6n+5)}{(2n+1)^2} = \frac{6}{4} > 1.$$

By Raabe's Test, the series is convergent for x = 1.

Again for x = – 1, the series is convergent.

($\therefore\ \Sigma\, a_n$ is convergent $\Rightarrow -\Sigma\, a_n$ is convergent).

Hence, the given power series is uniformly convergent in [–1, 1] (Abel's Theorem).

A Note on Absolute and Uniform Convergence

It is to be noted carefully that the *uniform convergence* of a series does not necessarily ensure its *absolute convergence*, nor conversely. For example, the series $\Sigma = \frac{z^2}{(1+z^2)^n}$ converges *absolutely*, but not uniformly (near z = 0).

Again the series $\sum_{n=1}^{\infty} \frac{(-1)^{n-1}}{z^2+n}$ is not absolutely convergent, since the series $\sum_{n=1}^{\infty} \frac{1}{|n+z^2|}$ is divergent. But for all real values of z, the terms of the series are alternately positive and negative and each term is less than the preceding one and so the sum of the series lies between the sum of first n terms and of its first (n + 1) terms.

Hence the remainder after terms is numerically less than the nth term, is.,

Hence, taking an integer m > 1/ε we have $|R_n| < \varepsilon$, for all values of n ≥ m and all values of z. And so the series is *uniformly convergent.*

UNIFORM CONVERGENCE OF SEQUENCES OF FUNCTIONS

It is natural to expect that the value of N depends on ε as well as on x *i.e.* for a given ε the values of N will be different for different elements x of E.

If for each ε > 0 it is possible to determine an N such that (2) holds for all $x \in E$ then we say that $\{f_n\}$ is uniformly convergent on E.

Definition 1:

Let $\{f_n\}$ be a sequence of real valued functions on a set E. We say that $\{f_n\}$ converges uniformly to f on E if for a given ε > 0, there exists a positive integer N such that

$$| f_n (x) - f (x) \} \leq \varepsilon \qquad (n \geq N, x \in E).$$

obviously here N depends on ε but not x. It may also be noted that if f_n converge uniformly to f on E then $\{f_n\}$ is also pointwise convergent on E.

Hurwitz Theorem:

Let the function fn (z) be analytic and non-zero in a domain D and let fn (z) converge to f(z) uniformly on every closed and bounded (i.e. compact) subset of D. Then f (z) is either identically zero or never equal to zero in D.

Proof:

Suppose that f (z) is not identically zero. Then we want to show that f (z) is never zero in D. Assume the contrary to be true, that is, assume that $f(z_0) = 0$ for some $z_0 \varepsilon D$. Since zeros of an analytic function are isolated, there exists a number r > 0 such that f (z) is defined and ≠ 0 for $0 < | z - z_0 | \leq r$. In particular f (z) ≠ 0 on the circle $| z - z_0 | = r$ which We denote by Γ. Let

$$\varepsilon = \min \{ | f (z) | : z \in \Gamma \}$$

so that $\varepsilon \leq | f(z) |$ for every $z \in \Gamma$. ...(1)

Also by hypothesis, fn (z) converges to f(z) uniformly on Γ.

Hence for sufficiently large n, we have

$$| f_n(z) - f(z) | < \varepsilon \qquad ...(2)$$

for every $z \in \Gamma$. From (1) and (2), we conclude that

$$| f_n (2) - f(z) | \leq | f (z) |$$

for all points z on Γ. It follows by Rouche's theorem that the functions (z) and $f_n (z) - f (z) + f (z) = f_n (z)$ have the same number of zeros inside Γ

But f(z) has a zero at $z = z_0$. Hence f_n (z) must also have a zero inside Γ. But this contradicts the hypothesis that f_n (z) is non-zero in D.

Therefore f(z) can never be zero in D.

CAUCHY'S CRITERIA FOR UNIFORM CONVERGENCE OF SEQUENCE OF FUNCTIONS

The sequence of functions $\{f_n\}$, defined on a set E, is uniformly convergent on E if and only if for every $\varepsilon > 0$, $\exists$ a positive integer N s.t.

$$m \geq N,\ n \geq N \Rightarrow$$

$$| f_n (x) - f_m (x) | \leq \varepsilon \quad \forall x \in E,$$

i.e. $\{f_n\}$ is uniformly convergent of E iff we are able to find a term fN after which if f_m and f_n are any two terms ($m \leq N$, $n \leq N$) then the difference of $f_n(x)$ and $f_m(x)$ is arbitrarily small.

Proof:

Let $\{f_n\}$ be uniformly convergent on E and let f be the limit function. Then by the definition there exists a positive integer N such that

$| f_n (x) - f(x) | \leq \varepsilon/2$, for $n \leq N$ and $\forall x \in E$

In a similar way if $m \geq N$ then

$$| f_n (x) - f(x) | \geq \varepsilon/2 \quad \forall x \in E$$

Thus, $| f_n(x) - f_m(x) |$

$$= |[f_n(x) - f(x)] - \{f_m(x) - f(x)\}|$$

$$\leq | f_n(x) - f (x) | + | f_m (x) - f(x) |$$

$$\leq \varepsilon/2 + \varepsilon/2$$

$\therefore | f_n(x) - f_m(x) | \leq \varepsilon.$

Conversely, if Cauchy's condition hold then the sequence of $f_n(x)$ converges for every x to a limit say f(x). Thus the sequence $\{f_n\}$ converges to f on E. We have to prove that the convergence is uniform.

Let $\varepsilon > 0$ be a given arbitrary number, we choose N such that

$| f_n(x) - f_m(x) | \leq \varepsilon$ for $n \geq N$, $m \geq N$ and $x \in E$

Now keeping x fixed letting $m \to \infty$ over $f_m(x) \to f(x)$, and $| f_n(x) - f(x) | \leq \epsilon$ for every $n \geq N$ and every $n \in E$.

Hence theorem.

Uniform Convergence of an Infinite Series

Definition: A series of functions Σf_n is said to converge uniformly on [a, b] if the sequence (S_n) of its partial sums defined by

$$S_n(x) = f_1(x) + f_2(x) + ... + f_n(x) = \sum_{i=1}^{n} f_i(x)$$

converge uniformly on [a, b].

In other words, a series of functions Σf_n converges uniformly to a function f on [a, b] if for any $\varepsilon > o$, and for all $x \in [a, b]$, there exists a positive integer m (dependent on ε only and independent of x) such that

$$| f_1(x) + f_2(x) + ... + f_n(x) - f(x) | < \varepsilon, \quad \forall\, n \geq m, \quad \forall\, x \in [a, b].$$

Necessary and Sufficient Condition

Theorem 1:

The necessary and sufficient condition for the uniform convergence of the series $\Sigma f_n\,(x)$ defined on E is that $\forall\, \varepsilon > 0$, however small, there exists a natural number N independent of x such that for all $n \geq N$ we have

$$| f_{n+1}\,(x) + f_{n+2}(x) + f_{n+3}\,(x) + ... + (f_{n+p}(x) | \leq \varepsilon$$

where p may have any positive integral value.

Proof:

The condition is necessary

Let $\Sigma f_n(x)$ be uniformly convergent on E. Then for a given $\varepsilon > 0$ we can find a natural number N such that $\forall\, n \geq N$ and $\forall\, x \in E$ we have

$$| s_n(x) - s(x) | \leq ½\, \varepsilon \qquad ...(1)$$

where $s_n(x) = f_1(x) + f_2(x) + ... + f_n\,(x)$

and also $| s_{n+p}(x) - s\,(x) | \leq ½\, \varepsilon$ ...(2)

Thus,

$$| f_{n+1}(x) + f_{n+2}\,(x) + ... + f_{n+p}\,(x) | = | s_{n+p}\,(x) - s_n(x) |$$

$$\leq | s_{n+p}(x) - s(x) | + |s_n\,(x) - s(x) |$$

$$\leq \varepsilon/2 + \varepsilon/2 = \varepsilon.$$

This proves the necessity part of the theorem.

The condition is also sufficient.

If the given condition is satisfied for all $x \in E$, we have

$$| s_{n+p}(x) - s_n(x) | \leq ½\, \varepsilon$$

or $s_n(x) - ½\, \varepsilon \leq s_{n+p}\,(x) \leq s_n\,(x) + ½\, \varepsilon$

$\forall\, n \geq N$ and $P \geq 0$.

Now keeping n fixed and letting $p \to \infty$, so that $s_{n+p}(x) \to s(x)$, then

$s_n(x) - \frac{1}{2}\varepsilon \le s(x) \le s_n(x) + \frac{1}{2}\varepsilon$

i.e. $| s_n(x) - s(x) | \le \frac{1}{2}\varepsilon < \varepsilon \ \forall \ n \ge N$ and $\forall \ x \in E$.

This shows that the series $\sum f_n(x)$ is uniformly convergent.

Theorem 2:

A series of functions $\sum f_n$ defined on [a, b] converges uniformly on [a, b] iff for each $\varepsilon > 0$ and for all $x \in [a, b]$, there exists a positive integer m such that

$| f_{n+1}(x) + f_{n+2}(x) + ... + f_{n+p}(x) | < \varepsilon \ \forall \ n \ge m, p \ge 1.$

Proof:

Let $\{s_n\}$ be the sequence of partial sums of the series $\sum f_n$. Then

$$s_n(x) = \sum_{i=1}^{n} f_i(x). \qquad ...(1)$$

Let $\varepsilon > 0$ be given.

Hence $\sum f_n$ is uniformly convergent on [a, b].

$\Leftrightarrow$ the sequence $\{s_n\}$ is uniformly convergent on [a, b]

$\Leftrightarrow |s_{n+p}(x) - s_n(x) | < \varepsilon \ \forall \ n \ge m, p \ge 1, \forall \ x \in [a, b]$.

(Cauchy's principle of uniform convergence)

$\Leftrightarrow |f_{n+1}(x) + f_{n+2}(x) + ... + f_{n+p}(x) | < \varepsilon$

$\forall \ n \ge m, \forall \ p \ge 1$ and $\forall \ x \in [a, b]$. [using (1)]

A Test for Uniform Convergence of Sequence

Theorem 3:

Let $\{f_n\}$ be a sequence of functions such that

$\lim_{n \to \infty} f_n(x) = f(x) \ \forall \ x \in [a, b].$

Let $M_n = \sup \{ | f_n(x) - f(x) | : x \in [a, b]\}$ ...(1)

Then $f_n \to f$ uniformly on [a, b] iff $m_n \to o$ as $n \to \infty$.

Proof:

(Necessary Condition) : Let $f_n \to f$ uniformly on [a, b].

Then for any $\varepsilon > 0$, there exists a positive integer m such that

$| f_n(x) - f(x) | < \varepsilon \ \forall \ n \ge m$ and $\forall \ x \in [a, b]$

$\Rightarrow \sup \{ | f_n(x) - f(x) | : x \in [a, b]\} < \varepsilon \ \forall \ n \ge m$

$\Rightarrow M_n < \varepsilon \ \forall \ n \geq m \Rightarrow | M_n - 0 | < \varepsilon \ \forall \ n \geq m.$

Hence $M_n \to 0$ as $n \to \infty$.

(Sufficient Condition) : Let $M_n \to 0$ as $n \to \infty$.

Then for any $\varepsilon > 0$, there exists some positive integer m such that

$| M_n - 0 | < \varepsilon \ \forall \ n \geq m \Rightarrow M_n < \varepsilon \ \ \forall \ n \geq m$

$\Rightarrow \sup \{ | f_n(x) - f(x) | : x \in [a, b]\} < \varepsilon \ \ \forall \ n \geq m$

$\Rightarrow | f_n(x) - f(x) | < \varepsilon \ \forall \ n \geq m, \quad \forall \ x \in [a, b].$

Hence, $f_n \to f$ uniformly on [a, b].

Theorem 4:

(Weierstrass's M-test). A series of functions Σf_n will converge uniformly (and absolutely) on [a, b] if there exists a convergent series ΣM_n of positive numbers such that for all $x \in [a, b]$

$| f_n(x) | \leq M_n$, f or all n

Proof:

Let $\varepsilon > 0$ be a positive number,

Since ΣM_n is convergent, therefore there exists a positive integer N such that

$| M_{n+1} + M_{n+2} + ... + M_{n+p} | < \varepsilon \ \ \forall \ \ n \geq N, \ \ p \geq 1$ ...(1)

Hence for all $x \in [a, b]$ and for all $n \geq N$, $p \geq 1$, we have

$| f_{n+1} + f_{n+2} + ... + f_{n+p} (x) \leq | f_{n+1} (x) | + | f_{n+2} (x) | + ...$

$+ | f_{n+p} (x) |$ ...(2)

$\leq M_{n+1} + M_{n+2} + ... + M_{n+p} < \varepsilon$ ...(3)

(2) and (3) imply that Σf_n is uniformly and absolutely convergent on [a, b].

Remark 1:

The converse is not asserted and is, in fact, not true, i.e., non-convergence of ΣM_n does not imply anything as far as Σf_n is concerned.

Remark 2:

Series which satisfy the M-test have been called normally convergent by Baire, to emphasise the fact that such series are uniformly as well as absolutely convergent. The terminology has the additional advantage of emphasising the fact that the test can be applied to nearly all series in ordinary everyday use.

UNIFORM CONVERGENCE AND CONTINUITY

Theorem 5:

If $\{f_n\}$ is sequence of continuous functions on [a, b] and if $f_n \to f$ uniformly on [a, b], then f is continuous on [a, b].

Prove that the uniform limit of a uniformly convergent sequence of continuous functions is continuous.

Proof:

Let c be any point of [a, b]. Let $\varepsilon > 0$ be given.

Since $f_n \to f$ uniformly on [a, b], so there exists a positive integer m in such that $\forall x \in [a, b]$,

$| f_n (x) - f(x) | < \frac{1}{3} \varepsilon \quad \forall n \geq m.$

In particular, $| f_m(x) - f(x) | < \frac{1}{3} \varepsilon \quad \forall x \in [a, b]$ ...(1)

$\Rightarrow | f_m(c) - f(c) | < \frac{1}{3} \varepsilon.$ ...(2)

Since f_m is continuous at c, there exists some $\delta > 0$ such that

$| f_m(x) - f_m(c) | < \frac{1}{3}\varepsilon \ \forall x \in]c - d, c + d[.$ ...(3)

Now

$| f(x) - f(c) | = | f(x) - f_m(x) + f_m(x) - f_m(c) + f_m(c) - f(c) |$

$\leq | f(x) - f_m(x) | + | f_m(x) - f_m(c) | + |f_m(c) - f(c) |$

$< \frac{1}{3} \varepsilon + \frac{1}{3} \varepsilon + \frac{1}{3} \varepsilon = \varepsilon \ \forall x \in] c - \delta, c + \delta$ [[using (1), (2), (3)]

$\therefore | f(x) - f(c) | < \varepsilon \ \forall \ x \in] c - \delta, c + \delta[.$

Thus, f is continuous at c. As $c \in [a, b]$ is arbitrary, f is continuous on [a, b].

Theorem 6:

If a series Σf_n converges uniformly to f in [a, b] where each f_n is continuous in [a, b], then f is continuous in [a, b].

Proof:

Since Σf_n converges uniformly to f on [a, b], so for $\varepsilon >$, there exists a positive integer m such that for all $x \in [a, b]$.

$| S_n(x) - f(x) | < \frac{1}{3} \varepsilon \ \forall \ n \geq m, S_n(x) = \sum_{r=1}^{n} f_r (x).$

Let c be any point of [a, b]. It follows that

$$| S_m(x) - f(x) | < \tfrac{1}{3}\ \varepsilon\ \ \forall\ x \in [a, b], \qquad ...(1)$$

and
$$| S_m(c) - f(c) | < \tfrac{1}{3}\ \varepsilon. \qquad ...(2)$$

Since each $f_n(x)$ is continuous at c, so

$S_m(x) = \sum_{r=1}^{n} f_r(x)$ is continuous at c.

For $\varepsilon > 0$, there exists some $\delta > 0$ such that

$$| S_m(x) - S_m(c) | < \tfrac{1}{3}\ \epsilon,\ \forall\ x \in [c - \delta, c + \delta]. \qquad ....(3)$$

$$| S_m(x) + S_m(x) | = | f(x) - S_m(x) + S_m(x) - S_m(c) + S_m(c) - f(c) |$$
$$\leq | f(x) - S_m(x) | + | S_m(x) - S_m(c) | + |S_m(c) - f(c) |$$
$$< \tfrac{1}{3}\varepsilon + \tfrac{1}{3}\varepsilon + \tfrac{1}{3}\varepsilon = \varepsilon\ \forall\ x \in\ ]\ c - \delta,\ c + \delta[$$

[using (1), (2), (3)]

$\therefore | f(x) - f(c) | < \varepsilon\ \ \forall\ x \in]\ c - \delta,\ c + \delta[$.

Hence, f is continuous at $c \in [a, b]$ and so in [a, b].

Notes:

1. The converse of Theorems 6 and 7 may not be true. For example, $\{f_n\}$ defined by $f_n(x) = n\ xe^{-nx^2}$ is a sequence of continuous functions is not uniformly convergent in [0, 1] but the point-wise limit f, given by $f(x) = 0\ x \in [0, 1]$, is a continuous function in [0, 1].
2. If the limit function of a sequence of continuous functions is not continuous on [a, b], then the convergence cannot be uniform.
3. If the sum function of a series of continuous functions is not continuous in [a, b], then the convergence cannot be uniform.

Theorem 7:

(Abel's test). If $b_n(x)$ is a positive, monotonic decreasing function of n for each fixed value of x in the interval [a, b], and $b_n(x)$ is bounded for all values of n and x concerned, and if the series $\sum u_n(x)$ is uniformly convergent on [a, b], then so also is the series $\sum b_n(x)u_n(x)$.

Proof:

Since $b_n(x)$ is bounded for all values of n and for x in [a, b], therefore there exists a number $K > 0$, independent of x and n, such that for all $x \in$ [a, b],

$$0 \le b_n(x) \le K, \qquad (\text{for } n = 1, 2, 3, ...) \qquad ...(1)$$

Again since $\Sigma u_n(x)$ converges uniformly on [a, b], therefore for any $\varepsilon > 0$, we can find an integer N such that

$$\left|\sum_{r=n+1}^{n+p} u_r(x)\right| < \frac{\varepsilon}{K}, \qquad \forall\ n \ge N,\ p \ge 1 \qquad ...(2)$$

Hence using Abel's Lemma, we get

$$\left|\sum_{r=n+1}^{n+p} b_r(x)u_r(x)\right| \le b_{n+1}(x) \max_{q=1,2,...p} \left|\sum_{r=n+1}^{n+q} u_r(x)\right|$$

$$< K\,\frac{\varepsilon}{K} = \varepsilon, \text{ for } n \ge N,\ p \ge 1,\ a \le x \le b.$$

$\Rightarrow \Sigma\, b_n(x)U_n(x)$ is uniformly convergent on [a, b].

Corollary 1:

A uniformly convergent series $\Sigma\, u_n(x)$ remains uniformly convergent on [a, b], if its terms are each multiplied by a function $a_n(x)$, $a \le x \le b$, provided that the sequence $\{a_n(x)\}$ is uniformly bounded on [a, b] (ie., $\exists\, K > 0$, such that $|\, a_n(x)\,| \le K$, for all x in [a, b] and for all n), and monotonic in n, for each $x \in [a, b]$.

Proof:

Under the given conditions, $\{a_n(x)\}$ converges point-wise. Let us write for each $x \in [a, b]$,

$$b_n(x) = \left\{\lim_{n\to\infty} a_n(x)\right\} - a_n(x),$$

or
$$a_n(x) - \lim_{n\to\infty} a_n(x),$$

according as $\{a_n(x)\}$ is monotonic increasing or decreasing. With this function $b_n(x)$, we deduce as above that the series $\Sigma\, b_n(x)\, u_n(x)$ converges uniformly on [a, b]. Also, since $\Sigma\, u_n(x)$ and hence $\Sigma\, [\lim a_n(x)]\, u_n(x)$ ($\because |\lim a_n(x)| \le K$, $a \le x \le b$) converges uniformly on [a, b]. The uniform convergence of $\Sigma\, a_n(x)\, u_n(x)$, then follows easily.

Corollary 2:

If $\sum_{n=1}^{\infty} a_n x^n$ is a (power) series which converges for all values of x, where $|\, x\,| < R$, then $\Sigma\, a_n x^n$ is uniformly convergent in [0, R] if and only if $\Sigma\, a_n R^n$ is convergent.

Proof:

Let $\Sigma\, a_n R^n$ be convergent, so that being a series of real numbers, it is uniformly convergent in [0, R].

Now, since $\Sigma\, a_n R^n$ is uniformly convergent, and $(x/R)^n$ is a positive monotonic decreasing bounded function of n, for each value of x in [0, R], therefore by Abel's test, the series $\Sigma\, a_n R^n (x/R)^n$ $\Sigma\, a_n x^n R^n$ is uniformly convergent on [a, b].

If the series $\Sigma\, a_n x^n$ is uniformly convergent in [0, R], it is obviously convergent at x = R.

Theorem 8:

If a series Σf_n converges uniformly to f on [a, b] and each f_n is continuous on [a, b], then f is integrable on [a, b] and

$$\int_a^b f\,dt = \sum_{n=1}^{\infty} \int_a^b f_n\,dt.$$

Proof:

By theorem 6, f is continuous on [a, b] and so f is integrable on [a, b].

Since each $f_n(x)$ is continuous on [a, b], so

$S_n(x) = \sum_{r=1}^{n} f_r(x)$ is also continuous and integrable on [a, b].

Further,

$$\sum_{r=1}^{n} \int_a^b f_r\,dt = \int_a^b \sum_{r=1}^{n} f_r dt. \qquad ...(1)$$

By the uniform convergence of the series, given any $\varepsilon > 0$, there exists positive integer m such that for all x in [a, b],

$$| S_n(x) - f(x) | < \varepsilon/(b-a) \ \forall \ n \geq m \qquad ...(2)$$

Now $\left|\sum_{1}^{n} \int_a^b f_r\,dt - \int_a^b f\,dt\right| = \left|\int_a^b \sum_{1}^{n} \int_a^b f_r\,dt - \int_a^b f\,dt\right|$, by (1)

$= \left|\int_a^b (S_n - f)\,dt\right| \leq \int_a^b |S_n - f|\,dt$

$< \dfrac{\varepsilon}{(b-a)}(b-a) = \varepsilon \quad \forall\ n \geq m$, using (2).

$$\therefore \lim_{n\to\infty} \sum_{r=1}^{n} \int_a^b f_r dt = \int_a^b f dt.$$

Hence, $\displaystyle\sum_{r=1}^{\infty} \int_a^b f_r dt = \int_a^b f dt.$

Theorem 9:

If a series Σf_n converges uniformly to f on $[a, b]$ and each f_n is integrable on $[a, b]$, then f is integrable on $[a, b]$. Further

$$\int_a^b f dt = \sum_{n=1}^{\infty} \int_a^b f_n dt.$$

In this case, we say that the series is integrable term by term.

Remark 1:

A sequence (series) may converge to an integrable limit without being uniformly convergent.

Remark 2:

If $f_n \to f$ (point-wise) and f is not integrable (where each f_n is integrable), then the convergence cannot be uniform.

Further, if

$$\lim_{n\to\infty} \int_a^b f_n dt \neq \int_a^b f dt$$

(where each f_n is integrable), then also the convergence cannot be uniform.

The similar results are also true for a series Σf_n.

Uniform Convergence and Integrability

Theorem 10:

If a sequence $\{f_n\}$ converges uniformly to f on $[a, b]$, and each f_n is integrable on $[a, b]$, then f is integrable o n $[a, b]$ and

$$\int_a^b f dt \lim_{n\to\infty} \int_a^b f_n dt.$$

Proof:

Let $\varepsilon > 0$ be given. Since $f_n \to f$ uniformly on $[a, b]$, there exists a positive integer m such that for all $x \in [a, b]$.

$$| f_n(x) - f(x) | < \frac{\varepsilon}{3(b-a)} \qquad \forall\ n \geq m. \qquad ...(1)$$

For n = m, we obtain

$$| f_m(x) - f(x) | < \frac{\varepsilon}{3(b-a)} \qquad ...(2)$$

Since f_m is integrable on $[a, b]$, there exists a partition P of $[a, b]$ such that

$U(P, f_m) - L(P, f_m) < \frac{1}{3}\varepsilon$ ...(3)

From (2), we get

$$f(x) - \frac{\varepsilon}{3(b-a)} < f_m(x) < f(x) + \frac{\varepsilon}{3(b-a)} \quad ...(4)$$

$$\Rightarrow f(x) < f_m(x) + \frac{\varepsilon}{3(b-a)}$$

$$\Rightarrow U(P, f) < U(P, f_m) + \frac{\varepsilon}{3(b-a)}.(b-a) \quad ...(5)$$

Again, from (4), $f(x) > f_m(x) - \frac{\varepsilon}{3(b-a)}$

$$\Rightarrow L(P, f) > L(P, f_m) - \frac{\varepsilon}{3(b-a)}(b-a) \quad ...(6)$$

From (5) and (6), we get

$$U(P, f) - L P, f) < U(P, f_m) - L(P, f_m) + \frac{1}{3}\varepsilon$$

$$< \frac{1}{3}\varepsilon + \frac{2}{3}\varepsilon = \varepsilon, \text{ by (3).}$$

Hence, f is integrable on [a, b].

Now, we prove the second part.

Since $f_n \to f$ uniformly on [a, b], there exists a positive integer N such that for all $x \in [a, b]$,

$$|f_n(x) - f(x)| < \varepsilon/(b-a) \quad \forall\, n \geq N. \quad ...(7)$$

Consider $\left|\int_a^b f_n dt - \int_a^b f_n dt\right| = \left|\int_a^b (f_n - f)\,dt\right|$

$$\leq \int_a^b |f_n - f|\,dt < \frac{\varepsilon}{(b-a)}(b-a) = \varepsilon, \text{ by (7)}$$

$$\therefore \quad \left|\int_a^b f_n\,dt - \int_a^b f_n\,dt\right| < \varepsilon \;\; \forall\, n \geq N.$$

Hence, $\lim_{n\to\infty} \int_a^b f_n dt = \int_a^b f dt$.

Hence, the theorem.

UNIFORM CONVERGENCE AND DIFFERENTIATION

The series $\sum \frac{\sin nx}{n^2}$ converges uniformly for all values of x, and every term, without exception, is continuous and differentiable. The series of differentials, $\sum \frac{\cos nx}{n}$, however, diverges at x = 0. The situation, therefore, seems to be different in the case of differentiation, and accordingly the theorem on term by term differentiation must be of a different stamp.

Theorem:

(A) *Let $\{f_n\}$ be a sequence of differentiable functions an [a, b] such that it converges at least at one point $x_0 \in [a, b]$. If the sequence of differentials $\{f_n'\}$ converges uniformly to G on [a, b] then the given sequence $\{f_n\}$ converges uniformly on [a, b] to f, and $f'(x) = G(x)$.*

(B) Let $\sum f_n$ be a series of differentiable functions of [a, b] and such that it converges at least at one point $x_0 \in [a, b]$. If the series of differentials $\sum f_n'$ converges uniformly to G on [a, b], then the given series $\sum f_n$ converges uniformly on [a, b] to f, and $f'(x) = G(x)$.

(The existence of f' is part of the conclusion.)

Proof:

(A) Let $\varepsilon > 0$ be any number.

By the convergence of $\{f_n(x_0)\}$ and uniform convergence of $\{f_n'\}$, for $\varepsilon > 0$, we can choose a positive integer N such that for all $x \in [a, b]$

$$| f_{n+p}(x_0) - f_n(x_0) | < \varepsilon/2, \qquad \forall\, n \geq N,\ P \geq 1 \qquad ...(1)$$

$$| f'_{n+p}(x) - f_n'(x) | < \varepsilon/2(b-a), \qquad \forall\, n \geq N,\ p \geq 1 \qquad ...(2)$$

Applying Lagrange's mean value theorem to the function $(f_{n+p} - f_n)$ for any two points x and t of [a, b], we get for $x < \xi < t$, for all $n \geq N$, $p \geq 1$

$$| f_{n+p}(x) - f_n(x) - f_{n+p}(t) + f_n(t) | = | x - t | \, | f'_{n+p}(\xi) - f_n'(\xi) |$$

$$< \frac{|x-t|\varepsilon}{2(b-a)} \qquad ...(3)$$

$$< \varepsilon/2 \qquad ...(3a)$$

and

$$| f_{n+p}(x) - f_n(x) | \leq | f_{n+p}(x) - f_n(x) - f_{n+p}(x_0) + f_n(x_0) |$$
$$+ | f_{n+p}(x_0) - f_n(x_0) |$$
$$< \tfrac{1}{2}\varepsilon + \tfrac{1}{2}\varepsilon = \varepsilon \qquad \text{[using (1), (3a)]}$$

$\Rightarrow$The sequence $\{f_n\}$ uniformly converges on [a, b].

Let it converge to f, say.

For a fixed x on [a, b] and for $t \in [a, b]$, $t \neq x$, let us define

$$\phi_n(t) = \frac{f_n(t) - f_n(x)}{t - x}, \ n = 1, 2, 3, ... \qquad ...(4)$$

$$\phi(t) = \frac{f(t) - f(x)}{t - x} \quad ...(5)$$

Since each f_n is differentiable, therefore for each n

$$\lim_{t \to x} \phi_n(t) = f'_n(x) \quad (6)$$

$$\therefore |\phi_{n+p}(t) - \phi_n(t)| = \frac{1}{|t-x|} | f_{n+p}(t) - f_{n+p}(x) - f_n(t) + f_n(x) |$$

$$= \frac{1}{|t-x|} | \{f_{n+p}(t) - f_n(t)\} - \{f_{n+p}(x) - f_n(x)\} |$$

$$< \frac{\varepsilon}{2(b-a)}, \quad \forall\, n \geq N, p \geq 1 \quad \text{(using (3))}$$

so that $\{\phi_n(t)\}$ converges uniformly on [a, b], for $t \neq x$.

Since $\{f_n\}$ also converges uniformly to f, therefore from (4).

$$\lim_{n \to \infty} \phi_n(t) = \lim_{n \to \infty} \frac{f_n(t) - f_n(x)}{t - x} = \frac{f(t) - f(x)}{t - x} = \phi(t)$$

Thus, $\{\phi_n(t)\}$ converges uniformly to $\phi(t)$ on [a, b], for $t \in [a, b]$, $t \neq x$.

Applying Theorem 7(A) to the uniformly convergent sequence $\{\phi_n(t)\}$ and using (6), we get

$$\lim_{t \to x} \phi_n(t) = \lim_{n \to \infty} f_n'(x) = G(x)$$

$$\Rightarrow \lim_{t \to x} \phi_n(t) = \text{exists},$$

and therefore, (5) implies that f is differentiable and

$$\lim_{t \to x} \phi_n(t) = f'(x)$$

Hence$f'(x) = G(x) = \lim_{n \to \infty} f'(x)$

This completes the proof of the theorem.

If in addition to the above hypothesis of the theorem, continuity of the functions f_n' is also assumed, then a much shorter proof of the theorem exists.

We now prove a simple version of the theorem for series; that for sequence may be written down on the same lines.

UNIFORM CONVERGENCE AND DERIVABILITY

Theorem:

Suppose a series Σf_n of derivable functions converges point-wise to f on [a, b], each f'_n is continuous on [a, b] and the series $\Sigma f'_n$ converges uniformly to a function G on [a, b]. Then

$f'(x) = G(x) \quad \forall\, x \in [a, b]$

$$\text{or } \frac{d}{dx}\left\{\sum_{n=1}^{\infty} f_n(x)\right\} = \sum_{n=1}^{\infty} \frac{d}{dx} f_n(x).$$

Further the given series $\Sigma f_n(x)$ converges uniformly to f on [a, b].

Proof:

Since the series $\Sigma f'_n$ of continuous functions converges uniformly to G on [a, b], therefore, its sum function G is continuous on [a, b]. Consequently $\int_a^x G(t)\,dt$ is differentiable and

$$\frac{d}{dx}\int_a^x G(t)\,dt = G(x)\ \forall\ x \in [a, b] \qquad ...(1)$$

We are given that

$$f(x) = \sum_{n=1}^{\infty} f_n(x),\ \ \forall\ x \in [a, b] \qquad ...(2)$$

Since each function f'_n being continuous is integrable on [a, b],

So we have

$$\int_a^x f'_n(t)\,dt = f_n(x) - f_n(a) \qquad \forall\ n \geq 1,\ x \in [a, b] \qquad ...(3)$$

From (2) and (3), we obtain

$$\sum_{n=1}^{\infty} \int_a^x f'_n(t)\delta = f(x) - f(a)\ \ \forall\ x \in [a, b] \qquad ...(4)$$

Since the series $\Sigma f'_n$ of continuous functions converges uniformly to G on [a, b], therefore we have

$$\int_a^x G(t)\,dt = \sum_{n=1}^{\infty} \int_a^x f'_n(t)\,dt,\ \ \forall\ x\ \in [a, b] \qquad \text{[Theorem 9]}$$

$$= f(x) - f(a) \qquad \forall\ x \in [a, b], \text{ by (4)}$$

$$\therefore \frac{d}{dx}\int_a^x G(t)\,dt = f'(x) \qquad \forall\ x \in [a, b]$$

Hence $f'(x) = G(x)\ \ \forall\ x \in [a, b]$, by (1)

$$\text{or } \ \frac{d}{dx}\left\{\sum_{n=1}^{\infty} f_n(x)\right\} = \sum_{n=1}^{\infty} f_n'(x) \qquad \forall\ x \in [a, b]$$

(ii) Finally we show that Σf_n converges uniformly to f on [a, b]

For any $x_0 \in [a, b]$, $\Sigma f_n(x_0)$ to $f(x_0)$ is point-wise convergent.

By the convergence of $\Sigma f_n (x_0)$ to $f(x_0)$ and uniform convergence of $\Sigma f_n'$ to f', for $\varepsilon > 0$, we can choose a positive integer m such that for all $x \in [a, b]$,

$$| S_n(x_0) - f(x_0) | < \tfrac{1}{2} \varepsilon \forall n \geq m, \quad ...(5)$$

$$\text{and} |S_n'(x) - f'(x)| < \frac{\varepsilon}{2(b-a)} \forall n \geq m, \quad ...(6)$$

$$\text{where} S_n(x) = \sum_{r=1}^{n} f_r(x).$$

Applying Lagrange's mean value theorem to the function $[\delta - (x) - f(x)]$ for any two points x_0, x of [a, b], there exists some $x \in]x_0, x[$ such that $\forall n \geq m$,

$$| \{S_n(x) - f(x) \} - \{S_n(x_0) - f(x_0) \} | - | x-x_0 | | S_n'(c) - f'(c) | <$$

$$\frac{\varepsilon|x-x_0|}{2(b-a)} < \frac{\varepsilon}{2}, \text{ [by (6)]} \quad ...(7)$$

Now,

$$| S_n(x) - f(x) | = | \{s_n(x) - f(X) \} - \{S_n(x_0) - f(x_0)\} + \{S_n(x_0) - f(x_0)\}|$$

$$< \tfrac{1}{2} \varepsilon + \tfrac{1}{2} \varepsilon = \varepsilon \quad \forall n \geq m \text{ and } \forall x \in [a, b].$$

(using (5) and (7))

Hence the series Σf_n converges uniformly to f on [a, b].

Remark 1:

The above theorem shows conditions under which a series can be differentiated term by term.

Remark 2:

It must be noted that for term by term differentiation of the series Σfn, the derived series $\Sigma fn'$ must be uniformly convergent and the given series Σf_n need only be point-wise convergent.

The above theorem can also be proved for a sequence of functions in the similar manner.

Theorem:

Suppose a sequence $\{f_n\}$ of differentiable functions converges point-wise to f on [a, b] and that each fn' is continuous on [a, b]. If the sequence $[f_n'\}$ converges uniformly to G on [a, b], then the given sequence $\{f_n\}$ converges uniformly to f on [a, b], and f' (x) = G (x) or

$$f'(x) = \lim_{n\to\infty} f_n'(x).$$

WEIERSTRASS'S M-TEST

The series $\Sigma u_n(z)$ converges uniformly and absolutely in a bounded closed domain D, if

(i) $|u_n(z)| \le M_n$ for every n and z in D, where M_n is a positive constant independent of z, and

(ii) the series ΣM_n is convergent.

Weierstrass's Approximation Theorem

Theorem:

If f is a real valued continuous function defined on a closed interval [a, b], then there exists a sequence of real polynomials $\{P_n(x)\}$ which converges uniformly to f(x) on [a, b].

Proof:

Without any loss of generality, we may suppose that [a, b] = [0, 1].

Let $g(x) = f(x) - f(0) - x\,[f(1) - f(0)],\ 0 \le x \le 1$.

Here g(0) = 0 = g)1) and further f(x) – g(x) is a polynomial of degree one.

If g(x) can be expressed as the limit of a uniformly convergent sequence of polynomials, then the same is true of f(x), since f(x) = [f(x) – g(x)] + g(x) and f(x) – g(x) is a polynomial.

So we may assume that f(0) = f(1) = 0.

Since f is defined on [0, 1], we may take

f(x) = 0 outside [0, 1].

We write $q_n(x) = c_n(1 - x^2)^n,\ n\in N$; ....(1)

where C_n is such that

$$\int_{-1}^{1} Q_n(x)\,dx = 1,\ n \in N \qquad ....(2)$$

$$\text{or } 1 = \int_{-1}^{1} C_n(1-x^2)^n\,dx = 2C_n \int_0^1 (1-x^2)^n dx$$

$$\ge 2C_n \int_0^{1/\sqrt{n}} (1-x^2)^n\,dx$$

$$\ge 2C_n \int_0^{1/\sqrt{n}} (1-nx^2)\,dx \quad [\because (1-x^2)^n > (1-nx^2) \text{ for } x \in [0, 1]]$$

$$\therefore 1 \geq 2\, C_n \left| x - \frac{1}{3} nx^2 \right|_0^{1/\sqrt{n}} = \frac{4C_n}{3\sqrt{n}} > \frac{C_n}{\sqrt{n}}$$

Thus, $C_n < \sqrt{n}$. Using in (1), we get

$$Q_n(x) < \sqrt{n}\,(1 - x^2)^n$$

or $$Q_n(x) \geq \sqrt{n}\,(1 - \delta^2)^n, \text{ where } \delta \leq |x| \leq 1. \quad ...(3)$$

Let $P_n(x) = \int_{-1}^{1} f(x+t)\, Q_n(t)\, dt,\ 0 \leq x \leq 1$ ...(4)

or $P_n(x) = \int_{-1}^{-x} + \int_{-x}^{1-x} + \int_{1-x}^{1}$ ...(5)

Now, $-1 \leq t \leq -x \Rightarrow -1 + x \leq t + x \leq 0 \Rightarrow x + t$ lies outside $[0, 1]$ and so $f(x + t) = 0$.

Again $1 - x \leq t \leq 1 \Rightarrow 1 \leq x + t \leq 1 + x \Rightarrow x + t$ lies outside $[0, 1]$ and so $f(x + t) = 0$.

Thus the first and third integrals on the R.H.S. of (5) vanish.

Consequently,

$P_n(x) = \int_{-x}^{1-x} f(x+t)\, Q_n(t)\, dt$, from (5)

or $P_n(x) = \int_0^1 f(t)\, Q_n(t-x)\, dt$,

which is a real polynomial of degree 2n in x, by (1).

We now proceed to show that the sequence $\{P_n(x)\}$ converges uniformly to f on [0, 1].

Since f is continuous on the closed interval [0, 1], f is bounded and uniformly continuous on [0, 1]. Thus, there exists some number $M > 0$ such that

$|f(x)| \leq M \quad \forall\ x \in [0, 1]$ ...(6)

Since f is uniformly continuous on [0, 1], for any $\varepsilon > 0$, there exists some δ, $0 < \delta < 1$ such that for any two points x_1, x_2 in [0, 1],

$|f(x_1) - f(x_2)| < \frac{1}{2}\varepsilon$, when $|x_1 - x_2| < \delta \leq 1$. ...(7)

For $0 \leq x \leq 1$, we have, by (4),

$$|P_n(x) - f(x)| = \left| \int_{-1}^{1} f(x+t)\, Q_n(t)\, dt - f(x) \right|$$

$$= \left| \int_{-1}^{1} \{f(x+t) - f(x)\} Q_n(t)\, dt \right|, \text{ by (2)}$$

$$\leq \int_{-1}^{1} |f(x+t) - f(x)|\, Q_n(t)\, dt$$

$$= \int_{-1}^{-\delta} + \int_{-\delta}^{\delta} + \int_{\delta}^{1}$$

Using (6) and (7), we get

$$| P_n(x) - f(x) | \leq 2M \int_{-1}^{-\delta} Q_n(t)\, dt + \tfrac{1}{2}\varepsilon \int_{-\delta}^{\delta} Q_n(t)\, dt + 2M \int_{\delta}^{1} Q_n(t)\, dt$$

$[\because | f(x + t) - f(x) | \leq | f(x+t) | + | f(x) | \leq M + M = 2M$, by (6)]

$$| P_n(x) - f(x) | \leq 2M \sqrt{n}\, (1 - \delta^2) \left[\int_{-1}^{-\delta} dt + \int_{\delta}^{1} dt \right] + \frac{1}{2}\varepsilon \text{ by (3)}$$

$= 2M \sqrt{n}\, (1 - \delta^2)^n [(1 - \delta) + (1 - \delta)] + ½\, \varepsilon$

$< 4M \sqrt{n}\, (1 - \delta^n) + ½\, \varepsilon$ $\qquad (\because 0 < \delta < 1)$.

Now, $0 < \delta < 1 \Rightarrow 0 < (1 - \delta^2) < 1 \Rightarrow \lim_{n\to\infty} (1 - \delta^2)^n = 0$.

Thus, there exists a positive integer N such that

$$(1 - \delta^2)^n < \frac{\varepsilon}{8M\sqrt{n}} \quad \forall\, n \geq N.$$

$\therefore | P_n(x) - f(x) | < ½\, \varepsilon + ½\, \varepsilon = \varepsilon \quad \forall\, n \geq N,$

where N is independent of

Hence, $\{P_n(x)\}$ converges uniformly to f(x) on [0, 1].

Corollary:

For any interval [–a, a], there is a sequence of real polynomials $\{P_n(x)\}$ such that $P_n(0) = 0$, and that

$$\lim_{n\to\infty} p_n(x) = | x |, \textit{ uniformly on } [-a, a].$$

Proof:

Since | x | is a continuous function on [–a, a], so there exists a sequence $\{Q_n(x)\}$ of real polynomials such that

$$\lim_{n\to\infty} Q_n(x) = | x | \quad \forall\, x \in [-a, a].$$

In particular, $\lim_{n\to\infty} Q_n(0) = 0$. $\qquad (\because 0 \in [-a, a])$

Let $P_n(x) = Q_n(x) - Q_n(0) \quad \forall\, n \in N,\ x \in [-a, a]$.

Hence $\lim_{n\to\infty} P_n(x) = | x | - 0 = | x | \quad \forall\, x \in [-a, a]$.

ABEL'S TEST FOR THE CONVERGENCE OF INTEGRAL OF A PRODUCT

If $\int_a^\infty f(x)\,dx$ converges and $\phi(x)$ is bounded and monotonic for $x > a$ then $\int_a^\infty f(x)\,.\,\phi(x)\,dx$ is convergent.

Example 1:

Test for the convergence of $\int_a^\infty e^{-x}\frac{\sin x}{x^2}\,dx$ *when* $a > 0$

Solution:

Let $f(x) = \frac{\sin x}{x^2}$ and $\phi(x) = e^{-x}$

Since $\left|\frac{\sin x}{x^2}\right| \le \frac{1}{x^2}$ and $\int_a^\infty \frac{1}{x^2}\,dx$ is convergent.

Therefore by comparison test $\int_a^\infty \frac{\sin x}{x^2}\,dx$ is also convergent.

Again e^{-x} is monotonic decreasing and bounded function for $x > a$

Hence by Abel's Test $\int_a^\infty e^{-x}\frac{\sin x}{x^2}\,dx$ is convergent

Example 2:

Test the convergence of $\int_a^\infty (1-e^{-x})\frac{\cos x}{x^2}\,dx$ *where as 0*

Solution:

$f(x) = \frac{\cos x}{x^2}$ and $\phi(x) = 1 - e^{-x}$

Here we have $\left|\frac{\cos x}{x^2}\right| \le \frac{1}{x^2}$ as $|\cos x| \le 1$

Since $\int_a^\infty \frac{1}{x^2}$ is convergent, therefore by comparison test $\int_a^\infty \frac{\cos x}{x^2}\,dx$ is also convergent Again $\phi(x) = 1 - e^{-x}$ is monotonic increasing and bounded function for $x > a$.

Hence by Abel's Test $\int_a^\infty (1-e^{-x})\frac{\cos x}{x^2}\,dx$ is convergent

DIRICHLET'S TEST FOR THE CONVERGENCE OF INTEGRATE OF A PRODUCT

If f(x) is bounded and monotonic $a \le x < \infty$ f $\lim_{x\to\infty} f(x) = 0$ Then thee integral $\int_a^\infty f(x)\,\phi(x)\,dx$ converges provided $\left|\int_a^\infty \phi(x)\ dx\right|$ is bounded as x takes all finite values.

Example 1:

Show that the integral

$$\int_0^\infty e^{-ax}\frac{\sin x}{x}\,dx,\ a \le 0 \text{ convergent}$$

Solution:

$$\int_0^\infty e^{-ax}\frac{\sin x}{x} = \int_0^\infty e^{-ax}\frac{\sin x}{x}\,dx + \int_a^{\infty/e^{-ax}}\frac{\sin x}{x}\,dx$$

Where $a > 0$

Since $\lim_{x\to 0} e^{-ax}\frac{\sin x}{x} = 1$ the integral $\int_0^a e^{-ax}\frac{\sin x}{x}dx$ is a proper integral and hence convergent.

Now it remains to test the convergence of $\int_a^\infty e^{-ax}\frac{\sin x}{x}\,dx$

Let $f(x) = \frac{e^{-ax}}{x}$ and $\phi(x) = \sin x$

Obviously the function $f(x) = \frac{1}{x^{ax}}$ is bounded and monotonic decreasing for all $x \ge 0$ and $\lim_{x\to\infty} f(x)\ \lim_{x\to\infty}\frac{1}{xe^{ax}} = 0$

Moreover $\left|\int_a^x \phi(x)\,dx\right| = \left|\int_a^x \sin x\,dx\right|$

$= |\cos a = \cos x| \le 2$ for all sin x value of x

Example 2:

Test the convergence of the integral

$$\int_a^\infty \frac{\sin x}{\sqrt{x}}\,dx,\ \textit{where } a > 0$$

Solution:

Let $f(x) = \frac{1}{\sqrt{x}}$ and $\phi(x) = \sin$

Now $\frac{1}{\sqrt{x}}$ is bounded and monotonic decreasing for all $x \ge a$ and $\lim_{x\to\infty}\frac{1}{\sqrt{x}} = 0$

Also $\left|\int_a^x \phi(x)\,dx\right| = \left|\int_a^x \sin x\,dx\right| = |\cos a - \cos x| \le 2$ for all finite value of x

[Note that the value of cone lies between –1 and 1]

$\left|\int_a^x f(x)\,dx\right|$ is bounded for all finite values of x

Hence by Drichlet's test the integral $\int_a^\infty \frac{\sin}{\sqrt{x}}\,dx$ is convergent

THE μ-TEST

Let f(x) be bounded and integrable in the interval (a, ∞) where a > 0

If there is number μ ϕ > 1 such that $\lim_{x\to\infty} x^{\mu} f(x)$ exists then $\int_a^\infty f(x)\,dx$ is convergent

If there is a number μ ≤ 1 such that $\lim_{x\to\infty} x^{\mu} f(x)$ exists and is non-zero then $\int_a^\infty f(x)\,dx$ is divergent and the same is true if $\lim_{x\to\infty} x^{\mu} f(x)$ is +∞ or –∞

While applying the μ test the value of μ is usually taken to be equal to the highest power of x in the denominator of the integrand minus the highest power of x in the numerator of the integrand.

ABSOLUTE CONVERGENCE

The infinite integral $\int_a^\infty f(x)$ is said to be absolute convergent if the integral $\int_a^\infty |f(x)|\,dx$ is convergent.

If the integral $\int_a^\infty f(x)\,dx$ is absolutely convergent it is necessarily convergent, but if the integral $\int_a^\infty f(x)\,dx$ convergent. If is not necessarily absolutely convergent. Thus absolute convergent gives a sufficient but not a necessary condition for the convergence of an infinite integral.

Example:

Show that $\int_1^\infty \frac{\sin x}{x^4}\,dx$ is absolutely convergent.

Solution:

The integral $\int_1^\infty \frac{\sin x}{x^4}\,dx$ will absolutely convergent if $\int_1^\infty \left|\frac{\sin x}{x^4}\right|\,dx$ is convergent.

Let $f(x) = \left|\frac{\sin x}{x^4}\right|$, then f(x) is bounded in the interval (1, ∞) we have

$$f(x) = \left|\frac{\sin x}{x^4}\right| \le 1/x^4 \sin x\ |\sin x| = 1$$

$\therefore$ By Comparison Test $\int_1^\infty f(x)\,dx$ is convergent if $\int_1^\infty \frac{1}{x^4}\,dx$ is convergent but the comparison integral $\int_1^\infty \frac{1}{x^4}\,dx$ is convergent because $\int_1^\infty$ Here $n = 4$ which is > 1

Hence $\int_1^\infty f(x)\,dx$ is convergent and so the given integral is absolutely convergent.

SOME MISCELLENEOUS SOLVED EXAMPLES

Example 1:

Show that the series

$$\frac{1}{a} - \frac{2a}{a^2 - 1^2}\cos\theta + \frac{2a}{a^2 - 2^2}\cos 2\theta \ldots\ldots$$

is uniformly convergent w.r.t. θ in any finite interval.

Solution:

We know

$| a^2 - n^2 | = | n^2 - a^2 | > \frac{1}{2} n^2,$ ...(1)

when n exceeds a certain integer N. Using (1), we get

$$\left|\frac{(-1)^n 2a \cos n\theta}{a^2 - n^2}\right| \ge 2\ |a|.1.\frac{2}{n^2}$$

$$= \frac{4|a|}{n^2}, \quad \forall\, n > N \text{ and } \forall\, \theta$$

Since $\sum M_n = \sum \frac{1}{n^2}$ is convergent, therefore by Weierstrass's M-test, the given series is uniformly convergent in any finite interval.

Example 2:

Show that the series $\sum_{n=0}^{\infty}(1-x)x^n$ *is not uniformly convergent on [0, 1].*

Solution:

The given series is

$(1 - x) + (1 - x)\,x + (1 - x)\,x^2 + ... + f_n(x) = (1 - x)\,x^n$.

For x = 1, the sum of the series = (x) = 0.

For x ≠ 1, the given series is a geometric series with common ratio x, so that the sum function is

$$f(x) = \frac{a}{1-r} = \frac{1-x}{1-x} = 1. \text{ Thus}$$

$$f(x) = \begin{cases} 1, & x \neq 0 \\ 0, & x = 0 \end{cases}$$

Thus, sum function is discontinuous on [0, 1] and so the given series is not uniformly convergent on [0, 1].

Example 3:

Let $f_n(x)\ \dfrac{x^n}{1+x^n}\ (0 \le x \le 1)$

Show that $\{f_n\}$ *converges point wise on [0, 1], if*

$$f(x) = \lim_{n\to\infty} f_n(x) \quad (0 \le x \le 1)$$

is there on N such that

$| f_n(x) - f(x) | \le ¼\ (n \ge N)$.

Solution:

$$f(x) = \lim_{n\to\infty} f_n(x) = \lim_{n\to\infty} \frac{x^n}{1+x^n} = 0 \qquad \text{if } (0 \le x \le 1)$$

$$= ½ \text{ if } (x = 1)$$

since $\lim_{n\to\infty} x^n = 0$ when $0 \le x < 1$

and $\lim_{n\to\infty} x^n = 1$ when $x = 1$

Let ε be any arbitrary small positive real number.

We have$| f_n(x) - f(x) | \le \varepsilon$ $\qquad (0 \le x < 1)$

If $\left|\dfrac{x^n}{1+x^n} - 0\right| \le \varepsilon$

or $\qquad$ if $x^n \le (1 + x^n)\,\varepsilon$

or $\qquad$ if $n^n\,(1 - \varepsilon) \le \varepsilon$

or $\qquad$ if $n^n \le \dfrac{1-\varepsilon}{\varepsilon}$

or $\quad$ if $\left(\frac{1}{x}\right) \geq \frac{1-\varepsilon}{\varepsilon}$

or $\quad$ if $n \log \left(\frac{1}{x}\right)^n \geq \log \frac{1-\varepsilon}{\varepsilon}$

or $\quad$ if $n \geq \dfrac{\log \frac{1-\varepsilon}{\varepsilon}}{\log\left(\frac{1}{x}\right)}$ $\quad (0 \leq x < 1)$

Thus, there exist a positive integer N for all $x \in [0, 1]$ *i.e.* given sequence converges at every point of [0, 1].

Again when $x = 1$

$$\left|\frac{x^n}{x^n+1} - \frac{1}{2}\right| \leq \varepsilon \text{ for all values of n.}$$

Hence the given sequence is point wise convergent on [0, 1].

Again, when $\varepsilon = ¼$

$$\text{Then} N = \frac{\log \frac{1-\frac{1}{4}}{\frac{1}{4}}}{\log\left(\frac{1}{x}\right)} = \frac{\log 3}{\log\left(\frac{1}{x}\right)}$$

Example 4:

Apply M_n test to show that $\{f_n\}$, the sequence of functions is non-uniformly convergent if

$f_n(x) - nx(1-x)^n (0 \leq x \leq 1)$

Solution:

We have

$$f(x) = \lim_{n\to\infty} f_n(x) = \lim_{n\to\infty} nx(1-x)^n$$

$$= \lim_{n\to\infty} \frac{nx}{(1-x)^{-n}} \quad \left(\text{Form } \frac{\infty}{\infty}\right)$$

$$= \lim_{n\to\infty} \frac{nx}{-(1-x)^{-n} \log(1-x)}$$

$$= \lim_{n\to\infty} \frac{x(1-x)^n}{\log(1-x)} = 0$$

since $1 - x < 1$

Thus, $f(x) = 0 \quad \forall\, x \in [0, 1]$

Now let

$$y = | f_n(x) - f(x) | = nx(1 - x)^n$$

For maximum value of y, $\frac{dy}{dx} = 0$

$$\therefore n(1 - x)^n - n^2x(1 - x)^{n-1} = 0$$

or $\quad x = \frac{1}{n+1}$

Also $\quad x = -$ve quantity when $x = \frac{1}{x+1}$

Thus, $\quad M_n$ = maximum value of y

$$= n\frac{1}{n+1}\left(1-\frac{1}{n+1}\right)^n$$

$$= \left(\frac{n}{n+1}\right)\left(\frac{n}{n+1}\right)^n$$

Now $\lim\limits_{n\to\infty} M_n = \lim\limits_{n\to\infty}\left(\frac{n}{n+1}\right)\left(\frac{1}{1+\frac{1}{n}}\right)^n = \frac{1}{e} \neq 0$

Therefore, the given sequence is non-uniformly convergent.

Example 5:

Show that the sequence $\{f_n\}$, where $f_n(x) = x^n$ is uniformly convergent on $[0, k]$, $k < 1$ and pointwise convergent on $[0, 1]$.

Now

$$f(x) = \lim_{n\to\infty} f_n(x) = \begin{cases} 0, & 0 \le x < 1 \\ 1, & x = 1 \end{cases}$$

Thus the sequence converges pointwise to a discontinuous function on $[0, 1]$.

Solution:

Let $\varepsilon > 0$ be given.

For $0 < x \le k < 1$, we have

$$| f_n(x) - f(x) | = x^n < \varepsilon$$

if $\left(\frac{1}{x}\right)^n > \frac{1}{\varepsilon}$

or if $n > \log(1/\varepsilon)/\log(1/x)$

This number, $\log(1/\varepsilon)/\log(1/x)$ increases with x, its maximum value being $\log(1/\varepsilon)/\log(1/k)$ in $]0, k]$, $k > 0$.

Now let N be an integer $\geq \log(1/\varepsilon)/\log(1/k)$.

$\therefore |f_n(x) - f(x)| < \varepsilon, \quad \forall\, n \geq N,\ 0 < x < 1$

Again at $x = 0$,

$|f_n(x) - f(x)| = 0 < \varepsilon, \quad \forall\, n \geq 1$

Thus for any $\varepsilon > 0$, $\exists$ N such that for all $x \in [0, k]$, $k < 1$

$|f_n(x) - f(x)| < \varepsilon, \quad n \geq N$

Therefore, the sequence $\{f_n\}$ is uniformly convergent in $[0, k]$, $k < 1$.

However, the number $\log(1/\varepsilon)/\log(1/x) \to \infty$ as $x \to 1$ so that it is not possible to find an integer N such that $| f_n(x) - f(x) < \varepsilon$, all $n \geq N$ and all x in $[0, 1]$.

Hence the sequence is not uniformly convergent on any interval containing 1 and in particular on $[0, 1]$.

Note: A point, like $x = 1$ which is such that the sequence is not uniformly convergent in any interval containing $x = 1$, is called a *point of non-uniform convergence.*

Example 6:

Show that the series

$$\frac{x}{x+1} + \frac{x}{(x+1)(2x+1)} + \frac{x}{(2x+1)(3x+1)} + \ldots\ldots.$$

in uniformly convergent in $]\,k, \infty\,[$, where k is a positive number. Show also that the series i s not uniformly convergent in $[0, \infty[$.

Solution:

We have

$$f_n(x) = \frac{x}{(nx+1)\,[(n-1)\,x+1]} = \frac{1}{(n-1)\,x+1} - \frac{1}{nx+1}$$

Now, $S_n(x) = f_1(x) + f_2(x) + \ldots. + f_n(x)$

$$= \left(1 + \frac{1}{x+1}\right) + \left(\frac{1}{x+1} - \frac{1}{2x+1}\right) + \ldots\ldots..$$

$$+\left(\frac{1}{(n-1)\,x+1}-\frac{1}{nx+1}\right)$$

$\therefore S_n(x) = 1 - \dfrac{1}{nx+1}$. The sum function is given by

$$f(x) = \lim_{n\to\infty} S_n(x) = \begin{cases} 1, & \text{if } x \neq 0, \\ 0, & \text{if } x = 0. \end{cases}$$

It is clear that the sum function f is discontinuous on [0, 1] and so the given series is not uniformly convergent in [0, ∞[.

Now we show that Σf_n is uniformly convergent on]k, ∞ [k > 0. Let ε > 0 be given. For x ≠ 0

$$|S_n(x) - f(x)| = \left|1 - \frac{1}{nx+1} - 1\right| = \frac{1}{nx+1} < \varepsilon,$$

if $n > \dfrac{1}{x}\left(\dfrac{1}{\varepsilon} - 1\right)$.

Now $\dfrac{1}{x}\left(\dfrac{1}{\varepsilon} - 1\right)$ decreases with x and has a maximum value

$$m_0 = \frac{1}{k}\left(\frac{1}{\varepsilon} - 1\right) \infty\ x, \infty k$$

Here m_0 is independent of x.

Thus, ∀ x ∈]k, ∞[, there exists a positive integer m(> m_0) such that $|S_n(x) - f(x)| < e \ \forall\ n \geq m$.

Hence, the given series is uniformly convergent on]k, ∞[, k > 0.

Example 7:

Show that the sequence $\{f_n\}$, $f_n(x) = nx\,e^{-nx^2}$ converges but not uniformly to f, where f(x) = 0 for all x ∈ [0, 1], and that

$$\lim_{n\to\infty} \int_0^1 f_n\,dx \neq \int_0^1 f\,dx.$$

Solution:

Here $f(x) = \lim_{n\to\infty} nx\,e^{-nx2} = 0 \ \forall\ x \in [0, 1]$.

$\therefore \int_0^1 f(x)\,dx = 0.$ Now $\int_0^1 f(n)\,dx = \int_0^1 nx\,e^{-nx^2}\,dx$

$$= -\frac{1}{2}\left|e^{-nx^2}\right|_0^1 = \frac{1}{2}(1-e^{-n})$$

$$\therefore \lim_{n\to\infty} \int_0^1 f_n dx = \lim_{n\to\infty} \frac{1}{2}(1-e^{-n}) = \frac{1}{2} \neq \int_0^1 f dx.$$

Since $\lim_{n\to\infty} \int_0^1 f_n\, dx \neq \int_0^1 f dx$, $\{f_n\}$ is not uniformly convergent to f on [0, 1].

Example 8:

Show that the series $\sum_{n=0}^{\infty} \frac{x^2}{(1+x^2)^n}$ *is not uniformly convergent for* $x \geq 0$.

Solution:

The given series is

$$x^2 + \frac{x^2}{(1+x^2)} + \frac{x^2}{(1+x^2)} + \frac{x^2}{(1+x^2)} + ...$$

For $x = 0$, $f_n(x) = 0\ \forall\ n$ so that the sum of the series is $f(x) = 0$.

For $x \neq 0$, the given series is a geometric series with common ratio $r =/(1 + x^2)$, so that the sum function is

$$f(x) = \frac{a}{1-r} = \frac{x^2}{1-(1/1+x^2)} = 1 + x^2. \quad \text{Thus}$$

$$f(x) = \begin{cases} 1 + x^2, & x \neq 0, \\ 0, & x = 0. \end{cases}$$

Clearly f is discontinuous on $[0, \infty[$ and so convergence is not uniform on $[0, \infty]$.

Example 9:

Let $\{f_n\}$ *be defined by* $f_n(x) = nx/(1+ n^2x^2)$ " $x \in [0, 1]$. *Show that* $\{f_n\}$ *is not uniformly convergent on* $[0, 1]$, *although*

$$\lim_{n\to\infty} \int_0^1 f_n(x)dx = \int_0^1 f(x)\ dx = \int_0^1 \lim f_n(x)dx,$$

$f(x)$ *being the point-wise limit of* $\{f_n\}$.

Solution:

Note that each $f_n(x)$ is continuous on [0, 1] and thus integrable on [0, 1]. $\{f_n\}$ is not uniformly convergent on [0, 1], but the point-wise limit of $\{f_n\}$ is $f(x) = 0\ \forall\ x \in [0, 1]$. Now

$$\int_0^1 f_n(x)dx = \int_0^1 \frac{nx}{1+n^2x^2} dx = \frac{1}{2n} \log(1+n^2)$$

$$\therefore \lim_{n\to\infty} \int_0^1 f_n(x)\,dx = \lim_{n\to\infty} \frac{\log(1+n^2)}{2n}$$

$$= \lim_{n\to\infty} \frac{1}{1+n^2} = 0 \qquad \text{(D Hospital's Rule)}$$

$$= 0 = \int_0^1 f(x)\,dx.$$

Example 10:

Show that the sequence $\{f_n\}$, where

$$f_n(x) = \begin{cases} n^2x, & 0 \le \le 1/n \\ -n^2x + 2n, & 1/n \le x \le 2/n \\ 0, & 2/n \le x \le 1 \end{cases}$$

is not uniformly convergent on [0, 1].

Solution:

We have $\lim_{n\to\infty} f_n(x) = 0 \quad \forall\, x \in [0, 1]$.

Thus the given sequence converges point-wise to f, where $f(x) = 0$ $\forall\, x \in [0, 1]$. Further each f_n and f are continuous on [0, 1]. Now

$$\int_0^1 f_n dx = \int_0^{1/n} n^2x\,dx + \int_{1/n}^{2/n} (-n^2x + 2n)\,dx + \int_{2/n}^1 0\,dx$$

$$= \frac{1}{2} - \frac{1}{2}n^2\left(\frac{4}{n^2} - \frac{1}{n^2}\right) + 2n\left(\frac{2}{n} - \frac{1}{n}\right) + 0$$

$$= \frac{1}{2} - \frac{3}{2} + 2 = 1.$$

Also $\int_0^1 f\,dx = 0$

Thus, $\lim_{n\to\infty} \int_0^1 f\,dx \ne \int_0^1 f\,dx.$

Hence, the given sequence is not uniformly convergent on [0, 1].

Example 11:

Show that the sequence $\{f_n\}$, $f_n(x) = nx\,(1 - x^2)^n$, converges but not uniformly to f, where $f(x) = 0$, for $0 \le x \le 1$, and that

$$\lim_{n\to\infty} \int_0^1 f_n\,dx \ne \int_0^1 f\,dx.$$

Solution:

We have $f_n(x) = 0 \quad \forall\, n$ if $x = 0$ or 1.

Now $0 < x < 1 \Rightarrow 0 < 1 - x^2 < 1$.

$$\text{Now } \lim_{n\to\infty} \frac{f_{n+1}(x)}{f_n(x)} = \lim_{n\to\infty} \frac{(n+1)\,x(1-x^2)^{n+1}}{nx(1-x^2)^n}$$

$$= \lim_{n\to\infty} \left(1+\frac{1}{n}\right)(1-x^2) \text{ for } 0 < x < 1$$

$$= (1 - x^2) < 1 \quad (\because 0 < x < 1)$$

$\therefore \lim_{n\to\infty} f_n(x) = 0$ for $0 < x < 1$.

Thus, the point-wise limit of $\{f_n\}$ is $f(x) = 0 \ \forall x \in [0, 1]$

$$\text{Now } \int_0^1 f_n(x)\,dx = \int_0^1 nx\,(1-x^2)^n\,dx$$

$$= -\frac{n}{2(n+1)} \left|(1-x^2)^{n+1}\right|_0^1 = \frac{n}{2(n+1)}$$

$$\therefore \lim_{n\to\infty} \int_0^1 f_n(x)\,dx = \frac{1}{2} \text{ and } \int_0^1 f(x)\,dx = 0.$$

Since $\lim_{n\to\infty} \int_0^1 f_n(x)\,dx \neq \int_0^1 f(x)\,dx$, $\{f_n\}$ is not uniformly convergent to f on [0, 1]

Example 12:

Show that the sequence $\{f_n\}$, $f_n(x) = x/(1+nx^2)$ *converges uniformly to a function f on [0, 1], and that the equation,* $f'(x) = \lim_{n\to\infty} fn'(x)$ *is true if* $x \neq 0$ *and false if* $x = 0$. *Why so?*

Solution:

The sequence $\{f_n\}$ converges uniformly to $f(x) = 0 \quad \forall x \in R$.

For $x \neq 0$, $f_n'(x) = \dfrac{1-nx^2}{(1+nx^2)^2} \to 0$ as $n \to \infty$,

so that $\lim_{n\to\infty} f_n'(x)$ is true for $x \neq 0$.

$$\text{For } x = 0,\ f_n'(0) = \lim_{x\to 0} \frac{f_n(x) - f_n(0)}{x-0} = \lim_{x\to 0} \frac{1}{1+nx^2} = 1$$

and $f'(0) = 0$. Thus

$\lim_{x\to\infty} f_n'(0) = 1 \neq f'(0)$ and so the given equation is false for $x = 0$. It is so because the sequence $\{f_n')$ is not uniformly convergent in any interval containing zero.

Example 13:

If $f(x) = \sum_{n=1}^{\infty} \frac{\sin nx}{n^2}$, *then prove that*

$$\int_0^{\pi} f(x)\,dx = 2\sum_{n=1}^{\infty} \frac{1}{(2n-1)^4}$$

Solution:

We have $\left|\frac{\sin nx}{n^3}\right| \le \frac{1}{n^3}\ \forall\ x.$

By Weierstrass's M-test, the given series is uniformly convergent for all x, in particular $0 \le x \le p$, and can be integrated term by term. Thus

$$\int_0^{\pi} f(x)\,dx = \int_0^{\pi}\left(\sum_{n-=1}^{\infty} \frac{\sin nx}{n^3}\right)dx = \sum_{n=1}^{\infty}\int_0^{\pi} \frac{\sin nx}{n^3}\,dx$$

$$= \sum_{n=1}^{\infty}\left(\frac{1-\cos n\pi}{n^4}\right) = 2\left(\frac{1}{1^4}+\frac{1}{3^4}+\frac{1}{5^4}+\ldots\right)$$

$$=2\sum_{n=1}^{\infty}\frac{1}{(2n-1)^4}.$$

Example 14:

Show that converges $\sum_{n=1}^{\infty} \frac{1}{1+n^2+n^4x^2}$ *uniformly for all values of x.*

Solution:

It is clear that

$$f_n(x) = \frac{1}{1+n^2+x^4n^2} < \frac{1}{n^2} \qquad \forall\ x \in R \text{ and } \forall\ n \in N.$$

Since $\sum M_n = \sum \frac{1}{n^2}$ is convergent, by Weierstrass's M-test, $\Sigma\, f_n$ is uniformly convergent for all $x \in R$.

Example 15:

Given $f(x) = \sum_{n=1}^{\infty} \frac{1}{n^2+n^4x^2}$, *justify the validity of*

$$f'(x) = -2x\sum_{n=1}^{\infty} \frac{1}{n^2(1+nx^2)^2}\text{"}$$

or

Show that the series $\sum_{n=1}^{\infty} \frac{1}{n^2+n^4x^2}$ *is uniformly convergent for all x.*

Solution:

It is clear that

$$f_n(x) = \frac{1}{n^2+n^4x^2} \leq \frac{1}{n^2} \quad \forall\ x \in R \text{ and } \forall\ x \in N.$$

Since $\sum M_n = \sum \frac{1}{n^2}$ is convergent, by Weiestrass's M-test, $\Sigma\, f_n$ is uniformly convergent for all $x \in R$.

We have $$f_n'(x) = \frac{2xn^4}{(n^2+n^4x^2)^2} = -\frac{2x}{n^2(1+nx^2)^2} \quad ...(1)$$

Let $g_n(x) = f_n'(x)$ so that $g_n'(x) = \frac{2+6x^2n}{1+nx^2}$.

Now $g_n'(x) = 0 \quad \Rightarrow \quad -2+6x^2n = 0$

$\Rightarrow \quad x^2 = 1/3n.$

Putting in (1), the maximum value of

$$|g_n(x)| = \frac{2}{\sqrt{(3n)}\, n^2(1+\frac{1}{2})^2} = \frac{3\sqrt{3}}{8n^{5/2}}$$

$$\therefore |g_n(x)| < \frac{1}{n^{5/2}} \quad \forall\ n.$$

Since $\sum M_n = \sum \frac{1}{n^{5/2}}$ is convergent, the series $\Sigma\, g_n = \Sigma\, f_n'$ is uniformly convergent for all $x \in R$ and consequently term by term differentiation of the series $\Sigma\, f_n$ is justified. Hence,

$$f'(x) = \sum_{n=1}^{\infty} f_n'(x) = -2x \sum_{n=1}^{\infty} \frac{1}{n^2(1+nx^2)^2}, \text{ using (1).}$$

Example 16:

Show that the function represented by $\sum_{1}^{\infty} \frac{\sin nx}{n^3}$ *is differentiable for every x and its derivative is* $\sum_{1}^{\infty} \frac{\cos nx}{n^2}$.

Solution:

Let $f_n(x) = \frac{\sin nx}{n^3}$

so that $f_n'(x) = \dfrac{\cos nx}{n^2}$

Since $|f_n'(x)| = \left|\dfrac{\cos nx}{n^2}\right| \le \dfrac{1}{n^2} \quad \forall x$

and $\sum M_n = \sum \dfrac{1}{n^2}$

is convergent, so by Weierstrass's M-test, the series $\Sigma f_n'$ is uniforml convergent for all values of x and consequently the series Σf_n can b differentiated term by term. Hence

$$f'(x) = \sum_1^{\infty} f_n'(x) = \sum_1^{\infty} \frac{\cos nx}{n^2}.$$

Example 17:

Show that the sequence $\{f_n\}$, where $f_n(x) = x - x^n/n$, converges uniform on [0, 1]. Show also that the s sequence $\{f_n'\}$ of differentials does not conver uniformly on [0, 1].

Solution:

$$\lim_{n\to\infty} f_n(x) \lim_{n\to\infty} \left(x - \frac{x^n}{n}\right) = x \quad \forall\, x \in [0, 1]$$

Thus, the point-wise limit of $\{f_n\}$ is f, $f(x) = x \;\; \forall\, x \in [0, 1]$.

Now, $|f_n(x) - f(x)| = \left|x - \dfrac{x^n}{n} - x\right| \le \dfrac{1}{n} \qquad \forall\, x \in [0, 1].$

$\therefore M_n = \sup \{ |f_n(x) - f(x)| : 0 \le x \le 1 \} = \dfrac{1}{n} \to 0$ as $n \to \infty$.

Hence, the sequence $\{f_n\}$ converges uniformly to f on [0, 1], whe $f(x) = \forall$ [0, 1]. We have $f'(x) = 1 \;\; \forall\, x \in [0, 1]$.

Thus $f'(1) = 1$. Now $f_n'(x) = 1 - x^{n-1} \;\; \forall\, x \in [0, 1]$ and $f_n'(1) = 0$. We see that $\lim\limits_{n\to\infty} f_n'(1) \ne f'(1)$

Hence, the sequence $\{f_n'\}$ does not converge uniformly on [0, 1].

Example 18:

Show that the sequence $\{f_n\}$, where

$$f_n(x) = \frac{1}{n^2} \log(1 + n^2x^2)$$

is uniformly convergent on [0, 1].

Solution:

We have $f_n'(x) = \frac{2nx}{1+n^2x^2}$.

Let $g_n(x) = f_n'()$ $\forall$ n.

Now $\lim_{n\to\infty} g_n(x) = \lim_{n\to\infty} \frac{2mx}{1+n^3x^2} = \lim_{n\to\infty} \frac{2x/n^2}{x^2+(1/n)^3} = 0,$

$\forall$ x $\in$ [0, 1], so that the point-wise limit is g(x) = 0 $\forall$ x $\in$ [0, 1].

Let $y = g_n(x) - g(x) = \frac{2mx}{1+n3x^2}$, so that

$$\frac{dy}{dx} = \frac{2n(1-n^2x^2)}{(1+n^3x^2)^2}$$

and so $\frac{dy}{dx} = 0 \Rightarrow x = \frac{1}{n^{3/2}}$

It can be verified that for this value of x, $y_3 < 0$.

Now, $M_n = \sup \{ | g_n(x) - g(x) | : 0 \le x \le 1\} = \frac{2n}{n^{3/2}(1+1)} = \frac{1}{\sqrt{n}}$
$\to 0$ as $n \to \infty$.

Hence, $\{g_n\} = \{f_n'\}$ converges uniformly to g, where g(x) = 0 $\forall$ x $\in$ [0, 1]. Also each function g_n is continuous on [0, 1].

We see that

$$\lim_{n\to\infty} f_n(x) = \lim_{n\to\infty} \frac{\log(1+n^2x^2)}{n^2} \left(\frac{\infty}{\infty}\right)$$

$$= \lim_{n\to\infty} \frac{3n^2x^2}{(1+n^3x^2)} \lim_{n\to\infty} \frac{3x^2}{2(3n^2x^2)} = 0$$

$\therefore \lim_{n\to\infty} f_n(x) = 0 \quad \forall$ x $\in$ [0, 1].

Thus, $\{f_n\}$ is a sequence of differentiable functions which converges point-wise to zero o n [0, 1]. The converges, $\{f_n\}$ converges uniformly to zero on [0, 1].

Example 19:

Prove that each of the series

$$\sum \frac{1}{n} \cos nx, \sum \frac{1}{n} \sin nx$$

converges uniformly in [α, $2\pi - \alpha$], where α is any fixed positive number less than π.

Solution:

(i) Let $b_n = \frac{1}{n}$ so that b_n is positive, monotonic decreasing function of n and converges uniformly to zero.

Let $u_n(x) = \cos nx$. Then

$$\sum_{r=1}^{n} u_r(x) = \cos x + \cos 2x + ... + \cos nx$$

$$= \frac{\cos\left\{\frac{1}{2}(n+1)x\right\} \sin\left\{\frac{1}{2}nx\right\}}{\sin\left(\frac{1}{2}x\right)}$$

$$\therefore \left|\sum_{r=1}^{n} u_r(x)\right| = \frac{|\cos\left\{\frac{1}{2}(n+1)x\right\}|\,|\sin\frac{1}{2}nx|}{|\sin(\frac{1}{2}x)|}$$

$$\leq \frac{1}{|\sin(\frac{1}{2}x)|} |\operatorname{cosec}(\tfrac{1}{2}x)| \quad \forall\, n \text{ and } \forall\, x \in [\alpha, 2\pi - \alpha],$$

where cosec $\frac{1}{2}$x) is bounded $\forall\, x \in [\alpha, 2\pi - \alpha]$.

Hence, by Dirichlet's test, $\sum \frac{1}{n} \cos nx$ converges uniformly in $[\alpha, 2\pi - \alpha]$.

(ii) Let $u_n(x) = \sin nx$. Then

$$\left|\sum_{r=1}^{n} u_r(x)\right| = \frac{|\sin\left\{\frac{1}{2}(n+1)x\right\}|\,|\sin\frac{1}{2}nx|}{|\sin(\frac{1}{2}x)|}$$

$$< |\operatorname{cosec}(\tfrac{1}{2}x)| \ \forall\, n \text{ and } \forall\, x \in [\alpha, 2\pi - \alpha].$$

Hence, by Dirichlet's test, $\sum \frac{1}{n} \sin nx$ converges uniformly in $[\alpha, 2\pi - \alpha]$.

Example 20:

Show that the series $\sum \frac{(-1)^n}{n} |x|^n$ *is uniformly convergent in* $-1 \leq x \leq 1$.

Solution:

Let $b_n(x) = |x|^n$ so that $b_n(x)$ is positive, monotonically decreasing and bounded in $-1 \leq x \leq 1$ (*i.e.*, $|x| \leq 1$).

Let $u_n(x) = \frac{(-1)^n}{n}$ so that the series is uniformly convergent

Hence, by Abel's test,

$$\sum b_n(x)\, u_n(x) = \sum \frac{(-1)^n}{x} |x|^n$$

is uniformly convergent in $-1 \le x \le 1$.

Example 21:

Discuss the uniform convergence of

$$1 + \frac{e^{-2x}}{2^2-1} - \frac{e^{-4x}}{4^2-1} + \frac{e^{-6x}}{6^2-1} - \ldots.$$

for all real $x \ge 0$.

Solution:

Neglecting the first term, we get

$$f_n(x) = \frac{(-1)^{n+1}\, e^{-2nx}}{(2n)^2-1}.$$

Let $b_n(x) = e^{-2nx}$ and $u_n(x) = \dfrac{(-1)^{n+1}}{(2n)^2-1}$

Now, $b_n(x)$ is a monotonic decreasing function of $n\ \forall\ x \ge 0$.

and $\lim\limits_{n\to\infty} b_n(x) = \lim\limits_{n\to\infty} \dfrac{1}{e^{2nx}} = 0 \quad \forall\ x \ge 0.$

Further, $\sum u_n(x) = \sum \dfrac{(-1)^{n+1}}{(2n)^{2-1}}$

$$= \frac{1}{2^2-1} - = \frac{1}{4^2-1} + = \frac{1}{6^2-1} - \ldots..$$

is an alternating series such that $u_{n+1} < u_n\ \forall\ n$ and $\lim\limits_{n\to\infty} u_n = 0.$

Using Leibnitz's test. $\Sigma\, u_n(x)$ is convergent.

Hence, by Dirichlet's test, the series $\Sigma b_n(x)\, u_n(x)$ *i.e.*, the given series is uniformly convergent for all $x \ge 0$.

Example 22:

Prove that the series $\sum (-1)^n \dfrac{x^2+n}{n^2}$ *converges uniformly in every bounded interval, but does not converge absolutely for any value of x.*

Solution:

Let $\Sigma u_n = \Sigma(-1)^n$, which oscillates finitely.

Let $b_n(x) = \dfrac{x^2+n}{n^2} < \dfrac{b^2+n}{n^2}$ $\quad \forall\ x \in [a, b]$

where [a, b] is any bounded interval.

It is clear that $b_n(x)$ is a positive, monotonic decreasing function of n for each x in [a, b], and converges uniformly to zero for $a \le x \le b$.

Hence, by Dirichlet's test, the series $\sum (-1)^n \dfrac{x^2+n}{n^2}$ converges, uniformly on [a, b].

Again $\left|(-1)^n \dfrac{x^2+n}{n^2}\right| = \dfrac{x^2+n}{n^2} \sim \dfrac{1}{n}$, which diverges.

Hence the given series is not absolutely convergent for any value of x.

Example 23:

Show that the series

$$\frac{2x}{1+x^2} + \frac{4x^2}{1+x^4} + \frac{8x^7}{1+x^8} + \ldots..$$

is uniformly convergent in $-1 < x < 1$.

Solution:

We have $u_n(x)$ = The nth, term of the series

$$= \frac{2^n x^{2^n-1}}{1+x^{2n}}$$

Then $| u_n(x) | = \left|\dfrac{2^n x^{2^n-1}}{1+x^{2n}}\right| \le 2^n, k^{2^n-1}$ ...(1)

for $| x | \le k < 1$

Thus to test the convergence of the series $\sum 2^n, k^{2^n-1}$ let $v_n = 2^n, k^{2^n-1}$

$$\therefore \lim_{n\to\infty}\left(\frac{v_n}{v_{n+1}}\right) = \lim_{n\to\infty} \frac{2^n, k^{2^n-1}}{2^{n+1} k^{2^{n+1}-1}}$$

$$\lim_{n\to\infty}\left[\frac{1}{2.k^{2n}}\right]$$

which tends to ∞ since k < 1

Hence by D' Alembert's ratio test, the series $\Sigma\ v_n$ is convergent.

So by Weierstrass's M-test the given series is uniformly convergent for $|x| \leq k$ 1.

Example 24:

Test for uniform convergence the series

$$\sum \frac{x}{n(1+nx^{-})}.$$

Solution:

Here $u_n(x)$ = The *n*th. term of the series

$$= \frac{x}{n(1+nx^2)}$$

The $u_n(x)$ is maximum if $\frac{d}{dx} u_n(x) = 0$.

or if $$\frac{n(1+nx^2)-2n^2x^2}{n^2(1+nx^2)^2} = 0$$

or if $$x = \pm \frac{1}{\sqrt{(n)}}.$$

So the maximum value f u_n (x) $= \frac{1/\sqrt{n}}{n[1+n.1/n]} = \frac{1}{2n^{3/2}} = M_n$ say

since $x = \frac{1}{\sqrt{n}}$ makes $u_n(x)$ a maximum.

But $\Sigma M_n = \Sigma \frac{1}{\sqrt{n}}$ is convergent.

Hence, it follows from Weierstrass's M-test that the given series is uniformly convergent for all values of x.

Example 25:

Prove that the series

$(1 - x) + x(1 - x) + x^2(1 - x) + \ldots$.

is absolutely convergent in the interval $-c \leq x < 1$ *where* $0 < c < 1$ *but that it is not uniformly convergent in this interval.*

Solution:

The given series is absolutely convergent in the given interval if the series

$|1 - x| \ |x| \, |1 - x| + |x^2| \, |1 - x| + \ldots$ ...(1)

is convergent for every value of x in that interval.

But the series (1) is a geometric series with $|x|$ (which is < 1) as its common ratio.

Thus, the sum to n terms of the series (1)

$$= \frac{|1-x|\,[1-|x|^n]}{1-|x|} \text{ which tends to } \frac{|1-x|}{1-|x|}$$

for every x in $-c \le x < 1$ as $n \to \infty$

This shows that the given series is absolutely convergent in the interval $-c \le x < 1$ where $0 < c < 1$.

To test the series for uniform convergence, we have

$S_n(x)$ = Sum to n terms of the original series

$$= \frac{(1-x)(1-x^n)}{1-x} = 1 - x^n \qquad ...(1)$$

$$\therefore S(x) = \lim_{n\to\infty} S_n(x) = \begin{cases} 1 \text{ when } -c \le x < 1 \text{ and } 0 < c < 1 \\ 0 \text{ when } x = 1 \end{cases}$$

Then for $-c \le x < 1$ and for a given $\in$ we have

$| S_n(x) - S(x) | \le \in$ if $| (1 - x^n) - 1 | \le \in$

$\Rightarrow$if $| x^n | \le \in$ or if $| 1/x |^n \ge 1/\in$

$\Rightarrow$if $n \log | 1/x | \ge \log 1/\in$

$$\Rightarrow \text{ if } n \ge \frac{\log 1/\in}{\log 1/|x|} \qquad ...(2)$$

Now (2) shows that if $x \to 1$, $n \to \infty$ so that it is not possible to choose a positive integer N such that $| S_n(x) - S(x) | < \varepsilon$ for every $n \ge N$ and for every x in $-c \le x < 1$.

So the convergence is non-uniform in the interval $-c \le x < 1$.

Note that $x = 1$ is a point of non-uniform convergence in the interval $-c \le x < 1$.

Example 26:

Show that the series

$$\sum_{n=0}^{\infty} \frac{(-1)^n x^{2^{n+1}}}{(2n+1)!} = x - \frac{x^2}{3!} + \frac{x^5}{5!} - ....$$

is uniformly convergent in every interval (a, b).

Solution:

Let M be any positive number greater than each of $| a |$ and $| b |$ so that for every x in (a, b) we have

$$\left|\frac{(-1)^n x^{2n+1}}{(2n+1)!}\right| \le \frac{M^{2n+1}}{(2n+1)!}$$

Now consider the series $M + \frac{M^3}{2!} + \frac{M^5}{5!} + \ldots.$ ...(1)

Since $e^M = 1 + m \frac{M^2}{2!} + \frac{M^3}{3!} + \ldots.$

and $e^{-M} = 1 - M + \frac{M^2}{2!} + \frac{M^3}{3!} + \ldots.$

we have $\frac{1}{2}(e^M - e^{-M}) = M + \frac{M^3}{3!} + \frac{M^5}{5!} + \ldots.$ ...(2)

(2) shows that the series (1) is convergent whatever the positive constant M may be.

Hence, by Weierstrass's M-test the given series

$\sum_{n=0}^{\infty} \frac{(-1)^n x^{2n+1}}{(2n+1)!}$ is uniformly convergent in (a, b)

Note that the above example justified the definition

$$\sin x = x \frac{x^3}{3!} + \frac{x^5}{5!} - \ldots + \frac{(-1)^n x^{2n+1}}{(2n+1)!} + \ldots.$$

Example 27:

Show that the series $\sum_{n=1}^{\infty} x^n(1-x^n)$ *is not uniformly convergent in the interval* $0 \le x \le 1$.

Solution:

The given series is $x(1-x) + x^2(1-x^2) + x^3(1-x^3) + \ldots.$

Thus $S_n(x) = (x + x^2 + x^3 + \ldots.. + x^n) - (x^2 + x^4 + x^6 + \ldots + x^{2n})$

$$= \frac{x(1-x^n)}{1-x} - \frac{x^2(1-x^{2n})}{1-x^2}$$

$$\therefore S(x) = \lim_{n\to\infty} [S_n(x)] = \begin{cases} \frac{x}{1-x} - \frac{x^2}{1-x^2} & \text{when } 0 < x < 1 \\ 0 & \text{when } x = 0 \text{ or } x = 1 \end{cases}$$

Then for $0 < x < 1$ and for a given ϵ we have

$$| S_n(x) - S(x) | \le \epsilon$$

$$\text{if } \left|\frac{x(1-x^n)}{1-x} - \frac{x^2(1-2^{2n})}{1-x^2} - \frac{x}{1-x} + \frac{x^2}{1-x^2}\right| \le \in$$

$$\Rightarrow \text{if } \left|\frac{x^{2n+2}}{1-x^2} - \frac{x^{n+1}}{1-x}\right| \le \in$$

$$\Rightarrow \text{if } \left|\frac{x^{2n+2} - (x+1)x^{n+1}}{1-x^2}\right| \le \in$$

$\Rightarrow$if $(x + 1)x^{n+1} - x^{2n+2} \le \in (1 - x^2)$ $\{$for $x < 1$ $(x + 1)\, x^{n+1} < x^{2n+2}$

$\Rightarrow$if $-(x + 1)x^{n+1} + x^{2n+2} \ge -\in (1 - x^2)$

$\Rightarrow$if $x^{2n+2} - (x + 1)\, x^{n+1} + (1 - x^2) \in \ge 0$

$$\Rightarrow \text{if } x^{n+1} \ge \frac{(x+1) \pm \sqrt{[(x+1) - 4\in(1-x^2)]}}{2}$$

$$\Rightarrow \text{if } (n+1) \ge \frac{\log\left[\frac{(x+1) \pm \sqrt{[(x+1) - 4\in(1-x^2)]}}{2}\right]}{\log x} \qquad \text{...(1)}$$

Now (1) show that when $x \to 1$, $n \to \infty$ so that it is not possible to find m such that $|\, S_n(x) - S(x)\,| \le \in$ for every $n \ge N$ and for every x in $0 < x \le 1$.

Here $x = 1$ is a point of non-uniform convergence of the series so that the series is non-uniformly convergent in $0 \le x \le 1$.

Example 28:

Prove that the series

$$\frac{1}{a} - \frac{2a}{a^2 - 1^2}\cos x + \frac{2a}{a^2 - 2^2}\cos^2 x - \ldots..$$

is uniformly convergent in any finite interval.

Solution:

Neglecting the first term we have

$$|\, u_n(x)\,| = \left|\frac{(-1)^{n-1}2a}{a^2 - n^2}\cos nx\right| \le \left|\frac{2a}{a^2 - n^2}\right| \qquad \text{...(1)}$$

But we have $n^2 - a^2 > \frac{1}{2}n^2$ if $\frac{1}{2}n^2 > a^2$

$\Rightarrow$ if $n > |a|\sqrt{2}$.

So if m is a positive integer just greater than $|a|\sqrt{2}$ then

$$|a^2 - n^2| = |n^2 - a^2| < \frac{1}{2} n^2 \text{ for every } n \geq m \qquad ...(2)$$

From (1) and (2) we have

$$|u_n(x)| \leq \frac{2|a|}{|a^2 - n^2|} < \frac{2|a|}{\frac{1}{2}n^2} \frac{4|a|}{n^2} \quad \text{for } n \geq m \qquad ...(3)$$

But $4|a| \Sigma 1/n^2$ is obviously convergent.

Hence the given series is uniformly convergent for $x \geq 0$ by Welerstrass's M-test.

Example 29:

Show that the series $\cos x + \frac{1}{2} \cos 2x + \frac{1}{3} \cos 3x + ...$ *converge uniformly in* $0 < a \leq x \leq b < 2\pi$.

Solution:

Let $u_n(x) = \cos nx$

and $v_n(x) = 1/n$.

Then $S_n(x) = \sum_{r=1}^{n} u_r(x) = \cos x + \cos 2x + \cos 3x + ... + \cos nx$

$$= \frac{\cos\left\{x + \frac{1}{2}(n-1)x\right\} \sin nx/2}{\sin x/2}$$

$$= \frac{\cos \frac{1}{2}(n+1)x \sin nx/2}{\sin x/2}$$

$$\therefore |S_n(x)| = \frac{|\cos \frac{1}{2}(n+1)x|\ |\sin nx/2|}{|\sin x/2|} \leq \frac{1}{|\sin x/2|}$$

$\leq |\operatorname{cosec} x/2|$

$< k$ where k is the least upper bound of cosec x/ 2 in the open interval $(0, 2\pi)$ for cosec x/2 is bounded for all values of x in $0 < a \leq x \leq b < 2\pi$,

Also the sequence $\{v_n(x)\} = \{1/n\}$ is monotonic decreasing converging uniformly to zero in $0 < a \leq x \leq b < 2\pi$.

Hence by Dirichlet's test the given series.

$\sum_{1}^{\infty} 1/n \cos nx$ is uniformly convergent in.
$0 < a \le x \le b < 2\pi$.

Example 30:

Test the series $\sum_{n=1}^{\infty} \frac{\sin nx}{n^p}$ *for uniform convergence in any finite interval.*

Solution:

(i) When $P > 1$, $\frac{\sin nx}{n^p} \le \frac{1}{n^p}$ ...(1)

as $|\sin x| \le 1$.

So if $u_n(x)$ = The *n*th term of the given series $= \frac{\sin nx}{n^p}$ and $M_n = \frac{1}{n^p}$

we have from (1) $|u_n(x)| \le M_n$.

But $\Sigma M_n = \sum \frac{1}{n^p}$ is convergent when $p > 1$.

Hence by Weierstrass's M-test it follows that $\sum \frac{\sin nx}{n^p}$ is uniformly convergent in any finite interval.

(ii) When $0 < p \le 1$ we have by taking $u_n(x) = \sin nx$ and $v_n(x) \frac{1}{n^p}$.

$$S_n(x) = \sum_{r=1}^{n} u_r(x) = \sin x + \sin 2x + \sin 3x \dots + \sin nx$$

$$= \frac{\sin\left(x + \frac{n-1}{2}x\right)\sin\frac{nx}{2}}{\sin\frac{x}{2}} = \frac{\sin\frac{n+1}{2}x\sin\frac{nx}{2}}{\sin\frac{nx}{2}}$$

$$\text{Hence } |S_n(x)| = \frac{\left|\sin\frac{n+1}{2}x\right| . \left|\sin\frac{nx}{2}\right|}{\left|\sin\frac{nx}{2}\right|} \le \frac{1}{\left|\sin\frac{x}{2}\right|}$$

or $|S_n(x)| \le |\operatorname{cosec} x/2|$ ...(2)

But cosec x/2 becomes infinitely great if

$x = 2m\pi$, $m = 0, 1, 2, 3, \dots$

Excluding these points from any finite interval we see that cosec x/2 is bounded for all the remaining values of that interval.

Also the sequence $\{v_n(x)\} = \left\{\frac{1}{n^p}\right\}$ is monotonic decreasing sequence converging to zero for $0 < p \leq 1$.

Hence by Dirichlet's test the series $\sum_{n=1}^{\infty} \frac{\sin nx}{n^p}$ is uniformly convergent in every interval from which the points $x = 2m\pi$, $m = 0, 1, 2$ .... are excluded.

(iii) When p = 0 the given series is reduce to the series $\sum_{n=1}^{\infty} \sin nx$.

Example 31:

Test the uniform convergence of series $\sum_{r=1}^{\infty} u_n(x)$ *near* $x = 0$ *(or in an interval including* $x = 0$*) where* $u_r(x) = x$ *and* $u_n(x) = x^{u(2n-1)} - x^{1/(2n-3)}$ *for* $n \geq 2$.

Solution:

Here $u_1(x) = x$

$u_2(x) = x^{1/3} - x$

$u_3(x) = x^{1/5} - x^{1/3}$

....

....

$u_n(x) = x^{1/(2n-1)} - x^{1/(2n-3)}$ (n ≥ 2)

Then $S_n(x)$ = Sum to n terms of the series $= x^{1/(2n-1)}$

$$\therefore S(x) = \lim_{n\to\infty} [S_n(x)] = \lim_{n\to\infty} [x^{1/(2n-1]}] = \begin{cases} 1 \text{ when } x \neq 0 \\ 0 \text{ when } x = 0 \end{cases}$$

So $\lim_{x\to 0} [S(x)] = 1$ since $S(x) = 1$ for $x \neq 0$.

Thus, $\lim_{x\to 0} [S(x)] \neq S(0)$ so that the sum function S(x) is discontinuous at x = 0 showing that the series is non-uniformly convergent in any interval that includes x = 0.

Example 32:

Examine for term by term integration

$S_n(x) = nx\, e^{-nx^2}$.

Solution:

$$S(x) = \lim_{n\to\infty} S_n(x) = \lim_{n\to\infty} \frac{nx}{e^{nx^2}}$$

$$= \lim_{n\to\infty} \frac{x}{e^{nx^2} . x^2} = 0$$

$S(x) = 0$ $\therefore \int_0^1 s(x)\, dx = 0.$

Also

$$\int_0^1 S_n(x)\, dx = \int_0^1 nx\, e^{-nx^2} dx = \left[-\frac{1}{2} e^{-nx^2}\right]_0^1$$

$$= \left[\frac{1}{2} - \frac{1}{2} e^{-n}\right]$$

Thus, $\lim_{n\to\infty} \int_0^1 S_n(x)\, dx = \lim_{n\to\infty} \left[\frac{1}{2} - \frac{1}{2}.1/e^n\right] = \frac{1}{2}$

$\therefore \int_0^1 S(x)\, dx \neq \lim_{n\to\infty} \int_0^1 S_n(x)\, dx.$

Thus, the series is not term by term integrable.

Example 33:

Test for uniform convergence and term by term integration the series for which nth partial sum $S_n(x)$ = nxe^{-ne^2} the limits of integration between 0 to 1.

Solution:

Here $S(x) = \lim_{n\to\infty} [S_n(x)] \lim_{n\to\infty} \left[\frac{nx}{e^{nx^2}}\right]$

$$= \lim_{n\to\infty} \left[\frac{nx}{1 + nx^2 + (n^2x^4)/2! + \ldots\ldots}\right] = 0$$

for all finite values of x.

Then in the interval $0 \le x \le 1$ we have

$$\int_0^1 S(x)\, dx = \int_0^1 0\, dx = 0 \qquad \ldots(1)$$

Also $\lim_{n\to\infty} \int_0^1 S_n(x)\, dx = \lim_{n\to\infty} \int_0^1 nx\, e^{-nx^2} dx$

$$= \lim_{n\to\infty} \left[\frac{e^{-nx^2}}{-2}\right]_0^1$$

$$= \lim_{n\to\infty} \left[\frac{1-e^{-n}}{2}\right]$$

$$= ½.$$

Since $\lim_{n\to\infty} \int_0^1 S_n(x)\, dx \neq \int_0^1 \lim_{n\to\infty} [S_n(x)]\, dx$, the series does not admit of term by term integration over the interval $0 \le x \le 1$. In fact $x = 0$ is a point of non-uniform convergence.

Note that the term by term integration is justified over the range (k, 1) where $0 < k < 1$. For we have

$$\lim_{n\to\infty} \int_k^1 S_n(x)\, dx = \lim_{n\to\infty} \int_k^1 nx\, e^{-nx^2} dx$$

$$= \lim_{n\to\infty} \left[\frac{e^{-nx^2}}{-2}\right]_k^1$$

$$= \lim_{n\to\infty} \frac{1}{2}\left[e^{-nk^2} - e^{-n}\right]$$

$$= 0$$

Thus, $\int_k^1 S(x)\, dx = \lim_{n\to\infty} \int_k^1 S_n(x)\, dx$ so that the series admits of term by term integration in (k, 1) where $0 < k < 1$.

Example 34:

Prove that $\int_0^1 \log \frac{1}{1-x}\, dx = 1$ *by expanding in powers of x and integrating term by term.*

Solution:

We have $\log \frac{1}{1-x} = -\log(1-x)$

$$= x + \frac{x^2}{2} + \frac{x^3}{3} + \dots + \frac{x^n}{n} + \dots \qquad \dots(1)$$

Then $\lim_{n\to\infty} \int_0^1 S_n(x)\, dx = \lim_{n\to\infty} \left[\int_0^1 \left\{x + \frac{x^2}{2} + \frac{x^3}{3} + \dots + \frac{x^n}{n}\right\} dx\right]$

$$= \lim_{n\to\infty} \left[\int_0^1 x\, dx + \int_0^1 \frac{x^2}{2} dx + \int_0^1 \frac{x^3}{3} dx + \dots + \int_0^1 \frac{x^n}{n}\, dx\right]$$

$$= \lim_{n\to\infty}\left[\frac{1}{1.2}+\frac{1}{2.3}+\frac{1}{3.4}+\ldots.+\frac{1}{n(n+1)}\right]$$

$$= \lim_{n\to\infty}\left[\left(1-\tfrac{1}{2}\right)+\left(\tfrac{1}{2}-\tfrac{1}{3}\right)+\left(\tfrac{1}{3}-\tfrac{1}{4}\right)+\ldots.+\left(\frac{1}{n}-\frac{1}{n+1}\right)\right] \quad \ldots(2)$$

$$= \lim_{n\to\infty}\left[\left(1-\frac{1}{n+1}\right)\right]=1$$

and $S(x) = \log\dfrac{1}{1-x}$ which is ∞ at $x = 1$

Hence, $\int_0^1 S(x)\,dx = \int_0^1 \log\dfrac{1}{1-x}\,dx$

$$= \lim_{\in\to\infty}\int_0^{1-\in}\log\frac{1}{x+1}\,dx$$

$$= \lim_{\in\to\infty}\left[\left\{x\log\frac{1}{1-x}\right\}_0^{1-\in} - \int_0^{1-\in}\frac{x}{1-x}\,dx\right]$$

$$= \lim_{\in\to\infty}\left[(1-\in)\log 1/\in+\left\{x+\log(1-x)\right\}_0^{1-\in}\right]$$

$$= \lim_{\in\to\infty}\left[(1-\in)\log 1/\in+\{1-\in+\log\in\}\right]$$

$$= \lim_{\in\to\infty}\left[-(1-\in)\log\in+1-\in+\log\in\right]$$

$$= \lim_{\in\to\infty}\left[\in\log\in+-\in\right] \quad \ldots(3)$$

$$\text{But } \lim_{\in\to\infty}[\in\log\in]\ \lim_{\in\to\infty}\left[\frac{\log\in}{1/\in}\right] \qquad \left(\text{from } \frac{\infty}{\infty}\right)$$

$$= \lim_{\in\to\infty}\left[\frac{1/\in}{-1/\in^2}\right] = \lim_{\varepsilon\to\infty}(-\in) = 0$$

$$\therefore \int_0^1 \log\frac{1}{1-x}\,dx = 1.$$

Since $\int_0^1 S(x)\,dx \lim_{n\to\infty}\int_0^1 S_n(x)\,dx = 1$, the term by term integration is justified i n (0, 1) and $\int_0^1 \log\dfrac{1}{1-x}\,dx = 1$.

Note that the sum function $\log\dfrac{1}{1-x}$ has infinite discontinuity at x = 1 so that the series is not uniformly convergent in any neighbourhood of x = 1 yet it admits of term by term integration.

Example 35:

Examine whether the series for which $S_n(x)$ $\frac{1}{n+n^3x^2}$ *is differentiable term by term.*

Solution:

We have $S(x) = \lim_{n\to\infty} [S_n(x)]$

$$= \lim_{n\to\infty}\left[\frac{1}{n+n^3x^2}\right] = 0 \quad \text{for all values of x.}$$

$\therefore \quad S'(x) = 0$

Also $\lim_{n\to\infty} [S'_n(x)] \lim_{n\to\infty}\left[\frac{-1}{(n+n^3x^2)^2 \cdot 2n^3x}\right] = 0$ for all values of x.

$\therefore \quad S'(x) = \lim_{n\to\infty} [S'_n(x)]$.

Hence, the term by term differentiation holds.

Note that the series of derivatives $\Sigma u_n'(x)$ is uniformly convergent for every real value of x since the sequence of $\{S'_n(x)\}$ is uniformly convergent as can be seen from the following working.

Here $|S'_n(x) - S'(x)| = \left|\frac{-1}{2n^5x(1+n^2x^2)^2} = 0\right|$

$= \frac{1}{2n^5x(1+n^2x^2)^2}$ which is < any preassigned ε_1

however small it may be, by choosing n independent of x and large enough for every x.

Hence the sequence $\{S'_n(x)\}$ is uniformly convergent for all real values of x and so the series $\Sigma u'_n(x)$ is uniformly convergent for every real value of x.

Example 36:

Show that the series

$$\frac{x}{x+1} + \frac{x}{(x+1)(2x+1)} + \frac{x}{(2x+1)(3x+1)} + \ldots$$

is uniformly convergent in (k, ∝; where k is any positive number. Show also that the series is non-uniformly convergent near the point x = 0.

Solution:

Here $S_n(x) = \sum_{n=1}^{n} u_n(x)$

where $U_n(x)$ = nth, term of the series.

$$= \frac{x}{x+1} + \frac{x}{(x+1)(2x+1)} + \frac{x}{(2x+1)(3x+1)} + ...$$

$$+ \frac{x}{\{(n-1)x+1\}\,(nx+1)}$$

$$= \left(1 - \frac{1}{x+1}\right) + \left(\frac{1}{x+1} - \frac{1}{2x+1}\right) + \left(\frac{1}{2x+1} - \frac{1}{3x+1}\right) + ...$$

$$+ \left(\frac{1}{(n-1)x+1} - \frac{1}{nx+1}\right)$$

$$= 1 - \frac{1}{nx+1} = \frac{nx}{nx+1}$$

$$\therefore s(x) = \lim_{n\to\infty} [S_n(x)] = \lim_{n\to\infty}\left(\frac{nx}{nx+1}\right) = \begin{cases} 1 \text{ when } x > 0 \\ 0 \text{ when } x = 0 \end{cases}$$

Then for $x > 0$ and for a given ε we have

$$| S_n(x) - S(x) | \le \varepsilon$$

if $\left|\frac{nx}{nx+1} - 1\right| \le \varepsilon$

or if $\left|\frac{-1}{nx+1}\right| \le \varepsilon$

or if $\frac{1}{nx+1} \le \varepsilon$ or if $nx + 1 \ge 1/\varepsilon$

or if $n \ge \frac{1-\varepsilon}{x\varepsilon}$ ...(1)

Also (1) shows that if $x\to 0$, $n\to\infty$ so that it is not possible to choose N such that $| S_n(x) - S(x) | \le \varepsilon$ for every $n \ge N$ and for every x in $(0, \propto)$.

So the convergence is non-uniform near $x = 0$.

However, if we consider the interval $(k, \propto)$ where k is any fixed number > 0 however large, then the maximum value of $\frac{1-\in}{x\in}$ is $\frac{1-\in}{k\in}$ so that we take N = any integer greater than $\frac{(1-\in)}{k\in}$ then $| S_n(x) - S(x) | \le \in$ for every $n \ge N$ and for every x in $(k, \propto)$.

Thus, the series is uniformly convergent in (k, ∝) where k > 0 and is non-uniformly convergent in (0, ∞).

Hence x = 0 is a point of non-uniform convergence of the series.

Example 37:

Show that the series $\sum \frac{x}{n(n+1)}$ *is non-uniformly convergent in (0, ∝).*

Solution:

$$S_n(x) = x\left[\frac{1}{1.2}+\frac{1}{2.3}+\frac{1}{3.4}+....+\frac{1}{n(n+1)}\right]$$

$$= x\left[\left(1-\frac{1}{2}\right)+\left(\frac{1}{2}-\frac{1}{3}\right)+\left(\frac{1}{3}-\frac{1}{4}\right)+...+\left(\frac{1}{n}-\frac{1}{n+1}\right)\right]$$

$$= x\left[1-\frac{1}{n+1}\right] = \frac{nx}{n+1}$$

Now, $s(x) = \lim_{n\to\infty} S_n(x) \lim_{n\to\infty} \frac{nx}{n+1} = x.$

We have $| S_n(x) - s(x) | \leq \in \quad (\in < 0)$

$$\Rightarrow \left|\frac{nx}{n+1} - x\right| \leq \in$$

$$\Rightarrow \left|\frac{-x}{n+1}\right| \leq \in$$

$$\Rightarrow \frac{x}{n+1} \leq \in$$

$\Rightarrow n + 1 \geq x/\in$ thus $n \geq x/\in - 1$.

Obviously, if the interval is (0, ∞), then no upper bound of N exists *i.e.* the given series is non-uniformly convergent in this interval, but if we take the interval (0, c) where c is any finite quantity however large, then series is uniformly convergent for in this case

N = integral part of $(c/\in - 1)$.

Example 38:

Show that the sequence $\{f_n\}$, *where*

$$f_n(x) = \frac{n^2x}{1+n^2x^2}$$

is not uniformly convergent on [0, 1].)

Solution:

$$\text{Here } f(x) = \lim_{n\to\infty} \frac{n^2x}{1+n^2x^2} = \frac{x/n}{(1/n^3)+x^2} = 0 \ \forall \ x \in R.$$

$$\text{Let} y = f_n(x) - f(x) = \frac{n^2x}{1+n^3x^2}.$$

$$\therefore \frac{dy}{dx} = \frac{(1+n^3x^2).n^2 - n^2x(2nx)}{(1+n^3x^2)^2} = \frac{n^2(1-n^3x^2)}{(1+n^3x^2)^2}$$

It can be verified that $y_2 < 0$ for $x = 1/n^{3/2}$.

Putting $x = 1/n^{3/2}$ in the value of y, we obtain

$M_n = \max |y| = \frac{1}{2}\sqrt{n} \to \infty$ as $n \to \infty$.

Hence the given sequence is not uniformly convergent on [0. 1]

Example 39:

Show that the sequence $\{f_n\}$, where

$$f_n(x) = \frac{nx}{1+n^2x^2}$$

is not uniformly convergent on any interval containing zero.

Solution:

$$\text{Here } f(x) \lim_{n\to\infty} \frac{nx}{1+n^2x^2} = \lim_{n\to\infty} \frac{x/n}{1/n^2+x^2} = 0.$$

$\therefore f(x) = 0 \quad \forall \quad x \in r.$

Consider any interval [a, b] containing 0.

$$\text{Let } y = f_n(x) - f(x) = \frac{nx}{1+n^2x^2}.$$

$$\therefore \frac{dy}{dx} = \frac{(1+n^2x^2).n - nx(2n^2x)}{(1+n^2x^2)^2} = \frac{n(1-n^2x^2)}{(1+n^2x^2)^2}$$

$$\text{Now } \frac{dy}{dx} = 0$$

$$\Rightarrow \quad x = \frac{1}{n} \in [a, b].$$

It can be verified that $y_2 < 0$ for $x = 1/n$.

So $M_n = \max. \ |y| = \frac{1}{2}$.

which does not tend to zero is $n \to \infty$. Hence the given sequence is uniformly convergent in any interval containing zero.

Example 40:

Show that the sequence $\{f_n\}$, where $f_n(x) = e^{-nx}$ is point-wise but not uniformly convergent in $[0, \infty[$. Also show that the convergence is uniform in $[k, \infty[$, k being any positive number.

Solution:

For $x \neq 0$, $f(x) = \lim_{n\to\infty} f_n(x) = \lim_{n\to\infty} \left(\frac{1}{e^{nx}}\right) = 0$

For $x = 0$, $f_n(x) = 1 \quad \forall\ n$ so that the point-wise limit is

$$f(x) = \begin{cases} 0, & x \neq 0, \\ 1, & x = 0, \end{cases}$$

We choose ε, $0 < \varepsilon < 1$.

For $x \in]0, \infty[$, we have

$| f_n(x) - f(x) | = | e^{-nx} - 0 | = 1/e^{nx} < \varepsilon$.

if $e^{nx} > 1/\varepsilon \Rightarrow nx > \log (1/\varepsilon)$

$\Rightarrow n > \frac{1}{x} \log (1/\varepsilon)$.

For $x = 0$, $| f_n(x) - f(x) |$

$= | 1 - 1 | = 0 < \varepsilon \quad \forall\ n \geq 1$.

Let m be a positive integer such that

$$m = \max. \left\{1, \frac{1}{x} \log (1/\varepsilon)\right\}. \qquad ...(1)$$

Then $m \to \infty$ as $x \to 0+$, so that there does not exist any positive integer m such that $\forall\ n \geq m$ and $\forall\ x \in [0, \infty[$,

$| f_n(x) - f(x) | < \varepsilon$.

Hence, the convergence is not uniform in $[0, \infty[$,

Let k be any positive number. Then by (1),

$m = \frac{1}{k} \log (1/\varepsilon)$. Thus $| f_n(x) - f(x) | < \varepsilon \quad \forall\ n \geq m, \quad \forall\ x \in [k, \infty[$.

Hence, $\{f_n(x)\}$ is uniformly convergent in $[k, \infty[, k > 0$.

Example 40(a):

Show that the sequence (e^{-nx}) is uniformly convergent in any interval [a, b], where a and b are positive numbers but only point-wise in [a, b].

Solution:

Do yourself.

Example 41:

Show that the series $\Sigma\{\log(n + 1)\}^{-x} \cos nx$ is uniformly convergent in $[\theta_1, \theta_2]$, where $0 < \theta_1 \le x \le \theta_2 < 2\pi$.

Solution:

When $x \in [\theta_1, \theta_2]$, $\{\log)n + 1)\}^{-x}$ is a positive monotonic decreasing function of n. Also since $\{\log (n + 1)\}^{-x} \le \{\log (n + 1)\}^{-\theta^1}$, the function $\{\log (n + 1)\}^{-x}$ tends uniformly to zero as $n \to \infty$.

$$\left|\sum_{r=1}^{n} \cos rx\right| \le \frac{1}{\sin(x/2)} \le \max\left(\frac{1}{\sin(\theta_1/2)}, \frac{1}{\sin(\theta_2/2)}\right),$$

both of which are independent of x and n.

Thus by Dirichlet's test the series $\Sigma \{\log (n + 1)\}^{-x} \cos nx$ is uniformly convergent in $[\theta_1, \theta_2]$.

Note 1: It is to be understood that θ_1 can be as close to zero and θ_2 as close to 2π as we please.

Note 2: If $\{v_n\}$ is a monotonic sequence of real numbers that converges to zero, then each of the series $\Sigma v_n \sin n\theta$, $\Sigma v_n \cos n\theta$, is uniformly convergent with regard to θ in the interval $[\alpha, 2\pi - a]$, where α is any fixed positive number less than π.

Example 42:

Prove that the series $\sum \frac{\cos n\theta}{n^p}$ and $\sum \frac{\sin n\theta}{n^p}$ converge uniformly for all values of $p > 0$ in an interval $[\alpha, 2\pi - \alpha[$, where $0 < \alpha < \pi$.

Solution:

When $p > 1$, Weierstrass's M-test at once proves that both the series converge uniformly for all real values of θ.

When $0 < p \le 1$, both the series converge uniformly in any interval $[\alpha, 2\pi - \alpha]$, $\alpha > 0$. This can be proved by taking $b_n = (1/n^p)$ and $u_n = \cos n\theta$ (or $\sin n\theta$) in Dirichiet's test.

$(1/n^p)$ is positive monotonic decreasing and tending uniformly to zero for $0 < p \le 1$, and

$$\left|\sum_{r=1}^{n} u_r\right| = \left|\sum_{r=1}^{n} \cos r\theta\right| = |\cos\theta + \cos 2\theta + ... + \cos n\theta|$$

$$= \left| \frac{\cos((n+1)/2)\,\theta \sin(n/2)\theta}{\sin(\theta/2)} \right| \le \text{cosec}\,(\alpha/2), \ \ \forall\, n,$$

for $\theta \in [\alpha, 2\pi - \alpha]$.

Thus, all the conditions are fulfilled and the series Σ (cos $n\theta/n^p$) and similarly Σ (sin $n\theta/n^p$) converge uniformly on $[\alpha, 2\pi - \alpha]$ where $0 < \alpha < \pi$.

Example 43:

Examine for uniform convergence on R, the sequence

$$\{f_n(x)\},\ f_n(x) = \frac{n^2x^2}{1+n^5x^4}.$$

Solution:

Do yourself.

Example 44:

Show that the sequence (f_n), where $f_n(x) = nx\, e^{-nx^2}$ *is not uniformly convergent on [0, 1].*

Solution:

$$\text{Here } f(x) = \lim_{n\to\infty} f_n(x)$$

$$= \lim_{n\to\infty} \frac{nx}{e^{nx^2}} \left(\frac{\infty}{\infty}\right)$$

$$= \lim_{n\to\infty} \frac{x}{x^2 e^{nx^2}} = 0 \qquad \text{" } x \in [0.\ 1]$$

$$\text{Let= } f_n(x) - f(x) = nx\,e^{nx^2} \qquad (\because f(x) = 0)$$

$$\therefore \frac{dy}{dx} = n\left[e^{-nx^2} + x(-2\,nx)e^{-nx^2}\right]$$

$$\text{Now } \frac{dy}{dx} = 0 \quad \Rightarrow \quad 1 - 2nx^2 = 0 \quad \Rightarrow \quad x = \frac{1}{\sqrt{2n}} \in [0, 1]$$

if can be verified that $d^2y/dx^2 < 0$ for this value of x.

$$\therefore M_n = \max.\ |\,y\,| = n.\ \frac{1}{\sqrt{2n}}\ e^{-1/2} = \sqrt{\frac{n}{2e}} \to \infty \text{ as } n \to \infty.$$

Thus, M_n does not tend to 0 as $n \to \infty$ and so the given sequence is not uniformly convergent in [0, 1].

Example 45:

Test the following sequence for uniform c convergence:

(i) $\left\{\dfrac{\sin nx}{\sqrt{n}}\right\}, 0 \le x \le 2\pi$

(ii) $\left\{\dfrac{nx}{1+n^3x^2}\right\}, 0 \le x \le 1.$

Solution:

(i) We have $\left|\dfrac{\sin nx}{\sqrt{n}}\right| \le \dfrac{1}{\sqrt{n}} \quad \forall\ x \in [0, 2\pi].$

$$\therefore \lim_{n\to\infty} \frac{\sin nx}{\sqrt{n}} = 0 \qquad \forall\ x \in [0, 2\pi].$$

Now, $|\ f_n(x) - f(x)\ | = \left|\dfrac{\sin nx}{\sqrt{n}} - 0\right| \le \dfrac{1}{\sqrt{n}} \quad \forall\ x \in [0, 2\pi]$

$$\therefore M_n = \sup \{\ |\ f_n(x) - f(x)\ | : 0 \le x \le 2p\} = \frac{1}{\sqrt{n}}$$

Since $M_n = \dfrac{1}{\sqrt{n}} \to 0$ as $n \to\infty$, so the given sequence is uniformly convergent on $[0, 2\pi]$

(ii) Here $f(x) = \lim\limits_{n\to\infty} \dfrac{nx}{1+n^3x^2}$

$$= \lim_{n\to\infty} \frac{(n/x^2)}{x^2+(1/n^3)} = 0 \qquad \forall\ x \in [0, 1].$$

Let $\quad y = f_n(x) - f(x) = \dfrac{nx}{1+n^3x^2}$

$$\therefore \quad \frac{dy}{dx} = \frac{(1+n^3x^2).n - nx(2n^3x)}{(1+n^3x^2)^2} = \frac{1-n^4x^2}{(1+n^3x^2)^2}$$

Now, $\dfrac{dy}{dx} = 0$

$$\Rightarrow \quad x = \frac{1}{n^2} \in [0, 1]$$

It can be verified that $y_8 < 0$ for $x = 1/\pi^2$.

So M_n Max. $|\ y\ | = \dfrac{1}{(1+n)} \to 0$ as $n \to \infty$.

Hence, the given sequence is uniformly convergent o n [0, 1].

Example 46:

If f is continuous on [0, 1] such that

$$\int_0^1 x^n f(x)\,dx = 0, \text{ for } n = 0, 1, 2, 3, ...$$

then show that f(x) = 0 on[0, 1].

Solution:

For any real polynomial,

$h(x) = a_0 + a_1x + a_2x^2 + ... + a_nx^n$

$$\int_0^1 h(x) f(x) = 0, \quad \text{[using (A)]} \qquad ...(1)$$

Since f is continuous on [0. 1], so by Weierstrass's approximation theorem, there exists a sequence $\{P_n(x)\}$ of real polynomials such that $\lim_{n\to\infty} P_n(x) =$ f(x) uniformly $\forall$ x $\in$ [0, 1]

$\Rightarrow \lim_{n\to\infty} P_n(x) = f(x) = f^2(x)$ uniformly $\forall$ x $\in$ [0, 1]

Since f is continuous on [0, 1], therefore

$$\int_0^1 f^2\,dx = \lim_{n\to\infty} \int_0^1 P_n f\,dx.$$

$$= 0, \text{ by (1)}$$

$\therefore f^2 = 0$ on [0, 1]. Hence f = 0 on [0, 1].

Example 47:

Show that the sequence $\{f_n\}$, where

$$f_n(x) = \frac{nx}{1+n^2x^2}, x \in R$$

is point-wise convergent but is not uniformly convergent in any interval containing zero.

Solution:

We know that 1, the given sequence is point-wise convergent with point-wise limit f, where

$f(x) = 0 \qquad \forall\, x \in R.$

Let, if possible, $\{f_n\}$ be uniformly convergent in [a, b] containing 0. By he above Remark, the point-wise limit is also the uniform limit. By the definition of uniform convergence, for ε = ½, there exists a positive integer m such that

$$\left|\frac{nx}{1+n^2x^2} - 0\right| < \frac{1}{4} \quad \forall\ n \geq m \text{ and } \forall x \in [a, b]. \qquad ...(1)$$

We can choose a positive integer k such that

$k \leq m$ and $1/k \in [a, b]$.

Taking $n = k$ and $x = 1/k$, we have

$$\left|\frac{nx}{1+n^2x^2} - 0\right| = \frac{1}{2} \qquad ...(2)$$

As (1) and (2) are contradictory statements, it follows that the given sequence is not uniformly convergent in any interval [a, b] containing 0, although it is point-wise convergent therein.

Hence the proved.

Example 48:

Consider the series

$$\sum_{n=0}^{\infty} f_n, \text{ where } f_n(x) = \frac{x^2}{(1+x^2)^n} \text{ (x real)}.$$

Solution:

At $x = 0$, each $f_n(x) = 0$, so that the sum of the series $f(0) = 0$.

For $x \neq 0$, it forms a geometric series with common ratio $1/(1 + x^2)$, so that its sum function $f(x) = 1 + x^2$.

Hence

$$f(x) = \begin{cases} 1 + x^2, & x \neq 0 \\ 0, & x = 0 \end{cases}$$

Each term of the series is continuous but the sum f is not.

Example 49:

Show that the sequence $\{f_n\}$, where

$$f_n(x) = \frac{nx}{1+n^2x^2}$$

converges point-wise to zero for all real x.

Solution:

$$\lim_{n\to\infty} f_n(x) = \lim_{n\to\infty} \frac{nx}{1+n^2x^2}$$

$$= \lim_{n\to\infty} \frac{x}{\frac{1}{n}+nx^2} = 0 \quad \forall\ x \in R.$$

Hence, the given sequence converges point-wise to zero for all real x.

Example 50:

Show that the sequence $\{f_n\}$, $f_n(x) = x^n$, is uniformly convergent in [0, k] k < 1 and only point-wise convergent in [0, 1].

Solution:

We know $\lim_{x\to\infty} x^n = 0, \quad \text{if } 0 \le x < 1,$

$= 1, \quad \text{if } x = 1.$

Thus the given sequence is point-wise convergent in [0, 1] and the point-wise limit f is given by

$$f(x) = \begin{cases} 0, & \text{if } 0 \le x < 1, \\ 1, & \text{if } x = 1. \end{cases}$$

Let us choose ε, $0 < \varepsilon < 1$. For $0 < x < 1$, we have

$| f_n(x) - f(x) | = | x^n - 0 | = x^n < \varepsilon.$

Now $x^n < \varepsilon \Leftrightarrow (1/x)^n > 1/\varepsilon \Leftrightarrow n \log(1/x) > \log(1/\varepsilon)$

$\Leftrightarrow n > (\log 1/\varepsilon) \div \log(1/x)$

For $x = 0$, $| f_n(x) - f(x) | = 0 < \varepsilon$, when $n \ge 1$.

Let m be a positive integer such that

$m = \max \{1, (\log 1/\varepsilon) \div \log(1/x)\}.$ ...(1)

Then $m \to \infty$ as $x \to 1$, so that there does not exists any positive integer such that $\forall\, n \ge m$, and $\forall\, x \in [0, 1]$,

$| f_n(x) - f(x) | < \varepsilon.$

Hence the convergence is not uniform in [0. 1].

Suppose k is any number such that $0 \le k < 1$.

Then, by (1), $m = \log(1/\varepsilon) \div \log(1/k)$.

$\therefore | f_n(x) - f(x) | < \varepsilon \quad \forall\, n \ge m$ and $\forall\, x \in [o, k]$.

Hence, $\{f_n\}$ is uniformly convergent in [0, k], k < 1.

Example 51:

The sequence $\{f_n\}$, where $f_n(x) = \dfrac{\sin nx}{\sqrt{n}}$, *(x real), has the limit.*

Solution :

$f(x) = \lim_{n\to\infty} f_n(x) = 0$

$\therefore f(x) = 0$, and so $f'(0) = 0$

But $\quad f'_n(x) = \sqrt{n} \cos nx$

so that $f'_n(0) = \sqrt{n} \to \infty$ as $n \to \infty$

Thus, at $x = 0$, the sequence $\{f'_n(x)\}$ diverges whereas the limit function $f'(x) = 0$, *i.e.*, the limit of differentials is not equal to the differential of the limit.

Example 52:

Show that the sequence $\{f_n\}$ where

$$f_n(x) = \frac{n}{n+x}, \quad x \geq 0$$

is uniformly convergent is any finite interval.

Solution:

Here, we have

$$f(x) = \lim_{n\to\infty} \frac{n}{n+x} = \lim_{n\to\infty} \frac{1}{x/n+1} = 1 \;\forall\; x \geq 0.$$

Then for an arbitrarily chosen positive number ε we have

$$| f_n(x) - f(x) | \leq e$$

if
$$\left| \frac{n}{x+n} - 1 \right| \leq \varepsilon$$

i.e., if $\left| \frac{-x}{x+n} \right| \leq \varepsilon$

or if $\frac{x}{x+n} \leq \varepsilon$

or if $n \geq x\left(\frac{1}{\varepsilon} - 1\right)$.

Obviously N increases with x and tends to ∞ as n tends ∞. Hence convergence is not uniform in (0, ∞). But if (0, k) is any finite interval where $k > 0$ however large then, N = any integer greater than or equal to $k\left(\frac{1}{\varepsilon} - 1\right)$ and $| f_n(x) - f(x) | \leq \varepsilon$ for every $n \geq N$ and every $x \in [0, k)$. This shows that the given sequence is uniformly convergent in [0, k].

Example 53:

Find the point-wise limit of $\{f_n\}$, where

$$f_n(x) = \frac{n}{x+n} \quad \forall\; x \geq 0.$$

Solution:

$$\lim_{n\to\infty} f_n(x) = \lim_{n\to\infty} \frac{n}{x+n} = \lim_{n\to\infty} \frac{1}{(x/n)+1} = 1.$$

Here the given sequence (f_n) is point-wise convergent for all $x \geq 0$ and the point-wise f is given by

$f(x) = 1 \quad \forall\, x \geq 0.$

Example 54:

Show that the sequence $\{f_n\}$, $f_n(x) = x^n$, is point-wise convergent in [0, 1].

Solution:

$$\lim_{n\to\infty} f_n(x) = \lim_{n\to\infty} x^n = \begin{cases} 0 & \text{for } 0 \leq x < 1, \\ 1 & \text{for } x = 1. \end{cases}$$

Hence the given sequence is point-wise convergent in [0. 1] and the point-wise limit f is given by

$$f(x) = \begin{cases} 0 & \text{when } 0 \leq x < 1, \\ 1 & \text{when } x = 1. \end{cases}$$

Example 55:

Show that the sequence $\{f_n\}$, where

$f_n(x) = n/(x + n)$

is uniformly convergent in [0, k] whatever k may be, but not uniformly convergent in [0, ∞].

Solution:

$$\lim_{n\to\infty} f_n(x) = \lim_{n\to\infty} \frac{x}{x+n} = \lim_{n\to\infty} \frac{1}{1+(x/n)}$$

$$= 1 \text{ for all } x \leq 0.$$

Thus, the sequence $\{f_n\}$ is point-wise convergent for all $x \leq 0$ and the point-wise limit is

$f(x) = 1 \quad \forall\, x \geq 0.$

Let $\varepsilon > 0$ be given. We have

$$|f_n(x) - f(x)| = \left|\frac{n}{x+n} - 1\right| = \frac{x}{x+n} < \varepsilon,$$

$$\text{if } \frac{x+n}{x} > \frac{1}{\varepsilon} \text{ or } n > x\left(\frac{1}{\varepsilon} - 1\right).$$

Consider the interval [0, k]. Let m be a positive integer;

$m > k\left(\frac{1}{\varepsilon}-1\right)$. Then

$| f_n(x) - f(x) | < \varepsilon \quad \forall\ n \geq m$ and $\forall\ x \in [0, k]$.

Hence, the given sequence is uniformly convergent in [0, k]. Now we show that $\{f_n\}$ is not uniformly convergent in $[0, \infty]$. Let m be a positive integer $> x\left(\frac{1}{\varepsilon}-1\right)$. Then $m \to \infty$ as $x \to \infty$ so that it is not possible to choose any positive integer m such that

$\forall n \geq m$ and $\forall\ x \geq 0$, $|f_n(x) - f(x) \} < \varepsilon$.

Hence the convergence is not uniform in $[0, \infty[$.

Let us Consider Few Examples

Note 1: If a sequence converges point-wise to f then for a given $\varepsilon > 0$, each point x_i of [a, b] determines an integer N_i such that

$| f_n(x_i) - f(x_i) | < \varepsilon$, for $n \geq N_i$

Consideration of all points of [a, b] gives rise to a sequence of integers $N_1, N_2, N_3, \ldots$

In case the sequence $\{N_i\}$ is bounded above, with supremum N, say, them (4) holds for all points of [a, b] when $n \geq N$ and so the given sequence $\{f_n\}$ converges uniformly on [a, b].

If no such N exists, the sequence $\{f_n\}$ is not uniformly convergent.

Note 2: *Uniform convergence ⇒ point wise convergence*

but not vice versa. However

Non-pointwise convergence ⇒ non-uniform convergence

i.e., a sequence which is not point-wise convergent cannot be uniformly convergent.

A series of functions Σf_n is said to converge uniformly on [a, b] if the sequence $\{S_n\}$ of its partial sums, defined by

$$S_n(x) = \sum_{i=1}^{n} f_i(x)$$

converges uniformly on [a, b].

Thus, a series of functions Σf_n converges uniformly to f on [a, b] if for $\varepsilon > 0$ and all $x \in [a, b]$ there exists an integer N (independent of x and dependent on ε) such that for all x in [a, b]

$| f_1(x) + f_2(x) + \ldots + f_n(x) - f(x) | < \varepsilon$, for $n \geq N$

Example 56:

State Weierstrass approximation theorem and assuming its validity for the interval [0, 1], prove it for any closed and bounded interval [a, b].

Solution:

Suppose f is continuous in [a, b]. The function defined by

$g(x) = f[a + (b - a)x\} - f(a) - x(f\{b) - f(a)\}$ ...(1)

is continuous on [0, 1].

By Weierstrass approximation theorem,

$P_n(x) \to g(x)$ uniformly on [0, 1].

Replacing a + (b – a) x by x, and using (1),

$$P_n\left(\frac{x-a}{b-a}\right) \to f(x) - f(a) - \frac{x-a}{b-a}\{f(b)-f(a)\}$$

Hence, $P_n(x) \equiv P_n\left(\frac{x-a}{b-a}\right) + f(a) - \left(\frac{x-a}{b-a}\right)\{f(b) - f(a)\}$

converges uniformly to f(x) on [a, b].

Example 57:

Show that $\sum \frac{(-1)^n x^{2n}}{n^p (1+x^{2n})}$ *converges absolutely and uniformly for all real values of x if p > 1.*

Solution:

$$| f_n(x) | = \left| \frac{(-1)^n x^{2n}}{n^p(1+x^{2n})} \right| = \frac{x^{2n}}{n^p(1+x^{2n})}.$$

Clearly $x^{2n} < 1+ x^{2n}$ $\forall x \in R$ and $\forall n \in N$.

$\therefore$ $\frac{x^{2n}}{1+x^{2n}} < 1$ $\forall x \in R$ and $\forall n \in N$.

Thus, $| f_n(x) | < \frac{1}{n^p} = M_n$ $\forall x \in R$, $\forall n \in N$.

Since $\sum M_n = \sum \frac{1}{n^p}$ is convergent ($\because p > 1$).

by M-test, the given series is uniformly and absolutely convergent for all real values of x if p > 1.

Example 58:

Show that the series $\sum_1^{\infty} \frac{x}{n(1+nx^2)}$ *converges uniformly for all real x.*

Solution:

Let $f_n(x) = \dfrac{x}{n(1+nx^2)}$

$$\therefore\ f_n'(x) = \frac{(1+nx^2) - x(2x^2)}{n(1+nx^2)} = \frac{1-nx^2}{n(1+nx^2)^2}$$

Now, $f_n'(x) = 0 \quad \Rightarrow \quad x = \pm\ 1/\sqrt{n}$.

It can be verified that $f_n'(x) < 0$ for $x = 1/\sqrt{n}$.

$$\therefore \text{Maximum value of } f_n(x) = \frac{1/\sqrt{n}}{n(1+1)} = \frac{1}{2n^{2/2}}$$

Thus, $f_n(x) < \dfrac{1}{2n^{3/2}} < \dfrac{1}{n^{3/2}} \quad \forall\ x \in R$ and $\forall\ n \in N$.

Since $\sum M_n = \sum \dfrac{1}{n^{3/2}}$ converges $\left(\because \dfrac{3}{2} > 1\right)$, so the given series is uniformly convergent for all real x.

Example 59:

Show that the series $\sum \dfrac{\cos n\theta}{n^p}, \sum \dfrac{\sin n\theta}{n^p}$ *converge uniformly for all values of* $p > 0$ *in* $[\alpha, 2\pi - \alpha]$, *where* $0 < \alpha < \pi$.

Solution:

Let $p > 1$ so that

$$\left|\frac{\cos n\theta}{n^p}\right| \le \frac{1}{n^p} = M_n.$$

Since $\sum M_n = \sum \dfrac{1}{n^p}$ $(p > 1)$ is convergent, so by Weierstrass's M-test, $\sum \dfrac{\cos n\theta}{n^p}$ is uniformly convergent $\forall\theta$.

For the case $0 < p \le 1$, we take $b_n = \dfrac{1}{p}$ so that b_n is positive, monotonic decreasing function of n and converges uniformly to zero. Let $M_n(\theta) = \cos n\theta$.

$$\left|\sum_{r=1}^{n} u_r(\theta)\right| \le \left|\operatorname{cosec} \frac{1}{2}\alpha\right| \ \forall\ n,\ \ \forall\theta \in [\alpha, 2\pi, -\alpha]$$

Hence, by Dirichlet's test, $\sum \dfrac{\cos n\theta}{n^p}$

converges uniformly in $[\alpha, 2\pi, -\alpha]$ for $0 < p \le 1$.

Similarly, we can do the second part.

Example 60:

Show that the following series are uniformly convergent in [–a, a], 0 < a < 1:

(i) $\sum_{n=0}^{\infty} x^n$, (ii) $\sum_{n=0}^{\infty} (n+1)\,x^n$, (iii) $\sum_{n=0}^{\infty} n^2x^n$,

Solution:

(i) $| x^n | = | x |^n \le a^n \quad \forall\, x \in [-\alpha, \alpha]$ *i.e.*, $| x | < \alpha$.

Let $M_n = \alpha^n$ so that $M_{n+1} = \alpha^{n+1}$

Now $\lim_{n\to\infty} \frac{M_{n+1}}{M_n} = a$, where $0 < \alpha < 1$.

By D' Alembert's Ratio Test, ΣM_n is convergent.

Hence, by M-test, Σx^n is convergent $\forall\, x \in [-\alpha, \alpha]$, where $0<\alpha<1$.

(ii) $| (n + 1)x^n | = (n + 1) | x |^n < \alpha^n (n + 1)$ $\qquad (\because | x | < \alpha)$

Let $M_n = \alpha^n (n + 1)$ so that $M_{n+1} = a^{n+1} (n + 2)$.

Now, $\lim_{n\to\infty} \frac{M_{n+1}}{M_n} = \lim_{n\to\infty} \frac{\alpha(n+2)}{(n+1)} = a < 1$.

By D' Alembert's Ratio Test, ΣM_n converges.

Hence, by M-test $\Sigma(n+1)\, x^n$ is uniform convergent in $[-\alpha, \alpha]$, where $0 < \alpha < 1$.

(iii) $| n^2.x^n | = n^2 | x |^n < \alpha^n n^2$.

Let $M_n = \alpha^n n^2$ so that $M_{n+1} = \alpha^{n+2} (n + 1)^2$.

Now, $\lim_{n\to\infty} \frac{M_{n+1}}{M_n} = \lim_{n\to\infty} \alpha\left(\frac{n+1}{n}\right)^2 = \alpha < 1$.

By D' Alembert's Ratio Test, Σm_n converges.

Hence, by M-test $n^2x^n)\, x^n$ is uniform convergent in $[-\alpha, \alpha]$, where $0 < \alpha < 1$.

Example 61:

Show that the sequence $\{f_n(x)\} = \{x^n\}$ is not uniformly convergent on [0, 1].

Solution:

Let $f_n(x) = x^n$.

For $x = 1$, $f_n(x) = 1$ and so that point-wise limit is 1.

For $x \in [0, 1[$, $\lim_{n\to\infty} f_n(x) = \lim_{n\to\infty} x^n = 0$.

Thus, the point-wise limit function of $\{x^n\}$ is

$$f(x) = \begin{cases} 0 & \text{in } [0, 1[, \\ 1 & \text{for } x = 1. \end{cases}$$

Thus f is not continuous on [0, 1] and so the convergence is not unifor on [0, 1].

Example 62:

Show that the series $\sum_{n=1}^{\infty} \frac{x}{1+n^2x^2}$ *is not uniformly convergent o [0, 1], while it is so on [½, 1].*

Or

Show that $\sum_{n=1}^{\infty} \frac{x}{1+n^2x^2}$ *is uniformly convergent in [δ, 1] for an δ > 0 but is not uniformly convergent in [0, 1].*

Solution:

Let $f_n(x) = \frac{x}{1+n^2x^2}$, $x \in [0, 1]$, $\delta > 0$.

$$\therefore |f_n(x)| = \left|\frac{x}{1+n^2x^2}\right| \leq \frac{x}{1+n^2\delta^2}$$

Let $M_n = \frac{x}{1+n^2\delta^2}\left(\sim \frac{1}{n^2}\right)$, so that ΣM_n is a convergent series and b M-test, $\Sigma f_n(x)$ is uniformly convergent in [δ, 1].

(ii) Let, if possible, $\Sigma f_n(x)$ be uniformly convergent on [0, 1].

By Cauchy's general principle of convergence, for δ = 1/6, there exis a positive integer m such that

$$| S_{n+p}(x) - S_n(n) | < \frac{1}{6} \quad \forall\, n \geq m,\ p \geq 1,\ \forall\, x \in [0, 1]$$

Example 63:

Show that $\int_1^{\infty} \frac{\sin x}{x^4}\, dx$ *is absolutely convergent.*

Solution:

The integral $\int_1^{\infty} \frac{\sin x}{x^4}\, dx$ will absolutely convergent if $\int_1^{\infty} \left|\frac{\sin x}{x^4}\right| dx$ convergent.

Let $f(x) = \left|\frac{\sin x}{x^4}\right|$, then f(x) is bounded in the interval (1, ∞) we have

$$f(x) = \left|\frac{\sin x}{x^4}\right| \leq 1/x^4 \sin x\ |\sin x| = 1$$

∴ By Comparison Test $\int_1^\infty f(x)\,dx$ is convergent if $\int_1^\infty \frac{1}{x^4}\,dx$ is convergent but the comparison integral $\int_1^\infty \frac{1}{x^4}\,dx$ is convergent because

$\int_1^\infty$ Here n = 4 which is > 1

Hence $\int_1^\infty f(x)\,dx$ is convergent and so the given integral is absolutely convergent.

Taking p = n = m, we obtain

$$|S_{2m}(x) - S_m(x)| < \frac{1}{6} \quad \forall\ x \in [0, 1]$$

$$\text{or } \frac{x}{1+(2m)^2x^2} + \frac{x}{1+(2m-1)^2x^2} + \ldots + \frac{x}{1+(m+1)^2x^2} < \frac{1}{6}$$

$$\text{or } \frac{mx}{1+(2m)^2x^2} < \frac{1}{6} \quad \forall\ x \in [0, 1]$$

Taking x = 1/m.

The above inequality becomes

$\frac{1}{5} < \frac{1}{6}$, which is impossible.

Hence $\Sigma f_n(x)$ is not uniformly convergent on [0, 1].

EXERCISES

1. *Show that the series* $\sum \frac{-(1)^{n-1}}{n}$ *is uniformly convergent in [0, 1].*

2. *Examine for uniform convergence on R, the sequence* $\{f_n\}$, $f_n(x) = \log(1 + n^3x^2)/2n^2$.

3. *Show that the series* $\sum_{n=1}^{n}(-1)^{n-1}x^4$ *is uniformly convergent for* $|x| \leq ½$.

4. *Prove that the series*

   (i) $\sum \frac{x^n}{n^2}$,

(ii) $\sum \frac{x^{2n}}{n^2+x^{2n}}$.

are uniformly convergent in [–1, 1].

5. *Discuss the uniform convergence of the series*

$$x^2 + \frac{x^2}{1+x^2} + \frac{x^2}{(1+x^2)^2} + \frac{x^2}{(1+x^2)^2} + ... \text{ in } [0, 1].$$

6. *Show that* $\sum \frac{\sin(x^2+nx^2)}{n(n+1)}$ *is uniformly convergent for all real x*

7. *Show that the following series :*

(i) $\sum_{n=1}^{\infty} n^2y^2$ (ii) $\sum_{n=1}^{\infty} \frac{x^4}{n-1}$.

(i) $\sum_{n=1}^{\infty} \frac{(-1)^n x^4}{n^2}$ (ii) $\sum_{n=1}^{\infty} \frac{x^n}{n!}$

are uniformly convergent for $|x| \le h$, $0 < h < 1$.

8. *Show that the sequence* $\{f_n'\}$ *where* $f_n(x) = \frac{x}{1+x^2x}$ *is not uniformly convergent on [0, 1].*

9. *Show that the series*

$x^4 + x^4/(1 + x^4) + x^4/(1 + x^4)^2 + x^4/(1 + x^4)^2 + ...$

is not uniformly convergent on [0, 1].

10. *Show that* $\sum_{n=1}^{n} (\sin x)^n$ *converges uniformly for*

$|x| \le h$, $0 < h < 1$.

11. *Show that* $\sum \frac{\sin n\theta}{n^p}$, $\sum \frac{\cos n\theta}{n^p}$ *are uniformly convergent for a real values of x if* $p > 1$.

12. *Show that the sequence* $\{f_n\}$ *defined on [0, 1] by*

$$f_n(x) = \begin{cases} n(1-nx), & 0<x<1/n \\ 0, & \text{otherwise} \end{cases}$$

converges point-wise but not uniformly to f, where $f(x) = 0 \ \forall x$ *[0, 1], and that*

$$\lim_{n\to\infty} \int_0^1 f_n dx \neq \int_0^1 f dx.$$

13. *Decide whether or not the sequence* $\{f_n'\}$ *converges uniformly on* $[0, 1]$ *where* $f_n(x) = x - \frac{x^n}{n}$.

14. *Show that* $\sum_{n=1}^{\infty} \frac{\cos nx}{n^2}$ *is uniformly convergent for all real values of* x.

15. *Show that the uniform sum of a series of continuous functions is continuous. Establish by on example that the point-wise limit of a sequence of continuous functions may be a continuous functions.*

16. *Show that the series* $\sum \frac{1}{n} \sin nx$ *converges uniformly in* $[0, 2\pi]$

17. *Prove that the series* $\sum \frac{x^4}{n(n+1)}$ *is uniformly convergent in 1 – 1..*

4

CALCULUS OF RESIDUES

RESIDUE AT A SINGLE POLE

We have already see that if z = a is simple pole of f(z), the residue at z = a is given by $\lim_{z \to a} (z - a) f(z)$.

Another form is obtained as follows

Let f(z) $\frac{\phi(z)}{\psi(z)}$, where $\psi(z) = (z - a) F(z)$, $F(a) \neq 0$.

Then $\lim_{z\to a}(z-a)\frac{\phi(z)}{\psi(z)}$

$$= \lim_{z \to a} \frac{(z-a)[\phi(a)+(z-a)\phi'(a)+...]}{\psi(a)+(z-a)\psi'(a)+...} \left[\text{the form } \frac{0}{0}\right]$$

$$= \lim_{z \to a} \frac{\psi(a)+(z-a)\phi'(a)+...}{\psi'(a)+...} \text{ since } \psi(a)=0$$

$$= \frac{\phi(a)}{\psi'(a)}.$$

RESIDUE OF A POLE OF ORDER GREATER THAN UNITY

Let z = a be a pole of order m of f(z) and suppose

$$f(z) = \frac{\phi(z)}{(z-a)^m}.$$

We then have, by the definition of a pole,

$$f(z) = \frac{\phi(z)}{(z-a)^m} = \psi(z) + \sum_{r=1}^{m} \frac{Mr}{(z-a)^r},$$

where $\psi(z)$ is regular at z = a,

or $\dfrac{\phi(z)}{(z-a)^m} = \psi(z) + \dfrac{M_1}{(z-a)} + \dfrac{M_2}{(z-a)^2} + \ldots + \dfrac{M_m}{(z-a)^m}$

$\therefore \phi(z) - \psi(z)(z-a)^m + M_1(z-a)^{m-1} + M_2(z-a)^{m-2} + \ldots M_m.$

Differentiating both the sides with respect to z, (m – 1) times, we have

$\phi^{(m-1)}(z) = \psi(m-1)(z)(z-a)^m + (m-1)\psi^{m-2}(z).m(z-a)^{m-1}$

$+\dfrac{(m-1)(m-2)}{2!}.\psi^{(m-3)}.(z)m(m-1).(z-1)^{m-1} + \ldots$

$+\psi(z)\dfrac{m!}{1!}(z-a) = M_1(m-1)$

$\therefore \psi^{(m-1)}(a) = M_1(m-1).$

Hence $M_1 = \dfrac{\phi^{(m-1)}(a)}{(m-1)!}$ which is the required residue at z = a.

In particular if $f(z) = \dfrac{\phi(z)}{(z-a)^2}$,

The residue at z = a is $\psi'(a)$ and if $f(z) = \dfrac{\phi(z)}{(z-a)^3}$,

The residue at z = a is $\dfrac{\phi''(a)}{2!}$ etc.

Formula:

Residue of $\dfrac{\phi(z)}{(z-a)^m}$ at $z = a$ is $\dfrac{\phi^{(m-1)}(a)}{(m-1)!}$.

Alternative Proof:

Let $f(z) = \dfrac{\phi(z)}{(z-a)^m}$. If z = a is a pole of order m, then $\phi(z)$ is regular at z = a.

Hence the residue at z = a,

= coefficient of $(z-a)^{-1}$ in f(z)

= coefficient of $(z-a)^{m-1}$ in $\phi(z)$

= coefficient of $(z-a)^{m-1}$ in

$$\left[\phi(a) + (z-a)\phi'(a) + \ldots + \frac{(z-a)^{m-1}}{(m-1)!}\phi^{(m-1)}(a) + \ldots\right]$$

$$= \frac{\phi^{(m-1)}(a)}{(m-1)!}.$$

Another Method:

Since residue at z = a is the coefficient of $\frac{1}{(z-a)}$ in the Laurent's expansion of f(z), the residue is the coefficient of 1/t in the expansion of f(a + t) as a power series where t is sufficiently small.

Example:

Find the residue of $\frac{1}{(z^2+1)^3}$ at z = i.

Solution:

$$\text{Let} f(z) = \frac{1}{(z+i)^3(z-i)^3} = \frac{\phi(z)}{(z-i)^3}$$

$$\text{where} \phi(z) = \frac{1}{(z+i)^3}.$$

Hence z = i is a pole of order three and the residue is $\frac{1}{2!}\phi''(i)$.

Now $\phi''(z) = \frac{12}{(z+i)^5}$ so that $\phi''(i) = \frac{12}{32i}$.

$$\therefore \text{ Residue} = \frac{2}{2!}.\frac{12}{32!} = \frac{3}{16i}.$$

Alternative:

$$\text{Residue} = \text{coefficient of } \frac{1}{t} \text{ in } \frac{1}{[(t+i)^2+1]^2}$$

$$= \text{coeffi. of } \frac{1}{t} \text{ in } \frac{1}{(t^2+2ti)^3}$$

$$= \text{coeffi. of } \frac{1}{t} \text{ in } -\frac{1}{8ti^3}\left(1+\frac{t}{2i}\right)^{-3}$$

$$= \text{coeffi. of } \frac{1}{t} \text{ in } -\frac{1}{8ti^3}\left\{1-3.\frac{t}{2!}+6.\left(\frac{t}{2i}\right)^2+\ldots\right\}$$

$$= -\frac{1}{8i}.\frac{6}{4i^2} = \frac{3}{16i}.$$

RESIDUE AT INFINITY

The definition of residue can be extended so as to include the point at infinity. We define residue at infinity as having given by the integral

$$\frac{1}{2\pi i}\int_C f(z)dz,$$

where as C is a circle enclosing within it all other singularities of f(z) and integral along C is performed in a clockwise direction, provided that this integral has a definite value. Taking the integral along C in an anti-clockwise direction, the residue at infinity is

$$-\frac{1}{2\pi i}\int_C f(z)dz.$$

An Important Observation

It can be easily seen that the residue at a finite point is zero if the function is analytic at that point but may not be so at infinity. For example, consider the function $\frac{1}{z-a}$ for residue at infinity. The only singularity of the function is a simple pole at z = a. The function is analytic at infinity.

$$\text{The residue at infinity} = -\frac{1}{2\pi i}\int_C \frac{1}{z-a}dz$$

$$= -\frac{1}{2\pi i}\int_0^{2\pi}\frac{rie^{i\theta}d\theta}{r.e^{i\theta}}, \text{ putting } z - a = re^{i\theta}$$

where C is the circle | z – a | = r

$$= -\frac{1}{2\pi i}.2\pi i = -1.$$

We have defined residue at infinity to be the value of the integral $\int \frac{1}{2\pi i} f(z)\,dz$, in clockwise direction round a large circle C which has in its interior all other sigularities. Putting $z = \frac{1}{Z}$, we get

$$\frac{1}{2\pi i}\int f(z)dz = \frac{1}{2\pi i}\int -f\left(\frac{1}{Z}\right)\frac{dZ}{Z^2}$$

taken in a counter-clockwise direction round a small circle about the origin.

Hence the residue off(z) at infinity.

$$= \frac{\text{Lim}}{Z\to a}\left[-\frac{Zf(1/Z)}{Z^3}\right] = \frac{\text{lim}}{Z\to a}[-zf(z)],$$

provided that this limit has a definite value.

Another Method:

Let f(z) have a pole of order m at infinity then f(1/Z) has a pole of the same order at Z = 0.

Expanding f(1/Z) by Laurent's formula near Z = 0, we get

$$f\left(\frac{1}{Z}\right)=\sum_{n=0}^{\infty}a_nZ^n+\sum_{n=1}^{m}\frac{b_n}{Z^n}.$$

Replacing Z by 1/z, the expansion of f(z) in the neighbourhood is given by z = ∞ is given by

$$f(z)=\sum_{n=1}^{m}a_nz^n+\sum_{n=0}^{m}a_nz^{-n}.$$

$$\int_C f(z)dz=\int_C\sum_{n=1}^{m}b_n2^n dz+\int_C\sum_{n=0}^{\infty}\frac{a_n}{z^n}dz$$

$$=\sum_{n=1}^{m}\int_C b_nz^ndz+\int_C\frac{a_n}{z^n}dz,$$

since the integral of the sim = sum of the integrals by the theorem of uniform convergence.

$$\int_C f(z)dz=\int_C\frac{a_1}{z}dz,\ \text{since all other integrals vanish}$$

$$=a_1\int_0^{2\theta}\frac{\rho.ie^{i\theta}d\theta}{\rho.e^{i\theta}},\ \text{putting } z=\rho.e^{i\theta}=2\pi ia_1.$$

Then the residue at infinity $=-\frac{1}{2\pi i}\int_C\frac{a_1}{z}dz=-a_1.$

Hence, the residue of f(z) at infinity is the coefficient of 1/z with its sign changed in the expansion of f(z) in the neighbourhood of z = ∞.

If f(z) is analytic at z = ∞, *i.e.* if $b_1 = b_2 = \ldots b_m = 0$, it still has a residue at infinity which is zero only when a1 = 0.

CAUCHY'S RESIDUE THEOREM

If f(z) is regular, except at a finite number of poles within a closed contour C and continuous on the boundary C, then

$$\int_C f(z)dz=2\pi i\Sigma R,$$

where ΣR is the sum of the residues of f(z) at its poles within C.

Proof:

Let $z_1, z_2, \ldots, z_n$ be the n poles within C. Let $\gamma_1, \gamma_2, \ldots, \gamma_n$ be the circles with centres $z_1, z_2, \ldots, z_n$ and each of radius ρ which is so small that all these circles lie entirely within C and do not overlap. Then f(z) is analytic in the region between C and the circles, so that we have by Cauchy's theorem

$$\int_C f(z)dz-\sum_{r=1}^{n}\int_{\gamma_1}f(z)dz=0$$

or $$\int_C f(z)dz=\int_{\gamma_1}f(z)dz+\int_{\gamma_2}f(z)dz+\ldots+\int_{\gamma_n}f(z)dz \quad \ldots(1)$$

Now if f(z) has a pole of order m_1 at $z = z_1$, we have

$$f(z) = \phi_1(z) \sum_{r=1}^{m_1} \frac{b_r}{(z-z_1)^r} \quad \text{where } \phi_1(z) \text{ is regular within and on } \gamma_1.$$

$$\therefore \int_{\gamma_1} f(z)dz = \int_{\gamma_1} \phi_1(z)dz + \int_{\gamma} \frac{b_1}{(z-z_1)}dz + \int_{\gamma} \frac{b_2}{(z-z_1)^2}dz$$

$$+ \ldots + \int_{\gamma_1} \frac{m_1}{(z-z)^{m_1}}dz$$

Since $\phi_1(z)$ is analytic within and on ϕ_1, therefore

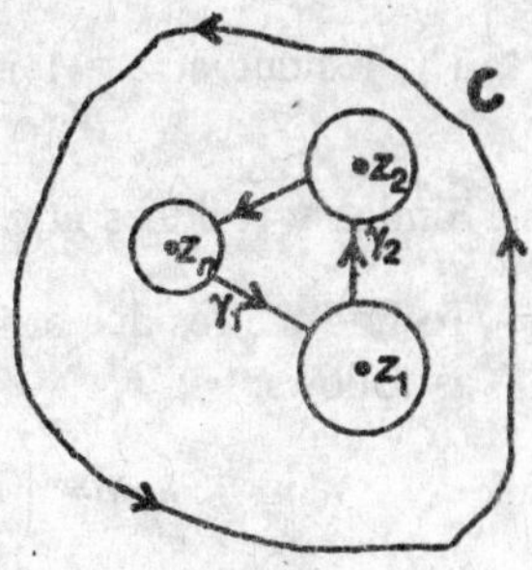

Fig. 4.1

$$\int_{\gamma_1} \phi_1(z)dz = 0$$

And putting $z - z_1 = \rho e^{i\theta}$ we get

$$\int_{\gamma_1} \frac{bm_1}{(z-z)^{m_1}}dz = \int_0^{2\pi} \frac{b_{m_1}.\rho i e^{i\theta}d\theta}{\rho^{m_1} e^{m_1 i\theta}}$$

$$= \frac{ib_{m_1}}{\rho^{m_1-1}}dz = \int_0^{2\pi} e^{-(m-1)i\theta}d\theta = 0, \text{ for } m_1 \neq 1$$

$$\text{and } \int_{\gamma_1} \frac{b_1}{(z-z_1)}dz = \int_0^{2\pi} \frac{b_1.\rho i e^{i\theta}d\theta}{\rho e^{i\theta}} = 2\pi i b_1$$

Hence $\int_{\gamma_1} f(z)dz = 2\pi i \times$ residue f(z) at $z = z_1$,

We then have from (1),

$$\int_C f(z)dz = 2\pi i \times (\text{sum of residues at } z_1, z_2, \ldots, z_n)$$

$$= 2\pi i \Sigma R.$$

Cor.:

If an analytic function has singularities at a finite number of points, then the sum of the residues at these points along with infinity is zero.

Proof:

Let C be a circle enclosing within it all the singularities excluding infinity. Then, we have

$$\frac{1}{2\pi i}\int_C f(z)dz = \text{ sum of the residues at all the finite singular points and}$$

$$-\frac{1}{2\pi i}\int_C f(z)dz = \text{ residue at infinity.}$$

Adding these, we get the required result. z

Example:

Evaluate the residues of $\frac{z^2}{(z-1)(z-2)(z-3)}$ *at z = 1, 2, 3 and infinity, and show that their sum is zero.*

Solution:

Hence $f(z) = \frac{z^2}{(z-1)(z-2)(z-3)}$ has simple poles at 1, 2 and 3.

The residue at z = 1 is $\lim_{z\to 0}(z-1)f(z) = \frac{z^2}{(z-2)(z-3)} = \frac{1}{2}$.

Similarly residues at z = 2 and 3 are –8 and $\frac{27}{2}$ respectively.

To find the residue at infinity, we expand f(z) in the neighbourhood of z = as follows:

$$f(z) = \left(1-\frac{1}{z}\right)^{-1}\left(1-\frac{2}{z}\right)^{-1}\left(1-\frac{3}{z}\right)^{-1}$$

$$= 1+\frac{6}{z}+ \text{higher powers of } \frac{1}{z}.$$

Hence the residue at infinity = –6.

∴ The sum of the residues at 1, 2, 3 and ∞.

$$= \frac{1}{2}-8+\frac{27}{2}-6 = 0.$$

EVALUATION OF REAL DEFINITE INTEGRALS

We have already discussed the notion of complex integration and of residue at a point. We now proceed to the evaluations of real definite integrals with the help of contour integration and the theorem of residues by properly choosing the intergrand and the contour. It may be noted that the integrals which can be thus evaluated can also be evaluated by other methods while there are many integrals which cannot be evaluated by contour integration. Before proceeding to the evaluation of definite integrals, we prove two useful theorems.

Theorem I:

If $\lim_{z\to a} (z-a) f(z) = A$, *and if C is the arc* $\theta_1 \le \theta \le \theta_2$ *of the circle* $|z-a| = r$, *then*

$$\lim_{r\to a} \int_C f(z)dz = iA(\theta_2-\theta_1)$$

Proof:

For a given ε, we can find b depending upon ε, such that

$|(z - a)f(z) - A| < \varepsilon$, for $| z - a | < \delta$.

Taking r less than δ, we have

$|(z - a)\ f(z) - A| < \varepsilon$, on the arc C.

$\therefore (z - a)\ f(z) = A + \eta$, where $| \eta | < \varepsilon$

or $\quad f(z) = \dfrac{A+\eta}{z-a}.$

$$\text{Then} \quad \int_C f(z)dz = \int_C \frac{A+\eta}{z-a}dz$$

$$= \int_{\theta_1}^{\theta_2} \frac{(A+\eta).re^{i\theta}.id\theta}{re^{i\theta}} \quad \text{putting } z - a = re^{i\theta}$$

$$= (\theta_2 - \theta_1)iA + (\theta_2 - \theta_1)i\eta$$

$$\text{or} \left| \int_C f(z)dz = iA(\theta_2 - \theta_1) \right| = (\theta_2 - \theta_1)\,|\,i\eta| < (\theta_2 - \theta_1)\varepsilon$$

$$\text{Hence} \lim_{r \to a} \int_C f(z)dz = iA(\theta_2 - \theta_1).$$

In particular if $z = a$ is a simple pole of f(z), A is the residue of f(z) at $z = a$. If C is a small circle $| z - a | = r$, we have $(\theta_2 - \theta_1) = 2\pi$ and we get

$$\int_C f(z)dz = 2\pi iA.$$

Particularly if$(z - a)\ f(z) \to 0$ as $z \to 0$, then

$$\int_C f(z)dz \to 0 \text{ as } z \to 0.$$

Theorem II:

If C is an arc $\theta_1 \le \theta \le \theta_2$ of the circle $| z | = R$ and if $\lim\limits_{R \to \infty} zf(z) = A$, then

$$\lim_{R \to \infty} \int_C f(z)dz = i(\theta_2 - \theta_1)A.$$

Proof:

For sufficiently large values of R, we have

$| zf(z) - A | < \varepsilon$

for $zf(z) = A + \eta$ where $| \eta | < \varepsilon$.

$$\therefore \int_C f(z)dz = \int_C \frac{A+\eta}{z}dz$$

or $$= \int_{\theta_1}^{\theta_2} \frac{(A+\eta)i\,Re^{i\theta}}{Re^{i\theta}}\,d\theta, \text{ putting } z = Re^{i\theta}$$

$$= Ai(\theta_2 - \theta_1) + \eta_1(\theta_2 - \theta_1)$$

or $$\left|\int_C f(z)dz - Ai(\theta_2-\theta_1)\right| = |\eta_i|(\theta_2-\theta_1)$$

$$= |\eta| . (\theta_2 - \theta_1) < (\theta_2 - \theta_1)\,\varepsilon,$$

$$\therefore \lim_{R\to\infty}\int_C f(z)dz = i(\theta_2-\theta_1).$$

In particular if $zf(z) \to 0$ as $R \to \infty$, then

$\int_C f(z)dz \to 0$ as $R \to \infty$.

INTEGRATION ROUND THE UNIT CIRCLE

We consider the integrals of the type

$$\int_0^{2\pi} f(\cos\theta, \sin\theta)d\theta,$$

where the integrand is a rational function of $\sin\theta$ and $\cos\theta$. If we write

$z = e^{i\theta}$, then $dz = ie^{i\theta}\,d\theta$ or $\frac{dz}{iz} = d\theta$

and $\frac{1}{2}\left(z+\frac{1}{z}\right) = \cos\theta$, $\frac{1}{2i}\left(z-\frac{1}{z}\right) = \sin\theta$, then

$$\int_0^{2\pi} f(\cos\theta, \sin\theta)d\theta$$

$$= \frac{1}{i}\int_C f\left[\frac{1}{2}\left(z+\frac{1}{z}\right), \frac{1}{2i}\left(z-\frac{1}{z}\right)\right]\frac{dz}{z}$$

$$= \int_C \phi(z)dz, \text{ say,}$$

where C is the unit circle $|z| = 1$.

Clearly $\phi(z)$ is a rational function of z. Hence by residue theorem

$$\int_C \phi(z)dz = 2\pi i \Sigma R_C,$$

where ΣR_C is the sum of the residues of $\varphi(z)$ at its poles inside C.

EVALUATION OF THE INTEGRAL

$$\int_{-\infty}^{\infty} f(x)dx.$$

Theorem:

If f(z) is a function which is analytic in the upper half of the z -plane except at a finite number of poles in it, having again no poles on the real axis and if further zf(z) tends to zero as | z | tends to infinity, then by contour integration.

$$\int_{-\infty}^{\infty} f(x) = 2\pi i \sum R^{+}$$

where $\sum R^{+}$ represents the sum of the residues at poles in the upper half plane.

Proof:

Conditions imposed upon f(z) ensure the convergence of the integral $\int_{-\infty}^{\infty} f(x)dx$. Such integrals can be evaluated by integrating f(z) round a contour C consisting of a semi-circle Γ of radius R large enough to include all the poles of f(z) and the part of the real axis from x = –R to x = R. Here the only singularities of f(z) in the upper half-plane are poles.

Hence by the residue theorem we have

$$\int_{C} f(z)dz = 2\pi i \sum R^{+}$$

$$\text{or } \int_{-R}^{R} f(x)dx + \int_{\Gamma} f(z)dz = 2\pi i \sum R^{+}, \quad \text{...(1)}$$

where $\sum R^{+}$ denotes the sum of the residues of f(z) at its poles in the upper half-plane. Now since zf(z) → 0 as | z | → ∞, it follows from theorem II of 5 that $\int_{\Gamma} f(z)dz = 0$.

$$\text{Also } \lim_{R\to\infty} \int_{-R}^{R} f(x)dx = P\int_{-\infty}^{\infty} f(x)dx,$$

where P denotes the principal value of the integral.

But since this integral is convergent, we can write

$$P\int_{-\infty}^{\infty} f(x)dx = \int_{-\infty}^{\infty} f(x)dx.$$

Hence proceeding to the limits when R→∞, we have from (1),

$$\int_{-\infty}^{\infty} f(x) = 2\pi i \sum R^{+}$$

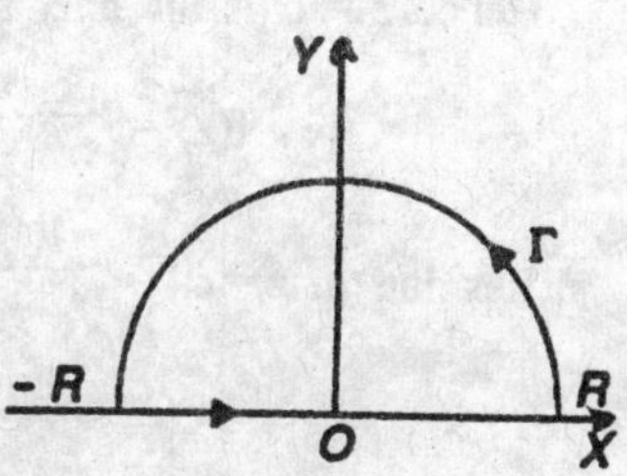

Fig. 4.2

Cor. :

Let $f(z) = \dfrac{P(z)}{Q(z)}$ where (i)

P(z) and Q (z) are polynomials such that (i) Q(z) = 0 has no real roots and (ii) the degree of P(z) is at least two less than that of Q(z) so that zf(z)→0 as | z | → ∞. Then

$$\int_{-\infty}^{\infty} \frac{P(z)}{Q(z)} dx = 2\pi i \sum R^{+}$$

SOME SOLVED EXAMPLES

Example 1:

(i) *Show that* $\int_0^{2\pi} \frac{d\theta}{a + b\cos\theta} = \int_0^{2\pi} \frac{d\theta}{a + b\sin\theta} = \frac{2\pi}{\sqrt{(a^2 - b^2}} a > b > 0.$

Solution:

Putting $z = e^{i\theta}$, $d\theta = \frac{bz}{iz}$, we get

$$I = \int_0^{2\pi} \frac{d\theta}{a + b\cos\theta} = \frac{1}{i} \int_C \frac{dz}{z\left[a + \frac{1}{2} b\left(z + 1/z\right)\right]}$$

$$= \frac{2}{i} \int_C \frac{dz}{bz^2 + 2az + b} = \frac{2}{i} \int_C f(z) dz$$

where C is the unit circle $|z| = 1$. The poles of f(z) are given by the roots of $bz^2 + 2az + b = 0$

$$\text{or } z = \frac{-2a \pm \sqrt{(4a^2 - 4b^2)}}{2b} = \frac{-a \pm \sqrt{(a^2 - b^2)}}{b}$$

$$\text{Let } \alpha = \frac{-a \pm \sqrt{(a^2 - b^2)}}{b}, \beta = \frac{-ab \pm \sqrt{(a^2 - b^2)}}{b}.$$

Since $a > b > 0$, we have $|P| > 1$.

But $|\alpha\beta| = 1$ $|a| < 1$.

Hence $z = \alpha$ is the only simple pole inside C. Also

$$f(z) = \frac{1}{b(z - \alpha)(z - \beta)}$$

$$\text{Residue (at } z = \alpha) = \lim_{z \to \alpha} (z - \alpha). \frac{2}{bi(z - \alpha)(z - \beta)}$$

$$= \lim_{z \to \alpha} \frac{2}{bi(z - \alpha)} = \frac{2}{bi(z - \beta)}$$

$$= \frac{2}{bi. \frac{2\sqrt{(a^2 - b^2)}}{b}} = \frac{1}{i\sqrt{(a^2 - b^2)}}$$

$$\text{Hence } \int_0^{2\pi} \frac{d\theta}{a + b\cos\theta} = 2\pi i. \frac{1}{i\sqrt{(a^2 - b^2)}} = \frac{2\pi}{\sqrt{(a^2 - b^2)}} \quad \text{... (1)}$$

Similarly $\int_0^{2\pi} \frac{d\theta}{1+a\sin\theta}$ can be evaluated. This is left as an exercise for the students.

(ii) *Show that* $\int_0^{2\pi} \frac{d\theta}{1+a\cos\theta} = \frac{2\pi}{\sqrt{(1-a^2)}}$, $a^2 < 1$.

Solution:

Replace b by a and a by 1 in (i).

(iii) $\int_0^{\pi} \frac{d\theta}{a+b\cos\theta} = \frac{1}{2}\int_0^{2\pi} \frac{d\theta}{a+b\cos\theta} = \frac{\pi}{\sqrt{(a^2-b^2)}}$

Solution:

Do yourself.

Example 2:

Evaluate $\int_0^{2\pi} \frac{d\theta}{(a+b\cos\theta)^2}$, $(a > b > 0)$.

Solution:

Putting $z = e^{i\theta}$, we get

$$I = \int_0^{2\pi} \frac{d\theta}{(a+b\cos\theta)^2} = \frac{1}{i}\int_C \frac{dz}{z[a+(b/2)(z+1/z)]^2}$$

$$= -4i\int_C \frac{z\,dz}{(bz^2+2az+b)^2}$$

$$= -\frac{4i}{b^2}\int_C \frac{z\,dz}{(z^2+(2a/b)z+1)^2} = -\frac{4i}{b^2}\int_C f(z)dz$$

where C is the circle $|z| = 1$.

Poles of order two of f(z) are given by the roots of

$$z^2 + \frac{2a}{b}z + 1 = 0$$

$$z = \frac{1}{2}\left[-\frac{2a}{b} \pm \sqrt{\left(\frac{4a^2}{b^2} - 4\right)}\right] = \frac{-a \pm \sqrt{(a^2-b^2)}}{b}$$

$$\text{Let } \alpha = \frac{-a+\sqrt{(a^2-b^2)}}{b},\ \beta = \frac{-a-\sqrt{(a^2-b^2)}}{b}$$

Since $a > b > 0$, $|\beta| > 1$. But $\alpha\beta = 1$ so that $|\alpha| < 1$.

Hence α is the only pole of order two inside C.

$$\text{Now } -\frac{4i}{b^2}f(z) = -\frac{4iz}{b^2(z-\alpha)^2(z-\beta)^2} = \frac{1}{(z-\alpha)^2}\phi(z).$$

$$\text{where } \theta(z) = -\frac{4iz}{b^2(z-\beta)^2}$$

Residue at the double pole z = α is

$$\phi'(\alpha) = -\frac{4i}{b^2}\left[\frac{(z-\beta)^2 - 2z(z-\beta)}{(z-\beta)^4}\right]_{z=a}$$

$$= -\frac{4i}{b^2}\left[\frac{(\alpha-\beta)-2\alpha}{(\alpha-\beta)^3}\right] = \frac{4i}{b^2}\frac{(\alpha+\beta)}{(\alpha-\beta)^3}$$

$$= \frac{4i}{b^2}\cdot\frac{-2a/b}{(8/b^3)(a^2-b^2)^{3/2}} = -\frac{ai}{(a^2-b^2)^{3/2}}$$

$$\text{Hence } \int_0^{2\pi}\frac{d\theta}{(a+b\cos\theta)^2} = 2\pi i\left[-\frac{ai}{(a^2-b^2)^{3/2}}\right] = \frac{2\pi a}{(a^2-b^2)^{3/2}}.$$

Example 3:

Prove that $\int_0^{\pi}\frac{d\theta}{(a+b\cos\theta)^2} = \frac{\pi a}{(a^2-1)^{3/2}}(a>1).$

Solution:

We have $\int_0^{\pi}\frac{d\theta}{(a+\cos\theta)^2} = \frac{1}{2}\int_0^{2\pi}\frac{d}{(a+\cos\theta)^2}.$

This is a particular case of Ex. 2 where b = 1.

$$\text{Hence } I = \frac{1}{2}\frac{2\pi a}{(a^2-1)^{3/2}} = \frac{\pi a}{(a^2-1)^{3/2}}.$$

Example 4:

Show that $\int_0^{2\pi}\frac{d\theta}{5+3\cos\theta} = \frac{\pi}{2}.$

Solution:

Proceed exactly a, in Ex. I, by putting the values of a and b.

Example 5:

Show that $\int_0^{\pi}\frac{1+2\cos\theta}{5+3\cos\theta}d\theta = 0.$

Solution:

We have $I = \int_0^{\pi} \frac{1+2\cos\theta}{5+3\cos\theta} d\theta = \frac{1}{2}\int_0^{\pi} \frac{1+2\cos\theta}{5+4\cos\theta} d\theta$

$$= \frac{1}{2i}\int_C \frac{1+z+\frac{1}{z}}{5+2\left(z+\frac{1}{z}\right)} \cdot \frac{dz}{z} = \frac{1}{2i}\int_C \frac{z^2+z+1}{z(2z^2+5z+2)} dz$$

$$= \frac{1}{4i}\int_C \frac{z^2+z+1}{z(z+\frac{1}{2})(z+2)} dz$$

where C is the unit circle $|z| = 1$.

The integrand has simple poles at $z = 0, -\frac{1}{2}, -2$ of which first two lie within C. Sum of the residues at 0 and $-\frac{1}{2}$

$$= \frac{1}{4i}\left[\lim_{z\to 0} \frac{z(z^2+z+1)}{z(z+\frac{1}{2})(z+2)} + \lim_{z\to \frac{1}{2}} \frac{(z+\frac{1}{2})(z^2+z+1)}{z(z+\frac{1}{2})(z+2)}\right]$$

$$= \frac{1}{4i}\left[1+\frac{\frac{1}{4}-\frac{1}{2}+1}{(-\frac{1}{2})(-\frac{1}{2}+2)}\right] = \frac{1}{4i}(1-1) = 0$$

Hence by residue theorem $I = 0$.

Example 6:

(i) Prove that $\int_0^{\pi} \frac{a\, d\theta}{a^2+\sin^2\theta} = \frac{\pi}{\sqrt{(1+a^2)}}, (a > 0).$

Solution:

Let $I = \int_0^{\pi} \frac{a\, d\theta}{a^2+\sin^2\theta} = \int_0^{\pi} \frac{2a\, d\theta}{2a^2+(1-\cos 2\theta)}$

$$= \int_0^{2\pi} \frac{a\, d\phi}{2a^2+1-\cos\phi} \qquad \text{putting } 2\theta = \phi$$

$$= \int_C \frac{a\, dz}{z[2a^2+1-\frac{1}{2}(z+i/z)]},$$

putting $z = e^{i\phi}$, where C is the unit circle $|z| = 1$

$$= \frac{2a}{i}\int_C \frac{dz}{[2z(2a^2+1)-(z^2-1)]}$$

$$= 2ai\int_C \frac{dz}{z^2 - 2(2a^2+1)z + 1} = 2ai\int_C f(z)dz.$$

Poles of f(z) are given by the roots of

$z^2 - 2(2a^2 + 1)\ z + 1 = 0$

or $z = \dfrac{2(2a^2+1) \pm \sqrt{[(2a^2+1)^2 - 4]}}{2} = (2a^2 + 1) \pm \sqrt{(4a^4 + 4a^2)}$

$= (2a^2 + 1) \pm 2a\sqrt{(a^2 + 1)}$

Let $\alpha = (2a^2 + 1) + 2a\sqrt{(a^2 +)}$, $\beta = (2a^2 + 1) - 2a\sqrt{(a^2 + 1)}$.

Clearly $|\alpha| > I$ and since $|\alpha\beta| = 1$, we have $|\beta| < 1$. Hence the only pole inside C is at $z = \beta$.

Residue (at $z = \beta$) $\lim_{z\to\beta} -\dfrac{2a}{i}.(z-\beta).\dfrac{1}{(z-\alpha)(z-\beta)}$

$$= -\frac{2a}{i(\beta-\alpha)} = -\frac{2a}{i(-4a)\sqrt{(a^2+1)}} = \frac{1}{2i\sqrt{(a^2+1)}}$$

$$\therefore \int_0^\pi \frac{a\,d\theta}{a^2 + \sin^2\theta} = 2\pi i, \frac{1}{2i\sqrt{(a^2+1)}} = \frac{\pi}{\sqrt{(a^2+1)}}$$

(ii) $\displaystyle\int_0^\pi \frac{a\,d\theta}{a^2 + \sin^2\theta} = \frac{1}{2}\int_0^\pi \frac{a\,d\theta}{a^2 + \sin^2\theta} = \frac{\pi}{1\sqrt{(1+a^2)}}$

Example 7:

Prove that $\displaystyle\int_0^{2\pi} \frac{\sin^2\theta}{a + b\cos\theta}d\theta = \frac{2\pi}{b^2}\{a - \sqrt{(a^2 - b^2)}\}$ *where* $a > b > 0$.

Solution:

Let $I = \displaystyle\int_0^{2\pi} \frac{\sin^2\theta}{a + b\cos\theta}d\theta.$

Putting $z = e^{i\theta}$. We get

$I = \dfrac{1}{i}\displaystyle\int_C \frac{[(1/2i).(z-1/z)^2}{a + \frac{1}{2}b(z+1/z)}.\frac{dz}{z}$ where C is the circle $|z| = 1$

$$= -\frac{1}{2i}\int_C \frac{(z^2-1)^2 dz}{z^2(2az + bz^2 + b)}$$

$$= -\frac{1}{2ib}\int_C \frac{(z^2-1)^2 dz}{z^2[z^2 + (2a/b)z + 1]} = -\frac{1}{2ib}\int_C f(z)dz.$$

Now f(z) has a double pole at z = 0 and simple poles at z = α and z = β, where α, β arc the roots of $z^2 + \frac{2a}{b}z + I = 0$

$$\text{or } z = \frac{1}{2}\left[-\frac{2a}{b} + \sqrt{\left(\frac{4a^2}{b^2} - 4\right)}\right]$$

$$\text{Let } \alpha = \frac{-a + \sqrt{(a^2 - b^2)}}{b}, \beta = \frac{-a - \sqrt{(a^2 - b^2)}}{b}.$$

Since a > b > 0, | β | > 1. But | αβ | = 1 so that | β | < 1. Therefore the poles inside the circle are a double pole at the origin and a simple pole at z = α.

$$\text{Residue (at } z = \beta) \lim_{z \to \alpha}(z - \alpha).\left[-\frac{1}{2ib}.\frac{(z^2 - 1)^2}{z^2(z - \alpha)(z - \beta)}\right]$$

$$= -\frac{(\alpha^2 - 1)^2}{2ib\alpha^2(\alpha - \beta)} = -\frac{1}{2ib}.\frac{(\alpha - 1/\alpha)^2}{(\alpha - \beta)}$$

$$= -\frac{1}{2ib}\frac{(\alpha - \beta)^2}{(\alpha - \beta)}. \text{ since } \frac{1}{\alpha} = \beta$$

$$= -\frac{1}{2ib}(\alpha - \beta) = \frac{1}{2ib}.\frac{2}{b}\sqrt{(a^2 - b^2)}$$

$$= \frac{i}{b^2}\sqrt{(a^2 - b^2)}$$

and residue at the origin

$$= \text{coefficient of } \frac{1}{z} \text{ in } -\frac{(z^2 - 1)^2}{2ibz^2(z^2 + (2a/b)z - 1)}, \text{ where z is small}$$

$$= \text{coefficient of } \frac{1}{z} \text{ in } -\frac{1}{2ibz^2}(1 - 2z^2 + z^4)\left(1 + \frac{2a}{b}z + z^2\right)^{-1}$$

$$= \text{coefficient of } \frac{1}{z} \text{ in } -\frac{1}{2ibz^2}(1 - 2z^2 + ...)\left(1 - \frac{2a}{b}z - ...\right)$$

$$= \frac{a}{ib^2} = -\frac{ai}{b^2}.$$

$$\therefore \int_0^{2\pi} \frac{\sin^2\theta \, d\theta}{a + 2\cos\theta} = 2\pi i\left[\frac{i}{b^2}\sqrt{(\alpha^2 - b^2)} - \frac{ai}{b^2}\right] = \frac{2\pi}{b^2}[a - \sqrt{(\alpha^2 - b^2)}].$$

Example 8:

Show that $\int_0^{\pi}\frac{\cos 2\theta\, d\theta}{1-2a\cos\theta+a^2}=\frac{\pi a^2}{1-a^2}(a^2<1)$.

Solution:

We have

$$=\int_0^{\pi}\frac{\cos 2\theta\, d\theta}{(1-2a\cos\theta+a^2)}=\int_0^{\pi}\frac{\cos 2\theta(1+2a\cos\theta+a^2)}{(1+a^2)^2-4a^2\cos^2\theta}$$

$$=\int_0^{\pi}\frac{(1+a^2)\cos 2\theta}{(1+a^2)^2-2a^2(1+\cos 2\theta)}d\theta+2a\int_0^{\pi}\frac{\cos 2\theta\cos\theta}{(1+a^2)^2-4a^2\cos^2\theta}d\theta$$

$$=\int_0^{\pi}\frac{(1+a^2)\cos 2\theta}{(1+a^2)^2-2a^2(1+\cos 2\theta)},$$ since the second integral is zero by the property of definite integrals,

$$=\frac{1}{2}\int_0^{2\pi}\frac{(1+a^2)\cos\phi\, d\phi}{1+a^4-2a^2\cos\phi},$$ putting $2\theta=\phi$

$$=\frac{1}{2i}\int_C\frac{(1+a^2)\frac{1}{2}(z+1/z)}{1+a^4-a^2(z+1/z)}\cdot\frac{dz}{z}$$ putting $z=e^{i\phi}$

where C is the circle $|z|=1$

$$=\frac{(1+a^2)}{4i}\int_C\frac{(z^2+1)dz}{[(1+a^4)z-a^2z^2-a^2]}$$

$$=\frac{(1+a^2)i}{4i}\int_C\frac{(z^2+1)dz}{z[z^2-(a^2+1/a^2)z+1]}$$

$$=\frac{(1+a^2)i}{4i}\int_C\frac{(z^2+1)dz}{z(z-a^2)(z-1/a^2)}=\frac{(a+a^2)i}{4a^2}\int_C f(z)dz,$$

Now f(z) has simple poles at $z = 0, a^2, 1/a^2$ of which the poles at $z = 0, a^2$ lie inside the circle since $a^2 < 1$.

Sum of the residues at these poles

$$=\frac{(1+a^2)i}{4i}\left[\lim_{z\to 0} z.f(z)+\lim_{z\to a^2}(z-a^2)f(z)\right]$$

$$=\frac{(1+a^2)i}{4a^2}\left[1+\frac{a^4+1}{a^2(a^2-1/a^2)}\right]$$

$$= \frac{(1+a^2)i}{4a^2}\left[\frac{2a^4}{a^4-1}\right] = \frac{a^2 i}{2(a^2-1)}$$

Hence $\displaystyle\int_0^{\pi} \frac{\cos 2\theta \, d\theta}{1-2a\cos\theta + a^2} = 2\pi i.\frac{a^2 i}{2(a^2-1)} = \frac{\pi a^2}{1} - a^2.$

Example 9:

Apply calculus of residues to prove that

$$\int_0^{2\pi} \frac{\cos 2\theta \, d\theta}{5+4\cos\theta} = \frac{\pi}{6}.$$

Solution:

We have $\displaystyle I = \int_0^{2\pi} \frac{\cos 2\theta \, d\theta}{(5+4\cos\theta)}$

$$= \text{real part of } \int_0^{2\pi} \frac{e^{2iq}}{(5+4\cos\theta)} d\theta$$

Now $\displaystyle I = \int_0^{2\pi} \frac{e^{2i\theta}}{(5+4\cos\theta)} d\theta = \int_C \frac{z^2}{[5+2(z+1/z)} d\theta$

putting $z = e^{i\theta}$, where C is the unit circle, $|z| = 1$.

$$I = \frac{1}{i}\int_C \frac{z^2 dz}{2z^2+5z+2} = \frac{1}{i}\int_C \frac{z^2 dz}{(2z+1)(z+2)}$$

$$= \frac{1}{2i}\int_C \frac{z^2 dz}{\left(z+\frac{1}{2}\right)(z+2)} = \frac{1}{2i}\int_C f(z) dz$$

Now f(z) has simple poles at $z = -\frac{1}{2}$ and $z = -2$ of which only $z = -\frac{1}{2}$ lies inside C.

Residue at $z = -\frac{1}{2}$ is $\displaystyle\lim_{z\to -\frac{1}{2}} \left(z+\tfrac{1}{2}\right).\frac{z^2}{2i\left(z+\frac{1}{2}\right)(z+2)} = \frac{1}{12i}$

$$\therefore \int_0^{2\pi} \frac{e^{2i\theta}}{(5+4\cos\theta)} d\theta = 2\pi i.\frac{1}{12i} = \frac{\pi}{6}.$$

Now equating real parts on both sides, we get $I = \pi/6$.

Example 10:

Prove that

$$\int_0^{2\pi} \frac{\cos^2 3\theta \, d\theta}{1-2p\cos 2\theta + p^2} = \pi \frac{1-p+p^2}{1-p} \qquad (0 < p < 1).$$

Solution

We have $I = \int_0^{2\pi} \frac{\cos^2 3\theta \, d\theta}{1-2p\cos 2\theta + p^2}$

$$= \frac{1}{2}\int_0^{2\pi} \frac{1+\cos 6\theta}{1-2p\cos 2\theta + p^2} d\theta$$

$$= \text{real part of } \frac{1}{2}\int_0^{2\pi} \frac{1+e^{2i\theta}}{1-2p\cos 2\theta + p^2} d\theta.$$

Now put $z = e^{i\theta}$ and consider

$$\frac{1}{2}\int_C \frac{1+z^6}{1-p(z^2+1/z^2)+p^2} \cdot \frac{dz}{iz} = \frac{1}{2i}\int_0 \frac{1+z^6}{z(1-pz^2)(1-p/z^2)}$$

$$= \frac{1}{2i}\int_C \frac{z(1+z^6)dz}{(1-pz^2)(z^2-p)} = \frac{1}{2i}\int_C f(z)dz,$$

where C is the circle $|z| = 1$. But f(z) has simple poles at $z = \pm 1/\sqrt{p}$, $\pm \sqrt{p}$ which $z = \pm\sqrt{p}$, lie within the circle $|z| = 1$, since $0 < p < 1$.

Sum of the residues at these poles

$$= \lim_{z\to\sqrt{p}} (z-\sqrt{p}f(z) = \lim_{z\to\sqrt{p}} (z+\sqrt{p})f(z)$$

$$= \lim_{z\to\sqrt{p}} \frac{1(1+z^6)}{(1-pz^2)(z+\sqrt{p})} + \lim_{z\to\sqrt{p}} \frac{z(1+z^6)}{(1-pz^2)(z-\sqrt{p})}$$

$$= \frac{\sqrt{p}.(1+p^3)}{(1-p^2)(2\sqrt{p})} + \frac{-\sqrt{p}.(1+p^3)}{(1-p^2)(-2\sqrt{p})} = \frac{1+p^3}{1-p^2}.$$

Hence $\frac{1}{2}\int_0^{2\pi} \frac{1+e^{6\theta i}}{1-2p\cos 2\theta + p^2} d\theta = 2\pi i.\frac{1+p^3}{1-p^2} = \frac{1-p+p^2}{1-p}\pi.$

Equating real parts on both sides, we get

$$I = \frac{1-p+p^2}{1-p}\pi.$$

Example 11:

Prove that $\int_0^{2\pi} \frac{(1+2\cos\theta)^n \cos n\theta}{3+2\cos\theta} d\theta = \frac{2\pi}{\sqrt{5}}(3-\sqrt{5})^n$

(n being a +ve integer)

Solution:

We have $$I = \int_0^{2\pi} \frac{(1+2\cos\theta)^n \cos n\theta}{(3+2\cos\theta)} d\theta$$

$$= \text{real part of } \int_0^{2\pi} \frac{(1+2\cos\theta)^n e^{n\theta i}}{(3+2\cos\theta)} d\theta.$$

Putting $z = e^{i\theta}$, we get

$$\int_0^{2\pi} \frac{(1+2\cos\theta)^n}{(3+2\cos\theta)} e^{n\theta i}\, d\theta = \int_C \frac{(2+z+z^2)^n}{(3+z+1/z)} \cdot \frac{dz}{iz},$$

where C is the circle $|z| = 1$.

$$= \frac{1}{i}\int_C \frac{(1+z+z^2)^n dz}{(1+3z+z^2)} = \frac{1}{i}\int_C \frac{(1+z+z^2)^n}{(z-\alpha)(z-\beta)} dz = \frac{1}{i}\int_C f(z)dz,$$

where α, β are the roots of the equation $z^2 + 3z + 1 = 0$,

whence $\alpha\beta = 1$, $\alpha = \frac{-3+\sqrt{5}}{5}$, $\beta = \frac{-5-\sqrt{5}}{5}$.

Clearly $|\beta| > |\alpha|$ so that $|\alpha| < 1$.

$\therefore$ The only pole of f(z) within C is at $z = \alpha$.

Residue of f(z) at $\alpha = \lim_{z\to\alpha} (z-\alpha)\, f(z)$

$$= \lim_{z\to\alpha} \frac{(1+z+z^2)^n}{(z-\beta)} = \frac{(1+\alpha+\alpha^2)^n}{(\alpha-\beta)}$$

$$= \frac{\left(1-\frac{3}{2}+\frac{\sqrt{5}}{2}+\frac{7-3\sqrt{5}}{2}\right)^2}{\sqrt{5}} = \frac{(3-\sqrt{5})^n}{\sqrt{5}}$$

Hence $$\int_0^{2\pi} \frac{(1+2\cos\theta)^n}{(3+2\cos\theta)} e^{n\theta i} d\theta = 2\pi o.\frac{1}{i}.\frac{(3-\sqrt{5})^n}{\sqrt{5}} = \frac{2\pi}{\sqrt{5}}.(3-\sqrt{5})^n$$

Equating real parts on both sides, we get

$$I = \frac{2\pi}{\sqrt{5}}(3-\sqrt{5})^n.$$

Example 12:

Prove that $$\int_0^{2\pi} e^{\cos\theta} \cos(n\theta - \sin\theta) d\theta = \frac{2\pi}{n!}$$

Solution:

$$1 = \int_0^{2\pi} e^{\cos\theta}.e^{-(n\theta-\sin\theta)t}d\theta$$

$$= \int_0^{2\pi} e^{\cos\theta+i\sin\theta}.e^{-n\theta i}d\theta = \int_0^{2\pi} e^{e^{i\theta}}.e^{-n\theta i}d\theta$$

$$= \frac{1}{i}\int_C \frac{e^z}{z^{n+1}}dz = \frac{1}{i}\int_C f(z)dz$$

putting $z = e^{i\theta}$, where C is the circle $|z| = 1$.

Clearly f(z) has a pole of order (n + 1) at the origin.

The residue of f(z) at the origin

$$= \frac{1}{n!}\left[\frac{d^n}{dz^n}.e^z\right]_{z=0} = \frac{1}{n!}$$

Hence $I = 2\pi i.\frac{1}{i}.\frac{1}{n!} = \frac{2\pi}{n!}$.

Equating real and imaginary parts,

$$\int_0^{2\pi} e^{\cos\theta}\cos(n\theta - \sin\theta)d\theta = \frac{2\pi}{n!}$$

and $\int_0^{2\pi} e^{\cos\theta}\sin(n\theta - \sin\theta)d\theta = 0$.

Example 13:

Prove that

(i) $\int_0^{\infty} \frac{dx}{(1+x^2)^2} = \frac{\pi}{4}$, (ii) $\int_0^{\infty} \frac{dx}{(x^2+1)^3} = \frac{3\pi}{8}$.

Solution:

We consider $\int_C \frac{dz}{(1+z^2)^2} = \int_C f(z)dz$ where C is the contour consisting of a large semi-circle Γ of radius R together with the part of the real axis from x = –R to R.

Then by residue theorem,

$$\int_C f(z)dz = \int_{-R}^{R} \frac{dx}{(1+x^2)^2} + \int_\Gamma \frac{dz}{(1+z^2)^2} = 2\pi i \sum R^+. \qquad \text{...(1)}$$

Since $\lim_{R\to\infty} zf(z) = \lim_{Z\to\infty} \frac{z}{(1+z^2)^2} = 0$, we have

$$\lim_{R\to\infty} \int_\Gamma \frac{dz}{(1+z^2)^2} = 0.$$

Also $\lim_{R\to\infty}\int_{-R}^{R}\frac{dx}{(1+x^2)^2}=\int_{-\infty}^{\infty}\frac{dx}{(1+x^2)^2}$

Then we have from (1),

$$\int_{-\infty}^{\infty}\frac{dx}{(1+x^2)^2}=2\pi i\sum R^+.$$

Now f(z) has double poles at z = ± i, of which z = i lies inside C.

Residue (at z = i) = ϕ' (i) where $\phi(z)=\frac{1}{(z+1)^2}$

$$=\left[-\frac{2}{(z+i)^3}\right]_{z=i}=\frac{1}{4i}$$

Hence we have from (1),

$$\int_{-\infty}^{\infty}\frac{dx}{(1+x^2)^2}=\int_{0}^{\infty}\frac{dx}{(1+x^2)^2}=2\pi i.\frac{1}{4i}=\frac{\pi}{2}$$

or $\int_{-\infty}^{\infty}\frac{dx}{(1+x^2)^2}=\frac{\pi}{4}.$

(ii) Consider the integral $\int_C\frac{dz}{(z^3+1)^2}=\int_C f(z)dz$, where C is the same contour as in (i). We have then

$$\int_C f(z)dz=\int_{-R}^{R}f(x)dx+\int_{\Gamma}f(z)dz=2\pi i\sum R^+ \quad ...(1)$$

Since $\lim_{Z\to\infty}zf(z)=0$, hence we have $\lim_{Z\to\infty}\int_{\Gamma}f(z)dz=0$

Proceeding to the limits as R→∞, we get from (1)

$$\int_{-\infty}^{\infty}f(x)dx=2\pi i\sum R^+. \quad ...(2)$$

Now f(z) has poles of order three at z = ± i, of which z = i lies in the upper half plane.

Residue (at z = i) is $\frac{1}{2!}\phi''$ (i), where $\phi(z)\ \frac{1}{(z+i)^3}$

$$=\left[\frac{1}{2!}.\frac{12}{(z+i)^5}\right]_{z=1}=\frac{6}{(2i)^5}=\frac{3}{16i}$$

∴ From (2), $\int_{-\infty}^{\infty}f(x)dx=2\pi i\frac{3}{16i}=\frac{3\pi}{8}.$

Example 14:

Prove that $\int_{-\infty}^{\infty}\frac{x^2-x+2}{x^4+10x^2+9}dx=\frac{5\pi}{12}.$

Solution:

We consider $\int_C \frac{z^2 - z + 2}{z^4 + 10z^2 + 9} dz = \int f(z)dz$,

where C is the contour by residue theorem,

$$\int_C f(z)dz = \int_{-R}^{R} f(x)dx + \int_{\Gamma} f(z)dz = 2\pi i \sum R^+ \quad \text{... (1)}$$

But $\int_{\Gamma} f(z)dz \to 0$ as $R \to \infty$, since $\lim_{z \to 0} zf(z) = 0$ or we may proceed independently as follows

On putting $z = Re^{i\theta}$, where z lies on the semi-circle, we obtain,

$$\int_{\Gamma} f(z)dz = \int_{\Gamma} \frac{z^2 - z + 2}{z^4 + 10z^2 + 9} dz = \int_{\Gamma} \frac{z^2 - z + 2}{(z^2 + 9)(z^2 + 1)} dz$$

$$= \int_0^{\pi} \frac{R^2e^{2i\theta} - Re^{i\theta} + 2}{(R^2e^{2i\theta} + 9)(R^2e^{2i\theta} + 1)} .Rie^{i\theta} d\theta.$$

$$\therefore \left| \int_{\Gamma} f(z)dz \right| = \left| \int_0^{\pi} \frac{R^2e^{2i\theta} - Re^{i\theta} + 2}{(R^2e^{2i\theta} + 9)(R^2e^{2i\theta} + 1)} .Rie^{i\theta} d\theta \right|$$

$$\leq \int_0^{\pi} \frac{|R^2e^{2i\theta}| + |-Re^{i\theta}| + 2}{\{|R^2e^{2i\theta}| - |-9|\} \{|R^2e^{2i\theta}| - |-1|\}} |R^2e^{i\theta}| d\theta$$

$[\because |a + b| \leq |a| + |b|$ and $|a - b| > |a| - |b|]$

$$i.e. \leq \int_0^{\pi} \frac{R^2 + R + 2}{(R^2 - 9)(R^2 - 1)} .Rd\theta,$$

$$i.e. \leq \frac{\pi(R^3 + R^2 + 2R)}{(R^2 - 1)(R^2 - 9)} \to 0 \text{ as } R \to \infty.$$

Hence we have from (1) on proceeding to the limits as $R \to \infty$,

$$\int_{-\infty}^{\infty} f(z)dz = 2\pi i \sum R^+.$$

Now f(z) has simple poles at $z = \pm i, \pm 3i$ of which $z = i$ and 3i lie inside C.

Sum of residues at these poles,

$$= \lim (z - i)f(z) + = \lim_{z \to 3i} (z - 3i)f(z)$$

$$= \frac{i^2 - i + 2}{(i^2 + 9)(2i)} + \frac{9i^2 - 3i + 2}{(9i^2 + 1)6i}$$

$$= \frac{1-i}{16i} + \frac{7+3o}{48i} = \frac{10}{48i} = \frac{5}{24i}.$$

$$\therefore \int_{-\infty}^{\infty} f(x)dx = 2\pi i, \frac{5}{24i} = \frac{5\pi}{12}.$$

Example 15:

Prove that $\int_{-\infty}^{\infty} \frac{x^2 dx}{(x^2+a^2)^3} = \frac{\pi}{8a^2}$ *provided that R (a) is + ve.*

What is the value of this integral when R (a) is, negative ?

Solution:

Consider $\int \frac{z^2 dz}{(z^2+a^2)^3} = \int f(z)dz$, where C is the same contour by residue theorem,

$$\int_C f(z)dz = \int_{-R}^{R} f(x)dx + \int_\Gamma f(z)dz = 2\pi i \sum R^+. \qquad ...(1)$$

Since $\lim_{z\to\infty} zf(z) = 0$, we have $\lim_{R\to\infty} \int_\Gamma f(z)dz = 0.$

$\therefore$ Proceeding to the limits, when $R \to \infty$, we get from (1),

$$\int_{-\infty}^{\infty} f(x)dx = 2\pi i \sum R^+. \qquad ...(2)$$

Now f(z) has poles at $z = \pm ai$ of order three, of which $z = ai$ lies inside C provided R (a) is positive.

Residue of f(z) (at z = ai) = coeff. of $\frac{1}{t}$ in f(t + ai)

$$= \text{coeff. of } \frac{1}{t} \text{ in } \frac{(t+ai)^2}{[(t+ai)^2+a^2)]^3}.$$

Now $\frac{(t+ai)^2}{(t^2+2ait)^3} = -\frac{1}{8a^3it^3}(t^2+2ait-a^2)\left(1+\frac{t}{2ai}\right)^{-3}$

$$= -\frac{1}{8a^3it^3}[t^2+2ait-a^2]\left[1-\frac{3t}{2ai}-\frac{6t^2}{4a^2}+...+\right]$$

$$\therefore \text{coeff. of } \frac{1}{t} \text{ in } f(t+ai) = -\frac{1}{8a^3i}\left[1-\frac{6ai}{2ai}+\frac{6a^2}{4a^2}\right] = \frac{1}{16a^3i}.$$

$$\therefore \text{Residue of f(z) (at z = ai)} = \frac{1}{16a^3i}.$$

$\therefore$ From (2), $\int_{-\infty}^{\infty} f(x)dx = 2\pi i.\frac{1}{16a^3 i} = \frac{\pi}{8a^3}$. ...(3)

When R(a) is –ve, pole within C is at z = –ai.

$\therefore$ In this case $\int_{-\infty}^{\infty} f(x)dx = -\frac{\pi}{8a^3}$. [replacing –a by a in (3)].

Example 16:

Evaluate $\int_0^{\infty} \frac{dx}{x^4 + a^4} (a > 0)$.

Solution:

Consider $\int_0^{\infty} \frac{dx}{x^4 + a^4} = \int_C f(z)dz$,

where C is the contour of § 7.

$$\int_C f(z)dz = \int_{-R}^{R} f(x)dx + \int_{\Gamma} f(z)dz = 2\pi i \sum R^+.$$

Since $\lim_{z\to\infty} zf(z) = 0$, we have $\lim_{R\to\infty} \int_{\Gamma} f(z)dz = 0$.

$$\lim_{R\to\infty} \int_{-R}^{R} f(x)dx + 2\pi i \sum R^+$$

$$\int_{-\infty}^{\infty} f(x)dx + 2\pi i \sum R^+. \quad ...(1)$$

Now f(z) has simple poles for values of a given by

$z^4 + a^4 = 0$ or $z^4 = a^4.\ e^{(2n+1)\pi i}$, n = 0, 1, 2, 3,

i.e. the poles are at $z = ae^{\pi i/4}, ae^{3\pi i/4}, ae^{5\pi i/4}, ae^{7\pi i/4}$ of which only first two lie in the upper half plane.

Let α denote any one of these poles, then $\pi^4 = -a^4$.

$$\text{Residue (at } z = \alpha) = \lim_{z\to\alpha}(z-\alpha)f(z)$$

$$= \lim_{z\to\alpha} \frac{(z-\alpha)}{z^4 - \alpha^4} \left[\text{form } \tfrac{0}{0}\right]$$

$$= \lim_{z\to\alpha} \frac{1}{4z^3} = \frac{1}{4\alpha^3} = \frac{\alpha}{4\alpha^4} = -\frac{\alpha}{4a^4}.$$

$$\therefore \text{ sum of the residues } = -\frac{1}{4a^4}(ae^{\pi i/4} + ae^{3\pi i/4})$$

$$= -\frac{1}{4a^3}(e^{\pi i/4} - e^{-\pi i/4})$$

$$= -\frac{1}{4a^3} 2i \sin\frac{\pi}{4} = -\frac{\sqrt{2}i}{4a^3}.$$

Hence we have from (1),

$$\int_{-\infty}^{\infty} \frac{dx}{x^4 + a^4} = 2\pi i\left(-\frac{\sqrt{2}i}{4a^3}\right) = \frac{\sqrt{2}\pi}{2a^3}$$

or $\displaystyle\int_0^{\infty} \frac{dx}{x^4 + a^4} = \frac{\sqrt{2}\pi}{4a^3}.$

Example 17:

Examine the convergence of

(i) $\displaystyle\int_0^1 \frac{\log x}{\sqrt{x}}$, (ii) $\displaystyle\int_0^{\pi/2} \frac{\log x}{x^4} dx \,(a < 1)$.

Solution:

(i) Since $\log x \mid \sqrt{x}$ is negative in]0, 1], we take

$$f(x) = -\frac{\log x}{\sqrt{x}} = \frac{\log 1/x}{\sqrt{x}}$$

Here 0 is the only point of infinite discontinuity.

Let $g(x) = \dfrac{1}{x^{3/4}}$ so that we have

$$\lim_{x\to 0+} \frac{f(x)}{g(x)} = \lim_{x\to 0+} x^{1/4} \log\frac{1}{x} = \lim_{x\to 0+} \frac{\log 1/x}{x^{-1/4}}$$

$$= \lim_{x\to 0+} \frac{x(-1/x^2)}{(-1/4)x^{-5/4}} \text{ is } \lim_{x\to 0+} x^{1/4} = 0$$

Since $\displaystyle\int_0^1 g(x)\, dx = \int_0^1 \frac{dx}{x^{3/4}}$ is convergent, so the given integral is convergent.

(ii) Since $\log x/x^a$ is negative when $0 < x <^1$, so we have

$$f(x) = \frac{\log x}{x^a} = \frac{\log(1/x)}{x^a}$$

Let k be a fixed number such that $a < k < 1$.

Let $g(x) = \frac{1}{x^2}$ so that $\frac{f(x)}{g(x)} = x^{k-a} \log\left(\frac{1}{x}\right) \to 0$ as $x \to 0+$

Since, $\int_0^1 g(x)\,dx = \int_0^1 \frac{dx}{g(x)} = (k < 1)$ is donvergent, so $\int_0^1 f(x)\,dx$ and hence, $\int_0^1 \frac{\log x}{x^a}\,dx$ is convergent if $a < 1$.

Again, $\int_0^{\pi/2} \frac{\log x}{x^a}\,dx = \int_0^1 \frac{\log x}{x^a}\,dx + \int_1^{\pi/2} \frac{\log x}{x^a}\,dx$

where the second integral on the R.H.S. is proper.

Hence, the given integral is convergent for $a < 1$.

Example 18:

Examine for convergence the integrals

(i) $\int_1^{\infty} \frac{\tan^{-1} x}{x^2}\,dx$, (ii) $\int_1^{\infty} \frac{x \tan^{-1} x}{(1+x^4)^{1/3}}\,dx$,

Solution:

(i) Let $f(x) = \tan^{-1} x/x^2$ and $g(x) = 1/x^2$ so that

$$\lim_{x\to\infty} \frac{f(x)}{g(x)} = \lim_{x\to\infty} \tan^{-1} x = \frac{\pi}{2}$$

Since $\int_1^{\infty} g(x)\,dx$ converges, so $\int_1^{\infty} f(x)\,dx$ converges

(ii) Let $f(x) = \frac{x \tan^{-1} x}{(1+x^4)^{1/3}} = \frac{x \tan^{-1} x}{x^{1/2}(1+x^{-5})^{1/3}}, g(x) = \frac{x}{x^{4/3}} = \frac{1}{x^{1/2}}$

$$\therefore \lim_{x\to\infty} \frac{f(x)}{g(x)} = \lim_{x\to\infty} \frac{\tan^{-1} x}{(1+x^{-4})} = \frac{\pi}{2}$$

Since $\int_1^{\infty} \frac{dx}{x^{1/3}}$ diverges, so $\int_1^{\infty} \frac{x \tan^{-1} x\,dx}{(1+x^4)^{1/3}}$ also diverges.

Example 19:

Show that the improper integral

$\int_0^{\infty} \log(1+2\sec hx)\,dx$ *is convergent.*

Solution:

$$\int_0^{\infty} f(x)\,dx = \int_0^1 f(x)dx + \int_1^{\infty} f(x)dx,$$

wheref(x) = $\log(1 + 2\sec hx)$

$$\text{We know see hx} = \frac{2}{e^2+e^{-2}} = \frac{2e^n}{e^{2n}+1}$$

Convergence at 0:

$$\lim_{x\to 0+} \log(1+2\sec hx) = \lim_{x\to 0+} \log 1+\frac{4e^x}{e^{2x}+1} = \log 3.$$

Thus 0 is not a point of infinite discontinuity and so $\int_0^1 f(x)\,dx$ is a proper integral.

Convergence at ∞:

We know log (1 + x) < x for all x ≥ 1

$\Rightarrow$ log (1 + 2 sec hx) < 2 sec hx

$$\Rightarrow \int_0^\infty \log(1+2\sec hx)\,dx < \int_1^\infty 2\sec hx\,dx$$

$$= \int_1^\infty \frac{4e^x}{e^{2x}+1}dx = 4\int_e^\infty \frac{dy}{1+y^2},\ y=e^x$$

$$< 4\int_e^\infty \frac{dy}{y^2}, \text{ which is convergent.}$$

Hence $\int_1^\infty f(x)\,dx$ is convergent and so the given improper integral is convergent.

Example 20:

Discuss the convergence of

$$\int_0^\infty \frac{x^{2m}}{1+x^{2n}} (m>0, n>0).$$

Solution:

Clearly 0 is not a point of infinite discontinuity of the integrand. We shall examine convergence at ∞ only.

$$\text{Let} f(x) = \frac{x^{2m}}{1+x^{2n}} \text{ and } g(x) = \frac{x^{2m}}{x^{2n}} = \frac{1}{x^{2(n-m)}}.$$

$$\therefore \lim_{x\to\infty} \frac{f(x)}{g(x)} = \lim_{x\to\infty} \frac{x^{2n}}{1+x^{2n}} = \lim_{x\to\infty} \frac{1}{1+(1/x^{an})} = 1$$

Since $\int_0^\infty g(x)\,dx$ converges iff 2 (n–m)>1, so

$$\int_0^\infty \frac{x^{2m}}{1+x^{2m}} \text{ converges iff } (n-m) > ½.$$

Example 21:

Test for convergence the integral

$$\int_0^1 x^p\left(\log\frac{1}{x}\right)^q dx.$$

Solution:

Taking $\log\left(\frac{1}{x}\right)=t$ or $x = e^{-1}$, we get

$$\int_0^1 x^p\left(\log\frac{1}{x}\right)^q dx = \int_0^\infty t^q e^{-(p+1)t}\, dt.$$

Here 0 is a point of infinite discontinuity, so we take

$$\int_0^\infty t^q\, e^{(p+1)}\, dt = \int_0^1 t^q e^{-(p+1)t}\, dt + \int_1^\infty t^q e^{-(p+1)t}\, dt.$$

Convergence at 0:

$$\text{Let } f(t) = t^q e^{-(p+1)t} = \frac{e^{-(p+1)t}}{t^{-q}}$$

Comparing with $\int_0^1 \frac{dt}{t^{-q}}$, we see that $\int_0^1 e^{-(p+1)t}\, t^q\, dt$ converges at 0 if $-q < 1$ or $q > -1$, for all values of p.

Convergence at ∞ :

Let $f(f) = t^q\, e^{-(p+1)t}$

$$g(t) = \frac{1}{t^2}$$

Now $\frac{f(t)}{g(t)} = \frac{t^{q+a}}{e^{(p+1)t}} \to 0$ as $t \to \infty$ for $p + 1 > 0$ and for all q.

Since $\int_1^\infty \frac{dt}{t^2}$ converges, so $\int_1^\infty t^q e^{-(p+1)t}\, dt$ converges for q and $p > -1$.

Hence, $\int_0^1 x^p\left(\log\frac{1}{x}\right)^q dx$ is convergent for $p > -1$, $q > -1$ and divergent for all other values of q.

Example 22:

Examine for convergence the integral

(i) $\int_0^\infty \frac{\sqrt{x}}{(1+x)^2} dx$, (ii) $\int_{-\infty}^\infty \frac{dx}{(1+x^3)^2}$

Solution:

(i) Let $f(x) = \dfrac{\sqrt{x}}{(1+x)^2}$ and $g(x) = \dfrac{1}{x\sqrt{x}} = \dfrac{1}{x^{3/2}}$ so that

$$\lim_{x\to\infty}\frac{f(x)}{g(x)} = \lim_{x\to\infty}\frac{x^2}{(1+x)^2} = 1$$

Thus, $\int_1^\infty f(x)\,dx$ and $\int_1^\infty g(x)\,dx$ have identical behaviour.

But $\int_1^\infty g(x)\,dx = \int_1^\infty \dfrac{dx}{x^{3/2}}$ converges, so $\int_1^\infty f(x)\,dx$ also converges.

(ii) $$\int_{-\infty}^{\infty}\frac{dx}{(1-x^2)^2} = \int_{-\infty}^{0}\frac{dx}{(1+x^2)} + \int_0^\infty \frac{dx}{(1+x^2)^2}$$

$$= 2\int_0^\infty \frac{dx}{(1+x^2)^2}$$

(Take $x = -y$ in the first integral)

Now, $$2\int_0^t \frac{dx}{(1+x^2)^2} = 2\int \cos^2\theta\,d\theta = \int (1+\cos 2\theta)\,d\theta,\ x = \tan\theta$$

$$= 0 + \frac{1}{2}(\sin 2\theta) = \theta + \frac{\tan\theta}{1+\tan^2\theta}$$

$$= \tan^{-1}x + \frac{x}{1+x^2} = \tan^{-1}t + t(1+t^2)$$

$$\therefore \lim_{t\to\infty}\frac{dx}{(1+x^3)^2} = \frac{\pi}{2}.$$ Hence $\int_{-\infty}^{\infty}\dfrac{dx}{(1+x^3)^2}$ converges.

Example 23:

Show that $\int_0^{\pi/2} \log \sin x\,dx$ *is convergent.*

Solution:

The function $f(x) = \log\sin x$ is non-positive in $[0, \pi/2]$, we consider the function $-f(x)$ for examining the convergence at 0.

Let $\quad g(x) = \dfrac{1}{x^m}$, where $m < 1$. Then we have

$$\lim_{x\to 0}\frac{-f(x)}{g(x)} = \lim_{x\to 0}(-x^m \log\sin x) = 0$$

So $\int_0^{\pi/2} -f(x)\,dx$ and $\int_0^{\pi/2} g(x)\,dx$ converge or diverge together.

Since $\int_0^{\pi/2} g(x)\,dx = \int_0^{\pi/2}\dfrac{dx}{x^m}$ is convergent for $m < 1$, so

$-\int_0^{\pi/2} \log \sin x \, dx$ is convergent.

Hence $\int_0^{\pi/2} \log \sin x \, dx$ is convergent.

Example 24:

Test the convergence of $\int_0^1 \frac{\log}{\sqrt{1-x^2}} dx$

Solution:

Do your self.

Example 25:

Show that $\int_{-\infty}^{\infty} e^{-x^2} dx$ converges.

Solution:

$$\int_{-\infty}^{\infty} e^{-x^2} dx = \int_{-\infty}^{0} e^{-x^2} dx + \int_0^{\infty} e^{-x^2} dx$$

Putting x = – y, we obtain

$$\int_{-\infty}^{\infty} e^{-x^2} dx = -\int_{\infty}^{0} e^{-y^4} dy + \int_0^{\infty} e^{-x^2} dx$$

$$= 2\int_0^{\infty} e^{-x^2} dx$$

Hence $\int_{-\infty}^{\infty} e^{-x^2} dx$ is convergent.

Example 26:

Show that $\int_0^{\infty} \left(\frac{1}{1+x} - e^{-n}\right) \frac{dx}{x}$ is convergent.

Solution:

$$\text{Let } f(x) = \left(\frac{1}{1+x} - e^{-n}\right)\frac{1}{x} = \left(\frac{1}{1+x} - \frac{1}{e^a}\right)\frac{1}{x}$$

$$\text{or} f(x) = \frac{e^x - (1+x)}{x(1+x)e^x} > 0 \text{ for } x > 0 \qquad [\because f(x) = 1 + x\frac{x^2}{2!} + ...1$$

Since $\lim_{x\to 0} f(x) = 0.$ 0 is not a point of infinite discontinuity.

We have $\int_0^{\infty} f(x)\, dx = \int_0^1 f(x)\, dx + \int_0^{\infty} f(x)\, dx, \int_0^1 f(x)\, dx$ being proper.

Now, we shall investigate the convergence of $\int_1^{\infty} f(x)\, dx$.

$$\text{Let } g(x) = \frac{1}{x^2} \quad \lim_{x\to\infty} \frac{f(x)}{g(x)} = \frac{e^x - (1+x)}{e^x}\left(\frac{x}{1+x}\right)$$

$$= \lim_{x\to\infty} \frac{e^x - (1+x)}{e^x} = 1 - \lim_{x\to\infty} \frac{1+x}{e^x} = 1 - \lim_{x\to\infty} \frac{1}{e^x} = 1$$

Thus, $\int_1^\infty f(x)\,dx$ and $\int_1^\infty g(x)\,dx$ converge or diverge together.

But $\int_1^\infty g(x)\,dx = \int_1^\infty \frac{dx}{x^2}$ converges. So. $\int_1^\infty f(x)\,dx$ converges

Hence $\int_1^\infty f(x)\,dx$ is convergent.

Example 27:

Show that $\int_0^\infty x^{n-1} e^{-x}\,dx$ *is convergent iff* $n > 0$.

Solution:

Let $f(x) = x^{n-1} e^{-m}$. Then 0 is a point of infinite discontinuity of f, if $n < 1$. Thus, we have to examine convergence at 0 and ∞. We take

$$\int_0^\infty f(x)\,dx = \int_0^1 f(x)\,dx + \int_1^\infty f(x)\,dx\,.$$

Convergence at 0:

Let $g(x) = \frac{1}{x^{1-n}}$. Then $\lim_{x\to 0} \frac{f(x)}{g(x)} = \lim_{x\to 0} e^{-n} = 1.$

So, $\int_0^1 f(x)\,dx$, $\int_0^1 g(x)\,dx$ have identical behaviour.

Now, $\int_0^1 g(x)\,dx$ converges iff $(1-n) < 1 \Rightarrow 0 < n$.

Convergence at ∞:

For given n and for large values of x_1 then we have

$$e^x > x^{n+1} \Leftrightarrow \frac{1}{e^{-x}} > x^{n-1}.x^2$$
$$\Leftrightarrow x^{x-1} e^{-n} < 1/x^2$$

Since $\int_1^\infty \frac{1}{x^2}\,dx$ converges, so $\int_1^\infty x^{n-1} e^{-n}\,dx$ converges $\forall$ n

Hence $\int_1^\infty x^{n-1} e^{-x}dx$ is convergent iff $n > 0$.

Remark:

The integral $\int_1^\infty x^{n-1} e^{-n}dx$ is called Gamma *Function. It is denoted by F(n).*

Example 28:

Discuss the convergence of

$$\int_{-\infty}^{\infty} e^{-(x-a/x)^2}\, dx.$$

Solution:

Let $f(x) = e^{-(x-a/x)^2}$. Then

$$\int_{-\infty}^{\infty} f(x)\, dx = \int_{-\infty}^{0} f(x)\, dx + \int_{0}^{\infty} f(x)\, dx$$

Putting x = – y, we see that

$$\int_{-\infty}^{0} e^{-(x-a/x)^2}\, dx = -\int_{\infty}^{0} e^{-(-y+a/y)^2}\, dy = \int_{-\infty}^{0} e^{-(y-a/y)^2}\, dy$$

$$\therefore \int_{-\infty}^{\infty} f(x)\, dx = 2\int_{0}^{\infty} e^{-(x-a/x)^2}\, dx$$

$$= 2\left[\int_{0}^{1} e^{-(x-a/x)^2}\, dx + \int_{1}^{\infty} e^{-(x-a/x)^2}\, dx\right]$$

We have $\lim\limits_{x\to 0} e^{-(x-a/x)^2} = 0$

$\int_{0}^{1} e^{(x-a/x)^2}$ dx is a proper integral.

Now we discuss convergence at ∞ only.

We know $e^{(x-a/x)^2} > (x - a/y)^2 \ \forall\ x \in R$.

$$\therefore \int_{1}^{\infty} e^{-(x-a/x)^2}\, dx < \int_{1}^{\infty} \frac{dx}{(x-a/x)^2}$$

$$\text{Now } \int_{1}^{\infty} \frac{dx}{(x-a/x)^2} = \int_{1}^{\infty} \frac{x^2 dx}{(x^2-a)^2}$$

Let $g(x) = x^2/(x^2 - a)^2$, $h(x) = \dfrac{1}{x^2}$. Then

$$\lim_{x\to\infty} \frac{g(x)}{h(x)} = \lim_{x\to\infty} \frac{x^4}{(x^3-a)^2} = \lim_{x\to\infty} \frac{1}{(1-a/x^2)^2} = 1$$

Since $\int_{1}^{\infty} h(x)$ dx is convergent, so

$$\int_{1}^{\infty} \frac{1}{(x-a/x)^2}\, dx \text{ is convergent}$$

$\Rightarrow \quad \int_1^{\infty} e^{-(x-a/x)^2} dx$ is convergent.

Hence $\int_{-\infty}^{\infty} e^{-(x-a/x)^2} dx$ is convergent.

Hence by (1), $\int_1^{\infty} \frac{x^{a-1} \log x}{1+x} dx$ is convergent iff n < 0.

Example 29:

Show that $\int_0^1 x^{n-1} \log x \, dx$ *converges iff* $n > 0$.

Solution:

Since log x is negative in [0, 1], so we consider

$$\int_0^1 -x^n \log x \, dx = \int_0^1 x^{n-1} \log\left(\frac{1}{x}\right) dx$$

Now, $\lim_{x \to 0} x^{n-1} \log\left(\frac{1}{x}\right) = 0$ if $n-1>0$

Thus, the given integral is proper if $n - 1 > 0$

Let $n - 1 \le 0$. In this case 0 is a point of infinite discontinuity.

Again, Let m be a positive number such that $(m + n - 1) > 0$.

Then, $\lim_{x \to 0} [-x^{m+n-1} \log x] = 0$

It follows that for any $\varepsilon > 0$. $\exists$ some $\delta > 0$ such that

$-x^{m+n-1} \log x < \varepsilon$ for $|x| < \delta$

$\Rightarrow -x^{m+n-1} \log x < \varepsilon/x^m$ for $|x| < \delta$

We know $\int_0^1 \frac{\varepsilon}{x^m} dx$ converges iff $m < 1$.

It is possible to choose a number m, $0 < m < 1$, such that

$(m + n - 1) = (m - 1) + n > 0$ iff $n > 0$.

Thus, $\int_0^1 -x^{n-1} \log x \, dx$ converges if $n > 0$.

For n = 0, given integral = $\int_0^1 \frac{\log x}{x} dx$. Now

$$\int_{\varepsilon}^1 \frac{\log x}{x} dx = -\tfrac{1}{2}(\log \varepsilon)^2 \to -\infty \text{ as } \varepsilon \to 0+$$

Thus, the given integral does not converge if n = 0,

For n < 0, we have

$x^{-1} < x^{n-1} \ \forall \ x \ \in [0, 1]$

$\Rightarrow x^{-1} \log x < x^{n-1} \log x \ \forall \ x \in [0, 1]$

Since, $\int_0^1 x^{-1} \log x \, dx$ diverges, so

$\int_0^1 x^{n-1} \log x \, dx$ also diverges for $n < 0$.

Hence, $\int_0^1 x^{n-1} \log x \, dx$ converges iff $n > 0$.

Example 30:

Discuss the convergence of

$\int_0^1 x^{m-1} (1-x)^{n-1} \log x \, dx$.

Solution:

Since the integrand is negative in [0, 1], so we shall test the convergence of

$$\int_0^1 -x^{m-1} (1-x)^{n-1} \log x \, dx = \int_0^1 x^{m-1} (1-x)^{n-1} \log \frac{1}{x} \, dx$$

Here 0 and 1 are the possible points of infinite discontinuity of $f(x) = -x^{m-1} (1 - x)^{n-1} \log x$. We take

$$\int_0^1 f(x) \, dx = \int_0^{1/2} f(x) \, dx + \int_{1/2}^1 f(x) \, dx.$$

Example 31:

Evaluate $\int_0^\infty \frac{x^2 dx}{x^6 + 1}$

Solution:

Consider $\int_C \frac{z^2 dz}{z^6 + 1} = \int_C f(z) dz$, where C is the contour. Then we have by residue theorem,

$$\int_C f(z)dz = \int_{-R}^{R} f(x)dx + \int_\Gamma f(z)dz = 2\pi i \Sigma R^+. \quad ...(1)$$

Since $\lim_{z \to \infty} z f(z) = 0$, we have $\lim_{z \to \infty} \int_\Gamma f(z)dz = 0$.

$\therefore$ Proceeding to the limits as $R \to \infty$, we have from (1)

$$\int_{-\infty}^{\infty} f(x)dx + 2\pi i \Sigma R^+. \quad ...(2)$$

Now f(z) has simple poles for values of z given by $z^6 + 1 = 0$ or $z^6 = e^{(2n+1)\pi i}$, where n = 0,1,2,3,4,5. Therefore the poles art at $z = e^{(\pi i)/6}$, $e^{(\pi i)/2}$, $e^{(5\pi i)/6}$, $e^{(7\pi i)/6}$, $e^{(3\pi i)/2}$, $e^{(11\pi i)/z}$, of which first three lie in the upper half plane

Let α denote any one of these poles.

Residue (at z = π)= $\left[\dfrac{z^2}{d/dz(z^6+1)}\right]_{z=\alpha}$

$$= \frac{\alpha^2}{6\alpha^5} = \frac{\alpha^3}{6\alpha^6} = -\frac{\alpha^3}{6}. \ [\because \alpha^6 = -1]$$

∴ Sum of the residues at these poles

$$= -\tfrac{1}{6}[e^{(\pi i)/2} + e^{(3\pi i)/2} + e^{(5\pi i)/2}] = -\tfrac{1}{6}[i - i + i] = -i/6.$$

We then have from (2),

$$\int_{-\infty}^{\infty} f(x)dx = 2\pi i\left(-\frac{i}{6}\right) = \frac{\pi}{3} \text{ or } \int_{0}^{\infty} f(x)dx = \frac{\pi}{6}.$$

Example 32:

Prove that $\displaystyle\int_{-\infty}^{\infty} \frac{dx}{(x^2+b^2)(x^2+c^2)^2} = \frac{\pi(b+2c)}{2bc^3(b+c)^2}$, (b > 0, c > 0).

Solution:

Consider the integral

$$\int_{-\infty}^{\infty} \frac{dx}{(x^2+b^2)(x^2+c^2)^2} \int_C f(z)dz,$$

where C is the contour of § 7. By the residue theorem,

$$\int_C f(z)dz = \int_{-R}^{R} f(x)dx = \int_\Gamma f(z)dz = 2\pi i \sum R^+. \quad \text{... (1)}$$

Since $\lim_{R\to\infty} zf(z) = 0$, we have $\lim_{R\to\infty} \int_\Gamma f(z)dz = 0$.

$$\therefore \lim_{R\to\infty} \int_{-R}^{R} f(x)dx = 2\pi i \sum R^+$$

$$\text{or } \int_{-\infty}^{\infty} f(z)dx = 2\pi i \sum R^+. \quad \text{...(2)}$$

Now f(z) has simple poles at z = ± bi and poles at z = ± ci of order two of which z = bi and z = ci lie in the upper half plane.

Residue (at z = bi) = $\lim_{z\to bi} (z-bi)f(z)$

$$= \lim_{z\to bi} \frac{1}{(z+bi)(z^2+c^2)^2} = \frac{1}{2bi(c^2-b^2)^2}$$

and residue (z = ci) = φ′(ci),

where $\phi(z) = \dfrac{1}{(z^2+b^2)(z+ci)^2}$.

Now log φ(z) = – log ($z^2 + b^2$) – 2 log (z + ci).

$$\therefore \frac{\phi'(z)}{\phi(z)} = -\frac{2z}{z^2+b^2} - \frac{2}{z+ci}$$

$$\text{or } \phi'(ci) = \phi(ci)\left[-\frac{2ci}{b^2-c^2} - \frac{2}{2ci}\right]$$

$$= \frac{1}{(b^2-c^2)(-4c^2)}\left[-\frac{2ci}{b^2-c^2} + \frac{i}{c}\right]$$

$$= \frac{1}{4c^2(b^2-c^2)}\left[\frac{2c^2i - b^2i + c^2i}{c(b^2-c^2)}\right] = \frac{(3c^2-b^2)i}{4c^3(b^2-c^2)^2}.$$

$$\text{Sum of the residues} = -\frac{1}{4b(c^2-b^2)^2} + \frac{(3c^2-b^2)i}{4c^3(b^2-c^2)^2}$$

$$= \frac{i}{4bc^3(c^2-b^2)^2}[2c^3 - 3c^2b + b^3]$$

$$= \frac{i(c-b)^2(b+2c)}{2bc^2(c^2+b^2)^2}, \text{ factorizing the numerator}$$

$$= -\frac{i(b+2c)}{4bc^2(c+b)^2}.$$

Hence we have from (2),

$$\int_{-\infty}^{\infty} f(x)dx = 2\pi i\left[-\frac{i(b+2c)}{4bc^2(c+b)^2}\right] = \frac{\pi(b+2c)}{2bc^3(b+c)^2}.$$

Example 33:

Examine the convergence of :

(i) $\int_0^1 \frac{x^n}{1+x}dx$ (ii) $\int_0^\pi \frac{\sqrt{x}}{\sin x}dx$

Solution:

(i) Consider $\int_0^1 \frac{x^n}{1+x}dx$.

This is a proper integral if $n \geq 0$ and an improper integral if $n < 0$ (0 being the only point of infinite discontinuity of the integrand).

For $n < 0$, we may take $n = -m (m > 0)$.

$$\therefore \int_0^1 \frac{x^n}{1+x}dx = \int_0^1 \frac{dx}{x^m(1+x)}$$

Let $f(x) = \frac{1}{x^m(1+x)}$ and $g(x) = \frac{1}{x^m}$. Then

$$\lim_{x\to 0+}\frac{f(x)}{g(x)} = \text{and} \lim_{x\to 0+}\frac{1}{1+x} = 1$$

Now $\int_0^1 g(x)\,dx = \int_0^1 \frac{dx}{x^n}$ convergence m < 1 or –n < 1 or n > – 1. Hence the given integral is convergent if n > –1.

(ii) Here 0 and π are the only points of infinite discontinuity of the integrand. Now

$$\int_0^\pi \frac{\sqrt{x}}{\sin x}\,dx = \int_0^1 \frac{\sqrt{x}}{\sin x}\,dx + \int_1^\pi \frac{\sqrt{x}}{\sin x}\,dx$$ convergence at 0

Let $f(x) = \frac{\sqrt{x}}{\sin x}$ and $g(x) = \frac{1}{\sqrt{x}}$. Then, we have

$$\lim_{x\to 0+}\frac{f(x)}{g(x)} = \lim_{x\to 0+}\frac{x}{\sin x} = 1$$

Since $\int_0^1 g(x)\,dx = \int_0^1 \frac{dx}{\sqrt{x}}$ converges,

Hence, $\int_0^1 \frac{\sqrt{x}}{\sin x}\,dx$ also converges,

Convergence at π

Let $f(x) = \frac{\sqrt{x}}{\sin x}$ and $g(x) = \frac{1}{x-\pi}$. Then

$$\lim_{x\to\pi-}\frac{f(x)}{g(x)} = \lim_{x\to\pi-}\frac{\sqrt{x}(x-\pi)}{\sin x}.\left(\frac{0}{0}\right)$$

$$= \lim_{x\to\pi-}\frac{\frac{3}{2}x^{1/2} - \frac{1}{2}\pi x^{-1/1}}{\cos x} = -\sqrt{\pi} \text{ (By L' Hospital's rule)}$$

Since $\int_1^\pi g(x)\,dx = \int_1^\pi \frac{dx}{(x-\pi)^1}$ is divergent,

so $\int_1^\pi \frac{\sqrt{x}}{\sin x}\,dx$ is divergent.

Hence, the given integral $\int_0^\pi \frac{\sqrt{x}}{\sin x}\,dx$ is divergent.

Example 34:

Examine the convergence of:

(i) $\int_0^\infty \frac{\sin^2 x}{x^2} dx$ (ii) $\int_0^\infty \frac{x^{n-1}}{1+x} dx$ (iii) $\int_1^\infty \frac{x^{n-1} \log x}{1+x} dx$

Solution:

(i) Let $f(x) = \sin^2 x/x^2$. Then

$$\int_0^\infty f(x)\, dx = \int_0^1 f(x)\, dx + \int_1^\infty f(x)\, dx$$

Now, $\int_0^1 \frac{\sin^2 x}{x^2} dx$ is a proper integral,

since $\lim_{x\to 0} \frac{\sin^2 x}{x^2} = 1$ and so 0 is not a point of infinite discontinuity.

We have $\frac{\sin^2 x}{x^3} < \frac{1}{x^4}$ $\forall\, x \in [1, \infty[$.

Since $\int_1^\infty \frac{1}{x^2} dx$ converges, so $\int_1^\infty \frac{\sin^2 x}{x^2} dx$ also convergence

Hence, the given Integral $\int_1^\infty \frac{\sin^2 x}{x^2} dx$ is convergent.

(ii) $\int_1^\infty \frac{x^{m-1}}{1+x} dx = \int_0^1 \frac{x^{m-1}}{1+x} dx + \int_1^\infty \frac{x^{m-1}}{1+x} dx$ convergence at 0

Let $f(x) = \frac{x^{m-1}}{1+x}$, $g(x) = \frac{1}{x^{1-m}}$

$$\therefore \lim_{x\to 0} \frac{f(x)}{g(x)} = \lim_{x\to 0}\left(\frac{1}{1+x}\right) = 1$$

Now $\int_0^1 g(x)\, dx$ converges if $1-m < 1$ i.e., $0 < m$.

Hence the given integral $\int_0^1 f(x)\, dx$ converges if $0 \Delta m$

Convergence at ∞

Let $g(x) = \frac{1}{x^{2-m}}$

$$\therefore \lim_{x\to\infty} \frac{f(x)}{g(x)} = \lim_{x\to\infty}\left(\frac{x}{1+x}\right) = 1$$

Since $\int_1^\infty \frac{dx}{2^{2-m}}$ converges if $2 - m > 1$ i.e., $1 > m$.

So $\int_0^\infty f(x)\, dx$ converges if $m < 1$.

Hence the given integral $\int_1^{\infty} \frac{x^{m-1}}{1+x} dx$ converges if $0 < m < 1$.

For large values of x, log x < x.

$$\therefore \int_1^{\infty} \frac{x^{a-1} \log x}{1+x} dx < \int_1^{\infty} \frac{x^a dx}{1+x} \qquad \ldots (1)$$

Let $f(x) = \frac{x^a}{1+x}$ and $f(x) = \frac{1}{x^{1-a}}$

$$\therefore \lim_{x \to \infty} \frac{f(x)}{g(x)} \lim_{x \to \infty} \frac{x}{1+x} = 1$$

Now $\int_1^{\infty} g(x)\, dx$ is convergent iff $1 - a > 1$

$\Rightarrow \int_1^{\infty} f(x)\; dx$ is convergent iff $0 > a$

Hence by (i) $\int_1^{\infty} \frac{x^{n-1} \log x}{1+x} dx$ is convergent iff $a < 0$.

Example 35:

Examine the convergence of:

(i) $\int_0^{\pi 2} \frac{\sin x}{x^n} dx$ (ii) $\int_0^1 x^{n-1} e^{-x}\, dx$

Solution:

(i) Here 0 is the only point of infinite discontinuity of the integrand.

Let $f(x) = \frac{\sin x}{x^n}$

and $g(x) = \frac{1}{x^{n-2}}$

$$\therefore \lim_{x \to 0+} \frac{f(x)}{g(x)} = \lim_{x \to 0+} \frac{\sin x}{x} = 1$$

Now $\int_0^{\frac{1}{2}} g(x)\, dx = \int_0^{\frac{1}{2}} \frac{dx}{x^{n-1}}$ converges if $(n - 1 < 1)\; a - 1$ i.e., $n < 2$

By second comparison test, the given improper integral is convergent if $n < 2$.

(ii) Consider $\int_0^1 \frac{e^{-x} dx}{x^{1-a}}$

Here 0 is the only point of infinite discontinuity of the integrand if $a < 1$.

Let f(x) $\frac{e^{-x}}{x^{1-a}}$ and $g(x) = \frac{1}{x^{1-a}}$

$$\therefore \qquad \lim_{x \to 0+} \frac{f(x)}{g(x)} = \lim_{x \to 0+} e^{-x} = 1$$

Now $\int_0^1 \frac{dx}{x^{1-a}}$ converges if 1 – a < i.e., 0 < a.

Hence, the given integral converges if a > 0.

Example 36:

Examine the convergence of

(i) $\int_0^1 \frac{dx}{\sqrt{x - x^2}}$ (ii) $\int_0^1 \frac{dx}{\sqrt{1 - x^2}}$ (iii) $\int_0^\pi \frac{dx}{\sin e}$

Solution:

(i) Notice that 0 and 1 are the only points of infinite discontinuity of the integrand in [0, 1]. We take 0 < ½ < 1.

Putting x = sin² θ, $\int \frac{dx}{\sqrt{x - x^2}} = 2\,\theta = 2\,\sin^{-1}\sqrt{x}$

$$= \lim_{\varepsilon \to 0} \int_\varepsilon^{1/2} \frac{dx}{\sqrt{x - x^2}} = \lim_{\varepsilon \to 0+} \left[2\,\sin^{-1}\left(\sqrt{\tfrac{1}{2}}\right) - 2\,\sin^{-1}\sqrt{\varepsilon}\right]$$

$$= 2\left(\frac{\pi}{4}\right) = \frac{\pi}{2}.$$

$$\lim_{\varepsilon \to 0} \int_{\frac{1}{2}}^{1-\varepsilon} \frac{dx}{\sqrt{x - x^2}} = \lim_{\varepsilon \to 0+} [2\,\sin^{-1}\sqrt{(1-\varepsilon)} - 2\,\sin^{-1}(\sqrt{\tfrac{1}{2}})]$$

$$= 2\left(\frac{\pi}{2} - \frac{\pi}{4}\right) = \frac{\pi}{2}$$

Hence, the given integral is convergent and

$$\int_0^1 \frac{dx}{\sqrt{x - x^2}} = \frac{\pi}{2} + \frac{\pi}{2} = \pi$$

(ii) It is easy to see that 1 is the only point of limits discontinuity of the integrand in [0, 1] we have

$$\int_0^{1-\varepsilon} \frac{dx}{\sqrt{1 - x^2}} = \left|\sin^{-1} x\right|_0^{1-\varepsilon} = \sin^{-1} = \frac{\pi}{2}$$

$$\therefore \lim_{\varepsilon \to 0} \int_0^{1-\varepsilon} \frac{dx}{\sqrt{1 - x^2}} = \lim_{\varepsilon \to 0+} \sin^{-1}(1 - \varepsilon) = \sin^{-1} 1 = \frac{\pi}{2}$$

Thus, the given improper integral is convergent with value ½π.

(iii) Notice that 0 and π are the only points of infinite discontinuity of the integrand in [0, π]. We take 0 < 1 < π. Now

$$\int_0^{1-\varepsilon} \frac{dx}{\sin x} = \left|\log \tan \tfrac{1}{2}x\right|_\varepsilon^1 = (\log \tan \tfrac{1}{2} - \log \tan \tfrac{1}{2}\varepsilon)$$

$$\to \infty \text{ as } \varepsilon \to 0+.$$

Thus $\int_0^1 \frac{dx}{\sin x}$ is divergent and consequently the given improper integral is divergent.

Example 37:

Show that, i m and n are positive integers, and m < n,

$$\int_0^\infty \frac{x^{2m}}{x^{2n}+1}dx = \frac{\pi}{2n \sin \{(2m+1)/2n\}\pi}.$$

Solution:

Consider $\int_C \frac{x^{2m}}{x^{2n}+1}dx = \int f(z)dz$, where C is the same contour we then have from residue theorem

$$\int_C f(z)dz = \int_{-R}^{R} f(x)dx + \int_\Gamma f(z)dz = 2\pi i \Sigma R. \quad \text{... (1)}$$

Since m and n are integers and m < n, the value of 2m is at east 2 less than the value of 2n. Hence $\lim_{z\to\infty} zf(z) = 0$.

It follows that $\int_\Gamma f(z)dz = 2\pi i \Sigma R^+$.

Proceeding to the limits, we get from (1)

$$\int_{-\infty}^{\infty} f(x)dx = 2\pi i \Sigma R^+. \quad \text{... (2)}$$

Now f(z) has simple poles for values of z given by

$z^{2n} + 1 = 0$ or $z^{2n} = e^{(2r+1)\pi i}$

where r = 0, 1, 2,... 2n – 1.

Therefore the poles are given by

$z = e^{\pi i/2n}, e^{3\pi i/2n}, \ldots e^{[(2n-1).\pi i/2n]},$

$e^{[(2n+1)\pi i]/2n}, e^{[(2n+3)\pi i]/2n}, \ldots, e^{[(4n-1)\pi i]/2n}$

Out of these 2n poles first n poles lie in the upper half-plane. Denote these poles by $\alpha_1, \alpha_2, \alpha_3, \ldots \alpha n$.

$$\text{Residue (at } z=\alpha) = \left[\frac{z^{2m}}{d/dz(1+z^{2n})}\right]_{z=\alpha}$$

$$= \frac{\alpha^{2m}}{2n\alpha^{2n-1}} = \frac{\alpha^{2m+1}}{2n\alpha^{2n}} = -\frac{\alpha^{2m+1}}{2n} \text{ since } \alpha^{2n} = -1.$$

Sum of the residues

$$= -\frac{1}{2n}[\alpha_1{}^{2m+1} + \alpha_2{}^{2m+2} + \ldots + \alpha_n{}^{2m+n}]$$

$$= -\frac{1}{2n}[e^{i\theta} + e^{3/\theta} + \ldots e^{(2n-1)/\theta}] \text{ where } \theta = \frac{2m+1}{2n}\pi$$

$$= -\frac{1}{2n}\frac{e^{i\theta}(1-e^{2ni\theta})}{(1-e^{2i\theta})} = -\frac{1}{n}.\frac{e^{i\theta}(1-e^{2ni\theta})(1-e^{2i\theta})}{(1-e^{2i\theta})(1-e^{-2i\theta})}$$

$$= -\frac{1}{2n}\frac{e^{i\theta} - e^{(2n+1)i\theta} - e^{-i\theta} + e^{(2n-1)i\theta}}{2-2\cos 2\theta}$$

$$= -\frac{1}{2n}\frac{2i\sin\theta - e^{2ni\theta}.2i\sin\theta}{4\sin^2\theta}$$

$$= -\frac{i}{4n\sin\theta}[2\sin^2 n\theta - 2i\sin n\theta\cos n\theta]$$

$$= -\frac{1}{2n}.\frac{\sin n\theta}{\sin\theta}[\cos n\theta + i\sin n\theta] = -\frac{i}{2n}.\frac{\sin^2 n\theta}{\sin\theta}$$

$$\text{since } \cos n\theta = \cos\frac{2m+1}{2}\pi = 0$$

$$= -\frac{i}{2n\sin\theta} \text{ since } (\sin n\theta)^2 = \left(\sin\frac{2m+1}{2}\pi\right)^2 = (\pm 1)^2 = 1.$$

Hence, we have from (2),

$$\int_{-\infty}^{\infty} f(x)dx = 2\pi i\left(-\frac{i}{2n\sin\theta}\right) = \frac{\pi}{n\sin\theta}$$

or
$$\int_0^{\infty}\frac{x^{2m}}{1+x^{2n}}dx = \frac{\pi}{2n\sin\left(\frac{2m+1}{2n}\right)\pi}$$

Example 38:

Prove by contour integration that

$$\int_0^{\infty}\frac{dx}{(a+bx^2)^n} = \frac{1}{2^n b^{1/2}}.\frac{1.3.5\ldots(2n-3)}{1.2.3\ldots(n-1)}.\frac{1}{a^{(n-1)/2}}.$$

Solution:

Consider $\int_C \frac{dx}{(a+bx^2)^n} = \int_C f(z)dz$, where C is the same contour by residue theorem, we get

$$\int_C f(z)dz = \int_{-R}^{R} f(x)dx + \int_\Gamma f(z)dz = 2\pi i \sum R^+. \quad ...(1)$$

Since $\lim_{z\to\infty} zf(z) = 0$, we get $\lim_{R\to\infty} \int_\Gamma f(z)dz = 0$, so that we get from (1) when $R \to \infty$.

$$\int_{-\infty}^{\infty} f(z)dz = 2\pi i \sum R^+. \quad ...(2)$$

Now f(z) has poles of nth order at $z = \pm\sqrt{\left(\frac{a}{b}\right)}\, i$ of which $z = \sqrt{\left(\frac{a}{b}\right)}\, i$ lies in the upper half-plane.

$$\text{Residue}\left\{\text{at } z = \sqrt{\left(\frac{a}{b}\right)} i\right\} \text{ is } \frac{1}{(n-1)!}\phi^{(n-1)}\left\{\sqrt{\left(\frac{a}{b}\right)} i\right\},$$

$$\text{where } \phi(z) = \frac{\left\{z - \sqrt{\left(\frac{a}{b}\right)} i\right\}^n}{(a+bz^2)^n} = \frac{1}{b^n\left\{z + \sqrt{\left(\frac{a}{b}\right)} i\right\}^n}$$

$$\text{Now } \phi^{(n-1)}(z) = \frac{1}{b^n}\cdot\frac{(-n)(-n-1)...[-n-(n-1)+1]}{\left\{z + \sqrt{\left(\frac{a}{b}\right)} i\right\}^{2n-1}}$$

$$= (-1)^{n-1}\frac{(n+1)...(2n-2)}{b^n\left\{z + \sqrt{\left(\frac{a}{b}\right)} i\right\}^{2n-1}}$$

∴ Residue at the pole

$$= \frac{1}{(n-1)!}(-1)^{n-1}\cdot\frac{n(n+1)...(2n-2)}{b^n\left\{2\sqrt{\left(\frac{a}{b}\right)} i\right\}^{2n-1}}$$

$$= \frac{n(n+1)...(2n-2)}{b^n\left\{2\sqrt{\left(\frac{a}{b}\right)}\right\}^{2n-1} i(n-1)!} \quad [\because i^{2n-2} = (-1)^{n-1}]$$

$$=\frac{1.2.3...(n-1)n(n+1)...(2n-2)}{\left\{2\sqrt{\left(\frac{a}{b}\right)}\right\}^{2n-1}.b^n(n-1)!(n-1)!}i$$

$$=\frac{1.3.5...(2n-3)2^{n-1}.1.2.3...(n-1)}{2^{2n-1}a^{n-(1/2)}.b^{1/2}.(n-1)!(n-1)!}i$$

$$=\frac{1.3.5...(2n-3)}{2^n b^{1/2}a^{n-(1/2)}.1.2.3...(n-1)}i$$

$\therefore$ From (2), $\int_{-\infty}^{\infty} f(x)dx=\frac{2\pi}{2^n b^{1/2}}.\frac{1.3.5...(2n-3)}{1.2.3...(n-1)}.\frac{1}{a^{n-(1/2)}}$

or $\int_0^{\infty} f(x)dx=\frac{\pi}{2^n b^{1/2}}.\frac{1.3.5...(2n-3)}{1.2.3...(n-1)}.\frac{1}{a^{n-(1/2)}}$

EXERCISES

Using the theory of residues evaluate the following intergrals:

1. If $a>0$, prove that $\int_0^{\infty}\frac{dx}{\left(x^2+a^2\right)^2}=\frac{\pi}{4a^3}$.

2. $\int_0^{\infty}\frac{dx}{x^4+1}$ **Ans.** $\frac{\pi\sqrt{2}}{4}$

3. $\int_0^{\infty}\frac{x^6dx}{\left(x^4+1\right)^2}$ **Ans.** $\frac{3\sqrt{2}}{16}\pi$.

4. $\int_0^{\infty}\frac{x\,dx}{\left(x^2+1\right)\left(x^2+2x+2\right)}$ **Ans.** $-\frac{\pi}{5}$.

5. $\int_0^{\infty}\frac{dx}{1+x^2}$ **Ans.** $\frac{\pi}{3}$.

6. $\int_0^{\infty}\frac{x^2dx}{\left(x^2+1\right)^3}$ **Ans.** $\frac{\pi}{16}$.

7. Prove that $\int_0^{\infty}\frac{2dx}{1+2x^2\cos\theta+x^4}=\frac{1}{2}\pi\sec\frac{1}{2}\theta$.

8. Show that $\int_{-\infty}^{\infty}\frac{x^2dx}{\left(x^2+1\right)\left(x^2+4\right)}=\frac{\pi}{3}$.

9. Show that $\int_{-\infty}^{\infty} \frac{dx}{\left(x^2+b^2\right)^{n+1}} = \frac{\pi}{(2b)^{2n+1}} \cdot \frac{2n!}{(n!)^2}$,

where n is a + ve integer.

10. Prove that $\int_{-\infty}^{\infty} \frac{x^6}{\left(a^4+x^4\right)^2} dx = \frac{3\sqrt{2}\pi}{16a} (a > 0)$.

21. Show that $\int_0^{2\pi} \frac{d\theta}{2+\cos\theta} = \frac{2\pi}{\sqrt{3}}$

12. Prove that $\int_0^{2\pi} \frac{\cos^2 3\theta \, d\theta}{5-4\cos 2\theta} = \frac{3\pi}{8}$

13. Show that, if | a | < 1,

$$\int_0^{2\pi} \frac{d\theta}{1+a^2-2a\cos\theta} = \frac{2\pi}{1-a^2}$$

and deduce the value of the integral when | a | > 1.

14. Evaluate

$$\int_{-\pi}^{\pi} \frac{a\cos\theta}{a+\cos\theta} d\theta, (a > 1)$$

by putting $z = e^{i\theta}$ and using the theory of residues.

Ans. $2a\pi\left[1-\frac{a}{\sqrt{a^2-1}}\right]$

15. Prove that

$$\left[\int_0^{2\pi} \frac{d\theta}{(a+b\cos^2\theta)^2} = \frac{\pi(2a+b)}{a^{3/2}(a+b)^{3/2}}, (a > b > 0)\right]$$

16. Show that

$$\int_{-\infty}^{\infty} \frac{dx}{(x^4+a^4)(x^4+b^4)} = \frac{\pi}{\sqrt{2}} \cdot \frac{a^2+ab+b^2}{a^3b^3(a^3+a^2b+ab^2+b^3)},$$

(a > 0, b > 0, a ≠ b).

17. Evaluate $\int_0^{2\pi} \frac{\sin n\theta \, d\theta}{1+2a\cos\theta+a^2}$ and $\int_0^{2\pi} \frac{\cos n\theta}{1+2a\cos\theta+a^2} d\theta$

($a^2 < 1$ and n being a +ve integer)

Ans. 0, $\frac{2\pi(-1)^n a^n}{(1-a^2)}$

18. Prove that

$$\int_0^{2\pi} e^{-\cos\theta}\cos(n\theta+\sin\theta)d\theta=(-1)^n.\frac{2\pi}{n!}$$

(n being a + ve integer)

19. Show that when R (a) > 0,

$$\int_0^{\pi}\tan(\theta+ai)d\theta=\pi i.$$

20. Show that, if m is real and $-1 < a < 1$, then

(i) $\int_0^{2\pi}\frac{e^{m\cos\theta}}{1+a^2-2a\sin\theta}$ $\{\cos(m\sin\theta)-a\sin(m\theta+\theta)\}\,d\theta$
$= 2\pi\cos ma.$

(ii) $\int_0^{2\pi}\frac{e^{m\cos\theta}}{1+a^2-2a\sin\theta}$ $\{\sin(m\sin\theta)+a\cos(m\sin\theta+\theta)\}d\theta$

$= 2\theta\sin ma.$

21. Use calculus of residues to evaluate the integral

$\int_0^{2\pi}\cos^{2n}d\theta$ where n is a +ve integer.

Ans. $\frac{(2n)!\pi}{2^{2n-1}(n!)^n}$.

22. Prove that

$\int z^2\log[(z+1)/(z-1)]\,dz$, taken round the circle $|z| = 2$, half the value $(4\pi i/3)$.